QSE
QUICK SMART ENGLISH

Advanced

TEACHER'S GUIDE

with

Photocopiable Resources

Maurice Forget

BROOKEMEAD ENGLISH LANGUAGE TEACHING

QSE Quick Smart English
Advanced
TEACHER'S GUIDE

Series editor: Duncan Prowse
Consultant: Rosemary Harris
Editors: Anna Whitcher Kutz, Picot Cassidy
Artist: Belinda Evans
Design: John Anastasio, Wendi Watson,
Lapiz Digital

Acknowledgements

Unit 2: © Gunther von Hagens, Institut for Plastination, Heidelberg/Germany. www.bodyworlds.com. **Unit 3:** Interviews by Kirsi Hantula. **Unit 5:** Courtesy of PETA: People for the Ethical Treatment of Animals. **Unit 8:** Voice of America. **Unit 9:** 'Seeing Eye Dog: 75th Anniversary' by Beth Finke. Originally broadcast January 28, 2004. Copyright 2004, Chicago Public Radio (www.chicagopublicradio.org). **Unit 12:** Click Online (August 5th 2004) BBC World Ltd. **Unit 13:** Extract from *Outfoxed: Rupert Murdoch's War on Journalism* © Carolina Productions. Footage from *The O'Reilly Factor:* Personal Story Segment with Jeremy M. Glick © Fox News Channel reproduced with due thanks to News Corporation Inc. **Unit 15:** The Nolan Show, BBC Radio Ulster. **Unit 16:** Original story by Anne Minard, for Arizona Public Radio (KNAU) in Flagstaff. **Unit 17:** With thanks for the provision of archive material to the European Space Agency – ESA. **Unit 18:** © Panos London / www.interworldradio.net. Abridged from 'Brazil: Computers in the Favelas' by Paula Gobbi. **Unit 19:** 'Laughter therapist visits Australia' with Dr Madan Kataria interviewed by Geoff Thompson first broadcast 26 February 2004 on PM for ABC Radio. Reproduced by permission of the Australian Broadcasting Corporation and ABC Online. © 2004 ABC. All rights reserved. The transcript is available at:
http://www.abc.net.au/pm/content/2004/s1054285.htm.

QSE Advanced Common European Framework Level B2-C1

QSE Series Title	Common European Framework	Cambridge ESOL	Michigan	TOEFL (New TOEFL)	Trinity College, London, ESOL	Edexcel London Test of English
Quick Start English (in preparation)	A1-A2	KET			ISE 0 GESE Grade 1, 2, 3	Level (A1) 1
Quick Smart English Pre-Intermediate	A2-B1	PET	BCCE		ISE I, GESE Grade 4, 5, 6	Level 1- 2
Quick Smart English Intermediate	B1-B2	FCE	ECCE	450-525 Target 485 (NT 163)	ISE II, GESE Grade 7, 8, 9	Level 2-3
Quick Smart English Advanced	B2-C1	CAE	ALCE	Target 525 (NT 197)	ISE III, GESE Grade 10, 11	Level 3-4

ISBN: 978-1-905248-26-1

Also available:
QSE Advanced Student's Book + DVD
ISBN 978-1-905248-00-1

Published by:
Brookemead English Language Teaching
P.O. Box 58230, London N1 1RP
www.brookemead-elt.co.uk

© Brookemead Associates Ltd. 2007, 2009
All rights reserved. No part of this publication may be reproduced, recorded, transmitted, or stored in any form whatsoever, without the prior written permission of the copyright holders.

Other books in the QSE Series:
QSE Pre-Intermediate (CEF A2-B1)
Student's Book, Workbook, Audio CDs,
Teacher's Guide with Photocopiable Resources

QSE Intermediate (CEF B1-B2)
Student's Book, Workbook, Audio CDs,
Teacher's Guide with Photocopiable Resources

CONTENTS

Materials Map (Student's Book, Workbook, Teacher's Guide, Audio, Video, Exams)	4
Introduction – Welcome to *QSE Advanced*	8
QSE and the Common European Framework of Reference (CEF)	8
QSE Advanced for exams	10
QSE Advanced and CLIL (Content and Language Integrated Learning)	12
QSE and Multiple Intelligences	12
English as a meme	13
QSE Advanced – At a glance	14
QSE Advanced – How the sections of each unit work	16
Internet sources and *QSE* illustrations	25
Unit 1 Teacher's notes and answer keys	26
Unit 2 Teacher's notes and answer keys	32
Unit 3 Teacher's notes and answer keys	38
Unit 4 Teacher's notes and answer keys	43
Unit 5 Teacher's notes and answer keys	49
Unit 6 Teacher's notes and answer keys	54
Unit 7 Teacher's notes and answer keys	60
Extended Reading 1 Teacher's notes and answer keys	65
Unit 8 Teacher's notes and answer keys	68
Unit 9 Teacher's notes and answer keys	75
Unit 10 Teacher's notes and answer keys	81
Unit 11 Teacher's notes and answer keys	88
Unit 12 Teacher's notes and answer keys	93
Unit 13 Teacher's notes and answer keys	99
Unit 14 Teacher's notes and answer keys	105
Extended Reading 2 Teacher's notes and answer keys	111
Unit 15 Teacher's notes and answer keys	114
Unit 16 Teacher's notes and answer keys	119
Unit 17 Teacher's notes and answer keys	125
Unit 18 Teacher's notes and answer keys	132
Unit 19 Teacher's notes and answer keys	138
Unit 20 Teacher's notes and answer keys	144
Extended Reading 3 Teacher's notes and answers key	149
Using the Student's **DVD-ROM**	152
Audio and Video Scripts Units 1-20	153
Exam Practice Listening Scripts (Tests 1-6)	169
Photocopiable Resources	
Introduction to Exam Practice	174
IGCSE Exam Practice (Reading, Writing, Speaking, Listening)	176
IELTS Exam Practice (Listening, Reading, Writing, Speaking)	204
CAE Exam Practice (Reading, Writing, Use of English, Listening, Speaking)	224
Placement Test	251
Exam Practice Answer Keys	253
Exam Practice Listening Scripts (Test 7)	256

QSE Advanced Teacher's Guide — MATERIALS MAP

Unit	Title	Subject / The BIG question	Reading	Language Banks Functions/ Grammar	Speaking
1	Buy now, think later	Advertising *Is advertising all a con?* SB8	Marketing: Decline of TV commercials; Celebrities out of a job SB9	Expressions used before challenging; Contradicting LB1 Prepositions WB94	TEAMWORK: Create a TV ad SB10,114 CONTROVERSY: Do spoof ads challenge advertisers? SB10 STRATEGIES: Mapping the presentation WB94
2	Express yourself	The arts *Are the arts relevant?* SB12	Arts: Monarchy and high culture; Spoils of war SB13	Signposting Sequencing (1); Inferring LB2 Word forms WB95	TEAMWORK: An art manifesto SB14, 114 CONTROVERSY: How does traditional art combine with modern motifs? SB14
3	The sky's the limit!	Ambitions *What would you do to succeed?* SB16	Film: Success stories: Jackie Chan, Shah Rukh Khan SB17	Downplaying; Justifying an argument LB3 Joining clauses WB96	TEAMWORK: A problem tree SB18, 114 CONTROVERSY: Does welfare work? SB18 STRATEGIES: Rhetorical questions WB96
4	Are you looking at me?	Bullying *Is bullying just part of life?* SB20	Youth culture: Satire: delinquent murders teacher; Steroid use among victims of bullying SB21	Modifying words; Expressing beliefs LB4 Word forms WB97	TEAMWORK: Stereotypes SB22, 115 CONTROVERSY: Is it survival of the fittest? SB22
5	Frills and thrills	Designer goods / Fashion *Are we all fashion victims?* SB24	Fashion: Japanese women and designer fashion; Metrosexual man SB25	Adjectives; Expressing opinions tentatively LB5	TEAMWORK: Re-design an ordinary object SB26, 115 CONTROVERSY: Haute couture SB26 STRATEGIES: De-emphasising WB98
6	Playing to win	Competitiveness *How important is winning?* SB28	Sport and leisure: Man versus machine; Sports and competitiveness SB29	The passive; Expressing reservations LB6, WB99	TEAMWORK: A reality TV show SB30, 115 CONTROVERSY: Can there be gender equality in sports funding? SB30
7	Profit and loss	Economic issues *Does economics really affect me?* SB32	Business: Farm subsidies; Virtual reality economy SB33	Intransitive and transitive verbs; Defending a point of view LB7, WB100	TEAMWORK: Finding the money for pensions SB34, 115 CONTROVERSY: What's the point of Fairtrade goods? SB34 STRATEGIES: Discussing graphs WB100
	Extended Reading 1	Equal opportunities SB36	Buffy the Vampire Slayer SB36		Interactive Task: Films SB37
8	Into the future	Future of the planet *Does the Earth need rescuing?* SB38	Environment: Gulf Stream; Viruses and epidemics SB39	Signposting: Arguments (1); Affirming LB8 Prepositions WB101	TEAMWORK: After natural disaster SB40, 116 CONTROVERSY: Can we really conserve fish stocks? SB40
9	Free to choose	Independence *Why do people want to be independent?* SB42	Society: Leaving home; Regional independence movements SB43	Signposting: Arguments (2); Interrupting LB9 Word forms WB102	TEAMWORK: Equipping an apartment SB44, 11 CONTROVERSY: Do we need government? SB4 STRATEGIES: Active and passive voice WB10
10	Do I get a say?	Individual and young people's rights *Can't we just do what we want?* SB46	Human rights: Slavery in Africa; Crackdown on anti-social behaviour SB47	Intensifiers; Challenging opinions LB10 Articles WB103	TEAMWORK: Choosing politicians SB48, 11 CONTROVERSY: Euthanasia SB48
11	Peace around the world	International events *Will we ever have peace?* SB50	International news: Chávez, Latin American revolutionary; Peaceful protest SB51	Tentative expressions; Evaluating viewpoints LB11	TEAMWORK: Conflict resolution SB52, 11 CONTROVERSY: EU and US – friends or rivals SB5 STRATEGIES: Power of three WB10

Key:
SB = Student's Book   TG = Teacher's Guide
WB = Workbook   PR = Photocopiable Resources

QSE Advanced MATERIALS MAP

Vocabulary	Listening Audio/Video	Writing	CLIL (Content and Language Integrated Learning)	Teacher's Guide Photocopiable Resources	Pages
Marketing, consumers, industry; Idioms WB94	**Audio**: Cigarette warning labels SB10	Review of an ad; Letter SB10 Sales email; Product description WB94	**Public relations**: Marketing, society and advertising, government regulation SB11	Teacher's notes and answer key TG26 IGCSE Exam PR176, 196, 203 CAE Exam PR244, 246 IELTS Exam PR208	Unit 1 SB8-11 WB94 TG26
High culture, pop culture, history; Idioms WB95	**Video**: The Body Worlds exhibition SB14	Biography of an artist; Letter about Elgin Marbles SB14 Diary entry: Music review WB95	**History of music**: African-Americans, civil rights SB15	Teacher's notes and answer key TG32 IGCSE Exam PR177, 193, 196 CAE Exam PR236, 244	Unit 2 SB12-15 WB95 TG32
Measures of social success; Idioms WB96	**Video**: Interviews about the American Dream SB18	Being a country's leader; Successful person's life SB18 Letter; Guide to speaking WB96	**Careers**: Jobs of the future SB19	Teacher's notes and answer key TG38 IGCSE Exam PR185, 192, 194, 196 CAE Exam PR242 IELTS Exam PR213, 221, 223	Unit 3 SB16-19 WB96 TG38
Forms of bullying; Idioms WB97	**Audio**: Bullying in the workplace SB22	Letter; Story about superhero SB22 Letter; Report on bullying WB97	**Psychology**: Prisoner rights; Effects of power SB23	Teacher's notes and answer key TG43 IGCSE Exam PR187, 196	Unit 4 SB20-23 WB97 TG43
Fashion trends; Idioms WB98	**Video**: PETA campaign against wearing fur SB26	On a shopping spree; Advice columnist answers SB26 Charity letter; Instructions WB98	**Consumer studies**: Maslow's Hierarchy of Needs; Manipulating desire SB27	Teacher's notes and answer key TG49 IGCSE Exam PR197 IELTS Exam PR217 CAE Exam PR244	Unit 5 SB24-27 WB98 TG49
Competitiveness, sports; Idioms WB99	**Audio**: Alternative beauty contests SB30	At the Olympics: New beauty contest SB30 Press release; Sports report WB99	**Physiology**: Effect of extreme sport on the body SB31	Teacher's notes and answer key TG54 IGCSE Exam PR192, 197 IELTS Exam PR223	Unit 6 SB28-31 WB99 TG54
Economics, trade; Idioms WB100	**Audio**: How war affects the economy SB34	Local economy; Fairtrade letter SB34 Article; Letter WB100	**Business Studies**: Reading data from a graph; Comparing prices SB35	Teacher's notes and answer key TG60 IGCSE Exam PR194, 197, 201 CAE Exam PR229, 243 IELTS Exam PR206, 221	Unit 7 SB32-35 WB100 TG60
Idioms SB36 Verbs for hand / arm movement SB37		Summary; Write an ending for the extract SB37		Teacher's notes and answer key TG65 IGCSE PR197	SB36-37 TG 65
Environment; Idioms WB101	**Audio**: *The Skeptical Environmentalist*: Bjorn Lomborg SB40	Letter to the EU; Preparing for disaster SB40 Science article; Space colony WB101	**Meteorology**: Climate change and El Niño SB41	Teacher's notes and answer key TG68 CAE Exam PR224, 241, 247 IELTS PR222	Unit 8 SB38-41 WB101 TG68
State institutions; Idioms WB102	**Audio**: Hanni, the seeing-eye dog SB44	Independence day; Student living away from home SB44 Article; Story WB102	**History**: Scottish independence SB45	Teacher's notes and answer key TG75 IGCSE Exam PR188, 198	Unit 9 SB42-45 WB102 TG75
Rights; Idioms WB103	**Audio**: Tough-discipline schools for 'problem' teenagers SB48	Mens'/womens' rights; Behaviour-modification school SB48 Letter; Summary WB103	**Law**: Rights for minority language speakers SB49	Teacher's notes and answer key TG81 IGCSE Exam PR198	Unit 10 SB46-49 WB103 TG81
News items; Idioms WB104	**Audio**: A tropical storm and flooding in Haiti SB52	Press release; An international event SB52 Email; Summary WB104	**Drama**: Anti-war drama SB53	Teacher's notes and answer key TG88 IGCSE Exam PR181, 188, 198 CAE Exam PR227	Unit 11 SB50-53 WB104 TG88

QSE Advanced Teacher's Guide

MATERIALS MAP

Unit	Title	Subject / The BIG question	Reading	Language Banks Functions/Grammar	Speaking
12	Click here!	Using the internet *Are we all online now?* SB54	Cyber news: Professional computer gamers; Internet dating SB55	Uncountable nouns; Deducing LB12 WB105	TEAMWORK: Creating a website SB56, 117 CONTROVERSY: What's the real cost of online gambling? SB56
13	What's in the news?	The media *Do you trust the media?* SB58	Media: Media mogul Berlusconi; Censorship SB59	Colloquialisms; Implying LB13	TEAMWORK: Fictional news stories SB60, 117 CONTROVERSY: Are journalists sometimes spies? SB60 STRATEGIES: Using quotes WB106
14	Heroes and villains	Role models *Do we need someone to look up to?* SB62	Pop culture: Eminem, pop culture icon; Christopher Reeve, disability campaigner SB63	Idiomatic and Softening expressions LB14 Joining clauses WB107	TEAMWORK: Role models for teenagers SB64, 117 CONTROVERSY: Is there a link between image and eating disorders? SB64
	Extended Reading 2	Lifestyles SB66	Snowboard Nirvana: A snowboarder's blog SB66		Interactive Task: Travel SB67
15	Family matters	Roles in the family *What's a normal family?* SB68	Family: New feminism; Fathers' rights SB69	Conditionals; Generalising LB15	TEAMWORK: Family and friends network SB70, 118 CONTROVERSY: Is it right to adopt from another country? SB70 STRATEGIES: Emphasising a point WB108
16	Let's change the subject!	School curriculum *Are students learning the right things?* SB72	Education: Rewriting the history books; Making the school system fairer SB73	Signposting: Sequencing (2); Asserting LB16 Gerund and infinitive WB109	TEAMWORK: Relevance of school subjects to everyday life SB74, 118 CONTROVERSY: Are single-sex schools better? SB74
17	Adventures in science	Scientific developments *Is science making life better?* SB76	Science and technology: Bionic suit; 'Spider-goats' super web material SB77	Expressions used to introduce assertions; Developing an argument LB17	TEAMWORK: Be a futurologist SB78, 118 CONTROVERSY: Where will cloning lead? SB78 STRATEGIES: Knowing what is important: key words WB110
18	The company we keep	Social issues *Are we doing enough to help?* SB80	National news: Hidden homeless; Waiting for medical treatment SB81	Expressions used to contradict; Summarising LB18 Wordforms WB111	TEAMWORK: New work opportunities for your community SB82, 119 CONTROVERSY: Should immigration be controlled? SB82
19	Stressed out!	Stress management *Are we seriously stressed?* SB84	Health: Prime Minister, fitness fan; Watching fish eases stress SB85	Language of empathy and sympathy; Calming LB19	TEAMWORK: How does fear turn into phobia? SB86, 119 CONTROVERSY: Dealing with stress or depression SB86 STRATEGIES: Anticipating questions WB112
20	Shock tactics	Young people's behaviour *Are all teenagers rebels?* SB88	Crime: Rock group with no drugs message; Jobs in the marijuana industry SB89	Language of caution; Eliciting feedback LB20 Verbs WB113	TEAMWORK: Creating programmes to help young people SB90, 119 CONTROVERSY: Should tattoos and body piercings be banned? SB90
	Extended Reading 3	Stereotypes SB92	Not all Natives are created equal SB92		Interactive Task: Stereotypes about older people and different ethnicities SB93
SB	Workbook SB94-113	Teamwork Scenarios SB114-119		Unit-by-unit Glossary SB120-128	
TG	Exam listening practice IGCSE PR200-203		IELTS PR204-208	CAE PR244-247	

Key:
SB = Student's Book   TG = Teacher's Guide
WB = Workbook   PR = Photocopiable Resources

QSE Advanced MATERIALS MAP

Vocabulary	Listening Audio/Video	Writing	CLIL (Content and Language Integrated Learning)	Teacher's Guide Photocopiable Resources	Pages
Computers, information technology; Idioms WB105	**Video:** Languages used on the internet SB56	Personal profile; Predictions for the internet SB56 Email; Game concept WB105	**Information technology:** Viruses and hacking SB57	Teacher's notes and answer key TG93 IGCSE Exam PR190, 198 CAE Exam PR229	Unit 12 SB54-57 WB105 TG93
TV, radio, newspapers; Idioms WB106	**Video:** TV news channel documentary SB60	Letter about pay-per-click journalism; Article review SB60 Article; Report WB106	**Media studies:** Media criticism; Control of free expression SB61	Teacher's notes and answer key TG99 IGCSE Exam PR199 CAE Exam PR231, 234	Unit 13 SB58-61 WB106 TG99
Personal qualities; Idioms WB107	**Audio:** Comic book superheroes SB64	Being a mentor; What is a 'bad' role model? SB64 Letter; Play outline WB107	**Literature:** Iconic writers: Maya Angelou and Jack Kerouac SB65	Teacher's notes and answer key TG105 IGCSE Exam PR195, 199 IELTS Exam PR213 CAE Exam PR227, 236, 239	Unit 14 SB62-65 WB107 TG105
Snowboarding SB67 Idioms SB66		Summary; Complete the missing section of the story SB67		Teacher's notes and answer key TG111	SB66-67 TG111
Family; Idioms WB108	**Audio:** Interview with a teenage mother SB70	Changes in families; A friend's wedding SB70 Email; Day in the life WB108	**Home economics:** Running a household with children SB71	Teacher's notes and answer key TG114 IGSCE Exam PR199 IELTS Exam PR223	Unit 15 SB68-71 WB108 TG114
School subjects; Idioms WB109	**Audio:** Creationism in Arizona schools SB74	Improving the school system; An exchange visit SB74 Diary entry; Essay WB109	**Physical education:** Learning through experience with outdoor activities SB75	Teacher's notes and answer key TG119 IGCSE Exam PR177, 199 IELTS Exam PR221 CAE Exam PR237, 242	Unit 16 SB72-75 WB109 TG119
Science; Idioms WB110	**Video:** Space debris SB78	Report; Scientific developments SB78 Article; Letter WB110	**Engineering:** New products and developments SB79	Teacher's notes and answer key TG125 IGCSE Exam PR179, 191, 202 IELTS Exam PR207, 222 CAE Exam PR239, 240, 245, 247	Unit 17 SB76-79 WB110 TG125
Social problems; Idioms WB111	**Audio:** Computer training for slum dwellers in Brazil SB82	Report on crime; Letter about healthcare SB82 Article; Report WB111	**Social studies:** Community development SB83	Teacher's notes and answer key TG132 IGCSE Exam PR183 CAE Exam PR243	Unit 18 SB80-83 WB111 TG 132
Ways of reducing stress; Idioms WB112	**Audio:** Laughter Clubs SB86	Coping with stress; Most stressful day SB86 Email; Article WB112	**Biology:** Effects of stress on the body and on behaviour SB87	Teacher's notes and answer key TG138 IGCSE Exam PR191 CAE Exam PR249	Unit 19 SB84-87 WB112 TG138
Types of teenage behaviour; Idioms WB113	**Audio:** Binge drinking SB90	Youth behaviour; Advice for a friend SB90 Email; Story WB113	**Poetry and music:** Analysing the meaning of a song SB91	Teacher's notes and answer key TG144 IGCSE Exam PR183, 192 IELTS Exam PR204 CAE Exam PR242, 250	Unit 20 SB88-91 WB113 TG144
Non-standard English SB93 Idioms SB92		Summary; New story about Big Glenn SB93		Teacher's notes and answer key TG149	SB92-93 TG149
					SB

Audio Tests 1-6 TG169-173, **Test 7** TG256   **Placement Test** PR251-252   **Exam answers** TG253-255   TG

QSE | Introduction | Teacher's Guide

Introduction - Welcome to *QSE Advanced*

- *Quick Smart English* is a topic-based English language course for levels B2 to C1 in line with the **CEF (Common European Framework)**.
- *QSE* uses affective, topical and sometimes controversial reading and listening material to present and revise structures and vocabulary and to develop communication skills.
- The language structures are those found in widely-accepted international curricula.
- The topic-based vocabulary is wide-ranging and based on real-life ideas and issues.
- The learning tasks include integrated skills activities, with a particular focus on speaking.
- Integrated **CLIL** (Content and Language Integrated Learning) activities are in each unit.
- Although *QSE Advanced* is not a dedicated exam preparation course, the structure and vocabulary practice, skills work, question types and supplementary test materials are all designed to help students prepare for international ESOL examinations.
- *QSE Advanced* is designed to cover a 70-80 hour course, although it can also be used in modules for skills development, in particular speaking practice.

QSE and the CEF

The structure and approach of the course are based on the Council of Europe's Common European Framework of Reference (**CEF**). Like the CEF, *QSE Advanced* takes a very broad view of what language students need to learn in order to use a foreign language and what knowledge and skills they need to develop so as to be able to communicate effectively. *QSE* aims to provide the widest possible cultural context, using examples from the great cultural diversity of global English (British, American, Australian, South African and others).

QSE helps to provide learners with strategies to activate general and communicative competences in order to carry out the activities and processes involved in the production and reception of texts and the construction of discourse dealing with particular themes.

The objectives, content and methods of *QSE* follow the guidelines of the **CEF**, aiming to equip students to deal with communicating in English, not only in English-speaking countries, but also in using the language as a *lingua franca* in other countries. *QSE* helps students to exchange information and ideas and to communicate their thoughts and feelings. Its wide range of topics, many of which are unusual in EFL courses, help students to achieve a wider and deeper understanding of the way other people live and think and of their cultural heritage. The methods of teaching language and learning with *QSE* are based on the needs, motivations, characteristics and resources of the learners themselves. The course is above all student-centred. The language learning activities are based on action-orientated tasks and relevant authentic texts (oral and written).

The topics (including the CLIL materials) help students to face the modern challenges of international mobility and closer co-operation, not only in education, culture and science but also in trade and industry. *QSE* aims to promote mutual understanding and tolerance, respect for identities and cultural diversity through more effective international communication.

The course visits all four **domains** identified by the CEF. The Public Domain, for example, is represented in many units including environmental issues in Unit 8, society in Unit 18 and economic issues in Unit 7. The Personal Domain is visited in Unit 10 (Young people's rights), Unit 9 (Independence) and Unit 20 (Young people's behaviour) among others. The Educational Domain features in Unit 16 (School curriculum), and the Occupational Domain appears in Unit 3 (Ambitions).

The CEF is a framework not only for language learning, but also for **assessment**, which is central to the methodology of *QSE*. *QSE Advanced* is compatible with preparation for a variety of international English examinations. *QSE Advanced* features a special set of exam preparation materials for the UCLES Cambridge suite of exams – CAE (Certificate in Advanced English) level, IELTS (International English Language Testing System) and IGCSE (International General Certificate of Secondary Education). Trinity College London recognises that *QSE* makes a valuable contribution to preparation for the Graded Examinations in Spoken English (GESE) and Integrated Skills Examination (ISE). Other levels of *QSE* are coordinated with other Cambridge exams – *QSE Pre-Intermediate* with **PET** level and *QSE Intermediate* with **FCE**. The chart below shows how the various levels of the *QSE* course have been planned to match the levels of the CEF and the requirements of international examinations.

QSE levels, the CEF and international examinations

QSE	Common European Framework (CEF)	UCLES (University of Cambridge ESOL)	Trinity College, London ESOL	Michigan / HAU	TOEFL (New TOEFL)	IELTS	Edexcel London Test of English
Quick START English (in preparation)	A1-A2	KET (Key English Test)	GESE Grade 1, 2, 3				Level (A1) 1
QSE Pre-Intermediate	A2-B1	PET (Preliminary English Test)	ISE 0, ISE I, GESE Grade 4, 5, 6	BCCE		3.0 to 4.0	Level 1-2
QSE Intermediate	B1-B2	FCE (First Certificate in English)	ISE II, GESE Grade 7, 8, 9	ECCE	450-525 Target 485 (NT 163)	4.0 to 5.5	Level 2-3
QSE Advanced	B2-C1	CAE (Certificate in Advanced English)	ISE III, GESE Grade 10, 11	ALCE	Target 525 (NT 197)	5.5 to 6.5 / 7.0	Level 3-4

QSE Advanced takes students from Level **B2** to **C1**. These are the **CEF Reference Levels Global Descriptors** for the two levels.

	B2 -------------------------------	----------------------------► C1
Listening	I can understand extended speech and lectures and follow even complex lines of argument provided the topic is reasonably familiar. I can understand most TV news current affairs programmes. I can understand the majority of films in standard dialect.	I can understand extended speech even when it is not clearly structured and when relationships are only implied and not signalled explicitly. I can understand television programmes and films without too much effort.
Reading	I can read articles and reports concerned with contemporary problems in which the writers adopt particular attitudes or viewpoints. I can understand contemporary literary prose.	I can understand long and complex factual and literary texts, appreciating distinctions of style. I can understand specialised linguistically complex articles and longer technical instructions, even when they do not relate to my field.
Spoken interaction	I can interact with a degree of fluency and spontaneity that makes regular interaction with native speakers quite possible. I can take an active part in discussion in familiar contexts, accounting for and sustaining my views.	I can express myself fluently and spontaneously without much obvious searching for expressions. I can use language flexibly and effectively for social and professional purposes. I can formulate ideas and opinions with precision and relate my contribution skilfully to those of other speakers.
Spoken production	I can present clear, detailed descriptions on a wide range of subjects related to my field of interest. I can explain a viewpoint on a topical issue giving the advantages and disadvantages of various options.	I can present clear, detailed descriptions of complex subjects integrating sub-themes, developing particular points and rounding off with an appropriate conclusion.
Writing	I can write clear, detailed text on a wide range of subjects related to my interests. I can write an essay or report, passing on information or giving reasons in support of or against a particular point of view. I can write letters highlighting the personal significance of events and experiences.	I can express myself in clear, well-structured text, expressing points of view at some length. I can write about complex subjects in a letter, an essay or a report, underlining what I consider to be the salient issues. I can select style appropriate to the reader in mind.

QSE for exams

QSE is not designed to be a specific exam-preparation course, but no teacher or class these days can ignore the fact that exams are a very important and almost unavoidable presence in the language classroom. All international exams today have been written or have been calibrated to fit into the levels and requirements of the CEF, however, styles of examination differ. As *QSE* is a course with a very strong emphasis on **spoken English** and developing **oral skills**, the author decided to use the syllabus of the **Trinity College, London, GESE** (Graded Examinations in Spoken English) and **ISE** (Integrated Skills in English) examinations for the core subject areas. However, we are aware that many students will take other exams, so there are many question types, tasks and exercises in the Student's Book and Workbook that provide exam practice in all four skills for several exam types. In addition, there are special photocopiable pages in this Teacher's Guide that practise the **University of Cambridge CAE, IELTS and IGCSE** – see details below. This makes *QSE* an ideal course for general study at the end of which students may go on to take a variety of exams, including those of Trinity and Cambridge.

QSE and Cambridge / Trinity / IELTS / IGCSE exam practice

QSE is not an exam-practice book; students taking any examinations should prepare by using actual sample papers before they sit any exams. However, *QSE* does provide a great deal of practice in every skill necessary for these.

Reading: Throughout the book there are many reading comprehension tasks, many of which are in specific exam formats, while the remainder practise the same skills in other formats. For example, the format of CAE Paper 1 Part 1 is specifically used in Units 3 and 17. Also, the IELTS Reading Passage 3 is covered in Units 5 and 18.

Writing: The Portfolio Writing section provides practice in CAE, IELTS and ISE-style writing tasks, as does the Portfolio Writing section in the Workbook. In particular, the ISE III Portfolio Writing tasks are seen throughout the book. Most can be used to simulate the Controlled Writing Tasks as well. The CAE exam practice pages for Units 4, 9 and 13 provide tasks in the precise format of the CAE exam, while IELTS Task 2 is practised in Units 1, 4 and 13.

Use of English
In almost every unit of the Workbook there is practice in CAE Paper 3 Use of English tasks. These are in abbreviated form, as it is not necessary to practise a complete exam paper for every activity. Each of the CAE exam practice pages provides tasks in the format of the Use of English paper and covers all question types.

Listening: Many of the listening activities in the units are based on CAE and IELTS-style tasks. With 80 minutes of audio and video material, *QSE* provides ample listening material.

There is also additional exam listening practice for IGSCE, CAE and IELTS on the DVD-ROM (see page 152 and 200–203, 204–208 and 244–247).

Speaking: All the speaking activities in the units practise the skills and functions necessary for the Cambridge CAE, IELTS, IGCSE and Trinity ISE III exam.

Exam practice pages

In this Teacher's Guide there are photocopiable exam practice pages from page 176, with an introduction about using the *QSE* Photocopiable Resources on page 174 of this Teacher's Guide. There are 27 pages for the **Cambridge Advanced English** exam, 20 pages for the **IELTS** exam and 28 pages for the **IGCSE** exam. You can use these pages at the same time as the main units, or separately for homework. Each set of materials can be marked by the teacher using the exam answers section.

QSE and the Trinity College London GESE and ISE exams

Because they are based on the structures, functions and subject areas of Trinity's Advanced (Grades 10 and 11) Graded Examinations in Spoken English (**GESE**) and Integrated Skills in English (**ISE III**) Examination (covering CEF levels **C1** and up), the units in the *QSE Advanced* coursebook provide a thorough preparation for students wishing to take either oral or integrated skills examinations at these levels.

The **READING** (Activity 2 of each unit) and **LISTEN / WATCH AND LISTEN** (Activity 4 of each unit) sections in the book familiarise students with the vocabulary specific to the subject areas in the Trinity examinations. Students then learn how to present and discuss their knowledge and ideas with the examiner in **TEAMWORK** (Activity 5), **CONTROVERSY** (Activity 6) and **the topic in English** (Activity 8) in each unit, using the appropriate structures and functions.

Students should select a **topic** that they are interested in, knowledgeable about and able to talk readily about. In preparing the topic, candidates should be actively discouraged from producing and memorising a written text, as this will have an adverse effect on the candidate's pronunciation and ability to use spontaneous spoken English. They should also prepare enough material to discuss the topic for up to five minutes. The discussion should provide opportunities for the candidate to use the language of the specific grade, for example at Grade 11 or ISE III, vague or imprecise language and expressions for downplaying.

In the Topic phase of the Trinity Advanced exams the candidate needs to be prepared to:
- Invite questions and comments from the examiner about the content of the presentation
- Engage the examiner in a discussion of some of the points made in the presentation
- Respond to the examiner's challenges and requests for clarification or elaboration.

Candidates may like to take with them into the exam one or more pictures, photos, models or other suitable objects to illustrate their prepared topics.

The **INTERACTIVE TASK** in the Student's Book (Extended Reading Sections 1, 2, 3) gives students the opportunity to prepare for the Interactive Task phase of the GESE and ISE exams at this level. Here candidates are expected to be able to:
- Take responsibility for the discourse with the examiner
- Use turn-taking to maintain a natural flow to the discourse
- Relate their own contributions with those of the examiner
- Negotiate toward a successful conclusion.

QSE and CLIL

One of the most significant aims of recent educational thinking in many countries has been to make learning a relevant preparation for the students' real lives in the widest sense. This can mean not just relevance to vocational training but also to personal development, citizenship, further education and the use of information technology. In addition, education reforms in many countries now encourage a greater emphasis on political, economic, historical and cultural world awareness, as globalisation affects everyone's lives.

QSE features a cross-curricular **CLIL** (Content and Language Integrated Learning) topic as part of every unit. Many reflect the nature of the modern syllabus with subjects like Business Studies, Law and Information Technology. The course approach to CLIL also reaches out more widely to embrace a range of topics that interest and are useful to students even if they are not being formally studied. These include ideas such as Psychology, Meteorology, Social Studies and Public Relations.

In *QSE,* CLIL is truly integrated so that it becomes a natural part of what we use language for – talking about the things that interest us.

The objective of the cross-curricular sections in this book is not to add to the students' own knowledge of subjects. Instead it is to equip students with an English-language strategy (and the relevant conceptual and linguistic tools) so that they can extend their understanding of the world through the use of a foreign language.

'CLIL is an approach to bilingual education in which both curriculum content – such as science or history – and English are taught together….. Hence it is a means of teaching curriculum subjects through the medium of the language still being learned.…. CLIL can also be regarded the other way round – as a means of teaching English through study of a specialist content. … CLIL is compatible with the idea of JIT education (i.e. Just In Time learning) and is regarded by some of its practitioners as the ultimate communicative methodology.' (David Graddol, *English Next*, British Council, 2006)

QSE and Multiple Intelligences

The theory of Multiple Intelligences, first posited by Dr Howard Gardner in 1983 and modified many times since then, has divided teachers and educators as much as it has brought them together. But this is really a matter of the details. Most educational theorists now agree that the long-established methods of teaching and testing, which only appealed to a learner's linguistic or logical-mathematical intelligences, work well for some students but exclude others whose intelligences are of a different type.

What we have tried to do in this book is address certain other aspects of the theory, particularly the distinction between interpersonal and intrapersonal intelligences. Students do not always want to interact with each other and provision needs to be made for 'lone' activities as well as pair and group work. Auditory learners will find plenty of stimulation in the varied audio material on the DVD-ROM. The video extracts on the DVD-ROM will attract visual learners, as will the photos that make the texts come alive.

We have also tried to balance giving teachers and learners what they like, expect and are used to and giving them something new and different, without making them alarmed or uncomfortable.

English as a meme

Content and Language Integrated Learning (CLIL) represents an evolution in second-language acquisition. It is an idea that is changing the way people learn English. One of the key concepts of CLIL is that, by changing the context in which a foreign language is learned, teachers can make it more relevant to the students' needs and thus more readily acquired.

In 1976, Professor Richard Dawkins of Oxford University suggested that there are units of cultural inheritance and transfer which he called 'memes'. He suggested that they work in a way that is similar to the way that genes pass on biological information. Memes are ideas (such as the Earth is flat) or fashions (like short skirts) or skills (such as skiing), which can be rapidly transmitted from one person to another.

The skill of speaking English as a foreign or second language is now a globally successful idea, or meme. Over a billion people worldwide are learning English as a foreign language. Dawkins and others think that memes reproduce by both mutation and recombination, rather like genes in the process of biological evolution itself. A mutation in thought may take centuries to take root. For example, Leonardo da Vinci's ideas on mechanical flight did not catch on in the 15th century because the technical environment of the time could not support them. Five hundred years later, the meme of flight is so commonplace we hardly question it.

Memes are also propagated by recombination, such as when existing ideas and skills come up against a new environment and adapt rapidly to suit it. Thus, mobile phones and the internet have dramatically changed the ways in which people communicate. We still talk and write, but now we do this instantly with people anywhere in the world. The result is an explosion of global communication — an extremely successful meme, evolved to fit the 21st-century environment.

CLIL may be another example of memetic recombination. The learning environment is filled with subjects like geography, history and physics. If language learning moves into these new environments, it becomes an improved meme — one that combines old ways of teaching with new situations and thus provokes students to acquire improved skills and new ideas.

Students not only learn *about* the subject of geography or maths with CLIL, they also turn the process upside down and learn the language *from* the subject. If they are already learning geography, discussing it in English enables them to recombine the subject with the second language, producing a form of learning that is better adapted to their environment. It's more fun, more relevant and more motivating, and like a gene or a meme, more successful.

QSE | Introduction | Teacher's Guide

QSE Advanced – at a glance

QSE Advanced consists of 20 separate units of five pages each (four pages in the main unit and a Workbook page), plus various additional materials, such as Extended Reading, Language Banks, Teamwork Scenarios and Glossary.

Every unit of the course works in the same way. The activities are varied, but the instructions are kept as simple and as similar as possible. This means that students only have to learn how to use the course in the first unit, and can then expect the same structure in the rest of the units. This makes it exceptionally clear and user-friendly, further defining the student-centred approach of the whole course.

Scope and sequence of the course:

Contents pages *Student's Book and Workbook* (see also Materials Map pages 4–7 of this Teacher's Guide)

Every unit consists of:

4 Student's Book pages

Page 1:
Viewpoint: Word Power, Reading, Speak Your Mind

Page 2:
Reading texts (two texts per unit)

Page 3:
Listen / Watch and Listen, Teamwork, Controversy, Portfolio Writing

Page 4:
CLIL, Further Discussion, Your Answer

1 Workbook page   *Teamwork Scenario*   *Language Bank*   *Student's DVD-ROM*

 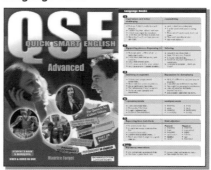 

Grammar, Vocabulary Use of English, Idioms, Writing, Speaking Strategies

Outline for Teamwork activity

20 Language Banks, on the cover flaps

Audio and video clips Printable transcripts

3 Extended Reading sections

Reading, Idioms, Identify the idiom / word,
Portfolio Writing, Interactive Task

Unit-by-unit Glossary in the Student's Book

Exam practice photocopiable pages in this Teacher's Guide

IGCSE exam practice: Reading, Writing, Speaking, Listening

IELTS exam practice: Reading, Writing, Speaking, Listening

CAE exam practice: Reading, Writing, Speaking, Listening, Use of English

QSE Advanced – how the sections of each unit work

MATERIALS MAP OF THE COURSE

Student's Book Contents pages 4–7
Teacher's Guide pages 4–7

The syllabus of **QSE Advanced** is based on an extensive survey of current international standards in EFL teaching. Increasingly these are based on the CEF, or, if non-European, they are now being aligned with it (for example the University of Michigan examinations). The topical basis of the course is the syllabus of Trinity College London, but it also takes into account the functional and structural requirements of the University of Cambridge ESOL syllabus.

Given that **communicative competence** is one of the main aims of the **QSE** course, care has been taken not to overload the students with grammar. There is an expectation by the author in coordination with the various exams that students at this level should have a thorough working knowledge of grammar by this point, however, the workbook does review key grammar points that may cause occasional mistakes. The Student's Book takes care to concentrate on skills work, particularly **speaking**.

The Contents pages show the scope and sequence of the whole book as well as each unit, with headings for **Topic** (or Subject), *The BIG question*, **Functions** (Language Banks), **Grammar**, **Reading**, **Listening**, **Speaking**, **Writing** and **CLIL**. These pages can be used as a quick reference for both students and teachers, including a list of **DVD tracks**.

STUDENT'S BOOK UNITS

The four colour pages of the Student's Book units contain all the main language input material of the course. There are many short units, rather than a few long ones, so there is lots of variety and interest for different tastes. There are **20 units**, plus three **Extended reading** sections. There is also a series of **Language Banks,** examples of functional language presented in meaningful and useful written or spoken examples. The **Language Banks** are on fold-out cover flaps for easy reference in class when students are working on any unit. The functions chosen for these Language Banks are taken from the Trinity College GESE syllabus, Grades 10 and 11.

The format of each unit is as follows:

Unit title and What's new?

Student's Book unit, page 1
The title gives a clue to the unit topic, and the **What's new?** box tells you what the unit covers. All three areas – Subject, Function and Grammar (where appropriate) – will prepare students for effectively tackling the speaking and writing requirements for the different exams. The Teacher's Guide includes extra questions (EQ) for every section to allow greater control of time and more intensive discussions as required.

1 *The BIG question* and Viewpoint

Every unit begins and ends with an important question related to the central unit theme and will be explored again at the end of the unit in the **Your Answer** section. The question is intended to immediately grab the attention of the students when it first appears. They are not asked to give an opinion at this stage. It is simply there to make them think. At the end of the unit, after consideration of the evidence in the unit and consultation with other students about their opinions, the class will be much more prepared and confident to answer the question.

Using *The BIG question:*

- Read the question out. Check students understand it by asking questions. You will get students to answer the question at the end of the unit for review.
- Ask students to write one or two sentences in their notebooks.
- Tell them that at the end of the unit you will ask them to reread their answers and see if they have changed their minds.

Viewpoint

Time: 5–10 minutes

Viewpoint gives some facts, quotes and photos to be used as a warm-up activity for the unit. The facts and quotes relate either directly or indirectly to the topics in the unit. There will be some background for these facts in the Teacher's Guide. Use the extra questions (EQ) in the Teacher's Guide to explore the significance of these facts. Students will often be asked to comment on or interpret the photo or illustration.

Note: These can be readily used by students in the topic presentation phase of the Cambridge CAE and Trinity Advanced Spoken Grade Examination interview.

1 WORD POWER

Time: 15–20 minutes

The **WORD POWER** section has two main aims:
- To introduce students to vocabulary and idioms relating to the subject area.
- To introduce and practise the phrases in the Language Bank, so that students are using this new vocabulary immediately in a communicative way by answering contextual questions. Answers to activities are in the Teacher's Guide.

Note: Teachers should stress to students that they should make every attempt to use the new vocabulary when they answer related questions.

This section is cross-referenced to the **Workbook** unit where there are extra activities.

2 READING

Student's Book unit, page 2
Time: 25 minutes

The second page of each unit has two reading texts: authentic articles from worldwide sources – print and online (newspapers, magazines, websites). The topics have been chosen in line with the specifications of the Trinity College spoken exams and other exam curricula. Occasionally the texts shock or surprise, but will always draw the attention of the reader. It also provides a strong motivation to read ELT materials as well.

The **Reading** activity is a communicative activity tied to the two articles. It helps students practise extensive and intensive reading skills.

The **Reading** section also aims to provide the students with material to help them deal with later activities in the unit, including **Your Answer** (Activity 10) to _**The BIG question**_ at the end.

There are various activities including:
- Vocabulary exercises: finding words in the article from definitions given and matching headlines with parts of the text.
- Summarising information in the articles.
- Evaluating or comparing the two articles.

Important! After skimming, students should read the article twice. The first time should be without the glossary to try to understand the meaning of the words in context. This can be done as a group to also practise pronunciation as well. The second time students could actively use the glossary list at the back of the book to confirm their understanding of the new vocabulary.

Using READING:

The comprehension activities:
- Read out the questions or ask students to read them silently. Ask questions to check comprehension.
- Put students into pairs or small groups to discuss their answers. Alternatively, give students time to think about their answers individually. Elicit answers, giving the answer yourself if necessary. Where appropriate, ask students to justify their answers by quoting the sentence(s) from the text.

Reading in class:
Ideally, students should be encouraged to read the articles before coming to class. This allows them time to read through the comprehension questions and think about their answers. However, the articles can also be read in class, which would simulate the time constraints of the various exams' reading comprehension. In either case, each student should have an opportunity to read part or an entire article aloud in class. The teacher should use this opportunity to check for possible pronunciation errors, which can be identified after the text has been read. Proper pronunciation is critical at this level.

Some extra suggestions for Reading:

- Students can be asked to read a text at home and do some preparatory work of their own, and then come to class with questions about the content.
- The teacher can pre-teach certain words and expressions in a dialogue of discovery with the class, and then the students can read the text in silence.
- In large groups, students can work in pairs or groups with a new text, using their own knowledge, dictionaries, and questions from the teacher.
- The teacher can assign the text to be read in small sections, a paragraph for example, each section to a different group. The different groups work on their fragment of text and then tell the rest of the class about it. One of them can read it aloud, as long as the others can't see the text themselves.

3 SPEAK YOUR MIND

Time: 20–30 minutes

This section is an innovative way of combining the chance to discuss the topic and also activate some key functional language. Four or five questions in this section give the class an opportunity to voice opinions on a wide variety of issues related to the unit's subject area. It is important to try to get students using the **Language Bank** phrases, where appropriate. Although this can be somewhat mechanical if pursued too rigorously, using the phrases will enable further practice and allow you to evaluate the accuracy of the phrasal usage.

This activity can be extended as long as class time allows. Use the extra questions (EQ) to help keep the discussion going if necessary.

It is also important to bear in mind that with any productive task, speaking or writing, successful completion of the task is more important than actually using the target functional language. In other words, if students carry out the task successfully, but don't use any of the target expressions, this is not a reason to criticise them!

Using SPEAK YOUR MIND:

- Go through the relevant **Language Bank**. Either read out the sentences yourself or ask students to read it out. Teach any new language.
- Read out the questions or ask students to read them out. Check comprehension by asking questions.
- Put students in pairs or small groups to discuss their answers. As students talk, walk round and listen to students, noting major errors. Alternatively, give students time to think about their answers individually.
- Elicit answers and encourage discussion. Make notes of students' major errors, particularly errors involving the target structure and vocabulary items. It's probably best to point out major errors after the discussion and write the correct versions on the board.
- It can prove to be very helpful, in a follow-up session, to briefly go through the activity again as a way of revising the language.

4 LISTEN / WATCH AND LISTEN

Student's Book unit, page 3
Time: 20–25 minutes

Listening is a vitally important language skill and it is important that listening material should sound authentic as well as interesting. The DVD-ROM includes 20 tracks, with a video or audio clip for each unit. The blue symbol (⓾) next to the title shows the track number on the DVD-ROM.

The **audio and video script** for the audio and video clips is also on the DVD as PDF files that can be opened on a PC and in the Teacher's Guide on page 153. See **Using the DVD-ROM** on page 152.

The clips have been carefully chosen for provocative content to stimulate discussion. They also reflect a global perspective with a mix of different accents from the UK and other English-speaking countries.

Using LISTEN / WATCH AND LISTEN:

- This section always has an opening discussion featuring questions relating to the issue in the listening activity. There is also a photo or photos as a prompt. The Teacher's Guide contains background information on the context of the track.
- The next question asks students to predict what may happen in the listening activity based on what they already know about the subject. At this point, you play the track for the first

time so students can answer a set of listening comprehension questions. These questions test the students' ability to find specific information. The students can answer these questions as a group. Answers are provided in the TG.
- In some of the listening activities there is a question to allow students to speculate on what will happen next in the clip. This helps students practise commenting on or imagining how the narrative might continue. The audio or video clip pauses for the teacher to discuss the question with the students.
- The final question asks students to address the underlying theme. You can again stress that students should try to practise the **Language Bank** phrases and new vocabulary from **Word Power.**

5 TEAMWORK

Time: 15 minutes

This section is a creative brainstorming activity. The idea is to help students become more spontaneous in generating ideas for discussion. This is particularly important in the interactive and conversation phases of the GESE. Each unit provides different brainstorming techniques that will be helpful outside the class.

The outline of the activity is explained in the **Scenario** section of the book. These activities are designed for pairs or groups of threes, which will maximise the students' speaking time. If you feel the students need more work on presentations, most Teamwork activities can be adapted so that the findings can be presented to another pair or the class. In addition, each unit provides important background information and additional questions to extend the activity as desired.

Using TEAMWORK:

- Divide students into pairs or groups, according to the numbers needed in the Teamwork activity.
- Ask students to read the Scenario and ask questions to check comprehension.
- Encourage students to enjoy themselves! Walk round and listen.
- Remember the golden rule of brainstorming – all ideas are valid and should be recorded. Editing, criticising or rejecting ideas should wait until after all ideas have been elicited.
- Students can present the results of their brainstorming session to the class.

6 CONTROVERSY

Time: 25–40 minutes

This is one of the most innovative sections of the **QSE Advanced** Student's Book. It deals with a deliberately controversial issue related to the topic of the unit to ensure that students practise using their argument skills in a debate. It is essentially an opinionated **role-play.** The roles are explained in abbreviated form on the page of the Student's Book.

Usually, the students divide into groups of four, but this is only recommended because it reflects the traditional number for debate teams. The activity will also work with groups of three, two or even one-on-one debates. Consider your class size and needs in making this decision.

Once the class is divided into groups, you can either let the groups pick a side for the debate or assign them a side. The students should have about five to ten minutes to brainstorm arguments for their side, then you can then let them begin debating.

In formal debating, usually one member from one side gives a statement, followed by a statement from a member of the other group, until all group members have spoken. Then each member can offer rebuttals in turn. However, you can let the debate be as formal or informal as you wish. You can find more rules about debating at:
   http://debate.uvm.edu/default.html
   www.debate-central.org
   www.qub.ac.uk/edu/nicilt/fd/fredebate.htm

The Teacher's Guide notes for each unit provide important background information and additional questions to extend the activity as required.

In many cases, students are being asked to take on the role of someone who may be outside their experience and, more importantly, who may have opinions and beliefs which are not the same as their own. There are two ways to deal with this:
a) Tell students that they don't have to play the role if they feel uncomfortable with it.
b) Tell students to try the role anyway, as it will be good communication skills practice and may come in useful in an examination.

The problem with the first of these solutions is that a lazy class can end up doing nothing at all! The problem with the second is that students may feel upset about having to express certain opinions, especially if there are cultural reasons why they object to taking a certain role. The teacher will know where there are sensitivities, and could opt to omit this activity, if it is too controversial. But controversy is the name of the activity!

Even so, we feel that the second option is the better one, and students can be mollified by knowing that the tasks are designed in a very systematic way to help them with their fluency.

Using CONTROVERSY:

- Divide students into groups.
- Make sure the students have time to familiarise themselves fully with their role. Ask questions to check comprehension.
- Ask students to look at the points made for each side, which they can pick up on, as well as adding their own ideas.
- Students have their debate. Encourage them to enjoy themselves! Walk round and listen.
- Ask the class for their comments, both positive and negative.
- Ask students for their real opinions.

7 PORTFOLIO WRITING

This section provides guidance for the students to carry out writing tasks. The tasks include emails, letters, articles, reports and creative writing. **Portfolio Writing** is a student-centred activity that many teachers and learners will find motivating and creative.

An ISE III writing portfolio should include the three best samples of the student's work; one from:

- Letters or emails
- Reports, articles or reviews
- Creative writing

Each unit provides sources for additional online or library research. This section helps students with the Topic discussion and Conversation phases.

This section can alternatively be used as a controlled writing activity by asking students to write the essay in class in a given time. This would help students with the Writing sections of the Cambridge CAE, IELTS and IGCSE.

Using PORTFOLIO WRITING:

Writing

- Let students choose either activity A or B for each unit.
- Writing activities should be done outside class.
- Actively encourage students to practise new vocabulary, phrases or idioms in their writing.
- Make sure students use the correct writing styles (formality, diction, etc.) and formats (letters, emails, etc.)
- Get students to use a thesaurus and dictionary actively.
- Get students to brainstorm ideas for their work in groups or pairs.

Corrections

- If students use a word processor, make sure they first try to write without using a spellchecker or a grammar check. They can do this by turning off the autocorrect function, or simply changing the 'text language' of the document.
- Students could correct each other's work in the next class before handing them in.
- Prepare a sheet with examples of mistakes from different students. Discuss in class how to correct these.

8 CLIL *in English*

Student's Book unit, page 4
Time: 20–30 minutes

In this section, the cross-curricular aspects of the central unit theme are explored. The title of each **CLIL** (Content and Language Integrated Learning) section makes this connection clear. Titles include **PSYCHOLOGY *in English*** or **BUSINESS STUDIES *in English***. This also addresses a major component in the Advanced Stage of the Trinity GESE – topic presentation and topic discussion.

The input material to be read is more dense and challenging (although it is always short) and different from the articles in the **Reading** section. Information is also presented as statistics, charts or maps, as well as more conventional reading texts. Cross-curricular material is more and more in demand by teachers and syllabi. We think there is great value in cross-curricular study, with students using English to accomplish tasks which refer directly to other aspects of their studies or work.

The activities are done in pairs and sometimes groups of three. In mirroring the small group size of one-on-one interviews, this activity allows for increased speaking time and reduces the students' fear of public speaking. The activity has two parts: a presentation followed by a discussion of the presentation and an associated question or questions. After the presentation, it is important that the others ask the presenter a question. This helps practise the situation that requires students to answer examiner questions about their chosen presentation. There will also be EQ or other material in the TG to help you begin or extend these sections.

Students who excel in the particular subjects under discussion in this section may of course find them easier to deal with. They will even be able to help the rest of the class who may not be as expert in these subjects as they are. For example in **ENGINEERING in English** in Unit 17 students who are engineers should be encouraged to show the rest of the class (and the teacher) what they know – as long as it is in English. The advantage of this is that these students can then help other students.

Using the CLIL section:
- Explain the task and check comprehension. Students work individually or in pairs or small groups to complete the task.
- Give the students between 10 to 15 minutes to read the text and prepare the material for a presentation. You can circulate at this point to answer any questions students may have and to discuss any background material which may be included in the TG. Encourage students to use the vocabulary from **Word Power,** where appropriate, and phrases from the **Language Bank.**

Note: The Workbook includes Speaking Strategies activities students can use to help them improve their presentation techniques.

Alternative suggestions:
- You can give the presentation part of this activity for homework to be presented in the next class. This allows for extra research but may cut back on presentation spontaneity.
- You can choose different students to make their presentation in front of the whole class. The more exposure that students have to public speaking, the better the students will do in the topic presentation, however, this may be fairly intimidating to some students and should be considered carefully.
- You can have the pairs join another pair to give their presentations again. This time ask the students to evaluate the presentation according to the content, speaking style, eye contact, body language and so on.

9 FURTHER DISCUSSION

Time: 20 minutes

This section allows students to address more questions about issues relating to the subject area. This section will help students in the conversation phase of the different exams.

The students work in pairs again to make sure they have more speaking time in class. You should again try to get the students to practise using the phrases from the **Language Bank** and the vocabulary in **Word Power,** where appropriate.

Using FURTHER DISCUSSION:
- Make sure that the students understand the questions they are going to discuss.
- Put students into pairs to discuss the questions.
- While students are discussing the points, walk round and monitor students' use of language and grammar. You can also help the discussions along by using the EQ in the TG.
- After students have finished discussing the questions in pairs, you could ask one or two pairs to re-enact their conversation in front of the class to present their ideas to the class or you can discuss the main points again as a class.
- Go through any significant errors and write the correct versions on the board.
- In a follow-up session, you could ask students to go through the conversation again with a different partner. This is a good way to revise the language.

10 *Your answer*

Time: 5 minutes

And finally, we come back to **The BIG question** which started the unit and which serves as a review of the unit as a whole. Students will now be in a much better position to answer it. To prove this, we recommend that, before you start using the book with your class, you experiment by reading **The BIG question** of a particular unit and making a note of what your answer would be on first reading. Then read and listen to the unit content, and read the question again. Is there anything you would change or add? We think so, and we are sure that students will benefit from this approach.

As usual with **QSE** activities, this section offers guidance, and even lists opinions that the students might feel happy to express themselves. Some students will of course prefer to express themselves in their own words, but the 'sample opinions' are valuable for equally opinionated but less articulate students.

Using YOUR ANSWER:

- Ask students to look back to **The BIG question** and the answers that they noted down. Ask them to think about their answers for a few minutes and whether their opinions have changed.
- Read out the questions and the answers or ask students to read them out. Explain that the answers are just examples – they don't have to agree with them.
- Put students into groups to discuss the questions. Walk round and listen, noting major errors.
- Afterwards, or alternatively, have a whole class discussion, encouraging students to reply to each other. You can also use the EQ in the TG to address any related issues.
- Point out major errors and write the corrected versions on the board.
- Ask students if their opinions have changed since they first answered **The BIG question**, and if so, why?
- For homework, ask students to write one or two paragraph answers to the questions.

EXTENDED READING

Time: 20–30 minutes

Three **Extended Reading** units are placed after units 7, 14 and 20. The authentic reading texts here are longer than the reading texts on page 2 of the main units. As the main units are heavily weighted toward speaking activities, these three units aim to balance out the amount of reading and writing practice. Each text is approximately a thousand words, which places them within the exam framework for the ISE III and the UCLES exams' long reading sections.

Each unit contains five activities. These units can be done in class or most often as homework. In either case, you will need to go through the answers in class. Answers are given in the Teacher's Guide.

Using the EXTENDED READING:

Reading

This activity is similar to the Reading activity in main units. The TG includes answers and EQ.

Idioms

At advanced level, it is important for students to be able to show a knowledge of and ability to use idioms. In this activity students find idioms in the text based on definitions. The students must then put the idioms into the appropriate gaps.

This activity asks students to read the text in more depth trying to find a certain number of idioms or phrases. To make sure students understand the meanings of these you can ask EQ when you are going through the answers.

Portfolio Writing

This section is similar to the main units. The first question in each of the three units complies with the ISE III Controlled Writing Task 1 requirements and the IGCSE Part 2. It can also help students summarise opinions about the subject area. The second question is a creative writing activity that is suitable for Trinity ISE and Cambridge CAE, IGCSE and IELTS. There is a third question in Extended Reading 3 that is not exam-specific, but it does challenge students to develop their ideas much further.

QSE Advanced

Interactive task

This activity is based specifically on the Interactive Task in the Trinity GESE. However, it is an excellent way for students taking other exams to develop their spoken abilities. A student is required to take the responsibility for maintaining interaction in a discussion for up to five minutes.

- Go through the relevant **Language Bank** as outlined in **Speak Your Mind** and **Controversy** notes above. Elicit ways of incorporating the functional language into the students' conversation.
- Put students into pairs or groups to make notes in preparation for the task. It can be helpful to ask one of the more confident groups to go through the task. As they do so, make notes of helpful new vocabulary and phrases. Afterwards, elicit / teach these items.
- Students then go through the task.
- Proceed as outlined above at the same stage in the **Speak Your Mind** and **Controversy** notes.

GLOSSARY

At the back of the Student's Book there is a unit-by-unit monolingual **Glossary** section. This contains approximately 20–40 head words per unit, with English-language explanations in the style of popular learner's dictionaries. This does not replace a dictionary, which students will need and should use frequently, but it does provide a quick reference to the most difficult vocabulary in a lexically rich book.

LANGUAGE BANKS

There are **20 Language Banks** (**LBs**) on the **cover flaps** of the Student's Book. In this way they can be kept open in front of the students for constant reference. There is a LB for each of the **functions** listed in the scope and sequence of the course (see Contents pages 4–7 of the Student's Book).

Students should be encouraged to use the LBs for ready reference in speaking activities particularly. Each LB can be used in conjunction with many different units of the book. However, each one is introduced and practised for the first time in the order of units shown in the contents. Reference to the new LB for each unit is usually made for the first time in Activity 1 **Word Power.** Thereafter students are expected to be able to use the LBs on their own initiative, and when prompted in the text.

WORKBOOK UNITS

The **QSE Advanced Workbook** section is designed to be done as homework, but you should go through the answers in class to discuss particular points, notably the idioms. There are four parts to each unit, with a Speaking Strategies activity that appears in every other unit (see below). Answers can be found in the Teacher's Guide.

The contents follow those of the Student Book units, the aim being to reinforce knowledge of the main themes as well as provide further practice with vocabulary and the **Language Bank** functions, language structures and writing skills in the main unit.

Using the WORKBOOK pages:

Word Power

This activity picks up from where the main unit **Word Power** leaves off. Students will need to make use of the vocabulary, phrases and / or idioms in the **Language Bank.**

Use of English

This activity gives students the chance to practise some key grammar points. This section usually has exercise material in the format of the Cambridge CAE, Paper 3, of Use of English. Students will find some of the grammar points covered in the Language Bank. Refer to the contents page for more information.

In most cases, this section will also be in the form of a text that will allow students the opportunity for further reading and more information on the subject area. If you feel it is appropriate and you have time in class, you can use the EQ to help you explore the issues brought up in the texts.

Writing

This section gives students even more opportunities to write for their ISE III Portfolios and practise their writing for use in Cambridge CAE, IGCSE and IELTS. Refer to the **Portfolio Writing** section above for tips on use. The choice of tasks is of the length and type specified in various exams. The writing tasks are diverse and include conversations, interviews, letters, emails and for / against opinion pieces. We hope to encourage students to appreciate the differences in register and style that are needed when writing for different purposes. The tasks here are useful ideas for homework, as they follow up work covered in the Student's Book unit.

Speaking Strategies

This section (which appears in every other unit) is very important for helping students to improve their presentation skills and their presentations in general. These are written activities, but they provide phrases, practical tips and techniques for organising presentations, opening lines, creating emphasis and creating rapport that can be used in the actual GESE topic presentation. After completing each Workbook unit, you should try to get students to incorporate these tips into their next presentation.

Idioms

As discussed above in the Extended Reading section, appropriate use of idioms is an important part of determining whether a student can communicate on a more advanced level. Idioms may appear last in the Workbook units, but they are certainly not least in the terms of importance. You should make sure that students answer the question: What do these mean? This will help you to determine whether they have a real grasp for the meaning and use or not.

There are several ways you can try to incorporate these idioms into communicative practice. Firstly, you can use the EQ in the Teacher's Guide, which will get students using the idioms in a real way. Secondly, you can ask students to use the idioms in writing tasks. Thirdly, you can try to organise the use of these idioms into a continuing 'competition', for example, whoever correctly uses the idioms first in the next class gets a point. You can keep track of these points over the course.

TEAMWORK SCENARIOS

This section contains the scenarios for the **Teamwork** activity in the main units. See **Teamwork** notes above.

QSE DVD-ROM and online material

The **Student's DVD-ROM** for *QSE Advanced* contains the video and audio clips and scripts and Using the DVD-ROM. The material from the Teacher's DVD-ROM is now available online at www.brookemead-elt.co.uk/downloads where there are over 250 pages of text files (PDF), including teacher's notes, answer keys, practice pages for the **CAE, IELTS** and **IGCSE** exams, plus audio files (MP3) for the exam practice **Listening Tests.** This means that teachers can in fact do without the printed copies of the Teacher's Guide if they wish to.

From the opening menu of the Student DVD-ROM, the teacher is able to scroll through to various menus, in addition to the audio and video clips:
1. **About** *QSE* – Information about the book and the *QSE* series.
2. **Using the DVD-ROM** – Instructions for use.
3. **Audio & Video Scripts** – All the transcripts of the video and audio clips.

Available online:
4. **Teacher's Notes** – All the pages of the Teacher's Guide in printable PDF files. These include the Introduction to the course, Contents, Materials Map, Teacher's Notes for all 20 Units and three Extended Reading sections.
5. **Exams (CAE, IELTS, IGCSE)** – All the printed pages of the exam materials for IGCSE, CAE and IELTS. There are seven audio files for the Listening Tests, with transcripts. There is a **Placement Test** for use at the beginning of the course. There is also an Introduction to using the exam materials.

QSE METHODOLOGY

The units are topic-based. The **topics** we have chosen are genuinely affective – stimulating, controversial and designed to make students want to express their own views in speaking and writing and to help them do it. Activities promote the sharing of ideas and opinions, the aim being to present both sides – or sometimes many sides – of a highly debatable issue. The issues chosen are those that affect everyone in our **globalised society** – from the highly personal (exams, ambition, education, finding a partner) to the most public of debates (environment, oil, peace, fame).

Vocabulary enrichment

Because all the topics are real life issues, and the input materials for them are from authentic sources, the vocabulary range is challenging. **QSE** is intentionally a rich source of new vocabulary for students' use. The benefit for students is that they have to deal with language they would actually meet in genuine written or spoken exchanges with native English speakers.

In addition, we provide activities to help students understand and activate new terms or concepts, both before they read or listen and afterwards. Then, after they have worked through the Student's Book activities, the Workbook section recycles and practises vocabulary items. This too helps learners to consolidate their knowledge and to become more confident in using the structures and expressions they have learnt.

Unit development

There is a systematic and structured development in each unit, which follows a logical cognitive pattern – words, ideas, grammar awareness, reading, discussion, listening, writing, followed by the cross-curricular (CLIL) information which relates the topic to other subjects the students may be studying. Finally, the wheel comes full circle and students, older and wiser, answer the question that started the whole thing off.

Internet sources

There are lists of **internet references** for further research in each of the unit-by-unit sections of this **Teacher's Guide**. We also recommend that teachers and students take advantage of the fantastic research and study opportunities offered by search engines such as Google. Online sources are correct at time of print. The publishers cannot guarantee that websites will not change. This is the reason why the internet links have not been printed in the Student's Book. Both teachers and students should be aware that all websites and online resources are constantly changing. They should be checked before they are used for educational purposes. **The contents of any online references cited in this book do not represent the opinions of or any manner of endorsement from the publishers, who cannot be responsible for any online content beyond their control.**

QSE illustrations

The illustrations in this book have been carefully chosen to be an affective resource in their own right. They are mainly news-style photographs, not included simply to decorate the page, but to be used as a resource. As in the best of printed and online competitive media, the pictures are designed to draw students' eyes when they open the book at a particular spread.

We suggest that, especially when you look at the opening double-page spread of the unit, you should start with an activity about the photos. Students can describe them but they may also want to comment on them.

In the **Viewpoint** and **CLIL** sections there are often graphs, diagrams and charts. Students going on to business English qualifications, such as the Cambridge BEC and IELTS for academic qualifications, have to be familiar with describing and using graphs in English.

Many forms of testing today require students to discuss and comment on images, and the pages of *QSE* provide ample opportunities for students to develop this form of **visual awareness,** which is such an important part of modern literacy and communication.

QSE Photocopiable Resources

On page 174 there is an introduction to the *QSE Advanced* Photocopiable Resources, which start on page 176 of this Teacher's Guide, for examination practice.

We hope you enjoy using *Quick Smart English Advanced* and find the ideas in this Teacher's Guide useful.

Maurice Forget

Ken Wilson, Mary Tomalin
Rebecca Robb Benne

Unit 1: Buy now, think later — Teacher's Guide

See pages 8–11 SB, 94 WB

WHAT'S NEW!

Communication Objectives:	Ss will be able to use: – contradicting expressions and expressions used before challenging. – advertising-related vocabulary, phrases and idioms.
Educational Objectives:	Ss will explore the social, economic and political impact of advertising in society.
Connected Topics:	– Corporate advertising – Types of advertising – Celebrity endorsements – Subtle advertising – Cigarette warning labels – Political advertising – Corporate image – Trends – Future of advertising – Private versus public media
Grammar:	Prepositions
Key Vocabulary:	junk mail, flyer, movie trailer, product placement, sponsorship, celebrity endorsement, pop-up ads, full-page ads, spam, brand names, launch, remedy, heartland, under siege, blindside, sticker, buzzword, big bucks, dump, execs, celebs, overshadow, high-profile, can, put the spotlight on, sticky situation, tarnish, surefire way, packet, spoof, slogan, sweatshop, corporal punishment, watchdog organisation

The BIG question: IS ADVERTISING ALL A CON?

This question deals with a common perception in the general public that advertising is somehow dishonest.

VIEWPOINT

Facts: The list of the ten largest global advertisers changes nearly every year depending on market factors for each industry. From the list, these companies work in the following industries: Procter and Gamble (beauty products, household goods, drugs, baby care etc), Unilever (foodstuffs, household goods, beauty products etc), General Motors (cars, trucks etc), Toyota (cars, trucks etc), Ford (cars, trucks etc), AOL / TimeWarner (internet services, magazines, movies etc), Daimler / Chrysler (cars, trucks etc), L'Oreal (beauty products etc), Nestlé (foodstuffs etc) and Sony (electronics, films, music etc).

Source: www.adage.com

EQ: *What do you think this money bought? Was this money well spent? What would you do with a billion euros?*

Quotes: William Penn Adair 'Will' Rogers (1879–1935) was a celebrated Cherokee Native American cowboy-humourist who worked in vaudeville, wrote for newspapers and acted in films.

EQ: *Do you agree with this quote? Some critics suggest that some industries rely on planned obsolescence (that is, they build products to fail after a set period of time). What do you think of this idea? Could products be made better?*

Quotes: John Wanamaker (1838–1922) was a US businessman responsible for creating the first US department store and pioneering truth in advertising.

EQ: *Why is this quote funny? How do advertisers target advertising to their customers? How often do adverts you are interested in make you want to buy something? What about adverts you are not interested in?*

Students should be encouraged to discuss whether products or lifestyles are being advertised. What does this say about emotions in advertising?

1 WORD POWER

A gets students to consider different types of advertising.

> **1 WORD POWER A**   Answers
>
> **1** Billboards, posters (near roads, pavements); celebrity endorsements (newspapers, radio, TV); classified ads (newspapers); full-page ads (magazines or newspapers); junk mail, flyers (in the post); movie trailers (cinemas, DVDs, TV); pop-up ads (internet pages / sites); product placement (films, TV); radio spots (radio, internet radio); spam (email inbox); sponsorship (sporting events); TV commercials (TV).
> **3** Government, politicians, charities, etc.

B gets students to practise contradicting phrases.

> **1 WORD POWER B**   Answers
>
> **1** Even a product placement in a top action film won't convince anyone to buy that. **Well, I don't see it that way, many people follow what their idols do. If Britney Spears drinks Pepsi, lots of kids will think it's good to drink Pepsi too.**
> **2** Brand names use bad English like *luv* and *kwik*. **But what about all the other brand names that use good English? Bad English is only used in a minority.**
> **3** Ad campaigns are only good if they're funny. **I understand what you're saying, but I think other types of campaigns can be interesting, entertaining or informative as well.**

ARTICLES
Gone in 30 Seconds

This article discusses recent trends in the marketing industry, with a discussion of how the dominance of traditional advertising, such as the 30-second TV commercial, has begun to wane. It is forcing advertisers to become more creative and allowing for more subtlety in the message. One driving force behind this trend is the development of new technologies, such as TIVO that allows TV viewers to record TV programmes and skip the TV commercials.

Another factor is the development of new ways of advertising like 'viral' advertising which relies on using the internet to spread messages among interested consumers by giving the message to important bloggers and websites. It is not clear yet whether these new forms of advertising will come to dominate the market or whether the subtler advertising will have the desired effect for advertisers.

EQ: *How has advertising developed with technology? Compare newspapers, radio, TV and the internet. With technology that allows TV viewers to skip commercials, will we see the end of advertising on TV?*

Companies Ditch Celebrity Endorsements

This article discusses the concept of the celebrity brand and its impact on advertising. Up to now brands have been defined as commercial products and services, but celebrities have begun to be thought of in the same way and packaged for media presentation. This has led some companies to re-think the usefulness of linking celebrities with their products.

EQ: *Do you see celebrities as brands? How are celebrities and products the same or different? What do you think of the celebrities discussed in the article?*

2 READING

A is a common skimming activity. It will help students writing the Use of English part of the CAE and the Trinity Controlled Writing ISE III section.

> **1 READING A**   Answers
>
> **1** primetime   **2** blindside   **3** buzzword   **4** logo

B gets students to formulate more complex arguments using specific information. You can get students to try using contradicting phrases again.

C 1 This inference question tries to get student to address the issue from the perspective of themselves and people they know.
2 This inference question requires students to think about the approaches of modern advertising. Students should try to provide concrete examples from TV, the internet, magazines or even the article.

Unit 1 — Buy now, think later — Teacher's Guide

See pages 8–11 SB, 94 WB

3 This inference question gets students to think about the personal point of view of the celebrities.

3 SPEAK YOUR MIND

This section covers the topics of celebrity endorsements, celebrities and companies in trouble and banned advertising (for example, alcohol, cigarettes).

A EQ: *What do you think of celebrities who talk about politics? Religion? Personal problems?*

B There are many celebrities who have been in trouble with the law: Michael Jackson, Kobe Bryant, Winona Ryder, O.J. Simpson, Hugh Grant, Robert Downey Jr. For more, see: www.thesmokinggun.com.

EQ: *What has led these celebrities to these problems? Do you think the law is applied in the same way to celebrities as to ordinary people? Do scandals hurt or help a celebrity's career? Why? / Why not?*

Some companies in trouble: Financial (Enron, WorldCom, Parmalat), Deaths (Union Carbide), Product Problems (Ford / Firestone for problems with tyres, Dow Corning for breast implants, ABB for asbestos) For more, see: www.bbc.co.uk/watchdog or www.multinationalmonitor.org.

EQ: *What are some common image / legal problems for companies? What leads companies into these situations? How should these companies be disciplined? How long do you think the public remembers these problems?*

C EQ: *What kinds of cigarette and alcohol adverts have you seen? Do you think these industries market to children or teenagers?*

4 LISTEN   DVD

This audio clip deals with Canada's controversial cigarette warning labels introduced in 2001. The tobacco industry has been quite outspoken about them and has tried unsuccessfully to challenge them in court. These new labels seem to have been quite effective at reducing smoking rates in Canada. The Canadian Cancer Society polled 2,000 smokers in 2001 and found that 43 per cent of smokers are more concerned about health effects, 21 per cent said the labels stopped them from taking a cigarette when tempted, and 18 per cent of smokers have asked for a different packet because of the label.

> **1 LISTEN A3, B1** Answers
>
> **A 3 Tobacco companies:** Would not be happy about people giving up smoking because of the warning labels (not mentioned in listening clip); **Smokers: Man 1** is shocked, but he is not sure these would stop him from smoking. **Woman 2** thinks they might help her quit smoking and finds them shocking. **Non-smokers: Woman 1** is in favour and thinks it would help her boyfriend quit because of the picture. **Man 2** hates smoking and thinks the labels are a good idea.
>
> **B 1** 360,000 people
> **2 Woman 1:** supports the idea; **Man 1:** against it; **Man 2:** supports it; **Woman 2:** supports it.
> **3** Smoking is seen as 'cool'.
> **4** These rates have dropped from 28 per cent to 18 per cent between 1999 and 2003.

5 TEAMWORK

This activity will give students a chance to create their own TV advert. Students should use their own experience and knowledge of fashion marketing to help them. The customer file includes some company information. Based on a creative thinking activity, the Idea Generator is to help students in their creative effort. Pairing seemingly unconnected ideas or words can lead to some original ideas. It is important to remind students not to be critical of any ideas until after all the brainstorming has run its course.

Sources:
The Blue Jean, Alice Harris.
www.diesel.co.uk
www.levi.com

6 CONTROVERSY

Political activists have become more creative in the way they criticise corporations. Given the budget available to corporations around the world, it takes something particularly shocking or new to catch a consumer's attention. One of these latest trends has been to co-opt the brand image of a product and use it to criticise the company. These have been highly controversial and have led companies to resort to legal action to protect their brand image. One example of this has been the case of Greenpeace and Exxon / Mobile. Exxon took Greenpeace into France for infringement of its trademark for its 'E$$O' campaign. The Greenpeace campaign against Esso, a trade name for Exxon in several countries, suggested that Esso was more concerned about money than the environment. Greenpeace won the case on appeal – the court said that freedom of speech allowed for this logo parody.

Sources:
www.adbusters.org
www.greenpeace.org

EQ: *What do you think of the companies in the ads? Should protestors be allowed to protest this way? Are these effective protest methods? Do they change your view of the products shown?*

7 PORTFOLIO WRITING

See the Introduction to the Teacher's Guide.

Sources:
www.pg.com
www.unilever.com
www.gm.com
www.toyota.com
www.ford.com
www.timewarner.com
www.daimlerchrysler.com
www.loreal.com
www.nestle.com
www.sony.com

8 PUBLIC RELATIONS *IN ENGLISH* (CLIL)

This activity was chosen because of the media discussion about the social responsibility of corporations. This is a difficult and complex issue. Nike is, by no means, a bad company nor an isolated case, but its experiences over the last decade with outsourced production in developing countries reflect the ethical difficulties faced by a global corporation. When a company makes the hard financial decision to change countries to lower costs, how is it able to decide which social, labour, environment standards to follow? Either way, the decision has real effects for both the corporate image, the workers involved and the consumers of the product. Nike now has a staff of 97 that just monitors conditions in its foreign factories.

EQ: *When a company moves its factory abroad, which labour, environmental or social standards should it follow: its home country or the developing country? Why? Who is to blame for sweatshops: the companies, consumers, sweatshop factories in developing countries, workers in developing countries, governments in developing countries?*

Sources:
Naomi Klein, *No Logo*.
www.nike.com
www.oxfam.org.au/campaigns/nike
www.videa.ca/resources/global_issues.html
www.cleanclothes.org
www.adbusters.org

9 FURTHER DISCUSSION

This section covers the topics of trends, the future of marketing, influence of advertising on the media, public versus private media.

A Try to get students thinking about the amounts of money first.

EQ: *Do you think news agencies (TV, newspapers) would ever not publish stories about advertisers in case they lose advertising revenue? If your business depended heavily on customers, what would you be willing to do to keep them happy?*

B Try to get students to analyse different public and private TV / radio stations.

EQ: *What are the advantages and disadvantages of public ownership? Does the government monitor or censor public TV or radio stations?*

C Try to get students to think of concrete examples of trends: hip hop, reality TV, etc.

EQ: *Could you ever start a trend by yourself? If so, how? If not, why not? What is meant by a 'trendsetter'? Give an example.*

Unit 1 — Buy now, think later — Teacher's Guide
See pages 8–11 SB, 94 WB

10 *Your answer:* IS ADVERSING ALL A CON?

This question attempts to address the very real concern about spending vast sums of money on advertising. The students should by this point have developed some very definite opinions on the subject. The students can look at the enormous cost in real money terms, at the effects marketing messages have on society, at the development of product image over product value, and corporate social responsibility with the right to conduct business. You can get students to imagine a world without advertising: products without labels; television without commercials; email without spam. What would it be like?

WORKBOOK

1 WORD POWER

This activity is a cloze-form version of the Use of English section of the CAE which gives students an opportunity to review their understanding of the use of prepositions in English. It also introduces students to further advertising-related issues.

1 WORD POWER			Answers
1 with **2** in / with **3** from / against **4** on **5** by			
6 on **7** to **8** into **9** with **10** at			

2 WRITING

A As spam often makes inflated claims for the products it is selling, you can encourage students to use hyperbole and very persuasive language.

Sources:
Antarctica, Peter Carey (Lonely Planet)
www.antarctica.ac.uk
www.aad.gov.au
www.antarcticconnection.com
www.coolantarctica.com

B This is a realia-based activity. You can encourage students to try to use advertising-style language.

3 SPEAKING STRATEGIES: Mapping the presentation

This activity is the first of several techniques to help students give better presentations. This one addresses the important issue of structure by giving several different ways of structuring a presentation.

3 SPEAKING STRATEGIES	Answers
1 Categorical: circles, triangles, squares; red, green, blue	
Commodities: grapes, oranges, soybeans, rice	
2 Chronological: past, present, future: 4000 BC, 1565, 1688–1715, 1970	
3 Compare/contrast: + vs. –, us vs. them: grapes, oranges (fruit) vs. soybeans, rice (vegetables/grain)	
4 Confucius principle: individual, family, community: how each relates to the person / town / country; how important each is to person / town / country.	
5 Geographical: north, south, east, west: France, Brazil, Thailand, Florida	
6 Hierarchical: top, middle, bottom	
7 Cost: champagne, oranges, soybeans, rice	
8 Sequential: first, secondly, thirdly / lastly	
9 History (4000 BC, 1565, 1688–1715, 1970)	
10 Status (champagne, oranges, soybeans, rice)	
11 Order first appeared in your country	

4 IDIOMS

See the Introduction to the Teacher's Guide.

4 IDIOMS	Answers
1 b **2** a **3** c **4** d **5** e	
1 jump on the bandwagon = choosing the popular side / whatever is most popular **2** give a blank cheque = allow someone to spend as much as they like **3** cost an arm and a leg = cost a lot of money, be very expensive **4** be seen dead = would never do something **5** round the clock = all hours, a lot of hours, day and night	

Ask students to use the idioms when answering these questions orally. This can be done as pair work or as a class.

- *Does advertising affect your buying habits very much?*
  - I must admit I do follow fashion trends a lot, but I don't think I *jump on the bandwagon* all the time.
  - I think cost is the most important factor. If it *costs an arm and a leg,* forget it.
  - Not always. They can sometimes advertise clothes that I *wouldn't be seen dead in.*
- *How should companies with bad reputations improve them?*
  - They could just sign a *blank cheque* to a PR company and say, 'Fix it.'
  - I think they need to *work around the clock* on their image.
- *Can advertising fix all problems?*
  - No, even if the US *wrote a blank cheque,* it couldn't solve the country's social problems overnight.
  - It can. But in some cases, it just *costs an arm and a leg.*

Unit 2 — **Express yourself** — **Teacher's Guide** — See pages 12-15 SB, 95 WB

WHAT'S NEW!

Communication Objectives:	Ss will be able to: – use inferring and signposting phrases. – use arts-related vocabulary, phrases and idioms.
Educational Objectives:	Ss will develop a critical appreciation for the arts.
Connected Topics:	– High culture vs. pop culture – Traditional art forms – Spoils of war – Music history – Life of the artist – Relevance of art – What is art?
Grammar:	Word forms Joining sentences in sequence using signposting phrases
Key Vocabulary:	artefact culture vulture muddy v commission v high / popular culture reign credentials integration umbrella organisation

The BIG question: ARE THE ARTS RELEVANT?

Here *Are the arts relevant?* questions the idea of the arts and what they represent.

VIEWPOINT

Facts: The British Museum information gives students some perspective on the enormous difference in the size of the collections in the Greek and British national museums. Using the information as a prompt, ask students to describe any experiences they have had in art galleries or museums.

EQ: *What are the main art galleries or museums in your country? Have you visited them this year, recently or ever? How important is it for a student's education to go to museums or art galleries? What do you like or dislike about being in a gallery or museum?*

The Van Gogh fact introduces the stereotype of the 'starving artist'. Using the information as a prompt, ask students to describe what the life of a typical artist would be like (lifestyle, looks, attitude). *What makes Van Gogh's art more popular now than in his lifetime?* This question addresses the situation that most artists are only popular after their deaths and often not understood or appreciated in their lifetime.

EQ: *The Portrait of the Artist survey in New Zealand found that on average artists made $20,700 a year compared to other New Zealanders who made $27,934. Does this fit your idea of the life of the artist? Why do you think artists make so little money? What motivates them to continue producing art? What art forms would give artists the greatest opportunity for success?*

Quote: Pablo Picasso (1881–1973) was a Spanish painter and sculptor. His quote introduces the idea of art as a means of self-expression and touches on the purity of creative ideas.

EQ: *What do you think Picasso meant (by this quote)? Do you agree that there is a connection between children and artists?*

1 WORD POWER

A Students consider 'what is art?' By trying to associate it with particular types of creative expression, they will begin to have a clearer idea and to express in their vocabulary what art means to them or even what art means to society in general. You can't discuss something until you can agree on a common definition.

B helps students to look at some vocabulary associated with the articles.

1 WORD POWER B		Answers
B 2 patron 3 performer		4 monarch
5 composer 6 collector		

C practises inferring in **Language Bank 2** how various people in **B** feel about the arts.

ARTICLES

Why the Queen is No Culture Vulture

This article is part of a larger debate on whether the Queen and the monarchy in general are still relevant today. It should be pointed out that the relevance of monarchs today is often a controversial subject in many countries. If you have the time or feel it is appropriate to explore this issue, you can ask: *In the 21st century should a country have a king or queen? What do monarchs do for a country?*

Elgin Marbles Campaign Launched

The case of the Elgin Marbles is a continuing diplomatic row between Greece and Britain. The Marbles were loaned to Greece for the 2004 Olympics, but it is unlikely that they will be returned permanently. If you have the time or feel it is appropriate to explore the issue, you can ask: *Does your country have any minor disagreements with other countries? How do history and geography affect diplomatic relations?*

2 READING

> **2 READING A, B, C** Answers
>
> **A** The Queen: has only bought 20 paintings in her reign; is not a fan of classical music (patron of orchestra but doesn't go very often); she collects glass animals rather than other artworks; not a fan of the arts.
>
> **B** Henry VIII was a passionate supporter of music and composers. The Queen is not really interested in the arts. / In Lord Elgin's time it was acceptable to buy the Greek sculpture and take it from Greece to London; now it would not be allowed.

C 1 It may help to mention that monarchs have traditionally commissioned works of art including music. In the Middle Ages artists could also be paid members of royal staff. If students are unsure, you can also ask: *How are pop albums produced today? How does this compare with the way music was produced in the past?*

C 2 If students are not sure how to answer this, you can ask: *Do you think it has something to do with... national pride, British self-identity as a former imperial power, its history or the reasons given by the museum?*

3 SPEAK YOUR MIND

This section covers the topics of the successful artist, modern art versus traditional art, the relevance of classical art forms, and art ownership versus cultural heritage.

A EQ: *What do you think their lives are like? How many artists do you think are successful?*

B EQ: *Should art only try to imitate real life or be realistic like a photo?*

C EQ: *Who watches / listens to opera, ballet or classical music? There has been some crossover between classical music and rock over the years. What do you think of this?*

D This discussion could be extended to include the return of lands and property.

EQ: *What would happen to Africa, Asia, Australia, Europe, North and South America, if all conquered lands were returned to the people who lived there before?*

 4 WATCH AND LISTEN DVD

The Body Worlds exhibition was created by German anatomist Gunther von Hagens to educate people about the anatomy of the human body. Although von Hagens says that his displays are simple educational tools rather than art, his descriptions, the display arrangements and exhibitions in art galleries belie this assertion. The exhibition continues to tour the world.

Source:
Body Worlds homepage: www.bodyworlds.com

Although the video clip documents the exhibit as visitors would view it, some students may not want to see it. It may be worth asking students about this after activities A and B. For these students, you can substitute an alternative silent activity: Write a letter (180–210 words) to Gunter von Hagens expressing their views about the Body Worlds exhibit.

> **4 WATCH AND LISTEN B** Answers
>
> **B** Gunther von Hagens gives the reasons:
> • education • The Renaissance

C The clip shows people looking at the exhibits. Students would probably answer the question by

Unit 2 — Express yourself — Teacher's Guide

See pages 12–15 SB, 95 WB

discussing something relating to what Von Hagens has said in the interview, mortality or just the exhibition itself.

> **4 WATCH AND LISTEN D** Answers
>
> D 1 Everyone is mortal. 2 Educational tool: it can help people understand their bodies better. Lesson about choices we make: unhealthy lifestyles can be presented in a very concrete way. 3 Renaissance anatomists: Leonardo da Vinci and Andreas Vesalius. 4 Vesalius was the first to assemble a skeleton, which he took from the grave.

E These questions will help students to explore how these seemingly divergent fields are in many ways connected. Example: *Painting has been helped by chemistry (how chemicals create different colours), physics (how light is defracted, colour wavelengths), biology / anatomy (how humans / animals move).*

Source:
www.asci.org

5 TEAMWORK

This activity relates to the idea that art can be radical in nature and the expression of ideas is at the core of a lot of modern art. When students look at the Scenario, try to make them think about how art develops or changes when an artist begins work with a particular idea in mind. Students' ideas can be funny, serious, entertaining or anything that interests them.

When you are finished, you could discuss: *Does this change your view of modern art? Do you think art takes itself too seriously? How might some famous works of art (for example: the Mona Lisa, David) have been different if they had been created with a different idea in mind?*

Source:
Futurist painters / manifestos: www.unknown.nu/futurism

6 CONTROVERSY

This activity opens up issues about the context of art. The meaning and value of art often exists within a certain society. It looks at traditional art forms in other countries (see also **A** in **9 Further Discussion** below) and how art is often relevant to the times.

EQ: *Why do you think the Afghan rug weavers created these rugs? Do you like these rugs? Why / Why not? If rug weavers from your country were to make rugs like these, what would the rugs look like?*

Source:
War rugs homepage: www.warrug.com

7 PORTFOLIO WRITING

See the Introduction to the Teacher's Guide.

A Sources:
Artist biographies: www.ibiblio.org/wm/
Nobel laureates: www.nobelprize.org/literature/laureates/index.html
Some important writer biographies:
www.xs4all.nl/~pwessel/writers.html#winners
Actor biographies: www.imdb.com/
(Note: 'Actor' used for men and women in a formal sense is becoming more common.)

B Sources:
Elgin Marbles: www.museum-security.org/elginmarbles.html
British Museum: www.thebritishmuseum.ac.uk/
National Archaeological Museum: www.culture.gr/2/21/214/21405m/e21405m1.html

8 HISTORY OF MUSIC *in English* [CLIL]

Music historians debate about when these musical forms started. Many of the musical forms also overlap, as musicians play many different types of music and are influenced by different music forms.

Civil rights has had a strong impact on the development of African-American music. Before the 1964 Civil Rights Act, African-American musicians could not go into the hotels or concert halls where they played. They had to use the back door and to leave as soon as they had finished playing. A lot of the 1960s and 1970s soul, R&B, blues and funk musicians sang songs about the hardship of life in the ghettos (segregated areas where African-Americans lived in many northern US cities) and racial inequalities. With the death of Martin Luther King, many blacks become angry with the system – race riots in 1967 and the development of the Black Panthers.

QSE Advanced   See pages 12–15 SB, 95 WB

A Begin by brainstorming with the class a list of different African-American musicians through the decades or musical styles.

Gospel: Thomas Dorsey (1899–1993), Mahalia Jackson (1911–72), James Cleveland (1931–91), Sam Cooke (1931–64), The Winans.

Jazz: Soloists: Louis Armstrong (1901–71), Billie Holiday (1915–59), Ella Fitzgerald (1917–96); Big Band / Swing: Edward 'Duke' Ellington (1899–1974), William 'Count' Basie (1904–84), Cabel 'Cab' Calloway (1907–94); BeBop / Cool / Fusion jazz: Charlie 'Bird' Parker (1920–55), Dizzy Gillespie (1917–93), Miles Davis (1926–91), Thelonious Monk (1917–82).

Blues: Mamie Smith (1883–1946), Robert Johnson (1911–38), Howlin' Wolf (1910–1976), Buddy Guy (b 1936) John Lee Hooker (1920–2001), Muddy Waters (1915–83), Etta James (b 1938), B.B. King (1925–), Stevie Ray Vaughn (1954–1990).

R&B (Rhythm and blues): James Brown (b 1933), Aretha Franklin (b 1942), The Temptations, The Supremes, Jackson 5, Stevie Wonder (b 1950), Ray Charles (1930–2004), Whitney Houston (b 1963), New Edition (1983–89), Boyz 2 Men.

Rock 'n' roll (Rock and roll): Chuck Berry (b 1926), Little Richard (b 1932), Jimi Hendrix (1942–70), Sly and the Family Stone, Michael Jackson (b 1958), Prince (b 1958), Bad Brains, Living Colour, Fishbone, Lenny Kravitz (b 1964), The Roots.

Soul: Aretha Franklin (b 1942), Otis Redding (1941–67), Percy Sledge (b 1940), Marvin Gaye (1939–84), Al Green (b 1946).

Funk: James Brown (1933–2006), Parliament / Funkadelic / P-Funk Allstars, Sly and the Family Stone, Herbie Hancock (b 1940), Stevie Wonder (b 1950), Earth, Wind & Fire.

Rap: Afrika Bambaataa, Run DMC, Public Enemy, NWA, BDP, MC Hammer, Tupac Shakur (1971–96), Salt-N-Pepa, Beastie Boys, De La Soul, Queen Latifah, The Fugees, Outkast.

B In its early years, blues and jazz were considered popular art forms, but today they are often considered high culture.

EQ: *Can you see any current music styles becoming high culture in a hundred years? Why / Why not?*

9 FURTHER DISCUSSION

This section covers: traditional arts in different countries; technology and the arts; the idea of the Renaissance man; controversial art and public funding. Encourage students to continue using the phrases in **Language Bank 2**.

A Students can brainstorm about what is traditional art in their country, then compare these with other countries. Examples: Japan (paper crafts, kimonos, textiles), Canada (Native American woodcarving, beadwork), Sweden (iron work, woodcarving, basket weaving), India (scroll painting, rug weaving, wood / sculpting).

B Encourage students to think about the uses of computers (architecture, music, drawing), industrial design (pop art), video (art), audio (music, installation art).

EQ: *How have computers changed writing? How have video cameras (film / TV) changed acting? How has modern printing changed art?*

C Ask students to think about how careers are often very specialised. Look at people who have tried to use different art forms (actors who are also artists or photographers (Leonard Nimoy, Dennis Hopper), musicians who are also writers (Henry Rollins, Leonard Cohen).

EQ: *Do you miss anything by specialising in only one area? What could other fields bring to another area (for example, music and medicine)?*

D EQ: *Should individuals have a say in what government spends its money on? Who should decide what art is?*

10 *Your answer:* ARE THE ARTS RELEVANT?

Arts funding is always a touchy issue with strong feelings on both sides especially about controversial art. You could ask students:

EQ: *Why do we create art? What does it tell us about society? What is the social value of art? Is it important enough that we should spend money on unpopular (financially unviable) art forms? How can we justify sponsoring art when there are so many social programmes that are short of money?*

Unit 2 — Express yourself — Teacher's Guide

See pages 12–15 SB, 95 WB

WORKBOOK

1 WORD POWER

This activity will introduce students to some art movements. It also gives students a chance to use the signposting expressions in **Language Bank 2** in a more natural way.

> **1 WORD POWER** — **Answers**
>
> **1** To begin with, the *Renaissance* (15th–16th centuries) was an important period of artistic and ideological revival. It mixed elements of classical style, scientific inquiry and Christian themes. Artists included Michelangelo, Da Vinci and Raphael.
>
> **Now that brings us to the next point** – the *Baroque* period (16th–17th centuries). It saw artists often trying to capture emotions and drama in their work. However, they often sought more realism in their art. Artists include Rubens, Rembrandt and Caravaggio.
>
> **Let's move on to the subject of** *Impressionism* (late 19th century). Here, art was used to convey subtle feelings or the impressions of the artist. It began to move away from the idea that art must represent actual things. Artists included Monet, Renoir and Cézanne.
>
> **Now that brings us to another important movement** – *Expressionism* (late 19th–early 20th centuries). The expressionists believed that direct communication of feelings can be shown, especially anxiety and despair. Artists included Van Gogh, Munch, Grosz, Dix and Beckmann.
>
> **Let's leave that and go to** *Surrealism* (early 20th century). Surrealism was strongly influenced by the psychological works of Freud and Jung. The art often sought to explore the subconscious. Artists include Breton, Dali and Man Ray.

2 USE OF LANGUAGE: Word forms

This activity introduces an important era for artistic, intellectual and political expression. You may want to discuss or mention the bohemian lifestyle – living hand-to-mouth outside society's traditional values (career, family, home ownership) usually in search of some greater truth for the sake of art.

The activity is based on an authentic activity used by the University of Cambridge Local Examinations Syndicate in the Certificate in Advanced English and Certificate of Proficiency in English.

> **2 USE OF LANGUAGE** — **Answers**
>
> 1 cultural 2 massive 3 movements
> 4 freedom 5 productive 6 happiest
> 7 sitting 8 imagine

3 WRITING

A Sources:
Among the Bohemians: Experiments in Living 1900–39, Virginia Nicholson
Women of the Left Bank: Paris, 1900–40, Shari Benstock
www.newbohemian.com

B Sources:
Jazz: A History of America's Music, Geoffrey C. Ward
www.allaboutjazz.com
Examples of music reviews:
www.rollingstone.com
www.downbeat.com
www.vibe.com

4 IDIOMS

See the Introduction to the Teacher's Guide.

> **4 IDIOMS** — **Answers**
>
> **1** She's a *budding artist*. We expect big things from her in the future.
> **2** I found the whole conversation went *over my head*. What did he mean by Existentialism?
> **3** You often need to keep an *open mind* when it comes to modern art.
> **4** I really think Picasso *was ahead of his time*.
> **5** He can't seem to write the last chapter of the book. I think he has *writer's block*.
> **6** You would have to pay a *king's ransom* if you want to buy that Matisse.
>
> **1** budding = developing, promising **2** to go over my head = so complex I don't understand **3** to keep an open mind = be objective **4** to be ahead of his time = very advanced in his ideas, way of thinking **6** to pay a king's ransom = pay a lot of money

© Brookemead Associates Ltd 2009 — Brookemead English Language Teaching

Ask students to use the idioms orally by answering these questions. These can be done as pair work or as a whole class.

Give some examples of radical new artists, writers or musicians. Ask:

- *How would you describe them and their work?*
  - They *are ahead of their time.*
  - Their stuff goes *over my head.*
- *Would you ever buy any of the following: a book of poetry, a Mozart CD, a war rug, a sculpture or a Picasso painting? Why?*
  - It would cost a *king's ransom* for a Picasso, so I'd never buy one.
  - You would need *an open mind* to want a war rug.
- *What difficulties do you imagine writers, artists and other creative individuals have in their work?*
  - I would imagine writers often get *writer's block.*
  - I imagine sometimes creative work can go right *over the heads* of the public.

Unit 3 — The sky's the limit! — Teacher's Guide — See pages 16–19 SB, 96 WB

WHAT'S NEW!

Communicative Objectives:	Students will be able to: – justify an argument and downplay expressions. – use ambition-related vocabulary, phrases and idioms.
Education Objectives:	Ss will explore a variety of issues relating to ambition, especially the root causes and effects.
Connected Topics:	– Race and future potential – Welfare and motivation – Fame and fortune – Biological drive – Asia's film industries – Ethics of success – The American Dream – Rejecting the system
Grammar:	Collocations Joining clauses Rhetorical questions
Key Vocabulary:	adversity, affluent, bioinformatician, burgeoning, celluloid elite, charismatic, consummate, data miner, deadpan, diminutive, elaborate *adj*, ferocity, flop *n*, floundering, forensic, grim, in the limelight, meteoric, persona, piety, rat race, rigorous, stint, token, wisecracking

The BIG question: WHAT WOULD YOU DO TO SUCCEED?

The question here asks what people are prepared to do to succeed in life.

VIEWPOINT

Facts: The information on poverty in the USA is based on US Census Bureau data. This study uses the US Census Bureau's definitions of poverty and affluence (ten times the poverty level). Source: 'Rags or Riches? Estimating the Probabilities of Poverty and Affluence across the American Adult Life Span' *Social Science Quarterly,* Vol. 82, No. 4, Dec 2001 Mark R. Rank et al.
www.weap.org/scholarship/rags_or_riches.pdf

   This point is brought up again in **4 Watch and Listen** and **9 Further Discussion A.**

EQ: *Name some successful African-Americans. Why are they successful? What influence do you think this has on the ambitions of young African-Americans?*

The quote is a common saying meaning you have to work hard to succeed.

EQ: *What do you think is meant by this quote? Do you agree with its meaning?*

The question under the graph addresses the essence of the rags to riches story that underpins most discussions about success. How do people get ahead?

1 WORD POWER

A asks students to consider symbols of success. By associating success with concrete or abstract constructs, students will have a clearer idea and vocabulary for what ambition and success means to them.

B gives practice in matching collocations linked to ambition and success.

1 WORD POWER B				Answers
2 b	3 e	4 c	5 d	6 a

C allows for further practice in using the collocations and **Language Bank 3** phrases.

ARTICLES
Chan the Man: The Early Years

This article is an extract from a longer piece on Jackie Chan's career. Mention to students that Jackie Chan was a huge star in Asia before moving

QSE Advanced See pages 16–19 SB, 96 WB

Unit 3
Teacher's Guide

on to Hollywood. He tried several times to break into the American market, before finding success there with *Rumble in the Bronx* (1996). Chan's movies often combine action and martial arts with comedy, but he does all his own stunts.

EQ: *What types of films do you like? Which tend to be the most popular in your country?*

The Shah of Bollywood

Bollywood films are often characterised by singing and elaborate dance choreography, while the musical has become less popular in American cinema. Unlike actors from other countries (Italy, China, UK), Indian actors have had little cross-over success in other countries. Some Indian films have been successful around the world; for example: *Bride and Prejudice* (2004), an adaption of Jane Austen's novel, *Pride and Prejudice*.

EQ: *Do you think there is discrimination against non-white actors in Hollywood? Why / Why not?*

2 READING

2 READING A				Answers
A 1 JC	2 neither	3 both	4 SRK	5 JC

C 1 You can bring up what talents or skills an actor may naturally possess (beauty, charisma, charm, intelligence) and may need to learn (fencing, martial arts, horse riding, singing).

C 2 It may help to discuss types of movies made, actors and directors, and then more general aspects of Hollywood, Bollywood or Hong Kong movies.

Hollywood – large budgets, special effects, American-centred plots.
Bollywood – musical aspect, dancing / singing, stylised acting.
Hong Kong – action and martial arts.

3 SPEAK YOUR MIND

This section covers childhood ambitions, future ambitions, making it in other countries, and taking risks and ambition.

A EQ: *Why do you think ambitions change as you get older? Do people change jobs and careers often in your country? What three careers would you like to have?*

B EQ: *How realistic do you think these goals are?*

C EQ: *Has anybody from your country gone on to become successful in other countries?*

D EQ: *Is risk-taking common in your country?*

4 WATCH AND LISTEN   DVD

The video interviews are with ordinary people in North Carolina. Generally, the interviewees express optimistic views of the system.

4 WATCH AND LISTEN B		Answers
B 1 C	2 B	3 B

C These questions will help students to explore the reality of the American Dream and aspects of success and failure.

5 TEAMWORK

The problem tree is a common tool to help people simplify rather complex problems. Visualising the problem in different stages from difficult to easy can provide a means for tackling these in a more productive order.

Example: *becoming an astronaut*

Difficult

You need many years of experience in a field related to space exploration.
You need to possess some skill valuable to the mission.
You need to have a good knowledge of science.
You need to pass many tests: physical, mental and emotional.
You need to undergo a lot of training.
You need to live in a country with a space programme.
You need to speak the language of that country.
You need to be physically fit.

6 CONTROVERSY

Welfare systems are always a heated issue, as they often take up a large percentage of a state's annual budget. The two main views are that:

• Welfare recipients are lazy and don't want to work.

BROOKEMEAD ENGLISH LANGUAGE TEACHING © Brookemead Associates Ltd 2009

- Welfare recipients should be given help to rebuild their lives.

Often these views overlap depending on social and political positions; for example, people who are economically vulnerable (lower and middle class) are often welfare's largest supporters, while people who are economically secure are often welfare's greatest critics.

7 PORTFOLIO WRITING

See the Introduction to the Teacher's Guide.

A Sources:
Learning to Lead: A Workbook on Becoming a Leader, Warren Bennis
The Time 100 leaders: www.time.com/time/time100/leaders
Leadership in Business: www.nwlink.com/~donclark/leader/leader.html

B Sources:
Goals! How to Get Everything You Want – Faster than You Thought Possible, Brian Tracy
Seven Habits of Highly Effective People, Stephen R. Covey
www.mygoals.com

8 CAREERS IN ENGLISH

Young people leaving school often need advice on careers. This activity is designed to give some perspective in this area, as some career choices will have a much better future than others.

---

8 CAREERS *in English*   **Sample answers**

A Reasons for choosing each job:

Bioinformatician: A relatively new field which combines a good knowledge of computer science and medical science. They can run complex computer models to test drugs before field trials.

Wireless engineer: Wireless equipment is set to become more and more common in the future, making these engineers in high demand.

Forensic accountant: Based on events in the US (Enron) and Europe (Parmalat), there is a growing need for accountants who can independently analyse the financial information in company reports and accounts.

Data miner: Customers prefer personal service, but in the age of large corporations, this can be difficult. Creating software that can tell companies what individual people like or dislike lets businesses personalise their services.

Home-care nurse: As the number of older people in the population grows, there will be a sharp increase in the need for nurses giving care at home.

AI programmer: Artificial intelligence is becoming closer to reality. Programmers are teaching computers how to learn like humans.

Adventure travel guide: Extreme sports and adventure travel are becoming more popular. There will be a greater demand for experienced professionals who can safely guide people in these trips.

Fuel-cell engineer: With oil supplies growing scarcer, hydrogen fuel cells will be the next important technological development for transport. Energy and car companies will be looking for people with this expertise.

Lawyer: Intellectual property rights are very important for many companies, for example the entertainment industry. Companies need lawyers to help stop people illegally downloading music from the internet and CD / DVD piracy.

Odd-job person: As there are more people who don't have time to do jobs for themselves or are too old to do them, there will be more demand for help around the house.

B EQ: *Which of these jobs would be likely to last longest? Why?*

9 FURTHER DISCUSSION

This section covers: fame, reasons for ambition, ambition and the law, rejecting society's expectations, and equality in society.

A You can begin this question by asking students to give examples of famous people in their country.

EQ: *Is being famous the same as being successful?*

B Ask students to think about what drives them to succeed. Is it parents, community values, personal expectations or something else?

C Students should consider whether success should be the ultimate goal.

EQ: *Does the end justify the means? Are successful people who commit crimes treated differently from ordinary criminals?*

D This brings in the idea of people who do not follow the usual way in society.

EQ: *Is dropping out of society just a luxury of developed countries?*

E This is one of the central issues in this unit. Try to get students to think about how life might be different for other people in their country or even in other countries.

EQ: *Does it really matter? Is there anything that society can or should do about this?*

10 Your answer: WHAT WOULD YOU DO TO SUCCEED?

The question relates in ways to the issue of ethics and ambition and how committed someone needs to be to succeed. Can you be ethical and ambitious? Are the sacrifices worth the gains? In part, it comes down to what the person and their culture values most. In some cultures, it is the family; in others success in career and life is the ultimate goal. This discussion of work-life balance will be looked at in greater depth in Unit 15.

WORKBOOK

1 USE OF LANGUAGE: Joining clauses

This activity introduces students to an extremely successful writer, J.K. Rowling, author of the Harry Potter books. At the same time, students will practise their knowledge of clauses. The activity itself is related to an authentic test activity used by the University of Cambridge Local Examinations Syndicate in the Certificate in Advanced English and Certificate of Proficiency in English.

1 USE OF LANGUAGE				Answers
1 that	2 who	3 who	4 After	5 where
6 whom	7 Although	8 while	9 After	10 which

2 WRITING

A Sources:
www.writing-world.com
Conversations with J.K. Rowling, Lindsey Fraser
www.jkrowling.com

B Sources:
The 100 Simple Secrets of Happy People, David Niven
Unlimited Power: The New Science of Personal Achievement, Anthony Robbins
www.motivation123.com
http://dir.yahoo.com/Business_and_Economy/Business_to_Business/Speakers/Motivational

3 SPEAKING STRATEGIES: Get rhetorical

This activity aims to get students to incorporate rhetorical questions into their presentations. It is a useful skill to emphasis points, strengthen arguments and build rapport with listeners.

3 SPEAKING STRATEGIES					Answers
1 b	2 e	3 c	4 d	5 f	6 a

4 IDIOMS

See the Introduction to the Teacher's Guide.

4 IDIOMS					Answers
1 e	2 f	3 a	4 b	5 d	6 c

1 down-to-earth = very practical, sensible
2 workaholic = addicted to work, working very long hours 3 control freak = likes to control everything people do 4 movers and shakers = important and influential people 5 stick-in-the-mud = dull, boring, unadventurous 6 shark = hard, focused on getting what he wants

Ask students to use the idioms orally by answering these questions. These can be done as pair work or as a whole class.

- *Do any of these idioms describe you? Do they describe people you know?*
  – I am a bit of a *control freak*. I like to be in charge of everything I do.

- *Which of these do you think would be successful in a career, family, or life in general?*
  – I don't think a *stick-in-the-mud* would be very successful in a career. They don't seem very motivated to do anything.

- *What kind of goals do you think each of them has?*
  – I think a *shark* would only be interested in winning at any cost – no matter what the area.

Unit 4 — Are you looking at me?

Teacher's Guide — See pages 20–23 SB, 97 WB

WHAT'S NEW!

Communication Objectives:	Ss will: – use modifying words and phrases for expressing beliefs. – use bullying-related vocabulary, phrases and idioms.
Educational Objectives:	Students will be able to understand the psychological, moral, social and legal implications of bullying.
Connected Topics:	– Satire and difficult issues – Dynamics of power – Steroids and other illegal drugs – Stanford Prison Experiment – Workplace bullying – Big versus small countries – Social Darwinism – Bullying and sports
Grammar:	Word forms and modifying words
Key Vocabulary:	anecdotal, bullying, cavort, Class A drugs, competition, detention, exclude, harassment, informant, irrefutable, intemperate, local education authority, multifarious, notorious, passive-aggressive behaviour, peremptorily, precipitous, psychopath, push-up, reinstate, sadistic, sketchy, survival of the fittest, teasing, truancy, unsubstantiated

The BIG question: IS BULLYING JUST PART OF LIFE?

While the unit title is framed as the typical challenge of someone who is behaving in aggressive way, as if just looking is an aggressive act in itself, *The BIG question* asks whether bullying is inevitable.

VIEWPOINT

Facts: The information is from a survey by ChildLine, a leading UK children's charity, and the UK government's Department for Education and Skills. They interviewed over a thousand pupils in Years 5 and 8 from 12 different schools from across the UK.

Source:
www.childline.org.uk/pdfs/bullysum.pdf

More statistics:
Two-thirds of bullying victims say they are bullied every day.
Two-thirds of bullying victims say their schools do nothing to help.
More than a third of bullying victims say bullying stopped after they told someone.

Source:
CBBC
http://news.bbc.co.uk/cbbcnews/hi/uk/newsid_2516000/2516997.stm

EQ: *Why do you think there is a difference between the rate of bullying in primary and secondary schools?*

Quote: Jimmy Carter Jr. (b 1924) was the 39th president of the USA from 1977–81. His administration supported social inclusion, human rights, peace in the Middle East and nuclear disarmament. Nowadays he is better known for his human rights work.

EQ: *Do you agree with Jimmy Carter's quote? How would you assess your country's treatment of its weakest and most helpless members?*

Poster: This poster is from an Australian anti-bullying website - www.sangrea.nte/bully. The students should be encouraged to think about self-esteem.

1 WORD POWER

A asks students to consider different types of bullies. By associating bullying with different social

Unit 4 — Are you looking at me?
Teacher's Guide
See pages 20–23 SB, 97 WB

roles, students will begin to make the association of bullying and abuse of power.

B Students find antonyms in the articles to complete the activity.

1 WORD POWER B				Answers
2 c	3 b	4 e	5 d	6 a

C This activity gives practice in using vocabulary from **B** and the phrases from **Language Bank 4**.

D More practice in using vocabulary and **Language Bank 4** phrases while discussing the issue of bullying from different points of view.

ARTICLES
Leave the Poor Psychopath Alone

This *Guardian* editorial was written after an incident at the Glyn Technology School in Surrey, UK. Two 15-year-old boys were caught throwing stones at school windows and were given a detention by the Physical Education teacher, Steve Taverner. The boys then left 44 threatening messages on the teacher's answering machine and mobile phone, including: 'You are going to die soon. You are going to get stabbed in the back of the head.' and 'You have five days to live.' The school's headmaster and governors decided to exclude the boys. After an appeal by the boys' parents, the appeals panel of the Surrey Local Education Authority overturned the verdict. The panel members chose not to listen to the tapes of the threats. Mr Taverner took sick leave for stress. The teachers at the school threatened to strike if the boys were allowed back. The UK Education secretary finally stepped in and reversed the appeal decision, so the boys have not returned to the school. The article was written directly after the appeal panel made its decision.

EQ: *How could this sort of incident happen?*

Drug Warning as Bullied Children turn to Steroids

This article expands on the worrying trend among secondary school boys in the UK and elsewhere. Steroids are often thought of as a sports-related problem, but they appear to be a social one as well. Some effects of abusing anabolic-androgenic steroids (male hormones) are: psychiatric effects (extreme mood swings, aggressive behaviour ('roid rage), extreme irritability, paranoia, delusions), high blood pressure / heart disease, liver damage / cancer, strokes / blood clots, stopping growth (adolescents), severe acne, baldness, nausea, insomnia. It also has effects on the reproductive system. Steroids can be taken orally or intravenously. Sharing needles when injecting can also increase the risk of HIV / AIDS and hepatitis.

EQ: *Is taking steroids as serious as taking other drugs like marijuana, LSD, cocaine or heroine?*

2 READING

B It might help to go through the article point by point. One key to understanding whether something is satirical is by deciding if the events can be taken seriously. You can get the students to discuss whether each of these events would ever happen.

The crime:
- Student killing a teacher.
- Mounting the head on 40-foot pole outside the teachers' room.
- Dancing around the pole naked, whooping and hollering and invoking the Antichrist.

Sample comment: *If it's a real crime, it would be one of the most bizarre and brutal this century.*

Reasons for committing the crime:
- Being punished: detention and exclusion
- According to Ms Bennett (Darren's mother): history of bullying by teacher for punishing Bennett for clear school and legal offences (truancy and possession of Class A drugs)

Sample comment: *These are rather absurd reasons to suggest that the murder was in any way justifiable.*

Response by the local school authority
- To overturn the exclusion because the threat of the student's rage was removed with the death of Mr McCreevey.
- To accept Ms Bennett's explanation and repeal the exclusion.

Sample comment: *The response of the local school authority in this fictional case is absurd and ridiculous. (The author is suggesting that the 'real' appeal verdict*

QSE Advanced   See pages 20–23 SB, 97 WB   Unit 4
Teacher's Guide

is similarly absurd and ridiculous.) It is against most normal ideas of justice.

EQ: *Why do people use satire? Think of some news events (especially controversial / unpopular ones). How could you speak about them in a satirical way?*

---

2 READING A, B   Answers

A 1 decapitate   **2** repercussion   **3** remonstrate   **4** precipitous

B 1 First article satirical: Events that are extreme and exaggerated are described as if they are normal, for example Darren killed his teacher but this was apparently justified because the teacher punished Darren for truancy and having illegal drugs, although this was what a teacher should normally do.

B 1: It may help to discuss the effects of steroids on the human body. (See effects of steroid abuse above.)

EQ: *Why do people take steroids (use and abuse)? What do they do? Should steroids be legal and easily obtainable? Would you take steroids if you were bullied?*

---

2 READING C2   Answers

C 2 The students are getting steroids from drug dealers pushing other drugs because they want to be bigger as a way of dealing with bullies.

---

3 SPEAK YOUR MIND

This section covers: the frequency of bullying, how bullying changes over time, the use of technology for bullying, bullying and physical violence, and the attitude of society to bullying.

A EQ: *How common is bullying in schools? Do schools take bullying seriously? How does / did your school deal with bullying?*

B EQ: *Do adults experience bullying too? If so, give examples. Is the type of bullying the same at different ages?*

C EQ: *Does the anonymity of an email or a mobile phone increase this kind of behaviour? How can it be dealt with?*

D EQ: *Is teasing just something harmless that everyone does?*

E EQ: *Would you defend someone from being bullied if it meant you might get injured? When should the authorities be brought in (for example: headmasters, police, employers)?*

4 LISTEN   DVD

Although bullying is not new to the workplace, it seems to have increased recently. With less job security, workers often feel they cannot protect themselves from a bully who might have control over their job. The most important point to be taken from this audio clip is that the problem of bullying in the workplace is due to the poor enforcement of existing workplace harassment policies in many companies.

---

4 LISTEN B, C   Answers

B • Bullying can take the form of shouting, swearing, fighting, passive aggressiveness (not talking to colleagues, not returning phone calls), rudeness, or disrespect.
• Bullies are often people with a special status, who are high up on the corporate ladder, or who have a special skill and are allowed to get away with their bad behaviour.
• To solve the problem, companies need to enforce their anti-bullying rules and adopt a zero tolerance policy.

C 1 A   **2** B

D Students might say that Roger's boss humiliated him.

E These questions will help students discuss how to deal with bullying.

5 TEAMWORK

Many of the victims of childhood and teenage bullying are targeted because of their physical appearance. The teenage years are often marked by trying to conform to social peers. While many personality traits can be adapted to 'fit in', differences in physical traits are not so easily changed. A study in Canada found that overweight or obese children were much more likely to be bullied. Obese girls were 90 per cent more likely to suffer from bullying than other girls. The study also found that victims were more likely to become bullies themselves.

EQ: *Do you think discrimination or racism is a form of bullying?*

6 CONTROVERSY

This issue is controversial as it touches on many topics that some might find difficult to talk about, although some nationalities may still consider themselves superior to others either morally, historically, financially, intellectually or militarily. It is important to mention a few obvious points before you begin:

1 People may be different around the world, but all people should be considered equal (one group of people is not by nature or design better than another).
2 Nationalism is good, but it also has an ugly side (too much nationalism can produce racism, prejudice and ignorance).
3 This activity is NOT an opportunity to target and attack different groups.

Sources:
On the Origin of Species, Charles Darwin
Social Darwinism in European and American Thought, 1860–1945, Mike Hawkins
Maus: A Survivor's Tale, Art Spiegelman
Anne Frank: Diary of a Young Girl, Anne Frank
The Prize, Marilyn LaCourt
www.en.wikipedia.org/wiki/Social_Darwinism
www.royalinstitutephilosophy.org/articles/midgley_genes.htm
www.darwinmag.com/read/060102/process.html

7 PORTFOLIO WRITING

See the Introduction to the Teacher's Guide.

A Sources:
www.education.guardian.co.uk/classroomviolence/story/0,12388,814816,00.html
www.news.bbc.co.uk/cbbcnews/hi/uk/newsid_2321000/2321379.stm
www.news.scotsman.com/topics.cfm?tid=572&id=1129982002

B Sources:
How to be a Superhero: Your Complete Guide to Finding a Secret Headquarters, Hiring a Sidekick, Thwarting the Forces of Evil, and Much More!!
Doctor Metropolis
www.bbc.co.uk/science/hottopics/superheroes

8 PSYCHOLOGY *in English* [CLIL]

The Stanford prison experiment was conducted by Dr Phillip Zimbardo and his team of psychology researchers at Stanford University in 1971. Everyone involved became identified with their roles to the point where the line between reality and experiment began to blur. Researchers became wardens and parole board members. Volunteers became guards and prisoners.

Many 'prisoners' began to believe that the experimental 'prison' was a real prison and that their situation was hopeless. Although they were overseen by the warden-researchers, the guards were free to use their own set of rules for the prison, and they began to develop harsher and harsher methods of control. The experiment was originally to last two weeks but it was shut down on Day 6 after a colleague of Dr Zimbardo witnessed the brutality and complete personality change in one of the more sadistic guards. It left a lasting impression on most of the people involved; many of the volunteers began careers in psychology, law, law enforcement and prisoner rights. See www.prisonexp.org.

EQ: *Do you think prison naturally leads to these kinds of abuse? What rights do prisoners have?*

9 FURTHER DISCUSSION

This section covers: victims becoming bullies, bullying and sports, how bullying happens, popularity and status, and powerful versus weaker countries.

A Begin by discussing what emotions the victims might be going through and how they can deal with them.

EQ: *A US Secret Service report found bullying to be a major factor in school shootings. Who is to blame in these cases: shooters, bullies, parents, schools, society or something else?*

QSE Advanced See pages 20–23 SB, 97 WB

Unit 4 Teacher's Guide

B Discuss what makes sports violent or aggressive. Some examples: boxing, martial arts, rugby, Australian Rules football.

EQ: *Do sports increase or decrease violence and aggression in society?*

C Discuss how people can be drawn into bullying.

EQ: *Do people get involved in bullying by doing something or doing nothing?*

D Ask students to think about how the search for popularity or social acceptance might be tied to bullying.

EQ: *Are popular people often bullies? Why / Why not?*

E This question will help students to think about bullying and relationships of power.

EQ: *Which countries do you think use their power to bully other countries?*

10 Your answer: IS BULLYING JUST PART OF LIFE?

This question relates to the issue of bullying in society. Is it just a phase of social development that we can't change, just part of our nature? You can get students to think about the nature of power and how it can be used and abused.

WORKBOOK

1 WORD POWER

This activity will give students the opportunity to review their understanding of key vocabulary found in the Student's Book. At the same time, students practise using modifying words.

1 WORD POWER	**Answers**

1 The gang in Raul's neighborhood **really / certainly** *intimidated* him when they walked past him in the street.
2 It is **basically / really / essentially / naturally** the role of parents to stop older brothers and sisters from *picking on* younger ones in the family.
3 The teacher **actually / really / essentially** seemed to *blame* the victim rather than the bully.
4 Mitsuko's threatening behaviour **actually / certainly** became so bad that the head teacher wanted to *exclude her from* school.
5 Sophia felt she was weak and **really / quite** *helpless* because her father shouted at her all the time.

2 USE OF LANGUAGE: Word forms

This activity introduces an interesting aspect of bullying: that it can be as prevalent among girls as among boys. The activity is based on an authentic test activity used by the University of Cambridge Local Examinations Syndicate in the Certificate in Advanced English and Certificate of Proficiency in English.

2 USE OF LANGUAGE	**Answers**

1 hidden 2 secretive 3 calling 4 understanding
5 actions 6 relationships 7 psychological
8 publicised

3 WRITING

A Sources:
www.bullying.org   www.bullying.co.uk
www.nobully.org.nz   www.antibullying.net

B Sources:
Taking The Bully By The Horns, Sam Horn
When You Work For A Bully: Assessing Your Options And Taking Action, Susan Futterman
www.bullyonline.org/workbully

4 IDIOMS

See the Introduction to the Teacher's Guide.

4 IDIOMS	**Answers**

1 f *played*   2 a *cross*   3 d *flogging*
4 b *driven*   5 e *went*   6 c *fight*

1 to play into someone's hands = to put yourself in a weak position 2 to cross swords = to provoke, argue with 3 to flog a dead horse = to do something that will have no effect 4 to drive someone over the edge = to push someone into doing something desperate 5 to go to great lengths = to make a lot of effort 6 to fight it out = to face someone about a problem

Unit 4 — Are you looking at me?
Teacher's Guide
See pages 20–23 SB, 97 WB

Ask students to use the idioms when answering these questions orally. This can be done as pair work or as a class.

- *Would you try to avoid a bully or confront him / her?*
  - I would try to *fight it out*.
  - I wouldn't want to *play into his / her hands*. I would avoid the bully.
  - I wouldn't *cross swords with* a bully. I'd likely stay away from him.
- *How much effort does it take to stop a bully?*
  - You might have to *go to great lengths* to stop a bully.
  - I imagine it might be like *flogging a dead horse* trying to get the school to take it seriously.
- *How might bullying affect someone emotionally?*
  - I would imagine it might *drive* some people *over the edge*.
  - I imagine always trying to avoid *crossing swords with* a bully would eventually leave someone feeling desperate and depressed.

Unit 5 — Frills and thrills — Teacher's Guide

See pages 24–27 SB, 98 WB

WHAT'S NEW!

Communication Objectives:	Ss will be able to: – express opinions tentatively and correctly use vivid adjectives. – use designer goods-related vocabulary, phrases and idioms.
Educational Objectives:	Ss will explore the origins, meaning and implications of fashion and designer goods.
Connected Topics:	– Fashion trends – Japan and designer goods – Metrosexual males and gender roles – PETA and animal products – Process of design – Haute couture – Hierarchy of needs – Cost versus price – Media and fashion demand – Art and design
Grammar:	Vivid adjectives Reported speech
Key Vocabulary:	beauty / grooming products, bling, brandstretching, cyclical, insurmountable, materialistic, metrosexual (man), minimalist, personal fulfilment, prestige, retro, sarong, suave, surge, tell-tale signs, vintage, way off the mark

The BIG question: ARE WE ALL FASHION VICTIMS?

The question here refers to the common expression 'fashion victim' for people who follow every fashion trend regardless of whether it is appropriate for them, but it asks students to reflect on whether we are all fashion victims, although some more than others.

VIEWPOINT

Fact: The huge shoe collection made by Imelda Marcos, wife of ex-Philippines President Marcos, caused a scandal because at the time she was spending so much on shoes many Filipinos lived in great poverty. When she and her husband fled the country in 1986, the shoes were put on display to show her extravagance and are now in the Marikina City Footwear Museum.

EQ: *What would be an excessive collection of clothes or shoes? Is collecting fashion something to admire?*

Quotes: Gore Vidal (b 1925) is an American novelist, essayist and screenwriter. The latter half of his career has focused mainly on political discussion, and he often criticises the American government.

EQ: *What does Gore Vidal mean by this comment? Do you agree with it? Do you think the attitude applies to you?*

Stella McCartney (b 1971) is a successful British fashion designer and the daughter of the former Beatle, Paul McCartney. Like her mother, Linda, and her father, she is a strict vegetarian and chooses not to use animal products in her designs.

EQ: *What do you think of celebrities who wear fur? Is fur glamorous? Do you think of fur or leather as dead animals? Why / Why not?*

The question about the photos can be addressed several ways: the difference between teenage and adult fashion; the difference between boys and girls, etc.

1 WORD POWER

A requires the students to actively express tentative expressions and adjectives from **Language Bank 5.** Although you can give the students some preparation time, this activity should stress the spoken use of the phrases so it should be more spontaneous.

B looks at the meanings of some more adjectives. It may be helpful to go through each word individually. Check that students understand, then ask whether the word is positive or negative. Remember to ask why.

Unit 5 — Frills and thrills — Teacher's Guide

See pages 24–27 SB, 98 WB

ARTICLES

Japanese Girls Go Crazy for Foreign Designer Goods

This article explores a long-term consumer trend in Japan. Although this article has been written by a foreign journalist, the question is also widely debated in Japan.

EQ: *How does the situation in your country compare to the situation in Japan?*

A New Male Market Emerges

This article addresses the recent phenomenon of the metrosexual man.

EQ: *Could this happen in your country?*

2 READING

Pronunciation note: mania [ˈmeɪnɪə] is pronounced differently from most words starting with 'm-a-n'. See: *ma*nage, *man*ner, *ma*ny.

A Matching headlines to the paragraphs requires students to read for gist. This type of activity is drawn from the Section 1 of the Reading part of the First Certificate in English exam.

2 READING A					Answers
1 c	2 f	3 e	4 b	5 a	6 d

B Reported speech is a grammatical structure that students should know how to use at this level. However, it may be helpful to review the rules.

How to report…	We report it…
A statement made recently	**Using verbs in present tense**
'I'm wearing a Gucci suit.'	→ He says (that*) he is wearing a Gucci suit.
A statement made in the past	**Using verbs in past tense**
'I bought a Louis Vuitton bag.'	→ She said (that*) she bought a Louis Vuitton bag.
Orders, advice or requests	**Using 'to'**
'Please sit down.'	→ He asked me *to* sit down.
'You should go to Paris for couture fashion.'	→ She advised me *to* go to Paris for couture fashion.
A question	**By changing the word order**
'Is that Prada?' 'When will the store open?'	→ She asked me if it was Prada. → He wanted to know when the store will open.

* Note: *that* is optional in reporting statements.

C 1 This can be a challenging question as it requires people to think about why we worry about how others see us.

EQ: *Is the demand for fashion all due to marketing? Do you think designer goods or fashion help or hurt people's self-esteem?*

C 2 It may be helpful to define what might be considered masculine and feminine things. In some cases, these are historical and cultural differences; for example: a Scottish kilt, South Pacific sarong.

EQ: *What are typical clothes for men and women? Why do we make distinctions between men's products and women's products? Do only women have fashion sense?*

3 SPEAK YOUR MIND

This section covers: the essence of fashion, the quality issue in designer goods, designing as a career, and what it means to use expensive toiletries.

A EQ: *What makes us want to buy new clothes so often? Why do we often find past fashions funny? Give examples.*

B EQ: *Name some designers or designer labels you have heard of. Which kinds of goods do they make?*

C EQ: *What do you think a designer's life is like?*

D Note: the question about men using grooming products refers to expensive 'designer grooming products' like moisturisers, not ordinary products like shampoo and deodorant.

EQ: *One assumption behind the 'metrosexual' man is that appearance-enhancing goods are very feminine. Do you agree? Why / Why not?*

QSE Advanced

See pages 24–27 SB, 98 WB

Unit 5
Teacher's Guide

4 WATCH AND LISTEN   DVD

This video material was produced by the People for the Ethical Treatment of Animals (PETA) in the USA. Note: the video contains some rather disturbing descriptions of the condition of animals in a fur farm and students should be told this before you watch.

The video talks about a highly publicised campaign: 'I'd rather go naked than wear fur'. While this campaign is a few years old now, the issue of fur has been back in the news with the trend in music videos for displays of wealth and status, in which many rappers and singers, including Jennifer Lopez, Beyoncé Knowles and Lil Kim, appeared wearing fur. Another incident involved the model Naomi Campbell. She had participated in the PETA 'I'd rather go naked…' campaign, but later appeared on a fashion show in Milan wearing fur.

EQ: *What did you think of the 'I'd rather go naked…' campaign?*

4 WATCH AND LISTEN B			Answers
B 1 A	2 C	3 C	

C The clip shows a homeless woman receiving a fur coat for the winter. Students would probably answer the question by thanking the person and commenting on how warm the fur coat is.

D Students have an opportunity to express their views about the PETA campaign.

5 TEAMWORK

This activity is based on a classic brainstorming technique widely used by groups when they are developing products and processes, for example, engineers and managers.

EQ: *Who might benefit from using SCAMPER? Why? Could you see yourself using SCAMPER in other studies?*

6 CONTROVERSY

This issue touches on an interesting question for a modern society based on equality. Do people with a lot of money have a responsibility to those who do not? Haute couture is for a small elite of very wealthy women, perhaps only 3,000 women in the whole world who afford to buy these clothes regularly. Couture is an extreme example of the maxim 'you get what you pay for'. Haute couture customers pay for the best in original design, fabrics, workmanship and service. It can take up to a thousand hours to make a hand-embroidered evening dress.

Sources:
The Art of Couture, Victor Skrebneski
Haute Couture, Harold Koda
The Wealth and Poverty of Nations: Why Some Are So Rich and Some So Poor, David Landes
www.fashion-era.com
www.pierrecardin.com
www.fashion.dior.com

7 PORTFOLIO WRITING

See the Introduction to the Teacher's Guide.

A Sources:
Confessions of a Shopaholic, Sophie Kinsella
The Lucky Shopping Manual: Building and Improving Your Wardrobe Piece by Piece, Kim France
www.shopping.com
www.shopping.yahoo.com

B Sources:
Male Impersonators: Men Performing Masculinity, Mark Simpson.
Both Feet on the Ground, David Beckham

8 CONSUMER STUDIES IN ENGLISH [CLIL]

The theories of American psychologist Abraham Maslow (1908-1970) are often considered the third force in psychology after psychoanalysis (Sigmund Freud) and behaviourism (B.F Skinner). His view of the causes of human behaviour centred on the need for humans to make decisions to fulfill certain needs. These needs are arranged in a hierarchy from the most basic up. Maslow focused on normal, healthy people, seeking to understand their motivations.

When looking at the Hierarchy of Needs, work from the bottom up.

- Physiological needs are the purely physical needs for basic human existence, including: oxygen, water, food, vitamins, minerals, sleep, physical activity, rest, excretion of waste and sex.

Unit 5 — Frills and thrills — Teacher's Guide

See pages 24–27 SB, 98 WB

- Safety needs relate to the mainly psychological need for structure in a chaotic world – safety, stability and protection. These could include a safe neighbourhood, stable relationships, job security, insurance, some savings.
- Social needs are the love and belonging needs that make people look for close relationships; for example: marriage, friends, children, or belonging to a group like a church or a gang. Careers come in here because of the human need for human interaction, and there may be associated problems with loneliness and social problems.
- The esteem needs are where Maslow believed that psychological problems in Western society often originate. He defined two types:
  - Higher esteem needs to do with self-esteem, the desire for self-confidence, achievement, independence and freedom.
  - Lower esteem needs relating to the respect of others, the need for fame, recognition, attention, reputation, dignity and dominance.
- Self-actualisation is the idea of becoming the best person you can be. Maslow estimated that perhaps only 2 per cent of people are capable of reaching this level. The idea is that once we have met all the other needs, we may still feel unfulfilled because we are trying to discover and fulfill the calling in life we are most suited for. For Maslow, people such as Albert Einstein, Eleanor Roosevelt and Aldous Huxley are examples of people who have reached this level.

EQ: *Do you think everyone has a calling in life? What do you think your calling in life might be? Do you think it is as difficult to reach the stage of self-actualisation?*

9 FURTHER DISCUSSION

This section covers: the process behind design; the media and fashion trends; art and design; the cost of designer goods, and status symbols.

A Ask students to begin by listing what items are considered designer goods and the adjectives they can use to describe them.

EQ: *(adjectives) How else can we describe these designer goods? How do trends affect designer goods?*

B Students can discuss the images on MTV, by analysing different music videos they have seen.

EQ: *Could these images influence what young people do? If so, should or can anything be done about it?*

C Ask students to think of some famous artists.

EQ: *If these artists were designers, how might they design various households items?*

D Students could start with specific examples: clothes, utensils, glassware, furniture and perhaps refer back to the **5 Teamwork** activity; for example, how replacing different materials might increase or decrease the costs.

EQ: *Fake designer goods are becoming more and more common. Where are these made and sold? Should making and selling fake designer goods be a crime? Would you ever buy fake designer goods?*

E Ask students to think about how we determine the value of anything.

EQ: *How is supply and demand related to status? How do you personally feel about owning designer goods?*

10 *Your answer:* ARE WE ALL FASHION VICTIMS?

This question asks student to focus on the values of Western society. Is materialism positive or negative? Is materialism a means to an end or is it an end in itself? If everyone in society does the same thing, can this action be considered wrong? What is normal and abnormal? Although these questions are meant to analyse society as a whole, students could consider their own buying habits.

WORKBOOK

1 WORD POWER

This activity will give students the opportunity for further practice of the adjectives and tentative expressions.

QSE Advanced See pages 24–27 SB, 98 WB

Unit 5
Teacher's Guide

> **1 WORD POWER** **Sample answers**
>
> **1A** exquisite **1B** Maybe we could think about buying it?
> **2A** dull **2B** It seems to me that we could get something better.
> **3A** spectacular **3A** Why don't you try it on?
> **4A** impractical **4B** Does that suggest we should buy a larger one?
> **5A** fresh and functional **5B** I tend to think it would work well at home.
> **6A** flashy **6C** Why don't we try somewhere else?

2 WRITING

2A Sources
Charity, Mark Peterson
Learning About Charity from the Life of Princess Diana, Caroline Levchuck
www.charitynavigator.org
www.charitychoice.co.uk

B Sources
New Complete Do-It-Yourself Manual Reader's Digest
The Book of Home Design Using IKEA Home Furnishings, Anoop Parikh
www.ikea.com

3 SPEAKING STRATEGIES: De-emphasising

This activity will help students who plan to de-emphasise contradictory points brought up by the invigilator.

> **3 SPEAKING STRATEGIES** **Answers**
>
> **1** j / g / i **2** f **3** g / i **4** a **5** b
> **6** e **7** h **8** d **9** j / i / g **10** k

4 IDIOMS

See the Introduction to the Teacher's Guide.

> **4 IDIOMS** **Answers**
>
> **1** b **2** d **3** a **4** c **5** e
>
> **1** keeping up with the Joneses = competing with other people by buying whatever is the latest fashion
> **2** trendsetter = someone who starts a fashion trend
> **3** empty existence = not emotionally or spiritually satisfying **4** to pay a pretty penny = to pay a lot of money **5** upmarket = more sophisticated

Ask students to use the idioms orally by answering these questions. These can be done as pair work or as a whole class.

- *How do you feel when you buy some new clothes?*
  – Mostly good, but you often have to *pay a pretty penny* for them, which is not so good.
  – I like being a *trendsetter,* so I always like it.
- *Do you think buying things makes you happy?*
  – I think always shopping and buying things might be an *empty existence.*
  – It's difficult to *keep up with the Joneses.* If that's all you worry about, I don't think you'd be happy.
- *Where would you place fashion on Maslow's Hierarchy of Needs?*
  – I think if you are talking about *upmarket* goods, it would be esteem needs.
  – In some countries, I think clothes are really about physiological needs, and staying warm. Being a *trendsetter* comes second.

Unit 6 — Playing to win
Teacher's Guide
See pages 28–31 SB, 99 WB

WHAT'S NEW!

Communication Objectives: Ss will be able to:
- express reservations and correctly use the passive verb form.
- use competitiveness-related vocabulary, phrases and idioms.

Educational Objectives: Ss will explore various examples, roles and effects of competition in society.

Connected Topics:
- The Olympics
- Artistic competition
- Intellectual competition of man and machine
- US athletes and sportsmanship
- Beauty contests
- Reality TV
- Men versus Women sports
- Hierarchical structures
- Extreme sports
- Nationalism and team spirit
- World records

Grammar: Passive verbs

Key Vocabulary:

beauty contest / pageant	drop-out rate	rub someone the wrong way
blister	etiquette	ruthlessly
blunder	flaunt v	sportsmanship
boast v	heat exhaustion	stakes were high, the
boorish	hierarchy	stem from
brute force	implement	sunstroke
cap v	landslide victory	team spirit
capitalise	motto	triathalon
dehydration	odds on	underdog
draw / tie n	reservation (doubt)	walkover
	rivalry	win hands down

The BIG question: HOW IMPORTANT IS WINNING?

The question here is framed to make students think about what motivates people in the search of success, and whether the end always justifies the means.

VIEWPOINT

Facts: The Academy of Motion Pictures Arts and Science has about 6,000 members most of whom are actors. The Academy Awards, or the Oscars, were first handed out in May 16, 1929.

EQ: *Do you think the Oscars represent the best movies of the year? Is it really possible to compare films or acting performances? What criteria should be used?*

Quotes: Vince Lombardi (1913–1970) was one of the most successful coaches in the NFL, the American football league. From 1959 to 1967, his Green Bay Packers won five championship titles.

EQ: *What do you think of the quote? What kinds of values would be associated with this statement?*

Dwight Whitney Morrow (1873–1931) was a US politician. He began as an investment banker with JP Morgan and Co, but World War II led him into political life.

EQ: *Do you agree with the quote? Is hard work always given credit? Do winners always deserve to win? Do losers always deserve to lose?*

1 WORD POWER

A gets students to think about some key ideas about competitiveness in terms of how these apply to competitors, and how sometimes apparently negative qualities can be useful for success in sport.

1 WORD POWER A						Answers
2 h	3 g	4 f	5 a	6 e	7 b	8 b

QSE Advanced — See pages 28–31 SB, 99 WB

Unit 6
Teacher's Guide

B gets students to practise expressing reservations. At the same time, it introduces new vocabulary and idioms relating to competition.

---

1 WORD POWER B — Answers

B 1 There will be a *landslide victory* in the election. **I'm not entirely sure about that. The opposition seems to be doing better in the polls.**
2 The Czechs will *win hands down* in ice hockey. **I know what you're saying, but I think they may still face some serious competition from the Canadians.**
3 Estonia *is odds on to win* the next song festival. **You have a point there, but I wouldn't discount Britain's or Sweden's entry.**
4 It was a *walkover* for our team; the score was 5-0. **That might be true, but they were missing their three best players.**
5 New Zealand will *come first* in the race. **That might be true (they have a strong team), but I wouldn't rule out the Australians.**

ARTICLES

Man Versus Machine Chess Match Drawn

This article discusses the continuing intellectual competition between man and machine. As chess is considered one of the most mentally challenging games, it was a natural choice for IBM's computer team to ask arguably the world's greatest chess player, Garry Kasparov. Kasparov was the world chess champion from 1985 to 2000. The X3D Fritz match was one in a series of matches between IBM supercomputers and Kasparov. The first match was with IBM's Deep Blue in 1986 which Kasparov won 3, drew 2 and lost 1. The second match with an updated Deep Blue ended with Kasparov losing 3.5 to 2.5. (Half points mean a draw.)

EQ: *'A chess genius is a human being who focuses vast, little-understood mental gifts and labors on an ultimately trivial human enterprise.'* (George Steiner) *Do board games like chess prove intelligence? Are these games worthwhile? Why / Why not?*

USOC: Be Good Sports

This article discusses the importance of sportsmanship in international sporting events. In recent years, the boisterous nature of American athletics has developed a rather bad reputation for the country abroad. The article discusses how the US Olympic Committee is trying to address the situation. It should be noted that much of this phenomena originated in basketball. 'Court talk' as it is known in the US is the very aggressive, almost violent banter between players on the basketball court. It is in some ways a psychological technique to intimidate opponents. Court talk has spread to other popular US sports and has become part of the American sporting experience.

EQ: *Is sportsmanship outdated? Does an athlete represent the values of a county? Why / Why? Are American athletes confident or arrogant?*

2 READING

A is a gap completion activity that will help students with Part 2 of the Reading section of the CAE exam.

---

2 READING A — Answers

A 1 D **2** B **3** E **4** A

B gives students the chance to express personal feelings and beliefs about competitors and competition.

---

2 READING B — Answers

B 1 a) The 4 × 100 relay was won by the US team.
b) Victory was achieved by Kasparov's long-term strategy.
c) Things had been made difficult in 2000 by boastful behaviour.
d) In closed games long-term strategy can be used by humans.

B 2 Up to a point Lloy Ball does support being modest, but he thinks boasting is just part of the American fighting spirit.

C asks students to infer about the situations posed in the articles.

1 It may be useful to have students discuss the significance of computers that may be smarter than humans.

EQ: *Is it a positive or negative development?*

2 It may be useful to generalise the question to all celebrities and discuss it.

EQ: *Can we know what kind of person a celebrity is based only on press reports?*

Unit 6 — Playing to win — Teacher's Guide

See pages 28–31 SB, 99 WB

3 SPEAK YOUR MIND

This section covers the topics of competitiveness, favourite sports team, intellect versus athleticism and the Olympics.

A EQ: *Which sports do you play or watch? Is amateur sports less competitive than professional sports?*

B EQ: *Which teams are most popular in your country? How else does money affect competition?*

C EQ: *Will computers and machines be better than humans in the future? Why / Why not? Do you like playing board games like chess or Trivial Pursuit? Why / Why not?*

D EQ: *Are the Olympics the ultimate in human achievement? Why do countries worry about the number of medals won?*

4 LISTEN   DVD

The photos try to show views of beauty that may challenge cultural standards. These include muscular women and plastic surgery beauty contestants.

---

4 LISTEN B, D   **Answers**

B (Sample answers) Relationships are a negative thing in the Miss America competition. Contestants must be single, without children and must sign pledges not to date during their reign. Mrs America allows contestants to be married.

Plastic surgery is discussed as a counterpoint to the other rules about relationships. The Miss America contest does not have any rule against it. In addition, there was recently the Miss Artificial Beauty in China where all contestants had undergone plastic surgery.

American values are discussed briefly in terms of the rules governing the current Miss America contest. Contestants need to be very pure (for example, no marriage, dating or children).

D 1 a) in Atlantic City
    2 b) married   c) two children
    3 d) plastic surgery
    4 e) the acceptance

---

5 TEAMWORK

This activity is designed to give students a chance to discuss both the most popular trend on television – reality TV and one of the most controversial shows on US TV. This activity is based on Celebrity Boxing 1 & 2, in which pairs of well-known, lesser celebrities are pitted against each other. The first show was watched by 15.5 million viewers and featured several matches including one between Tonya Harding (the US figure skater implicated in the assault of a rival US skater) and Paula Jones (a woman who claimed to have had an affair with former President Bill Clinton). The second event featured several matches including a match between Joey Buttafuoco (his young lover killed his wife) and professional female wrestler, Chyna. As reality show formats are often bought by other countries, it is possible that this show will appear elsewhere.

EQ: *What kinds of reality TV shows are there in your country? How are reality TV shows different from other shows? What do reality TV shows say about its viewers, producers and contestants? Would you ever want to be on reality TV?*

6 CONTROVERSY

The debate over equality in funding for women's sports is an offshoot of the larger issue of equality and women's rights. Although you should try to keep the students on the topic of sports and competition, the discussion is likely to incorporate these larger issues of equality. You should therefore be prepared to field questions about women's rights. It may also be worth discussing the professional status of women in different sports; for example: tennis, football, basketball. Note also the way that sports leagues make a distinction between men's and women's sports by adding 'women's' or 'ladies'.

EQ: *Do you think women and men will ever be considered equal in sports? Should they be? Why don't men and women play in the same leagues?*

Sources:

Out of Bounds: Women, Sport and Sexuality, Helen Lenskyj

www.dol.gov/oasam/regs/statutes/titleix.htm

www.olympic.org/uk/organisation/missions/women/index_uk.asp
www.wta.com
www.lpga.com
www.nwhlhockey.com

7 PORTFOLIO WRITING

See the Introduction to the Teacher's Guide.

A Sources:
Athens to Athens: The Official History of the Olympic Games and the IOC, 1896-2004, David Miller
Tales of Gold, Patrick Collins
www.olympic.org

B Sources:
Pageant: The Beauty Contest, Keith Lovegrove
www.msgoldenamerica.com

8 PHYSIOLOGY *in English* [CLIL]

The triathlon was first created in Mission Bay, California in 1974. Since then, the triathlon has been the benchmark distance for creating ultra-sporting events. Today, there are double, triple, quadruple, quintuple and decatriathlons from Finland to Mexico. The World Championship Decatriathlon was first run in 1995. While it is rather difficult for the average person to understand fully the physical and mental anguish involved, you can get some kind of an idea by reading British ultra-athlete Bobby Brown's blog entry on his website: www.bobbysrun.co.uk/ironman.html. It took him two years to fully recover.

The fastest time for a man was set by Fabrice Lucas in 1997 with a time of 8 days, 0 hours and 26 seconds. The fastest time for a woman was set by Silvia Andonie in 1992 with a time of 10 days, 9 hours, 14 minutes, 52 seconds.

EQ: *Imagine you just finished the event. What would it feel like? Could you see yourself ever competing in this sport?*

Sources:
Going Long: Training for Ironman-Distance Triathlons, Joe Friel
Triathlete magazine.
www.iutasport.com

9 FURTHER DISCUSSION

This section covers the topics of competition in artistic endeavours, the role of sports on the world stage, the value of sport versus intellect, and record keeping.

A This question picks up from the Oscars statistic and the question in **Viewpoint**.

EQ: *How do subjectivity and objectivity enter into competitions? Are contest judges ever unbiased? Why / Why not? Why do commercially successful authors like Stephen King or Danielle Steele never seem to win awards?*

B Try to discuss the relative values of sport and intellectual ability.

EQ: *How do time, money, energy and society change this relationship?*

C Try to discuss concrete aspects of nationalism.

EQ: *How do you show your nationalism? What are other examples of nationalism you have seen or heard of? Which of the following are acceptable and why: chanting 'We're number 1', painting your country's flag on your face, or booing the actions of other countries' competitors?*

D Try to get students to consider examples of national or world records for different sports.

EQ: *Which sports records have you heard about? Who holds the world record in…?*

10 *Your answer:* HOW IMPORTANT IS WINNING?

This question attempts to personalise the entire discussion. Here it would be helpful to get students to give concrete examples from school, work, sports, hobbies, computer games, or elsewhere. You can remind students about the winning paradigm that there is only one winner.

EQ: *If there can be only one winner, should everyone else feel like losers? Why / Why not? How do / should you feel when you lose? Does participation or 'giving it 110 per cent' have any effect on these feelings?*

Unit 6 — Playing to win — Teacher's Guide

See pages 28–31 SB, 99 WB

WORKBOOK

1 WORD POWER

This activity will give students the opportunity to review some key unit vocabulary and further practice using the phrases in **Language Bank 6**.

> **1 WORD POWER** — **Sample answers**
>
> 1 I think the opposition party is heading for another *landslide victory* in the polls. **I'm not sure about that...**
> 2 The Russian team will *win hands down* in this competition. **That might be true, but...**
> 3 I don't think you can expect rivals to be *good sports*. **You have a point there, but...**
> 4 The Australian swimmer was the *favourite*. **I'm not entirely sure about that.**
> 5 Any competition leads to *team spirit*. **You have a point there but...**
> 6 The game show proved to be a *walkover* for her. **That might be true, but...**

2 USE OF LANGUAGE: The passive

This activity introduces the students to some biographical information about Arnold Schwarzenegger and his strong competitive streak. It will also give further practice with the passive verb form.

> **2 USE OF LANGUAGE** — **Answers**
>
> 1 He was thought to be a little crazy,
> 2 a year in the Austrian military had to be served.
> 3 he would not be given permission
> 4 Arnold was not deterred,
> 5 Although the contest was won,
> 6 Mr Europe, the Best Built Man in Europe and the International Powerlifting Championship would be entered and won by him.
> 7 the event would be dominated by Arnold.
> 8 This would be capped

3 WRITING

A Sources:
Drug Testing in Sports, David L. Black, ed.
Drug Testing: Issues and Options, Robert H Coombs, ed.
www.olympic.org/uk/organisation/commissions/medical/index_uk.asp
www.drugtestingnews.com

B Sources:
The Best American Sports Writing of the Century, David Halberstam, ed.
Associated Press Sports Writing Handbook, Steve Wilstein
www.news.bbc.co.uk/sport2/hi/default.stm
www.espn.go.com

4 IDIOMS

See the Introduction to the Teacher's Guide.

> **4 IDIOMS** — **Answers**
>
> 1 e 2 d 3 b 4 a 5 f 6 c
>
> 1 the name of the game = the most important thing / aim 2 to play the game = to take part 3 a sporting chance = a chance to win 4 to give someone a run for their money = to make it difficult for someone to win 5 a whole new ball game = the situation was completely changed 6 to throw in the towel = to give up / in, admit defeat

Ask students to use the idioms when answering these questions orally. This can be done as pair work or as a class.

- *What would happen if your class played a football match against Real Madrid?*
  - I don't think we would *give them a run for their money.*
  - I am guessing that we'd have to *throw in the towel* after the first ten minutes.

- *What does it take to get ahead in … (business / sport / school)?*
  - I think practice is *the name of the game*. The more practice you get, the better you'll be.
  - If you want to succeed, you have *to play the game*.
  - I think today *it's a whole new ball game*, a team needs lots of money to be the best.

- *Do you ever feel sorry for losers?*
  - I do, when I know they don't *have a sporting chance* like when too many players are injured.
  - I don't. You should know when *to throw in the towel* and accept defeat.

Unit 7 — **Profit and loss** — **Teacher's Guide** — See pages 32–35 SB, 100 WB

WHAT'S NEW!

Communication Objectives:	Ss will be able to: – defend a point of view and correctly use transitive and intransitive verbs. – use economics-related vocabulary, phrases and idioms.
Educational Objectives:	Ss will explore the impact of different economic indicators on the global economy.
Connected Topics:	– Consumer spending – Unemployment – Agricultural subsidies – Internet economy – War and economic progress – Fair trade and free trade – Oil and other commodities – Privatisation and nationalisation – Black market goods
Grammar:	Transitive and intransitive verbs
Key Vocabulary:	across the board, assets, black economy, close a deal, commodity, concession, decrease v, depression, fair trade, free trade, free-market economy, gross domestic product, gross national product, inflation, privatisation, recession, robust, scrap, subsidy, spawn v, target, transaction, watchdog

The BIG question: DOES ECONOMICS REALLY AFFECT ME?

This question deals with the distance that many people feel from the larger economic issues.

VIEWPOINT

Facts: The statistic on consumer spending shows how dependent the USA and the world economies are on US consumers' spending habits. Consumers in the US are spending more and more using consumer debt (credit cards and mortgages). Many economists worry that this level of consumer debt will lead to problems, as consumers may not be able to maintain this level of debt.

Quotes: Jay Leno is a popular late-night talk show host in the US with the long-running Tonight Show.

EQ: *Do you agree with the quote? Do we take unemployment rates seriously enough? Why do unemployment rates not have the same emotional impact as the effects of unemployment on individuals?*

1 WORD POWER

A asks students to use intransitive verbs in **Language Bank 7** to describe the graph in **Viewpoint**. In the economy, when the GDP is high, generally output is higher, unemployment is lower, and demand for products / commodities is often higher.

1 WORD POWER A — *Sample answers*
After 1980 growth declined / decreased / went down, but by 1985 GDP had gone up / increased again. / In the 1990s growth went down at first, then increased / went up around 1995. In the late 1990s growth increased sharply but dropped in 2000. After 2005 it stopped expanding until 2007.

B introduces new economics-related vocabulary that will be discussed in the unit and gives students practice in defending or rejecting the statements. Note: 'I can't accept that' and 'I think you might be mistaken' are most often used as interjections and should go at the beginning of the sentences.

1 WORD POWER B — *Sample answers*
1 If you look at the facts, you can see that the bubble collapse DID affect the economy.
2 It seems clear that we DID have a recession from 1988–1991.
3 I think you might be mistaken. Commodities would NOT have sold better in 1991 than 1984.

© Brookemead Associates Ltd 2009 — BROOKEMEAD ENGLISH LANGUAGE TEACHING

4 Perhaps you are overlooking the fact that high growth that year would mean relatively low unemployment. Unemployment rates would probably have been highest in 1982.
5 I can't accept that. We do NOT see steady growth from 1990 to 1998.

C gives students an opportunity to discuss aspects of economics.

ARTICLES

Farm Subsidies Key as WTO Works on Trade Plan

This article discusses an important international trade issue: farm subsidies for farmers in developed countries. As much of the developing world relies on agriculture as a major source of employment and income, levels of poverty and development will not change significantly until the issue of subsidies is resolved. In the developing world, farmers can produce much more cheaply but they have no subsidies to help them.

EQ: *Will free trade solve all the problems in developing countries? Why do developed countries promote free trade but keep farm subsidies?*

Virtual World Grows Real Economy

As will be further discussed in Unit 12, playing games on line is increasing. Cheaper high-speed internet access means there are now a few dozen video games played by multiple players on different types of PC and gaming consoles. Computer industry analysts are predicting even more in future decades.

EQ: *Do you see Norrath as a real economy? Why / Why not? How do you feel knowing that Norrath as a virtual economy is wealthier than over a hundred other real countries?*

2 READING

2 READING A   Answers

A 1 Switzerland (get most) **2** European Union (37%) **3** United States (18%) **4** New Zealand (get least)

2 READING B, C   Answers

B 3

C 1 (Sample answers) Less competitive farmers in developed countries would want to keep farm subsidies, as without subsidies they could go out of business. Large agri-businesses receive much larger amounts of subsidies compared to small farmers, but these large-scale farming operations are also highly profitable. Farmers from developing countries would not have to compete against artificially low prices from developed countries and would earn more, and poverty levels would go down. US and EU food manufacturers would be likely to begin importing more commodities from developing countries, as these would be cheaper.

C 2 You can bring up the issue of both the real internet economy and the virtual economy in Everquest's Norrath. For virtual economies, discuss with students the importance that they place on entertainment activities like video games.

EQ: *How important are video games to you? Would you ever make real-life purchases to help you in a video game?*

C 3 It is a simple question of supply and demand. The 'platinum pieces' are in demand, and the good players are willing to supply these. This is what happens in real economies.

3 SPEAK YOUR MIND

This section covers: trends in the economy, effects of social or political developments in the world on the economy, tax and IT industry compared to agriculture.

A EQ: *Do you ever read the financial pages of a newspaper or watch reports about the economy on television?*

B EQ: *How has the 2004 Asian tsunami affected the economies of Asian countries? How has the Iraq war affected the world economy?*

C EQ: *Should everyone pay the same rate of tax?*

D EQ: *How have computers affected business? Do many people work in agriculture in your country?*

4 LISTEN — DVD

The photo is of an American soldier in Iraq. You can try to get students to think about current conflicts around the world. The dichotomy is that industry usually benefits (military, oil, (re)construction), but war often has a financial impact on the ordinary people through destruction of buildings and infrastructure.

> **4 LISTEN B, C** — Answers
>
> **B** 1 S 2 C 3 N 4 S
>
> **C** 1 Like a jolt / shock of electricity to get the economy started. 2 Women took on jobs in industry, but there were still labour shortages. 3 Not clear yet; it had a bad effect on the Iraqi economy and an impact on the price of oil (negative), and on consumer and business confidence.

5 TEAMWORK

For many students, pensions and retirement may not seem relevant to their daily lives. It will affect them, however, because when they start work they will have to pay for pensioners and towards their own pensions when they retire. Many of the options in the activity would have a direct effect on students and their lives; for example, cuts in education or healthcare, and people having to retire later.

6 CONTROVERSY

The Fairtrade movement began in 1986 in the Netherlands when Max Havelaar created the first Fairtrade label for coffee from Mexico. There are now 19 different international Fairtrade organisations, under the umbrella organisation Fairtrade Labelling Organisations International.

For many developing world farmers, it has been a lifeline. Different food commodity markets have dropped since the late 1990s; for example, in the coffee market between 1994 and 2001, the price of robusta beans (used for instant coffee) dropped from 180 cents / lb to 17 cents / lb. For a cappuccino in a London café costing £1.75, a grower might get around 5p. As a result, many farmers have had to abandon their fields or in some cases even turned to growing illegal crops like coca or opium poppies, which provide more income.

Fairtrade pays a premium price to producers for all products carrying its label, so coffee growers can make more through Fairtrade than ordinary markets.

Sources:
www.fairtrade.org.uk
www.fairtrade.org.uk/downloads/product_prices.xls

7 PORTFOLIO WRITING

See the Introduction to the Teacher's Guide.

A Sources:
www.cia.gov/cia/publications/factbook
news.bbc.co.uk/1/hi/country_profiles/default.stm
www.economist.com/countries

B Sources:
The No-Nonsense Guide to Fair Trade, David Ransom
The Conscious Consumer: Promoting Economic Justice through Fair Trade, Rose Benz Ericson
www.fairtrade.org.uk
www.fairtradefederation.com

8 BUSINESS STUDIES *in English* [CLIL]

The airline industry has had a lot of financial difficulties since 2001. After the World Trade Centre attacks (11 September 2001) many in North America and Europe were afraid to travel by air, then there was an outbreak of SARS (Sudden Acute Respiratory Syndrome) in some Asian countries. The second war in the Persian Gulf (the Iraq War) began in March 2003, and some travellers cancelled their bookings. The real problem for the airline industry, however, was the rapid rise in oil prices. (Note: The price of oil has always been calculated in US dollars.)

Mention to students the dramatic oil price rise. To stay in business airlines have begun to cut costs by cutting jobs and wages. Many have also added fuel surcharges to the price of air tickets.

EQ: *Has your attitude to air travel changed since the 11 September attacks, SARS and the war in Iraq? If you were the head of an airline, what would you do to manage the present situation?*

QSE Advanced — See pages 32–35 SB, 100 WB — Unit 7 Teacher's Guide

9 FURTHER DISCUSSION

This section covers: unemployment, moving jobs to other countries, the black economy, the privatisation debate.

A This question picks up on the quote in **Viewpoint.**

EQ: *Is the government doing enough to create jobs? What can the government do about unemployment? What kind of help do unemployed people get?*

B Discuss the outsourcing trend to countries like China (manufacturing) and India (IT / customer helplines).

EQ: *Is your country very competitive in getting new companies? What would you think of major companies from your country moving away for cheaper taxes? Is paying taxes a patriotic thing to do?*

C Discuss which kinds of goods are produced or imported illegally (computer software, CDs, DVDs, brand name clothing)? (Note: *Black economy = black market* AmEng)

EQ: *Do you see piracy (software, brand-name clothing, CDs) as theft? Why / Why not? Would you buy these goods?*

D Ask students to consider examples of privatised or government-controlled companies where they live.

EQ: *Why do you think businesses might be more efficient than governments?*

10 *Your answer:* DOES ECONOMICS REALLY AFFECT ME?

This question aims to take the idea of economic issues from the abstract to the personal. Students might question how their life might be affected if there was a deep recession, stock market crash or banking crisis; for example, unemployment, bankruptcies, cutbacks in the public sector (effects on education or healthcare), freezing of bank accounts, ability to buy a home. The students can think of what they can actually do to stimulate the economy — spend more, buy a house, invest more, start their own business (creating jobs), further education or training, pay taxes.

WORKBOOK

1 USE OF LANGUAGE: Transitive and intransitive Verbs

This activity will introduce students to the tremendous growth in the Chinese economy. At the same time, this will get students to review the key grammatical structure of the transitive and intransitive verbs. The activity is based on an authentic test activity used by the University of Cambridge Local Examinations Syndicate in the CAE and CPE in English.

> **1 USE OF LANGUAGE** Answers
> (Several verbs possible)
> **1** rose / increased / expanded / grew / went up
> **2** declining / decreasing / dropping / going down
> **3** pushed up / increased / expanded / boosted
> **4** go up / increase / expand / grow
> **5** went up / was up / increased / expanded / grew
> **6** went up / were up / increased / expanded / grew
> **7** declined / decreased / dropped / was down
> **8** cut / decrease

2 WRITING

A Sources:
Job Creation in America: How our Smallest Companies Put the Most People to Work, David Birch
Green Job Creation in the UK, Victoria Wiltshire
www.europa.eu.int/scadplus/leg/en/s02304.htm
www.tbr.co.uk/consultancy/projects/dti_job_generation

3 SPEAKING STRATEGIES: Discussing graphs

This activity will help students who are using graphs in language presentations to use the appropriate phrases for pointing out key facts and figures.

> **3 SPEAKING STRATEGIES** Answers
> **1** e **2** d **3** a **4** c **5** b

Unit 7 — Profit and loss — Teacher's Guide

See pages 32–35 SB, 100 WB

4 IDIOMS

See the Introduction to the Teacher's Guide.

> **4 IDIOMS** — Answers
>
> 1 b   2 d   3 a   4 e   5 f   6 c
>
> 1 to fall off the back of a lorry = to be stolen
> 2 to be the driving force behind = to be the main force pushing or making changes
> 3 cracks in the relationship = first difficulties in the relationship
> 4 to be caught in the poverty trap = to be poor and not able to change this
> 5 to be in the red = to be in debt
> 6 to have a windfall = to receive some good luck, often money (sometimes a large amount) unexpectedly

Ask students to use the idioms orally by answering these questions. These can be done as pair work or as a whole class.

- *What do you think of Kofi Annan's attempts to put poverty at the top of the UN agenda?*
  - I think it's good that he was *the driving force behind* this measure.
  - Many people around the world are caught in *the poverty trap*. You need some large organisations to help if you want things to change.
- *How would it affect the economy if your city were chosen to host the Olympics?*
  - I think it would be like having a *windfall*. A lot of money would be spent on new facilities and lots of jobs would be created.
  - I think there might be *some cracks in the relationship* with other parts of the country.
  - If we were in *the red* before, we wouldn't be afterwards.
- *How does poor government regulation affect the economy?*
  - I think it allows for a black economy to develop; more people sell things that have fallen off *the back of the lorry*.
  - I think it can cause some *cracks in the relationship* between business and government when government does decide to take tougher actions.
  - I think a country can quickly be in *the red* if it doesn't collect taxes efficiently.

ER 1 — Buffy the Vampire Slayer — Teacher's Guide
See pages 36–37 SB

WHAT'S NEW?

Communication Objectives: Ss will be able to use phrases or grammar from:
- Unit 1: Contradicting expressions / Expression used before challenging
- Unit 2: Signposting phrases: Sequence / Inferring
- Unit 3: Expressions for downplaying / Justifying an argument
- Unit 4: Modifying words / Expressing beliefs
- Unit 5: Adjectives (grammar) / Expressing opinions tentatively
- Unit 6: The Passive (grammar) / Expressing reservations
- Unit 7: Intransitive and Transitive verbs (grammar) / Defending a point of view

Educational Objectives: Ss will explore the issue of equal opportunities for both genders.

Connected Topics:
- Vampire mythology
- Superheroes
- Unconventional occupations
- Historical inequalities

Grammar: Phrasal verbs   Idioms

Key Vocabulary:

alacrity	flank *v*	remains
be clued into	flaw	scowl
come to one's senses	fleeting	skull and crossbones
cope	frown	spot *v*
countenance	glower	stagger
cremate	headstone	stake
crooked	husk	stand one's ground
crumbling	jargon	stranded
dart *v*	lay to rest	stuffed
denial syndrome	lumber	taut
depleted	lunge	undertaker
easy pickings	newbie	vamp
eccentric	no muss, no fuss	wadded
exterminator	prey	yank *v*
feeding frenzy	prowess	
ferocity	puffy	

EXTENDED READING: Background Information

This extract was taken from an original novel called *Prime Evil* based on the popular American TV series *Buffy the Vampire Slayer*, which ran for seven seasons. The programme is about an ordinary California high school student who was chosen by some higher powers to be the only killer (slayer) of vampires on Earth. She is endowed with incredible strength and speed, but she can be killed. Buffy is not entirely alone, however, she gets help from a Watcher (an advisor), who also happens to be the school librarian. Her friends also help her fight various vampires and demons.

EQ: *– Have you seen this television programme before? What do you think of the idea of the programme? Who do you think this programme appeals to more: men or women? Why? Why would either group want to watch this show?*
– How does having a female lead instead of male lead character make this programme different?
– Do you believe in the supernatural (vampires, ghosts, werewolves)? Why do people believe in these? Why do you think these myths have survived so long?

1 READING

A is a common skimming activity. It will help students writing the Reading part of the CAE, the Trinity Controlled Writing ISE III section, IELTS Reading Part 2, and IGCSE Reading Parts 1 and 3.

ER 1 — **Buffy the vampire slayer** — Teacher's Guide — See pages 36–37 SB

1 READING A, B, C — Answers

A 287 lb: the weight of Big Jack Perkins, the latest vampire victim (para 19, page 37)
Jelly: peanut butter and jelly (or jam in Br Eng) is a popular sandwich filling the USA (para 13, page 36)
Butterflies: tattoo pattern (para 3, page 36)
Car: a motorist's car has broken down near the graveyard (para 22, page 93)

B 1 Joyce is not able to help Buffy in her dangerous job. Joyce wants to make sure that the few things that she can help with are done to the fullest; that is, making Buffy eat so much.
2 Two reasons: people in Southern California drive their cars everywhere and people generally realised that the streets were dangerous at night (too many people never returned from walking the dog).
3 She heard that he Big Jack Perkins had been attacked and killed when closing up Tom's Tattoo Emporium.

C (Sample answers) **1** Vampire myths include: You need to 'kill' vampires by staking them through the heart. Vampires die, but come back from the grave. Vampires drink blood, so they bite people with fangs and kill people. Sunlight can kill vampires.

2 IDIOMS

This activity follows the specifications of the Trinity syllabus Grades 10 and 11 which call for students to have a good understanding of and ability to use various idioms. The correct use of idioms will help students in other exams as well.

2 IDIOMS — Answers

A 1 to be laid to rest **2** to come to terms with
3 easy pickings **4** to meet someone's match
5 to take a break

B 1 Six hours of studying? You should *take a break* and come on and play tennis with us.
2 They had trouble *coming to terms* with the death of their grandmother.
3 The zebra *was easy pickings* for the lions as it stood alone in the tall grass.
4 Oscar Wilde, Jim Morrison and Edith Piaf *were laid to rest* in the same cemetery in Paris.
5 The chess champion had *met his / her match* in the latest supercomputer.

3 UP IN ARMS

This section follows the specifications of the Trinity syllabus Grades 10 and 11, which call for students to have a good understanding of and ability to use various phrasal verbs. It may be worthwhile to practise these verbs further. The correct use of phrasal verbs will help students in other exams as well.

As these verbs all deal with physical movements, you could get students to play 'charades'. Write the different verbs on small pieces of paper. Put the pieces of paper in a cup or box. Ask a student to pick out one piece of paper and to act out the verb (without talking), while other students try to guess it.

3 UP IN ARMS — Answers

set down	throw away
wiped off	pull
dipped in	shove
served	threw
reached for	grab
set aside	yank
stack *something*	claw
clear *(the table)*	grip
flip open something	threw someone's arms around
dump	
hesitate *(pause in action)*	drive *(a stake)*
place back	brush off
roll	fist

4 PORTFOLIO WRITING

A You should remind the students that this is a first-person point of view, for example, Joyce might say: 'I cooked Buffy dinner before she went out.'

A Sources:
Buffy the Vampire Slayer: Prime Evil, Diana G. Gallagher. London: Pocket Books, 2000.
The Elements of Style, William I. Strunk.
http://owl.english.purdue.edu

B Sources:
How to Write Short Stories, S. Peterson.
www.bbc.co.uk/cult/vampires
www.short-stories.co.uk
www.classicreader.com/toc.php/sid.6

5 INTERACTIVE TASK

This activity is directly based on the Interactive Task phase of the Trinity Language Spoken Exam Grades 10 and 11. It would also be useful practice for developing stronger communicative skills and confidence for Parts 3 and 4 of the spoken phase of the CAE English exam.

This activity requires students to lead the conversation, which can be a challenge for some students. It is important that you go round the room to monitor the students' communicative leadership in this activity. They should be commenting and asking their partner questions. Silence is not an option; it is up to them to keep the dialogue active and flowing if, and when, their partner begins to falter. They should already have experience with leading the dialogue during **Teamwork**, presentation and **Further Discussion** activities in previous units.

To help in general, you can get students to think of the different brainstorming activities they have encountered so far in the Teamwork activities.

Comment 1: If students seem to have trouble beginning, you can help them by suggesting that they brainstorm some well-known action films. Have they seen these films?

Comment 2: If students are having trouble beginning, you can help them by suggesting they brainstorm more strong fictional women figures from films and television. Are they the same as or different from ordinary women?

Unit 8 — Into the future — Teacher's Guide — See pages 38–41 SB, 101 WB

WHAT'S NEW!

Communication Objectives:	Ss will be able to: – use expressions for affirming and signposting words: arguments. – use vocabulary, phrases and idioms related to the future of the planet.
Educational Objectives:	Ss will explore current theories about possible global catastrophes.
Connected Topics:	– History of natural disasters – Natural disasters – Population problems – Overfishing and ecology – Global warming – El Niño – End of the Gulf Stream – Technology as a panacea – Destruction of the rainforest – Religion and the end of the world – Super-bugs (new flu strains) – Global destruction as a film plotine – The Environmental Skeptic
Grammar:	Verbs and prepositions Adverbial clauses
Key Vocabulary:	abrupt, agent, allegiance, antibiotics, asteroid, biodiversity, bioweapon, blaze *n*, blueprint, catastrophic, climatologist, contaminated, deliberate, depletion, emissions, epidemic, eradicate, glacier, global warming, grade, halt, helping hand, ice cap, infectious, ozone layer, patch, perpetrator, rampaging, (return) with a vengeance, rogue, routine, sanitation, shortage, subsidy, surge, sustainable, swill, trawler, trigger, ulterior motive, virulent

THE BIG question: DOES THE EARTH NEED RESCUING?

This question is related to the continuing political conflict between environmentalists and industry, and an apparently growing apathy in the general public over the extent of the problem.

VIEWPOINT

Facts: The previous mass extinctions include:

- Ordovician-Silurian extinction: 439 million years ago, caused by the decrease and increase of water level by glacier formation killing 60 per cent of marine genera
- Late Devonian extinction: 364 million years ago, unknown causes killing 57 per cent of marine genera Permian-Triassic extinction: 251 million years ago, caused by asteroid impact killing 95 per cent of all species
- End Triassic extinction: about 200 million years ago, caused by massive volcanic eruptions killing 52 per cent of marine genera
- Cretaceous-Tertiary extinction: about 65 million years ago, caused by asteroid, volcanic eruptions or global warming, killing 47 per cent of marine genera and 18 per cent of land families.

(Note: Hierarchy of organisms: kingdom, phylum, class, order, family, genus – pl. genera, specie – pl. species.)

Source:
http://biology.about.com/od/evolution

QSE Advanced   See pages 38–41 SB, 101 WB   Unit 8   Teacher's Guide

EQ: *Does this worry you at all? Is there anything that can be learned by these previous catastrophes? How are these previous catastrophes different from what might happen? Would humans survive?*

About half of the people aged 10–19 are poor. A quarter of them survive on less than $1 dollar a day. These young people also represent half of all new HIV infections. Young girls are often marrying and having children at too young an age. In 2000, a special UN summit developed the Millennium Developments Goals (MDGs), which had, among others goals, to halve poverty by 2015. These goals are already behind schedule.

Source:
www.unfpa.org/swp/swpmain.htm

EQ: *Does this information make you optimistic or pessimistic? Why? How can young people help with the problems with the Earth? Do you think most young people care about the future of the Earth? How often do you think about the environment and other problems? What effect would worrying about things all the time have on someone?*

Quotes: Richard Buckminster 'Bucky' Fuller (1895–1983) was an American designer, architect and inventor known for his geodesic domes. Later, the spherical molecules, carbon-60, were nicknamed 'bucky balls' after his geodesic designs.

EQ: *How well do you understand how the Earth works? Do you see humans as the drivers of the planet? Are we good or bad drivers?*

Photos: The photos are linked to questions to encourage students to think about overpopulation and the destruction of the environment.

1 WORD POWER

A gets students to consider the most likely threats to life on Earth and the causes for the next mass extinction. This activity can be extended by getting students to agree or disagree with other students. If they agree, they should try to use the affirming phrases from **Language Bank 8.**

B gets students to practise the affirming phrases from **Language Bank 8.** Note: Mention to students that they may need to adapt the phrases in Language Bank 8 replacing 'you' with 'pessimists' in these phrases.

---

1 WORD POWER A, B   **Answers**

A Control over: nuclear war, overpopulation, global warming, pollution, thinning of the ozone layer, shortage of fresh water, infectious diseases, loss of biodiversity. (Sample answers) Well, most other mass extinctions have resulted from asteroid impacts, therefore, I think it would probably be the most likely. – **I have to admit, you are probably right there.** / I would guess that overpopulation will be the reason. We are able to sustain life at the moment with over 6 billion people, however, the number of humans is expected to grow to 9 billion by 2050. – **That's a good point.**

B (Sample answers) **1 I completely agree with** the pessimists who say politicians are not doing enough about / to stop pollution. **2 I have to admit** the pessimists are probably right there when they say that politicians aren't doing enough to stop nuclear war.

ARTICLES

North America, Europe May Cool in Warmer World

This article takes up a much less discussed point about the possible impact of future global warming. If the Earth heats up by a few degrees along the Equator, it will heat up many degrees more in northern regions and at the poles. Initially, the climate would be warmer in northern regions, causing the melting of the polar ice caps. This would slowly release millions of litres of fresh water into the oceans, and the rising water could flood many coastal cities.

There is another worse consequence. Scientists have come to understand that the Gulf Stream that supplies Europe and eastern North America with warmer weather could shut down, making Europe and eastern North America much colder. This would have a significant impact on agriculture (imagine no grape growing in France), trade (frozen sea ports and rivers in Northern Europe) and energy costs (energy needs for heating would increase; many houses are not insulated).

EQ: *What's the warmest and coldest weather you have experienced? How might your city be different if it were 10°C warmer or colder throughout the year? Do you think politicians in your country or others take global warming seriously?*

Unit 8 — Into the future
Teacher's Guide
See pages 38–41 SB, 101 WB

Open to Attack

This article discusses developments regarding infectious diseases. Besides the two cases mentioned in the article, anthrax and foot-and-mouth disease, there have been several cases of infectious disease since 2001. Severe acute respiratory syndrome (SARS) in 2003 killed 10 per cent of the 8,096 people infected in 28 countries. Avian influenza ('bird flu') in 2003 / 2004 killed 58 per cent of the 88 people infected in three countries. If this bird flu virus begins to spread through human-to-human contact, a pandemic may be possible. Already a problem in the UK and other European countries, Bovine spongiform encephalopathy (BSE, also called 'mad cow disease') was detected in 2003 in Canada and the United States. In 2005, a killer Asian influenza virus was accidentally sent in a standard lab testing kit to labs in 18 countries. It could have caused a pandemic similar to 1957 in which between 1 to 4 million people died. People born after 1968 have little or no immunity to the virus.

EQ: *Which diseases around the world worry you? (e.g. AIDS, malaria, Ebola, dengue fever, tuberculosis, leprosy) How likely is it for someone from your country to contract these diseases? What is the relationship between poverty and disease?*

2 READING

A is a reading comprehension activity that requires students to find the correct multiple choice response. Questions 1 and 2 refer to the first article, 'North America, Europe May Cool in Warmer World'. Question 3 refers to the second article, 'Open to Attack'.

B This question gets students to consider the reasons for experimenting with germs (viruses and bacteria). You may want to help them by asking leading questions.

EQ: *Should governments be experimenting with lethal viruses (e.g. Ebola, Small Pox, Avian Flu)? If so, what can be learned from these experiments? If not, why not? There are permanent nuclear and chemical weapons inspectors, but no permanent biological weapons inspectors. Why do you think this is?*

2 READING A			Answers
A 1 b	**2** a	**3** a	

3 SPEAK YOUR MIND

This section covers the topics of global warming, the Kyoto Protocol, rainforest depletion and epidemics.

A Global warming – **EQ:** *What effects will global climate change have on you and your country? How would the projected 50 cm to 2 m increase in sea levels by 2100 affect your country? What impact would this have on countries near sea level like the Netherlands, the Maldives or Bangladesh? Does global warming worry you? Why / Why not?*

B Kyoto Protocol – **EQ:** *Carbon dioxide (CO_2), methane (CH_4) and nitrous oxide (N_2O) are the three main 'greenhouse' gases (six gases in total). Where and how are they produced? (e.g. CO_2 – cars, humans / animals, industry; CH_4 – industrial livestock (cows, pigs), rotting vegetation (hydro-electric dams); (N_2O) – cars, industry, industrial agriculture.) Do you support cutting greenhouse gases? Even if it hurts the economy or means losing your job? Which is more important – the economy or the environment? Why? Is it possible to have a healthy economy and a healthy environment?*

C Rainforest – **EQ:** *Why are plants and trees important to the world climate? Is deforestation a problem in your country? Why / Why not? When the environment conflicts with human development, which usually wins? Which should win? Why?*

D Epidemics – The 1918–19 Spanish Influenza pandemic killed between 20 and 50 million people around the world—that is more people who died than were killed in World War I. About 10 per cent of the global adult population died.

EQ: *Will the next pandemic be natural or manmade? How would more air travel increase its spread? Are we ready to deal with a global pandemic? Global warming is expected to spread tropical diseases (malaria, yellow fever) to warmer Northern countries. What impact might this have?*

QSE Advanced — See pages 38–41 SB, 101 WB

Unit 8
Teacher's Guide

> **3 SPEAK YOUR MIND A** — Answers
>
> **A** (Sample answer) Greenhouse gases insulate the Earth's atmosphere. This traps the heat given off by the sun. Temperatures rise around the world / globally.

4 LISTEN — DVD

This audio clip deals with Bjorn Lomborg, a controversial Danish professor of statistics. After reading a book by American economist Julian Simon, Lomborg, a self-professed green, tried to debunk Simon's theories that the Earth was in fact getting better. As Lomborg wrote in his 2001 book, *The Environmental Skeptic* (note AmE spelling), he actually found Simon's arguments to be statistically sound. He contends that mortality rates, consumption rates, natural resource supplies and several other points are getting better. He has many notable critics especially for his suggestion that the money to be spent on the Kyoto Protocol (up to $350 billion) would be better spent elsewhere. Lomborg suggests in a pure cost-benefit analysis it would be better to spend that amount of money on bringing clean drinking water to developing countries.

> **4 LISTEN B** — Answers
>
> **B** 1 Greenpeace 2 American economist 3 debunked
> 4 Kyoto Protocol 5 $350 6 sanitation
> 7 comparisons 8 ice cream
>
> **C** (Sample answer) Lomborg might say that he thinks global warming is real but we only have a limited amount of money to spend so the Kyoto Protocol looks too expensive for the results we might get.

5 TEAMWORK

This activity is based on the situation in Yellowstone National Park, which stretches across three US states – Idaho, Montana and Wyoming. The last time Yellowstone Supercaldera exploded 640,000 years ago, it left a giant crater, killed everything within 1,600km, and spread volcanic ash across western North America. Today, Yellowstone is a fairly active geological region, with active geysers, hot springs and between a thousand and three thousand earthquakes every year. More recently, geologists have discovered a large bulge, about the length of seven football pitches, beneath Yellowstone Lake, which is evidence of a build-up of gas or magma. The scenario is based on what geologists believe would have happened during the last eruption, however, make sure that students know that geologists are only moderately concerned. The odds of another caldera-size eruption are less likely than winning a lottery.

Source:
www.nps.gov/yell, http://volcanoes.usgs.gov/yvo

6 CONTROVERSY

The issue of overfishing is a very serious global issue. A large part of this problem is created by governments which give large subsidies to commercial fishing fleets. The World Wildlife Fund estimates that government subsidies account for almost 20 per cent of the value of the world's annual commercial fish catch, an estimated $76–$80 billion. The countries which subsidise most are Japan, the USA, China and others from the EU. An example of what may happen can be seen in Canada's east coast cod fishery. Once the largest supply of cod in the world, this fishery closed completely in 1992 due to depleted stocks, and these stocks have still not recovered. The problem does not have any easy solution, but many national politicians want to keep subsidies because they do not want to lose votes from fishing communities if jobs are lost.

EQ: *Do you go fishing or eat fish often? How would unemployed fishermen earn a living? What problems would coastal communities face? Is fish farming the solution? What would happen if there were no fish left?*

Source:
www.fao.org, www.wwf.org

7 PORTFOLIO WRITING

See the Introduction to the Teacher's Guide.

A Sources:
The End of the Line: How Overfishing is Changing the World and What We Eat, Charles Clover

Unit 8 — Into the future — Teacher's Guide
See pages 38–41 SB, 101 WB

Fish, Markets and Fishermen: The Economics of Overfishing, Suzanne Ludicello
www.panda.org/stopoverfishing, http://archive.greenpeace.org/oceans/globaloverfishing/deadahead.html

B Sources:
Catastrophe: Risk and Response, Richard A. Posner
www.aoml.noaa.gov/general/lib/hurricbro.html
www.bt.cdc.gov/disasters, www.unep.org

8 METEOROLOGY *in English* [CLIL]

The El Niño Southern Oscillation (ENSO) has an enormous effect on global weather patterns. El Niño (Spanish for 'the child') was named after the Infant Jesus by early Peruvian fishermen who noticed the unusually warm water around Christmastime. El Niño (ENSO warm episode) pushes warm water from Australia / SW Pacific Ocean to the west coast of South America. La Niña (also called the 'Little girl', 'El Viejo', anti-El Niño, or a cold episode) pushes cold water from Antarctica up towards the west coast of South America and toward Australia. These warm / cold movements have alternated regularly in past centuries with fairly even numbers of warm and cold years; since 1950, however, climatologists have noticed a trend in which El Niño occurred 31 per cent to 23 per cent for La Niña (the remaining time was normal). Since 1990 El Niño occurred five times compared to two for La Niña. Some climatologists, such as Kevin Trenberth of the US National Center for Atmospheric Research, believe that global warming is contributing to more frequent and intense warm episodes, but computer models cannot yet prove this conclusively.

The effect of more El Niños has led to dramatic changes in weather. Oceania, north and east Australia, SE Africa, NE South America, the Indian sub-continent, western North America and the southern Caribbean had extremely dry weather, causing fires and droughts. Other regions, such as the SE United States, Central Africa, NW and SE South America and Northern Europe, saw more floods and landslides.

EQ: *Do you think El Niño has affected your country? Have there been very wet or very dry years? Have you ever had floods, landslides, droughts or large fires? If so, what happened? If not, what effect would these have? How might changing weather patterns affect your country?*

Sources:
Our Affair with El Niño, S. George Philander
El Niño: The Weather Phenomenon that Changed the World, Ross Couper-Johnston
www.cpc.ncep.noaa.gov, www.pmel.noaa.gov, www.cdc.noaa.gov

9 FURTHER DISCUSSION

This section covers the topics of: Malthus' population theory, reliance on technology, religion and apocalyptic beliefs, and apocalyptic film plots.

A Try to get students to consider the current 6 billion population and the projected 9 billion by 2050 and the resources available on the Earth.

EQ: *What effects does human overpopulation have? How large is your country's population? Is it increasing or decreasing? What social, economic and political effects might this have? Genetically modified (GM) foods may provide a solution to world hunger. Do you agree with GM food production?*

B This question looks at the belief that technology can solve most of humanity's problems.

EQ: *Give some examples where technology has solved world problems. Give examples where technology has created world problems. Given that most technology is developed for business purposes, is there a market for saving the environment?*

C Some conservative US politicians openly advocate anti-environmental policies on religious grounds. See also www.apocalypsesoon.org and www.raptureready.com.

EQ: *What do different religions believe about the end of the world? The environmental movement is a 20th century phenomenon. Most religions are many centuries old. How can you reconcile ancient beliefs with the modern world?*

D Some apocalypse movies: *Armageddon, The Core, Deep Impact, Independence Day, Godzilla, Outbreak, Hellboy, 28 Days Later, The Day after Tomorrow, Terminator 1, 2 and 3, Constantine, Dr. Strangelove, Planet of the Apes, Mad Max.*

QSE Advanced   See pages 38–41 SB, 101 WB

Unit 8
Teacher's Guide

EQ: *Why do you think the media is so interested in doomsday scenarios? Are films about the end of the world just light entertainment or just in bad taste?*

10 <u>Your answer:</u> DOES THE EARTH NEED RESCUING?

This question tries to get students to address the main theme of the unit: Are they optimistic or pessimistic about the future of the Earth? Optimists can discuss what will lead to these improvements (e.g. technology, human activity) and whether the Earth's looming environmental catastrophe has been overstated (e.g. the environmental sceptic, Malthus and GM foods). Pessimists can discuss what can be done locally and globally to help (e.g. grassroots action, changing government policy, ending subsidies).

WORKBOOK
1 WORD POWER

This activity will give students the chance to practise signposting words for arguments from **Language Bank 8**.

1 WORD POWER	Answers
1 Although / Whereas 2 As a result	
3 Similarly 4 However / But	
5 In the same way / Similarly / As a result.	

2 USE OF LANGUAGE: Verbs and prepositions

This activity gives information about the problems relating to geomagnetic reversal, the process in which the Earth's magnetic poles are reversing. The magnetic field around the Earth protects all life from lethal cosmic radiation. During these reversals, the field weakens and cosmic radiation can shower the Earth killing everything. The activity is based on an activity type for the CAE and CPE exams.

2 USE OF LANGUAGE					Answers
2 1 to 2 of 3 by 4 in 5 during 6 up					
7 off 8 with 9 from 10 up 11 about, by					

3 WRITING

A Sources:

OECD, Energy to 2050: Scenario for a Sustainable Future
Global 2050: A Basis for Speculation, John Cole
www.futurist.com, www.census.gov/ipc/www/worldpop.html
www.wfs.org

B Sources:

Terraforming: Engineering Planetary Environments, Martyn J. Fogg
A Traveller's Guide to Mars, William K. Hartmann
www.redcolony.com
www.bio2.com

4 IDIOMS

4 IDIOMS	Answers
1 e 2 a 3 d 4 c 5 f 6 b	
1 the tip of the iceberg = only a small part of the whole (often used for a problem) 2 to turn over a new leaf = to change one's ways / what you do 3 a recipe for disaster = very likely to lead to a very negative result 4 to go against the grain = to go against your or other people's wishes 5 a small world = for unexpected connections between people or things that seemed unknown to each other / unconnected 6 a ray of hope = some hope	

Ask students to use the idioms when answering these questions orally. This can be done as pair work or as a class.

- *How worried are people in your country about environmental problems?*
  – I think they've *turned over a new leaf* since the 1960s. Many people are concerned about the environment today.
  – It's such *a small world.* I wouldn't have thought that something like El Niño so far away could affect the weather here.
  – I think you are *going against the grain* if you are not worried about the environment.

Unit 8 — Into the future — Teacher's Guide

See pages 38–41 SB, 101 WB

- *Does it bother you that so many species are dying out?*
  - I think there is still *a ray of hope* that things will improve. I mean at least everyone is discussing it it now.
  - I've heard that the loss of species today is just *the tip of the iceberg* compared to the future. Millions of species could die because of global warming.
  - Yes, I think it would *a recipe for disaster* if today's species died out.

- *Do you think there will be a global pandemic in your lifetime?*
  - I think you would *go against the grain* not to say 'yes' when so many scientists are predicting it.
  - I think there is still *a ray of hope* that a pandemic could be contained, as SARS was in 2003.

Unit 9 — Free to choose — Teacher's Guide
See pages 42–45 SB, 102 WB

WHAT'S NEW!

Communication Objectives:	Ss will be able to: – use interrupting expressions and signposting phrases relating to arguments. – use independence-related vocabulary, phrases and idioms.
Educational Objectives:	Ss will explore the value of having personal and national independence.
Connected Topics:	– Newly independent countries – Moving out for the first time – Rates of independence between genders – Italian *mammoni* – Responsibilities and place to live — own apartment – Independence movements – Physical challenges to independence – Anarchy – Scottish independence – Financial dependence – Terrorism and freedom fighting
Grammar:	Word forms Pronouns
Key Vocabulary:	accessible elated reliable acquaintance family nest redress autonomy futile step up barter grievance sue ceasefire handiwork tempered cold-blooded handout trustworthy credibility leave the nest unfurnished deplore male chauvinist upkeep devolution proclivity violate dump *v* rebel *v* yearn

The BIG question: WHY DO PEOPLE WANT TO BE INDEPENDENT?

This questions deals with the fundamental drive in both individuals and among nations to seek independence.

VIEWPOINT

Cartoon: The issue of nest-leaving has been studied quite actively within the European Union. It is believed to have significant effects on consumer buying habits and the long-term financial status of older individuals. EU policy makers need to understand the typical EU household dynamics if they aim to develop workable policies for across the region.

Sources:
www.eco.rug.nl/~espe2002/Mazzuco.pdf
www.iza.org/iza/en/papers/transatlantic/1_kluve.pdf
www.demogr.mpg.de/Papers/Working/WP-2001-038.pdf

EQ: *Why do you think there are such differences between these countries? Would you want to be still living at home at 30 years old?*

Facts:
- East Timor: Having been colonised by the Portuguese, invaded by the Japanese and occupied by the Indonesians, East Timor became independent following several decades of resistance to Indonesia rule. Some 250,000 East Timorese are believed to have died.
- Serbia and Montenegro: Yugoslavia underwent a bloody civil war through the early 1990s with atrocities committed by all sides. Note: In 2006 people in Montenegro voted to become independent of Serbia.
- Tuvalu and Tongo: Both former British protectorates, they became independent in the 1970s. They did not seek UN recognition until recently.

Unit 9 — Free to choose — Teacher's Guide
See pages 42–45 SB, 102 WB

- Andorra: It has been a co-principality since 1278 ruled by France and Spain. In 1993, it became a parliamentary democracy with two heads of state represented by France and Spain.
- Eritrea: Annexed by Ethiopia in 1962, Eritrea fought a 30-year war of independence. Another border war began with Ethiopia in 1998 to 2000.

Source:
CIA World Factbook. www.cia.gov/cia/publications/factbook/index.html

EQ: *Why do you think these countries sought UN recognition? Why does it matter if other countries recognise your existence or not?*

Quote: Bill Cosby became a US cultural icon through his work in stand-up comedy and television. Although he is most remembered for *The Cosby Show* and *Fat Albert* TV programmes, he is also a noted educational philanthropist and an outspoken leader in the African-American community.

EQ: *Why is this quote funny? Is it unnatural for children to return home?*

1 WORD POWER

A gets students to consider vocabulary related to independence.

> **1 WORD POWER A**   **Answers**
> government, decentralisation, legitimate, nationalism, freedom, emancipation, individualist

B gets students to practise signposting phrases and the vocabulary in **A**.

ARTICLES

Mummy's Boys (and Girls)

This article discusses the interesting Italian cultural phenomenon whereby grown children tend to leave the parental home considerably later than in other EU countries. Although among Western countries, this may be unusual, close family ties into adulthood predominate elsewhere. In parts of the Middle East, Asia and Africa, clan structures underline the question of residence. For instance, in Saudia Arabia, tradition and traditional architecture make it common for newlyweds to set up home within a family compound. Also Saudi women usually don't leave their parental home until after marriage.

As was seen in the reading text for Unit 5, Japanese children often get financial help and live at home longer due to the high cost of living. Historically speaking, the situation was not that different in the past in most Western countries where adult children tended to live with their parents until marriage.

EQ: *Is independence from parents seen positively or negatively in your culture? Why? How is adult independence similar to or different from teenage rebellion?*

Surprising ceasefire

This article discusses a very controversial issue that exists in both North Ireland and Spain. In both cases, groups have sought independence from a government power they do not recognise.

- **Basque region:** The Basque people are an indigenous group located in four Spanish and three French provinces. They have a long history in the region, but much of the current nationalist fervour stems from the Spanish civil war era. After the 1937 Basque government defeat, General Franco introduced laws repressing minority cultures across Spain. In 1959, the *Euskadi Ta Askatasuna* ('Basque Country and Liberty'), or ETA, was formed. Although initially ETA was peaceful and popular during the Franco years, it quickly turned to armed resistance and lost public support as Spain became democratic. Over thirty years, ETA has been responsible for the deaths of 817 people.
- **Northern Ireland:** In 1801, the kingdoms of Ireland and Great Britain joined under the Act of Union to become the United Kingdom. In 1921, the Government of Ireland Act allowed the different counties of Ireland to opt out of Union. Six counties in the North Ireland province of Ulster were largely for the Union and chose to stay in it. This has lead to the ongoing situation between Ulster Unionists and Irish Republicans. With militant groups formed on both sides, there have been over 3,500 deaths since 1969.

EQ: *What do you think of these groups? Do you think attitudes to terrorism have changed over the years?*

2 READING

A covers an important language skill that might not be present in some countries. The polite way to interrupt is to wait until the person takes a breath and use one of the appropriate phrases in **Language Bank 9**.

B reflects an upper intermediate structural understanding highlighted by both Trinity and Cambridge exams. Students need to work out what the pronouns refers to in the text.

---

2 READING B **Answers**

1 'It' refers to the fact that Italian children leave home so late in life.
2 'It' refers to the situation of Italian students (who) don't graduate until their late twenties.
3 'It' refers to the child not paying for housekeeping even though they can afford to pay.
4 'He' refers to the 29-year old man who sued his parents to support him.
5 'They' refers to the mothers of these young women.

C will help the students focus their arguments about the two main types of independence in the unit.

D 1 This question tries to personalise the issue of the *mammoni*. However, if the issue is difficult for students, culturally or otherwise, you may want to discuss the issue more in terms of the society as a whole.

D 2 This question requires students need to know a bit about their country's history. It would help to provide students with concrete examples. For instance, how would the United States be different if Britain was still in charge? How would France be different if Nazi Germany was still in control? It may require you to give a hypothetical scenario as well.

EQ: *At what age do most children move out in your country? How does this compare with other countries?*

Do daughters move out before sons in your country? Why / Why not?

3 SPEAK YOUR MIND

This section covers the topics of causes of leaving home, community values, and independence movements.

A EQ: *Have you moved out of your parent's home? If so, what has it been like? If not, why not? What motivated you or would motivate you to leave home for the first time? What difficulties can someone expect when they first move out?*

B EQ: *Do you see this as positive or negative thing? Why? Is it possible to have independence in a culture which stresses very strong family and community ties? Do you think globalisation is affecting these ties?*

C EQ: *Are there or have there been any independence movements in your country or countries nearby? If so, what effect have they had? Do you view independence movements positively or negatively? Why? Give examples. Should all people have independence? Why / Why not?*

4 LISTEN   DVD

This audio clip deals with Beth Finke and her guide dog Hanni as they cross the busy Chicago streets. Ms Finke lost her sight at the age of 26 after developing complications from diabetes. She has written a book, *Long Time, No See,* about her experiences of learning how to live without her eyesight. She is regular contributor to public radio in the US. It is worth visiting her website, www.bethfinke.com, to read more about her life and listen to other audio clips. Note: When Beth is out on the street, she is describing how she and Hanni work together, and sometimes she is talking to the dog. 'Lab' is short for Labrador (a breed of dog).

A You can try to get students to think about the five senses and what it would mean to lose each. Likewise, you can discuss what it would be like to lose the use of different parts of the body.

4 LISTEN B, C Answers

B 1 Guide dogs don't understand street lights.
2 Guide dogs can identify danger.
3 Guide dogs are not meant to be guard dogs.
4 Guide dogs can lead someone down the street.

C 1 mix (of Labrador and Golden Retriever)
2 She waits for the lights to change, listens to the traffic stop, waits for next light then can go.
3 It means to wait for the traffic lights to change from one direction then the other direction.
4 (Sample answer) Beth needs to correct Hanni a lot, but she uses an encouraging tone of voice, almost as if she is taking to a child. It could be unsafe to let Hanni do whatever she wanted. Beth talks normally to the listeners.

5 TEAMWORK

This activity was designed to give students an opportunity to discuss the reality involved in being independent for the first time. Because this activity is supposed to represent an authentic situation, it might be helpful for students to have access to local newspapers (classifieds section for rentals or used furniture), home furnishing catalogues (www.ikea.com), or home decoration magazines to remind them about things they might like to have or need. It would also be useful to get the students to think about the apartment room by room. For example, in the kitchen, the friend will need plates, cups and saucers, pots and pans and so on.

Sources:
Mr. Thrifty's How to Save Money on Absolutely Everything, Jane Furnival
Leaving the Nest: The Complete Guide to Living on Your Own, Dorinne and Richard Armstrong
www.interiordec.about.com/od/firstapttips

6 CONTROVERSY

Anarchism is a related group of political philosophies characterised by their opposition to an imposed authority (government) and social hierarchy. Fundamentally, they have an optimistic belief that left to their own devices, humans could operate together without need of a higher power. Its origins are not entirely clear, possibly dating back to Athens in 404 BC.

Modern anarchy shares many of its basics ideas with communism, and early anarchists often worked with communists. Some anarchists have in the past advocated the violent overthrow of government. This was the case of the young anarchist, Gavrilo Princip, whose assassination of Archduke Franz Ferdinand of Austria helped trigger World War I. Like communism, anarchy was an enigma that was feared in the West. By the 1950s, it had by and large begun to fade into academic obscurity. However, it has had something of a renaissance with the Sex Pistols 1976 song *Anarchy in the UK*. Today, it is common to see black-clad anarchists protesting at various International Economic Forums like the World Trade Organisation meetings. It should be pointed out to students that some, but not all, anarchists advocate violent overthrow of government.

EQ: *What do you think of anarchy? Would the world work without governments? Why / Why not? Would it be a better place?*

Sources:
Anarchism: A Documentary History of Libertarian Ideas: From Anarchy to Anarchism (300CE to 1939), Robert Graham
The Philosophy of Punk Rock: More than Noise!! Craig O'Hara
http://dwardmac.pitzer.edu/Anarchist_Archives
http://www.greenanarchy.org

7 PORTFOLIO WRITING

See the Introduction to the Teacher's Guide.

A Sources:
Africa Since Independence: A Comparative History, Paul Nugent
A History of Cyprus: From Foreign Domination to Troubled Independence, Stavros Pantelli
The Oxford History of the British Empire: 20th Century, Vol. 4., ed. Judith Brown
www.cia.gov/cia/publications/factbook
www.economist.com/countries

B Sources:
The Real Freshman Handbook, Jennifer Hanson
Freshman Dorm series, Linda A. Cooney
www.personal.u-net.com/~ic/fr_guide.html
Most universities also have webpages regarding life on campus.

8 HISTORY *in English* [CLIL]

There is archaeological evidence pointing to the first inhabitants of Scotland arriving around 8000 BC, however, the first written history of Scotland dates back to the Roman rule of Britain. The Romans invaded around AD 79. Having met with fierce resistance from the Northern Celtic tribes, mainly Scots and Picts (the ancestors of modern Scots), Roman emperor Hadrian had a wall built to divide the south from the Northern barbarians in AD 122. When the Germanic tribes (Angles, Saxons, etc.) invaded in 440, the Celts were pushed further north. Between 843 and 1034, the Celtic tribes were consolidated under a single Scottish kingdom. Much of the consolidation in this period was over fears of the Viking invaders. While most of the Viking raids happened south of Scotland, the Vikings did occupy parts of Eastern Scotland and the Orkney Islands. In 1314, Robert Bruce succeeded in creating a Scottish kingdom independent of England. Historians sometimes date the beginnings of Scotland as a country back to 834, but it did not become fully independent of English control until Robert Bruce. Note: Great Britain includes England, Scotland and Wales. The United Kingdom includes Great Britain and Northern Ireland.

EQ: *What did you know about Scottish people and Scotland, or its history before? Does this change your opinion at all?*
The 'modern' Scottish independence movement was largely peaceful. Is peaceful independence the exception to the rule? How does the Scottish experience compare to your country's history?
Robert Bruce is a hero to many Scots. Do ancestors really have any connection to the reality of modern life? The Scottish diaspora (emigrant communities) can be found today in Australia, Canada, the United States and other countries. Was there a diaspora from your country in other countries? How similar are diaspora communities to their mother country? Give examples.

Sources:
www.britannia.com/celtic/scotland/history_scotland.html
www.rampantscotland.com/history.htm
www.bbc.co.uk/scotland/history
www.scotshistoryonline.co.uk/

9 FURTHER DISCUSSION

This section covers the topics of financial independence, distance from the family, and terrorism versus freedom fighters.

A EQ: *If a country accepts financial help (IMF, aid, etc.), is it really independent? With globalisation and the integration of the world economy, is any country truly independent?*

B Try to discuss the need for family bonds.

EQ: *Does absence really 'make the heart grow fonder'? How would moving to another country affect your sense of belonging to your family, culture and country?*

C EQ: *How would you define terrorism? Is national independence more important than human life? Why do terrorist groups often target civilians?*

10 *Your answer:* WHY DO PEOPLE WANT TO BE INDEPENDENT?

This question tries to get students to think about the underlying themes in this unit. The students can address this question any number of ways. It can be looked at in terms of:

- Nationalism – why do we care whether we belong to one country or another
- Economics – having a place to live in, being able to earn a living
- A purely emotional level – the sense of belonging and owning something of one's own. Try to get students to think about the deeper meaning of personal and national independence. You may even get them to answer the hypothetical question: *What if you had no independence?*

WORKBOOK

1 USE OF LANGUAGE: Word forms

This activity introduces another perspective on the issue of independence with the case of Nicaragua in the 20th century. The activity is based on an authentic test activity used by the University of Cambridge Local Examinations Syndicate in the CAE and CPE.

Unit 9 — Free to choose — Teacher's Guide

See pages 42–45 SB, 102 WB

---

1 USE OF LANGUAGE — Answers

1 leaving 2 nationalised 3 immunisation
4 democratically 5 assassination

2 WRITING

A Sources:
Most countries have government internet sites dealing with the history of their country, however, you can encourage students to write this from an emotional perspective. This also ties in with the unit's *The BIG question*.
www.cia.gov/cia/publications/factbook
www.economist.com/countries

B Sources:
You can encourage students to write this as either a humorous satirical piece or as a serious thought exercise. Some examples of city states:
www.visitsingapore.com
www.visitmonaco.com
www.tuvaluislands.com
www.vatican.va

3 SPEAKING STRATEGIES: Using the active and passive voices

The passive voice is identified by the use of the verb 'to be' and with the (optional) use of 'by', for example *He was struck by a car*. It is often used in formal writing to put some distance between the speaker and the action in the sentence.

4 IDIOMS

See the Introduction to the Teacher's Guide.

---

4 IDIOMS — Answers

1 d   2 b   3 e   4 c   5 a

1 to reach a turning point = to come to a key / important moment 2 an eye-opener = a surprising experience 3 a red-letter day = a memorable, important or very happy moment 4 a golden opportunity = an excellent opportunity 5 a close-knit family = a family whose members are very close to each other

Ask students to use the idioms when answering these questions orally. This can be done as pair work or as a class.

- *How important is family to you?*
  – We are *a close-knit family* so it is very important.
  – It was *a real eye-opener* when my uncle died. I didn't realise how important family was to me until then.
- *What will it be like / what was it like to move out for the first time?*
  – I think it will be *a golden opportunity* to prove to my parents that I can take care of myself.
  – It was certainly *a red-letter day*. My mum cried when I left for college. My dad was very proud.
  – It was *an eye-opener* for sure. I hadn't realised how hard it might be.
- *How do people feel about independence movements in your country?*
  – Given the negative public feeling towards these groups, it would be *a golden opportunity* for them to try peaceful political means.
  – I think the bombings have been *a real eye-opener* for many people who didn't take these issues seriously.

Unit 10 — **Do I get a say?** — **Teacher's Guide** — See pages 46–49 SB, 103 WB

WHAT'S NEW!

Communication Objectives:	Ss will be able to use: – expressions for challenging arguments and opinions. – intensifiers. – vocabulary, phrases and idioms related to individual rights.
Educational Objectives:	Ss will explore the issue of individual rights.
Connected Topics:	– Road to individual rights – Dilemma of the political prisoner – Limits of free speech – Minority language rights – Prisoner rights – The state versus the individual – Slavery in the 21st century – Power, wealth and status and – Immigration laws and human rights equality of rights – Political elites and the – The right to bear arms right to hold office – Differences between countries' rights – Euthanasia
Grammar:	Adverbs Reported speech Articles
Key Vocabulary:	assembly hunger strike sinister asylum storm of controversy regime acquaintance detain demise indigenous spate tolerant chore roots prevalence quick to jump on

The BIG question: DO I GET A SAY?

This expression used when people are arguing and want to give their point of view draws students' attention to the desire of individuals to feel they are allowed to give their opinion or have some control over their lives.

VIEWPOINT

Facts: This was part of the Teens and Freedom survey conducted by USA Today's USA Weekend. 219,350 students aged 13 to 19 from across the US were asked about their views on many different subjects.

Source:
www.usaweekend.com/97_issues/970504/970504 teen_cov.html

EQ: *Do you think the situation is similar in your country? Why do you think young people feel this way? When you were a teenager, did you feel your parents restricted your freedom too much? If so, how? If not, why not?*

Separation of state and religion is often a divisive issue in many countries. Conservative groups often prefer greater government adherence to religious principles. Liberal groups often prefer religion to be totally excluded from government. Much of the debate revolves around whether the religious rules (Biblical – 'ten commandments', canonical laws, Koranical) should apply in the legal systems. While most governments do explicitly state a true separation, there is often an implicit historical acknowledgement of religious doctrines.

Source:
Pew Research Institute, 'Views of a changing world, 2001' 2002. p. 115. From: http://people-press.org/reports/pdf/185.pdf

EQ: *Do you agree that 'it's necessary to believe in God to be moral and have good values'? This dichotomy suggests that non-believers or believers of different faiths are immoral. Do you agree?*

Quote: Hubert Humphrey (1911–78) was a US Vice President from 1965–69 under President Lyndon Johnson. Although a social reformer, he is more

Unit 10 Do I get a say?
Teacher's Guide
See pages 46–49 SB, 103 WB

remembered for his support for the Vietnam War and losing the 1968 presidential election to Richard Nixon.

EQ: *Why is this quote funny? What does this imply about free speech? Do you think everyone should be heard? Do you like to listen to different points of views?*

The picture is symbolic of the restrictions that many young people feel in the transition from childhood into adulthood.

1 WORD POWER

A gets students to consider different individual rights.

1 WORD POWER A								Answers
1 b	2 h	3 d	4 c	5 f	6 e	7 i	8 a	9 g

Notes:
The plural of *paparazzo* is *paparazzi*.

Under the United Nations' Universal Declaration of Human Rights (1948).

Article 3: *Everyone has the right to life, liberty and security of person.* (This is the case referred to in Exercise 1 for 1b.)

It should also be noted that in the US and UK, the expression 'right to life' is often used by anti-abortion campaigners as a way of emphasising their belief in the rights of the unborn child.

B gets students to practise expressions for challenging arguments and opinions and the vocabulary in **A**.

1 WORD POWER B	Sample answer
Paparazzi arrested for spying on a celebrity: **The evidence simply doesn't support your argument. Where's the proof? My client took the pictures while the person was on a public beach.**	

ARTICLES
Slavery in Niger – Battling Against The Odds

This article discusses a controversial and taboo subject in parts of Africa. Although banned by international treaties – the League of Nations 1926 Slavery Convention, UN's 1948 Universal Declaration of Human Rights and the UN's 1956 Supplementary Convention on the Abolition of Slavery, slavery still exists around the world, from the trafficking of women and children in the sex trade, forced unpaid labour by prisoners, and various other forms of indentured service.

The case in Niger is especially troubling given that slavery is officially banned according to the 1999 Niger Constitution and Penal Code, yet an estimated 8 per cent of the population are still slaves. According to the local anti-slavery group Timidria, local and state governments have been allowed slavery to continue; the slave-owning classes often refuse even to acknowledge it exists. However, education and public-awareness campaigns seem to be bringing about change, as can be seen with the case of Assibit.

Source:
www.antislavery.org

EQ: *Why do you think slavery continues into the 21st century? What can be done to stop it? Do you think people in your country are aware of or care about the problem?*

Police Powers Extended in Yob Crackdown

This article discusses a very controversial law in the UK. British tabloids have for many years used examples of yob violence to create sensationalist headlines. The police have found the law useful for cracking down on the troublemakers within their jurisdictions. Aimed at nuisance neighbours and rowdy youth, the law does away with the entire due process procedure, which remains a crucial civil rights issue. Police or city council can basically ban individuals from being in an area by issuing a anti-social banning order, or ASBO. One family in Scotland was even banned from their own house because of their continued rowdy behaviour.

Note:
ASBO is pronounced [azbō].

EQ: *What do you think of this law? Do you have the same kinds of problems as in the UK? What can police in your country do if some troublemakers refuse to abide by laws? Do you think ASBOs would work or be needed in your country?*

2 READING

A is a gap completion activity that will help students with Part 2 of the Reading section of the CAE exam.

2 READING A   Answers

A 1 B   2 E   3 C   4 A

B gives students a chance to practise reported speech.

C 1 This question tries to contextualise the issue of slavery in terms of how the slave-owning classes would view the issue. It requires the students to attribute beliefs and emotions not inherent in the text. You may need to ask the obvious related question: *Why do the slave owners and others in society not want to talk about this issue?*

C 2 gets students to speculate from their own experience. This requires only anecdotal evidence.

C 3

3 SPEAK YOUR MIND

This section covers the topics of status of rights in the student's country, free speech, the right to free movement, slavery, and dealing with anti-social behaviour.

A EQ: *Describe the historical development of individual rights in your country. Has everyone always had the same rights as you have now? Do people really care about their rights today? If you did not have all these rights, would you miss them?*

B EQ: *Should hate speech or any kind of speech be censored? Why / Why not?*

C EQ: *If you could live anywhere, where would you choose?*

D EQ: *How and why were slaves used? Many countries and people are wealthy today from the work of slaves. Should descendents of slaves be paid by descendents of slave owners for their ancestors' unpaid labour? Why do you think former slave-owning nations such as the USA or Brazil refuse to discuss the topic of reparation payments to African slave descendants?*

E EQ: *Is it fair to target all young people for the actions of a few?*

4 LISTEN   DVD

This audio clip is about the Tranquillity Bay WWASP facility in Jamaica. WWASP is only one chain of schools among a group of schools for so-called troubled young people. Many others often employ military-style boot camps. In many cases, these schools are located away from the continental US, which frees them from United States laws. These laws would for instance not allow beatings, forced confinement, kidnapping, starvation and other behaviour-modification measures. The sole purpose of these measures is to force the 'students' at these schools to submit to the will and authority of their superiors, the staff and parents. It is not dissimilar to the basic training for US Marines.

Parents are often not given access to the children during the treatment. They get the end result, but they are often unaware or unconcerned about any abuses – the ends justify the means. As for the students, there have been a number of suicides and accidental deaths at different schools over the years, including the 2004 suicide of a girl at a Montana WWASP facility.

4 LISTEN B   Answers

B 1 B   2 C   3 A

D You should try to get students to understand the situation from the parents' point of view.

5 TEAMWORK

This activity is loosely based on the ancient Greek *'boule'* system. The *boule* was the city council for the city-states. In democratic city-states like Athens, the *boule* positions were chosen in a random lottery from the city's aristocrats. These city councillors would then be required to run the daily affairs of the city for one year.

Although students should be given freedom to create whichever types of candidates they want, they should try to analyse how these people's background might affect the rule of law. Given this analysis, they should try to focus more on authentic or realistic people.

Sources:
The Greeks, H.D.F. Kitto
www.ancientgreece.com
www.bbc.co.uk/schools/ancientgreece/main_menu.shtml

Unit 10 — Do I get a say? — Teacher's Guide — See pages 46–49 SB, 103 WB

6 CONTROVERSY

Euthanasia became a national issue in the Netherlands following the case of Dr. Geertruida Postma in 1973. She gave her mother a lethal injection of morphine following her mother's prolonged suffering after a brain haemorrhage. Postma was convicted of voluntary euthanasia but received only a suspended sentence. The court laid the groundwork for what later became the conditions on which a person may be allowed to choose to die: an incurable illness, unbearable (mental or physical) suffering, a request to die, to be in the final stage of illness and the consent of the physician. The Termination of Life on Request and Assisted Suicide Act was passed into law in the Netherlands in 2002.

EQ: *What do you think about euthanasia? What are the laws in your country? If someone should choose euthanasia, under what circumstances should it be allowed? Some Dutch politicians worry that this right may lead to euthanasia tourism. Is this a real fear?*

Sources:
Euthanasia (Just the Facts Series), Robert Pool
Negotiating a Good Death: Euthanasia in the Netherlands, Linda A. Jackson
www.nvve.nl/english
www.euthanasia.com
www.kevork.org

7 PORTFOLIO WRITING

See the Introduction to the Teacher's Guide.

A Sources:
The Future of Women's Rights: Global Visions and Strategies, Joanna Kerr
www.un.org/Overview/rights.html
www.hrw.org/women
http://iwraw.igc.org

B Sources:
www.wwasp.com
www.nospank.net
http://fornits.com/anonanon/docs/wwasp/mvm

8 LAW *in English* [CLIL]

Although there has been some cultural friction between the Francophones in Quebec and the Anglophones in the rest of Canada, a tenuous balance had been managed through power sharing in the national government. However, this changed in the 1960s when Quebec underwent the Quiet Revolution. A combination of events lead to a polarisation in Quebec politics, stressing Quebec's right to separate administrative powers such as tax collection. The French-speakers fumed at the indifference displayed in several well-publicised labour disputes, while much of Canada was unaware of the growing resentment.

The desire for recognition shifted to a demand for independence. By the end of the decade, a pro-independence terrorist group called the *Front de liberation du Québec* (FLQ) had begun a bombing and kidnapping spree leaving the Quebec Labour Minister, Pierre Laporte, murdered. Although the FLQ was quashed by instituting martial law, the demands for independence continued to grow. By 1976, the *Parti Québecois* was elected in Quebec with a mandate to hold an independence referendum.

After several failed independence referendums, several failed attempts at constitutional reconciliation and a generally buoyant economy in Quebec, the independence movement has stalled. Although the French language is not a direct cause of this dispute, the French language and its place in Canadian society is symbolic of the larger constitutional dispute. So for many Quebeckers, controlling language rights is necessary to exhibit some sense of control in a process they feel to be outside their control.

EQ: *How are minority languages treated in your country? How should they be treated? What is the significance of a language being defined as an official language?*
Many international companies use English as their official company language. What do you think of this practice?

Sources:
http://archives.cbc.ca/IDD-1-73-1297/politics_economy/bill101
www2.marianopolis.edu/quebechistory
www.cric.ca/en_html/guide/language/quebec.html

Note:
The EU now spends over €800 million every year on translation or €2.55 for every person in the EU. The

EU employs over 2,500 interpreters and translators (more than a hundred per language). Every year, the EU translates over two million pages of text. Most translations between smaller language groups are done through a 'relay language' like English, French or German. The top four languages by population are German (24%), French (16%), English (16%) and Italian (16%). The most spoken languages are English (47%), German (32%) and French (28%).

Source:

http://europa.eu.int/translation_enlargement/index_en.htm

EQ: *Should the EU use all 20 official languages? Wouldn't it make more sense for everyone to just use one* lingua franca? *Why / Why not? How might only using a second language affect democracy?*

9 FURTHER DISCUSSION

This section covers the topics of individual rights, equality in the eyes of the law, and the right to bear arms.

A This question is meant to analyse how different countries view individual rights and different governments legislate different rights. It is not necessary to expand on each point unless you feel it is appropriate.

EQ: *Which does your country hold as rights? Do you approve of your country's individual rights in this case? What values does this suggest of your country? How would you view countries which value different individual rights than your country? Is there a right and wrong way to legislate individual rights? At what age, are / should these activities be accessible in your country: property ownership, sexual consent, voting, matrimony, operating a vehicle, use of alcohol / cigarettes, gambling?*

B Try to get students to think in concrete terms.

EQ: *Give examples of politicians, wealthy or other powerful individuals who have been in trouble with the law. What happened to them? Do you think they receive the same justice as a poor person who cannot afford an expensive legal defence?*

C Try to get students to imagine what living in gun culture might be like.

EQ: *Would you feel safer? Why / Why not? There is a popular pro-gun slogan 'guns don't kill people, people kill people'. Do you agree?*

10 *Your answer:* CAN'T WE JUST DO WHAT WE WANT?

This question tries to get students to think about the relationship between individuals and individual rights and society as a whole. The question targets one of the fundamental philosophical dichotomies of human existence. On the one hand, you have the idea first proposed by Rene Descartes in *Meditations on First Philosophy* (1641). By rationally subtracting what could not be explained by logic, Descartes was limited to being able to prove only his own existence. So does society even exist for us? Moreover, should we care? By extension, do we actually have any obligations to others? This is contrasted with the point brought up in John Donne's famous line from *Mediations XVII*: 'No Man is an Island unto Himself.' At heart, humans are social animals and need society. Much of what we have accomplished as a human species is due to our ability to cooperate and live relatively harmoniously with each other. How do we maintain this cooperation – by limiting human freedoms, our individual rights?

WORKBOOK

1 WORD POWER

This activity will give students the chance to practise the intensifiers and phrases for challenging arguments and opinions from **Language Bank 10**. The answers below are only examples, there is more than one answer possible for each.

> **1 WORD POWER** **Sample answers**
> **1** Everyone I know agrees (**wholeheartedly**) with me, we (**definitely / absolutely**) need to restrict immigration. **That can't be true. What about me? I disagree with you.**
> **2** It goes (**completely / entirely**) against our country's beliefs to restrict freedom of speech.

Unit 10 — Do I get a say? Teacher's Guide   See pages 46–49 SB, 103 WB

Regardless of that, the fact remains the country needs to restrict free speech sometimes. / **If you look at the facts, they would show** that our country has at times needed to restrict free speech.

3 Police should (**definitely / clearly**) have (**absolutely / totally / completely**) unlimited power to stop terrorists. **That can't be true. What about** the right to privacy? / **The evidence simply doesn't support your argument. Where's the proof?** Do the benefits outweigh the costs?

4 It's (**absolutely / definitely / totally / completely / entirely / clearly**) wrong to tax inheritance. It goes (**utterly / completely / entirely / totally / completely**) against the right to property. **The evidence doesn't support your argument.**

5 I (**totally / completely / fully**) disagree, criminals don't deserve any rights. **Regardless of** whether they deserve them, if you take them away, it becomes a slippery slope argument. / **That can't be true. What about** people who commit very minor crimes?

6 It is (**extremely**) important to have people from a variety of backgrounds as candidates for political office. **Regardless of that, the fact remains that** you need a lot of money to run for office.

2 USE OF LANGUAGE: Articles

This activity introduces the issue of individual rights in the age of the internet. The activity is based on an authentic test activity used by the University of Cambridge Local Examinations Syndicate in the CAE and CPE.

2 USE OF LANGUAGE				Answers
1 the	**2** a	**3** -	**4** -	**5** the
6 The	**7** the	**8** an	**9** a	**10** -

3 WRITING

A Sources:
Many developed countries have organisations campaigning to lower the voting age to 16. *Taking Back the Vote,* Jane Eisner.

www.votesat16.org.uk
www.youthrights.org/votingage.shtml
www.youthvote.org/

B Sources:
You can find assessments and other information about rights for most countries at:
www.cia.gov/cia/publications/factbook
www.amnesty.org
www.unhchr.ch/html/intlinst.htm
www.ilhr.org

4 IDIOMS

See the Introduction to the Teacher's Guide.

4 IDIOMS					Answers
1 b	**2** f	**3** c	**4** e	**5** a	**6** d

1 a sacred cow = person or thing that is above criticism or attack **2** a kangaroo court = an unofficial or illegal court **3** not to see eye to eye = to disagree, have different ideas **4** to sit on the fence = not to join any side / be uncommitted in a controversy **5** to put the clock back = to go back in time, make things as they were before **6** to come face to face with = to make direct personal contact with

Ask students to use the idioms when answering these questions orally. This can be done as pair work or as a class.

- *How does justice in your country compare to other countries?*
  – I don't know a lot about other countries, but I have heard that some countries often use *kangaroo courts* for political dissidents.
  – I think some countries really *put the clock back* on individual rights.
  – I haven't *come face to face* with courts in other countries so I couldn't tell you for sure.

- *How would you react if some individual rights were taken away?*
  – I would definitely not *sit on the fence*. I think I would protest right away.
  – I think we have already *seen the clock put* back on some rights in our country.

– Well, I think it would really depend on which ones. I mean some rights are like *sacred cows,* while others are not.

- *What would you say to someone who thought their rights were more important than yours?*
  – I'd probably tell them that we *don't see eye to eye* on this issue.
  – I haven't really *met* anyone like that *face to face,* but I would guess I would have to object.
  – I would have to explain that rights are universal. To think that one person's rights are more important than another's leads to unjust government and *kangaroo courts.*

Unit 11 — **Peace around the world** — Teacher's Guide — See pages 50–53 SB, 104 WB

WHAT'S NEW?

Communication Objectives:	Ss will be able to: – use expressions for evaluating different standpoints and tentative expressions. – use vocabulary, phrases and idioms related to international events.
Educational Objectives:	Ss will address issues of the impact of events that have occurred within recent years.
Connected Topics:	– Nobel Peace Prize – Diplomacy – Events making headlines – European Union – Conflicts around the world – Natural disasters – Peaceful solutions – EU versus US – Anti-war theatre – Technology and warfare – Civilians and war – Rogue states
Grammar:	Adjectives — Collocations — Idioms
Key Vocabulary:	abduct / be at odds / bulwark / civilian / counterpoint / coward / credit worthiness / crude / draft *n* / envoy / extradition / foe founding member / immunity / initiative / intent on / irritant / largesse / mission / obliterate / pet project / profiteer / recall *v* / reclaim *v* repressive / rival / secular / surpass / suspend a law / uprising / void / windfall / withhold / witness *v*

The BIG question: WILL WE EVER HAVE PEACE?

This question deals with the fundamental issue of the innate nature of humans. Are we by nature violent beings?

VIEWPOINT

Facts: Reasons for winning Nobel Peace Prize: Shirin Ebadi for promoting children and women's rights in Iran; Mohamed El Baradei for trying to identify a nuclear weapons programme in Iraq before the US invasion in 2003; Wangari Maathai's work with deforestation relates to a larger more complex issue of the roots of warfare. In many instances, war happens when resources are scarce.

Source: http://nobelprize.org/peace/

EQ: *What is the significance of the Nobel Peace Prize? Should people promoting peace be recognised? Should these people have been recognised? Are Peace Prize recipients as well known as war leaders?*

Quote: Lester B. Pearson (1897–1972) was the Prime Minister of Canada from 1963 to 1968. He won the Peace Prize for ending the Suez Canal crisis.

EQ: *How important is diplomacy for your country? Internationally? Can you think of any instance where diplomacy helped solve a possible conflict? If so, what happened? Do you think diplomacy and talking about issues really solves anything?*

1 WORD POWER

A gets students to practise their knowledge of adjectives and word partners.

QSE Advanced — Unit 11 Teacher's Guide
See pages 50–53 SB, 104 WB

1 WORD POWER A — Answers

1 c   2 a   3 b   4 h   5 g   6 f   7 d   8 e

nature	natural	disaster
diplomacy	diplomatic	envoy
population	popular	uprising
terror	terrorist	attack
region	regional	conflict
finance	financial	crisis
politics	political	corruption
peace	peaceful	protest

B 1 gets students to look at how these common world events have affected the own country.
2 gets students to create dialogues using phrases from **Language Bank 11**. It would be worthwhile to have students role play these dialogues together.

ARTICLES

Chavez, Seeking Foreign Allies, Spends Billions

This article discusses the growing tensions between Venezuelan president Hugo Chavez and the United States. The United States is strongly opposed to Chavez because of his left-leaning policies. An admirer of Fidel Castro, Chavez supports wealth redistribution and is opposed to US economic policy in Latin America. Many Latin Americans blame US policies for the continuing widespread poverty in the region. Chavez is trying to export his Bolivarian Revolution to other countries in the region by giving these countries financial help to offset US influence.

EQ: *What do you think of Hugo Chavez? Should countries with great inequalities of wealth try to redistribute this wealth? How would you feel about this if you were one of the poor or one of the very wealthy?*

Hope Ends 29-year March of Mothers of the Plaza de Mayo

This article discusses the legacy of the Mothers of the Plaza de Mayo. Formed at the beginning of the 'Dirty War' in Argentina, these women worked tirelessly to protest against the injustice that was happening in their country. Their non-violent protests have eventually led to a slow and steady recognition in Argentina of a need to reconcile the past.

EQ: *How would you react in these women's position? Would you continue this long?*

2 READING

A is a skimming activity that will help students with the Reading section in the CAE exam.

2 READING A — Answers

A For: Fidel Castro (friend and political ally), Brazilians (supports Samba parades), poor Mexicans (eye surgery), poor US citizens (subsidized heating fuel).
Against: US government (anti-communist history), George Bush (has had war of words with Chavez), Antonia Ledezma (political opponent), Heritage Foundation (right-wing think tank)

B relates to a type of question in the Trinity exam which requires students to speculate on the unstated feelings of people. You should make sure students provide some information from the article to support their opinions.

C 1 This question touches on United States' foreign policy in Latin America and the rest of the world. Students will get to practise the conditional here.
2 You can give the students some help by pointing to several countries which have had to deal with this problem: South Africa after apartheid, post-Cold War Russian / US relations, Germany after reunification.

3 SPEAK YOUR MIND

This section covers the topics of recent world events, UN peace-keeping, citizen's protests, what makes good and bad government.

A EQ: *How do you think the world has changed because of these events? How have these events affected your country? Have there been any significant events in your country which have affected the world? Do you think people will care about these events 25 years from now?*

B EQ: *What conflicts are going on at the moment? Does your country provide UN peace-keeping troops?*

C EQ: *Have you ever protested against anything? Did it help? What issues do you feel strongly enough about to protest?*

D EQ: *Are all governments good, bad or something in between? How good is your present government? Why?*

Unit 11 — Peace around the world — Teacher's Guide

See pages 50–53 SB, 104 WB

4 LISTEN   DVD

While much of the world is aware of the 2004 Asian Tsunami, few save neighbouring Caribbean countries remembers the impact of the torrential flooding that hit Haiti and the Dominican Republic in the same year. While both countries had significant losses from the event, the floods were worse in Haiti due to the deforestation in the mountains and its endemic poverty. It is by far the poorest country in the Western hemisphere with 80 per cent of the country living in poverty and 3.5 per cent of its 8.1 million inhabitants living with HIV / AIDS.

A Photos: Some disasters: hurricanes / typhoons, flooding, mudslides, tsunamis, earthquakes, avalanches, ice storms, tornados, hailstorms, lightning storms.

4 LISTEN C		Answers
C 1 60 cm	2 10–20	3 wood and propane

5 TEAMWORK

This activity is designed to get students to think about reasons for war and to brainstorm creative ways of resolving these issues. Students can create whichever solutions they want. The third part of this activity is controversial.

6 CONTROVERSY

Relations between the United States and the European Union can be difficult. Recently, the US government has emphasised a need for a more dominant role for the US in world politics, placing US interests over those of possible rivals. While several countries including the UK and Italy have been able to maintain close ties, on trade the EU and US have had several bitter disputes on issues such as GM (genetically modified) foods, internet trade, Boeing / Airbus subsidies and steel tariffs as well as disagreements over the handling of international conflicts and diplomatic issues.

The US today prefers bilateral agreements and negotiations to take advantage of its immense military and economic advantage compared to the EU, which continues to favour multilateral institutions like the United Nations. The reality remains that the US and the EU need each other for trade and for security.

Sources:
Transatlantic Economic Disputes: The EU, the US and the WTO, Ernst-Ulrich Petersmann
Managing EU-US Relations, Rebecca Steffenson
www.eurunion.org
http://europa.eu.int/comm/external_relations/us/intro
www.useu.be

EQ: *Why do you think the US and the EU seem at odds today? What do you think the future relationship between the two powers will be like? Are the US and the EU right in their current attitudes toward each other? Which one do you think developing countries favour? Why?*

7 PORTFOLIO WRITING

See the Introduction to the Teacher's Guide.

A Sources:
See local newspapers for examples of announcements. Entertainment announcements are likely the best examples.

B Sources:
See the website of most major media outlets for examples of world event coverage.
www.bbc.co.uk
www.guardian.co.uk
www.cnn.com

8 DRAMA *in English* [CLIL]

Theatre and the arts in general have often expressed divergent viewpoints. Anti-war protest pieces have existed since the beginning of Western theatre in ancient Greece. Present-day activism does not come without a price. Actors, especially film actors like Susan Sarandon and Tim Robbins, have come under considerable criticism for expressing anti-war views in the United States over the Iraq War.

EQ: *Does anti-war theatre have as much impact as protest rallies? Do you think old anti-war plays are still relevant? Why / Why not? What do you think of street theatre as a form of protest? How political or activist are actors and theatre groups in your country? Should actors give their political views in public?*

Think of five things people often protest about. Choose one and develop a short plot summary for a drama or comedy that protests against it.

Note:
The quote from *Hair* is derived from a 1967 anti-speech by civil-rights activist Stokely Carmichael.

Sources:
The Oxford Dictionary of Plays, Michael Patterson
www.sfmt.org/
www.lysistrataproject.com/
www.thawaction.org

9 FURTHER DISCUSSION

This section covers involvement in conflicts, civilians in war, technology and war, and rogue states.

A Try to get students to think about their country's role in world politics and its role in any international disputes, whether as a combatant, a peacekeeper or negotiator.

EQ: *Was your country right to join this? Can you foresee any future possible conflicts? What effect does being the victor or loser in a battle have on a country? What effect does being the aggressor in a conflict have on a country? Can a country ever escape its past?*

B Try to get students to think about the reality of living in a war zone.

EQ: *What would it be like to live in a war zone? Why are civilian deaths so under-reported?*

C Try to get students to think about new weapons developed since medieval times.

EQ: *Name five early (medieval) weapons and five modern weapons. Which weapon / military vehicle has had the biggest impact: knife, horse, gun, chemical weapon, fighter jet, tank, nuclear bomb, submarine, aircraft carrier? How has the nuclear bomb changed international diplomacy and war?*

D Some countries considered rogue nations by the US: Syria, North Korea, Iran, Sudan and Cuba.

EQ: *What do you think of Syria, Iran, North Korea, or Cuba? Are they dangerous? Should people in your country be worried about them?*

10 Your answer: WILL WE EVER HAVE PEACE?

This question tries to get students to address the most fundamental question regarding peace. There are obviously many obstacles to overcome ranging from dictatorships to ignorance and greed. Beyond this, we need to ask the fundamental question: is it in human nature to be peaceful? Is war a normal means of solving international conflict? Is war an extension of the violence in society? Do people care when wars are fought in far off countries?

WORKBOOK

1 WORD POWER

This activity will get students to practise evaluating different standpoints and using tentative expressions from **Language Bank 11**.

---

1 WORD POWER **Sample answers**

1 **Historically speaking,** regional conflicts have often been a threat to stability in the world. **Perhaps, it's hard to say.**
2 **If you look at it from another perspective,** I am optimistic that the world will always send money and help after natural disasters. **Maybe you're right. Who knows?**
3 **While I respect your position, I think** peace comes from understanding others; globalisation will help increase both. **Well, I guess we'll have to wait and see.**
4 **If you look at it from another perspective,** the UN needs forces for peace-making as well as for peace-keeping. **Well, I'm not so sure.**
5 **If I were playing devil's advocate, I'd say** all elections should be monitored by international observers. **Perhaps, it's hard to say.**
6 **On the other hand, you need to consider that** civilians should never be caught up in wars. **Maybe, you're right. Who knows?**
7 **While I respect your position, I think** peaceful protest is the best way to change things. **Maybe you're right. Who knows?**
8 **While I respect your position, I think** political corruption nearly always leads to a financial crisis. **Well, I'm not so sure.**

Unit 11 **Peace around the world** Teacher's Guide See pages 50–53 SB, 104 WB

2 WRITING

A Sources:
Peacemonger, John Murray.
We did Nothing: Why the Truth Doesn't Always Come Out When the UN Goes In, Linda Polman
www.un.org/Depts/dpko/dpko/index.asp

B Sources:
The Penguin Companion to the European Union, Timothy Bainbridge
http://europa.eu.int
www.euobserver.com

3 SPEAKING STRATEGIES: The power of three

This activity is one of the techniques to help students give better presentations. This provides students with a great way to make their presentations more interesting and compelling.

3 SPEAKING STRATEGIES					Answers
1 d	2 c	3 b	4 f	5 a	6 e

4 IDIOMS

See the Introduction to the Teacher's Guide.

4 IDIOMS				Answers
1 f	2 a	3 e	4 c	5 b

1 to bury the hatchet = to make resolve differences, make peace **2** to build a bridge = to make contact to resolve differences / conflicts **3** to reopen old wounds = to go back / to bring up old differences / reasons for past conflict **4** to pick up the pieces = to begin to sort things out after something difficult has happened **5** to explore every avenue = to try / investigate any possibilities

Ask students to use the idioms when answering these questions orally. This can be done as pair work or as a class.

- *How does history affect international relations?*
  – Many countries have trouble *burying the hatchet* over old grievances.
  – I think many countries prefer to *build bridges* when there are obvious economic benefits.
  – I think it is hard not to *reopen old wounds* whenever a dispute happens. Look at China and Japan.
- *How will the EU develop in the future?*
  – I hope they will *explore every avenue* of cooperation with the US.
  – I think the EU has sometimes been left *to pick up the pieces* in former Communist countries.
- *What can your country do to help find peace in the Middle East?*
  – I hope we could help *build bridges* between warring parties.
  – I think we could help them to *explore every avenue* towards a peaceful resolution.
  – I hope we could help *pick up the pieces* when the conflicts are resolved.

Unit 12 — Click here! — Teacher's Guide
See pages 54–57 SB, 105 WB

WHAT'S NEW?

Communication Objectives:	Ss will be able to: – use expressions for deducing and using uncountable nouns. – use vocabulary, phrases and idioms related to using the internet.
Educational Objectives:	Ss will address issues of internet technologies and some evolving reasons for internet use.
Connected Topics:	– Languages use on the net – Computer security – Online gaming – Using the internet – Internet access rights – Online dating – Webpage design – Gambling online – Hackers – Computer viruses – Protecting children online – Mobile internet – Spam mail
Grammar:	Uncountable nouns
Key Vocabulary:	Anglocentric, broadband connection, casual, Chinese characters, console, daring, dot-com, epaulette, execute, face off, frantically, gambling, gauge, google, hacker, intervene, hairdo, landmark, log on, lose one's head, lure, mecca, netiquette, packed, pro, prospect, roll out, search engine, six-figure income, social engineering, spectator sport, spyware, take off, tax haven, texting, the one, tunic, venue, video conference, virtual

The BIG question: ARE WE ALL ONLINE NOW?

Here the students should think about 'we' in the context of the whole world.

VIEWPOINT

Graph: Although the British Council estimates that about half the world population will speak English by 2015, other reports suggest that it will begin to decline by 2050 to be overtaken by Hindi-Urdu and Arabic. Currently, there are 514 million English speakers in the world (as a first or second language). This is second only to Mandarin Chinese with 1,075 million (as a first or second language).

Source:
www.glreach.com/globstats/index.php3

EQ: *Why is English so common on the internet? Does this give English-speaking people or companies an unfair advantage in the world? Do you think English will continue to dominate the internet in the future?*

Facts: The cost includes internet protection (firewalls, anti-virus software), dedicated IT specialists, IT consulting fees, damage and repair of networks after a virus infection, fraud from Trojan software, spyware and social engineering (phishing), equipment theft and denial of service attacks (stop a website from operating).

Source:
Trend Micro, Inc.

EQ: *Name some viruses or worms that you have heard of. What do / did they do? How might they cost people, businesses or the government? Who should pay these costs: businesses, governments, jailed hackers, consumers?*

Unit 12 — Click here! — Teacher's Guide

See pages 54–57 SB, 105 WB

Quote: This is a play on the old adage: Give a man a fish and you feed him for a day. Teach him to fish and you will feed him for a lifetime.

EQ: *How much of a distraction is the internet? Which is the most common reason to use the internet: education, business work, personal work or entertainment? Why?*

1 WORD POWER

A 1 gets students to discuss common uses of the internet.

2 gets students to practise using uncountable nouns.

B gets students to practise using the deducing phrases from **Language Bank 12**.

---

1 WORD POWER B Sample answers

1 I think we can assume that / My conclusion about this would be that / This leads me to believe that hackers are a continuing problem.

2 It's fair to say that / My conclusion about this would be that / This leads me to believe that he is a fairly well-known individual.

3 This would clearly suggest that / My conclusion about this would be that countries that have invested in broadband, like Korea, have an advantage.

ARTICLES

Don't Tell the Kids: Computer Games Can Make You Rich

This article discusses the enormous cultural phenomenon in South Korea and other Asian countries surrounding internet gaming. Massive Multiplayer Online Role-Playing Games (MMORPGs) allow many people to play the same game simultaneously via the internet. As the article states, game consoles used to be very expensive leading to a rise in demand for games that could be played online.

Internationally, online gaming attracts tens of millions of users. Yahoo! Games and MSN Games can have up to 150,000 to 200,000 players at a time, with over half being adult women. The success of online gaming has even spawned the World Cyber Games with more than 700 contestants from over sixty countries. Korea continues to be a leader in the trend; the games market there reached some $4.3 billion in 2005.

EQ: *Do you think video games are as competitive as sports? Do video games work as a spectator sport? What kind of training do you think these competitors undertake? Why would Samsung or Coca-Cola want to sponsor these online gaming events?*

A Few Emails and She Knew He Was The One

This article deals with the increasing interest in online dating. The largest US internet dating site, Match.com, boasts over 4.5 million users with new users every day. Online dating was in many ways a natural progression from the computer dating craze of the 1980s. It combines the ease of a search engine with the anonymity of the internet. The case discussed in the article also demonstrates the growing acceptability amongst the younger generation compared to older generations.

EQ: *How easy or difficult is it to meet people where you come from? Do you think everyone has a perfect match waiting for them somewhere? Would you or anyone you know try online dating?*

2 READING

A is a skimming activity that will help students with one of the Reading sections of the CAE exam.

---

2 READING A, B Answers

A Lim = 1, 4

B (Sample answers) **1-2** Andy / Katrina have fallen in love. **3** Katrina's grandmother doesn't know that Katrina met Andy through a website because Katrina thinks she wouldn't understand. **4** Katrina's grandmother doesn't know anything about Venus. She might not approve of her granddaughter meeting her husband through the internet.

C 1 This question relates to a type of question in the Trinity exam which requires students to speculate and conclude on the unstated feelings of people. You may want to extend the discussion by asking: *Would you want to be a professional gamer? What would be some benefits or drawbacks? Is professional gaming something you could do for the rest of your life?*

2 This question requires students to speculate on the unstated reasons for the past negative impression given to dating services. You should try to get students to look at the deeper issue of finding someone. Does admitting you are lonely mean you are unwanted or something else? What are the rules of attraction? How does dating / relationships relate to a person's ego / self-confidence?

3 SPEAK YOUR MIND

This section covers the topics of internet use, rights to internet access, online gaming and online dating.

A EQ: *Do the benefits of the internet outweigh any negative aspects? Does the internet unite or divide people?*

B EQ: *Should the internet be free (i.e. cost nothing)? How can we bring the internet to people who don't have it? Why do you think some countries are afraid of total internet access for their citizens? How should the internet be controlled or monitored?*
The United States FBI has a computer program called Carnivore which can monitor and access emails anywhere. What do you think of this?

C EQ: *What is the appeal of playing a character in a virtual world? How similar or different are video games to movies? Why?*

D EQ: *Would you ever date someone you met online? Do you think these relationships last?*

4 LISTEN AND WATCH   DVD

This video clip was produced by the BBC for the weekly computer show *Click Online*. It covers a difficult issue that may actually prove rather explosive. While the American-based Internet Corporation for Assigned Names and Numbers (ICANN) actively seeks an international agenda, there are some logistical problems arising with the idea of incorporating other language scripts into the internet addresses. The main reason is a huge disparity between meanings of a single character across different languages. Unfortunately, this has the potential to eventually lead to a separate internet developing in China.

---

4 LISTEN AND WATCH B, C, D   Answers

B Many people are unhappy with not having their own language available. They want to use them. Japanese and Korean use Chinese characters with different meaning. There might be a separate Chinese internet.

C (Sample answers) I would hope they could find a compromise. / Or what if we never find a solution that makes everyone happy? / Maybe, the UN could help provide a framework.

D 1 In the early days, it was English-speaking, but now it's multicultural.
2 150,000 and it is growing.
3 Same word, different companies in different countries.
4 More than 100 million.

5 TEAMWORK

This activity is designed to get students to work with authentic material in the form of a web page. This activity should be used to develop the students' impression of what is possible online. It will also give them the chance to think about what goes into web page design. Students should be given the freedom to create whichever type of web page they want. To extend the activity you can ask: *Do you have your own web page? If so, what's it like? If not, why not? Have you ever designed web pages before? How difficult do you think it is? Do you think it is a very creative medium? Is there still information you can't find online?*

Sources:
The Complete Idiot's Guide to Creating a Web Page and Blog, Paul McFedries
www.webstyleguide.com
http://www.wpdfd.com

6 CONTROVERSY

Online gambling started in 1994. The island state of Antigua and Barbuda passed the Free Trade and Processing Zone Act which allowed the government the right to issue licences for online gambling. With later developments in securing payments, visual graphics and different gambling software, online gambling spread to dozens of countries. In 2004, online gamblers lost $237 billion to gambling companies worldwide, with 12 million online users. Some countries have recently passed laws to ban online gambling. Although politicians often claim that they are only worried about a lack of regulation, many critics believe the actions are simply an attempt to regain lost tax revenue, however, even the critics admit that there remains the same problem – gambling addiction. Many governments supportive of online casinos are often reluctant to discuss the negative aspects of gambling.

Sources:
The Complete Idiot's Guide to Online Gambling, Mark Balestra
www.gamblingonlinemagazine.com
www.onlinegambling.com/online-gambling-news.htm

EQ: *How common is gambling in your country? Do you ever gamble? What can be some problems associated with gambling? Should gambling be made illegal? What kind of help is available to addicted gamblers? Do you think of lotteries or contests as gambling? Why / Why not?*

7 PORTFOLIO WRITING

See the Introduction to the Teacher's Guide.

A Sources:
Online Dating: The Early Years, Cosmo Fox
The Rules for Online Dating, Ellen Fein
www.pearmatch.co.uk/personals/online-dating.html

B Sources:
Futurenet: the Past, Present and Future of the Internet as Told by its Creators and Visionaries, Sally Richards
Networks and Netwars: The Future of Terror, Crime and Militancy, John Arquilla
Future Active: Media Activism and the Internet, Graham Meikle
www.elon.edu/predictions/RecentSubmissions.aspx

8 INFORMATION TECHNOLOGY *in English* [CLIL]

Further examples of hackers and what they do.

Some Cracking Techniques

- Buffer overflow: Too much data sent to a site can leave a hole for the hacker to enter.
- Sniffing: Software that monitors information passed between networked computers.
- Vulnerability scanning: Checking for holes in the firewall or computer programs.
- Spoofing: Forging a computer authentication source address; tricks a server into allowing access.
- Cracking open wireless networks using 'wardriving' (scanning neighbourhoods for open wireless networks).

Famous Hackers / Crackers

1988: Robert Morris sends out first worm, nearly shuts down the internet. Fined US $10,000 and 3 months probation.
1988: Kevin Mitnick stole equipment and access codes to make long-distance phone calls (A year in prison.)
1993: Kevin 'Dark Dante' Poulsen and friends rig phone lines to win a radio call-in contest. (Three years in prison.)
1994: Matthew Bevan and Richard Pryce crack US military. Bevan is cleared. Pryce gets €1,200 fine.
1994: Vladimir Levin steals $400,000 from Citibank. (Three years in prison and a US $240,015 fine.)
1998: Hao Jinglong and Hao Jingwen (twin brothers) hack into a Chinese bank and stole 720,000 yuan ($87,000). They were sentenced to death.
2000: Russians Alexei V. Ivanov and Vasiliy Gorshkov extort money from US companies by threatening to shut down their sites. (Three years in a US prison and fine of $700,000.)
2003: Lynn 'Danny-boy' Htun breaks into US computer security companies' websites. Arrested at London's InfoSecurity Fair.

EQ: *How big of a problem are hackers in your country? Why do hackers want to break into computers? Have there been any examples of hacking into business or government computers in your country?*
Hackers are often portrayed as heroes in literature and movies. Do you see them that way? Why / Why not? Why would someone want to write a computer virus? Do you think hackers and virus writers are punished strongly enough? Should governments / businesses hire or pay known hackers to help protect their secure networks?

Sources:
A Complete Hacker's Handbook, Dr. K
The Art of Computer Virus Research and Defense, Peter Szor
www.2600.com
www.defcon.org
www.vmyths.com

9 FURTHER DISCUSSION

This section covers favourite web pages, surfing the net safely, mobile internet access, and political hacking.

A Try to get students to think about concrete examples.

EQ: *What do you consider are effective web page designs? Give examples of different web pages. Do you prefer lots of graphics or just text? What are the five pages you visit most? Why? What are the most innovative features available on web pages today?*

B Try to get students to think about dangers that might exist online for children or teenagers, such as viewing pornography; the case of the German cannibal Armin Meiwes, who found his willing victim online, or sexual predators.

EQ: *Is it possible to prevent children from viewing pornography? Do you trust people are who they say they are online? Why / Why not? Do you think the police and politicians are doing enough? What recommendations would you make to parents about this issue?*

C Try to get students to think about how mobile internet access might be helpful.

EQ: *How might mobile internet access help with: getting directions, transport, shopping, finance, personal safety or entertainment? Would you be willing to pay money to watch TV, play games or download music on your mobile phone?*

D Try to get students to think about which governments have been unpopular in recent years.

EQ: *Why are some countries targeted for political hacking? Think of different important websites, what could happen if some of these sites are hacked into? Can anything be done to stop this? Is hacking a legitimate form of protest?*
Some hackers are now hacking for profit, that is, pay us or we crash your site. What do you think about this development?

10 *Your answer:* ARE WE ALL ONLINE NOW?

This question tries to get students to consider the reality of the internet. In many respects, the net remains the domain of wealthy, industrialised nations, creating a digital divide between them and developing countries. However, the net also provides many opportunities for developing countries, for example outsourced call centres and software development in India to hardware manufacturing in China.

What if the net wasn't there tomorrow? As many businesses rely so heavily on the net and computers, any stoppage to the net would in effect shut down the world economy. It is one reason why many are worried about the amount of spam online. See the Workbook section.

EQ: *What would happen if the internet stopped working tomorrow? Do you think everyone gets fair access to the internet? What advantages would an internet user (in the developed world) have over a non-internet user (in the developing world)?*

WORKBOOK

1 WORD POWER

This activity will get students to practise using new vocabulary from the unit and the deducing phrases from **Language Bank 12**.

---

1 WORD POWER Answers
1 googled   2 broadband   3 downloading
4 hackers   5 chat rooms   6 surfing

1 I googled / *used the Google search engine for* all my research info. **This would clearly suggest that** a lot of students use it for their research.
2 Korean *broadband connections* are so good, you can watch TV online. **It's fair to say that** many countries will probably follow South Koreas's lead.
3 A lot of people don't consider *downloading / using the internet to get* music without paying is a criminal activity. **My conclusion about this would be that** people don't see the crime affecting other people. Here, it only seems to hurt companies.
4 Many companies produce special software to protect computer networks against *hackers*. **It's fair to say that** this should help with the problem.
5 *Chat rooms* can be fun, but also a bit risky. **This leads me to believe that** people are so curious they will take risks sometimes.
6 In my spare time I spend hours *surfing* the internet / *looking at websites on* the internet. **My conclusion about this would be that / This would clearly would suggest that** you don't get enough exercise.

Unit 12 — Click here! — Teacher's Guide
See pages 54–57 SB, 105 WB

2 USE OF LANGUAGE — Answers

This activity introduces the problem of spam mail. The activity is based on an authentic test activity used by the University of Cambridge Local Examinations Syndicate in the CAE and CPE.

> **2 USE OF LANGUAGE** — Answers
>
> 1 research 2 productivity 3 equipment
> 4 junk   5 progress   6 excitement
> 7 help   8 money   9 mail
>
> **Note:** Other uncountable (or sometimes uncountable) nouns in the text: email, news, history, hope, postage.
>
> Other uncountables in the text show in bold italics:
> A growing amount of (0) _traffic_ on the internet is now caused by spam. A type of (1) __ suggests that spam accounts for over 40 per cent of all emails globally. If you consider that annually each employee receives about 2,100 junk emails and each takes about 6 seconds to delete, you can understand just how much (2) __ is lost. In the same way, if corporate servers need to hold that much extra *email*, this means companies are buying a lot of extra (3) __ just to store a lot of useless (4) __. There has been some (5) __, with spam filters keeping out some spam. So what else can be done? Well, there was plenty of (6) __ about the *news* that a lot of (7) __ is on the way and spam will be soon be *history*. Although several solutions are being explored, a lot of (8) __ and *hope* is being placed on exploring the idea which gives each email an identifiable 'postage' stamp. If the email is returned as spam, the sender will have to pay a few cents for *postage*. A lot of returned (9) __, say ten million, would indeed make spamming very expensive.

3 WRITING

A Sources:
The Rough Guide to the Internet 2005, Peter Buckley
http://netforbeginners.about.com/od/internet101
www.internet101.org

B Sources:
Designing Virtual Worlds, Richard Bartle
Game Design Workshop, Tracy Fullerton

www.vancouver.wsu.edu/fac/peabody/game-book/Coverpage.html
www.gamedev.net/reference

4 IDIOMS

See the Introduction to the Teacher's Guide.

> **4 IDIOMS** — Answers
>
> 1 d   2 f   3 e   4 a   5 b   6 c
>
> 1 to go haywire = to go crazy, be out of control
> 2 to bring to a standstill = to make something stop
> 3 to be a lone wolf = to live or act on your own
> 4 Sparks will fly = there will be trouble / an argument
> 5 to start from scratch = to start from the very beginning
> 6 to be a bit of an unknown quantity = to be something / someone that people don't know about

Ask students to use the idioms when answering these questions orally. This can be done as pair work or as a class.

- *What can be done about spam mail?*
  – I'm not sure, but if they can't do something it might eventually *bring* the internet *to a standstill*.
  – That's *a bit of an unknown quantity*.
  – It will make *sparks fly* if they don't do something soon.
- *Why do hackers do what they do?*
  – I think he's just *a lone wolf*. He has something to prove.
  – I think knowing they can make computers *go haywire* is just a power trip.
  – I think it's *a bit of an unknown quantity*.
- *How would a problem with the internet affect your city or country?*
  – Business would *go haywire* trying to rely on ordinary mail.
  – I think many basic services would be *brought to a standstill*.
  – It's *a bit of an unknown quantity*.

Unit 13 — **What's in the news?** — Teacher's Guide — See pages 58–61 SB, 106 WB

WHAT'S NEW?

Communication Objectives:	Ss will be able to: – use expressions for implying and colloquialisms. – use vocabulary, phrases and idioms related to the media.
Educational Objectives:	Ss will address issues of censorship, freedom of the press and media ownership.
Connected Topics:	– Sensationalism – Public versus private media – Television content – Life of a journalist – Political parties and the media – Journalists and the intelligence community – Censorship and dystopian novels – Media as a component of democracy – Technology and the media – Entertainment journalism – Fake stories
Grammar:	Prepositions Colloquialisms
Key Vocabulary:	ban, biased, caste system, clone, constrained, disinformation, distort, drive, dumbing down, dystopia, exile, fake, foreign correspondent, free press, headlines, impact, install, integrity, legitimate, lowest common denominator, mass media, media freedom, point the finger, ranking, real time, sensational, slippery slope argument, slogan, spin

The BIG question: DO YOU TRUST THE MEDIA?

VIEWPOINT

Facts: Reporters without Borders published these findings in 2005. The index is based on surveying journalists, researchers and legal experts about many areas affecting press freedom (censorship, pressure, media monopolies, arrest and murder of journalists).

Source:
http://www.rsf.org/rubrique.php3?id_rubrique=554

EQ: *Can you draw any conclusions about why some countries have more or less press freedom? Was there anything surprising about these figures? How do you think Reporters without Borders analyses press freedom?*

Quote: Rose Macauley (1881–1958) was a British novelist and essayist known for satirising middle-class life.

EQ: *Is Macauley being serious, ironic or something else? Why? Do you believe everything you read / see / hear about in the media? Why / Why not?*

1 WORD POWER

A gets students to practise their knowledge of prepositions.

1 WORD POWER A		Answers
1 for	2 in, from	3 with
4 of	5 about	6 at

B gets students to analyse differences between broadsheet (more serious news providers) and tabloid (more sensational news providers) journalism and practise using colloquialisms in **Language Bank 13**.

Unit 13 What's in the news?   Teacher's Guide   See pages 58–61 SB, 106 WB

1 WORD POWER B — Answers

1 Arrested **for** *pinching cop* car
2 Pensioner bought shares **in** *dodgy* deal **from** best *mate*
3 *What's up* **with** the Prime Minister?
4 Cost of living too *pricey*? *Fed up with* (Tired **of**) being *broke*?
5 Politicians *touchy* **about** electoral *scam*
6 Do *blokes* do their fair share **at** home?

B 2 (Sample answers)
Based on this third headline, **you could get the impression that** there was some problem with the Prime Minister. (Headline 3)
I would suggest that the fourth headline deals with the cost of living. (Headline 4)
I believe that refers to men not helping with housework. (Headline 6)

ARTICLES

Italy Trail in Press Freedom

This article discusses the debate about the controversial former Italian Prime Minister Silvio Berlusconi and press freedom in Italy. Many in the media suggested that Italy's wealthiest man had a serious conflict of interest because of his media ownership and should have divested some of his holdings. Between his ownership of Mediaset and his party's control of state-run RAI (the Italian public broadcaster) he controlled 90 per cent of Italian TV.

While Berlusconi rejected claims that this had led to press censorship, several cases involving RAI gave cause for concern. When Berlusconi publicly stated dislike of the criticisms aired against him by the respected journalists Enzo Biagi, Michele Santoro and comedian Daniele Luttazzi, RAI ended its relationship with all three. In November 2003, Sabina Guzzanti's satirical programme was taken off the air after she criticised one of Berlusconi's companies. By and large, the Italian public seems largely ambivalent about Berlusconi's media ownership. In fact, many see his ability to run a large corporate empire as evidence of his leadership skills.

EQ: *Would it worry you if your country's leader owned 90 per cent of the media in your country?*

Pay-Per-Click Journalism

This article discusses an interesting phenomenon, which seems set to upset the traditional roles in print journalism of editor and journalist. While many detractors worry that this will inevitably lead to dumbing down or the lowest common denominator in journalism, it could lead to greater choice. No longer will an editor choose what should be printed, but the public will choose themselves.

The Korean internet newspaper, Ohmynews (http://english.ohmynews.com/), has taken this one step further with letting the public write their own stories. Ohmynews has some 32,000 citizen-reporters averaging several million hits per day. The popularity of the site has shaken the Korean press.

EQ: *Do you think the public is only interested in sensational news? What kind of news stories interest you? What news stories have interested you the most recently?*

2 READING

A is a skimming activity that will help students with the Use of English section of the CAE exam.

2 READING A — Answers

Mediaset, main private TV company in Italy; controls a large share of publishing and newspaper market, including Mondadori, Italy's largest book and magazine publishing group, and *Il Giornale*, a leading national newspaper.

B requires students to analyse and imply similarities and differences between unrelated people. You should encourage the students to cite actual examples from the text and to use implying phrases in **Language Bank 13.**

C 1 This question relates to a type of question in the Trinity exam which requires students to speculate and conclude on the unstated feelings of people.
2 This question requires students to discuss the role editors play in choosing the news that is printed. You can help students by introducing words such as *censorship, bias* and *tabloid journalism*.

EQ: *What does it take to become a journalist or editor? Do you think an editor's education and experience gives them the right / ability to choose the stories that matter to the public? Do editors make the right choices?*

3 SPEAK YOUR MIND

This section covers the topics of news sources and current events, television content, life of a journalist, political control over the media and media as a pillar of democracy.

A EQ: *What are the advantages or disadvantages of getting your information from only one source? Name some current events. How might these stories be reported on differently by different networks? How is news reporting different and similar between television, radio, newspapers, news magazines and the internet?*

B EQ: *The average American watches over four hours of TV per day. How does this compare to your country? Is television an important part of your free time activities? Why / Why not? Should television viewing be restricted in any way? Can television be educational? Do you think television influences you in any way?*

C EQ: *What would it be like to interview famous people? To report from war zones? To break an important story? Do you think there is a difference between TV and newspaper journalists' jobs?*

D EQ: *How might news stories sound different if different political parties reported them? Give examples. Should you know everything? Can a country be democratic without a free press?*

4 LISTEN   DVD

This video clip is part of the controversial documentary, *Outfoxed: Rupert Murdoch's War on Journalism* by director Robert Greenwald. *Outfoxed* analyses the rise of the Fox News Channel, the 24-hour US cable news channel owned by Australian-born media tycoon, Rupert Murdoch.

Fox News was created to counter what conservatives viewed as an inherent liberal bias in the media and is one of the first news networks to openly support the political agenda of a single party, the right-wing US Republican party. Although it uses the slogan 'Fair and Balanced', Fox News often mixes journalism and conservative opinions that may blur the lines between conservative opinion and facts.

While cable news remains a small market (Fox has just over 1 million viewers) critics argue that the network has created a shift in US media towards the right. Greenwald and others also worry about the extent of Murdoch's total media empire. Murdoch's company News Corporation owns 9 satellite TV networks, 100 cable channels, 40 TV stations, 40 book companies, 175 newspapers and 1 movie studio. News Corp. is estimated to reach an audience of 4.7 billion.

B The text inside the box is a special review of the *Outfoxed* video clip. It was written in the first person by the author and publisher of *Quick Smart English*. This unusual step of reviewing a video clip in this way in an EFL textbook was to ensure this book's compliance with the fair use of copyrighted material. Students should be strongly encouraged to compare this style of journalism with that of journalists in their own country.

C You decide: Was this programme reporting news in a biased or fair way? After watching this, what do you think of Fox News' slogan, 'Fair and balanced'?

5 TEAMWORK

This activity is designed to get students to develop ideas for fictional story lines. This activity is designed to aid students in their creative effort and is based on an actual creative thinking activity. By pairing seemingly unconnected ideas or words, the resulting connection can lead to some original ideas. It should be viewed as both a fun activity and a serious attempt to think about the importance of truth in journalism. Students should be given the freedom to create whichever type of headlines or story ideas they want.

Sources:
Weekly World News. Bat Boy Lives!: The WWN Guide to Politics, Culture, Celebrities, Alien Abductions, and the Mutant Freaks that Shape our World.
www.weeklyworldnews.com

6 CONTROVERSY

In 1976, the US Senate Select Committee on Intelligence discovered that more than fifty American journalists had worked as CIA agents during the Cold War. The Committee condemned the practice, but during the next twenty years, the CIA simply limited the practice. In 1996, the US Council on Foreign Relations suggested that the law limiting the use of journalists as spies should be re-examined. In response, former CIA director John Deutch told Congress that there was no need to change the law because under the guidelines the CIA director still had the right to approve the use of journalists as spies when needed.

This use of journalists appears to be the norm among major powers rather than the exception. Colonel Stanislav Lunev, a defector from Russia's military intelligence, stated in 2000 that at least half of all Russian journalists working in Washington and the US were spies. According to Major General Yury Kobaldze of Russia's SVR, "There is no essential difference between the work of a spy and a journalist; both collect information in the same way – just the end consumers are different. Journalists make the best spies; they have more freedom of access than diplomats. The Americans' moral stand on not using journalists is artificial, and not a little duplicitous."

Sources:
The Thin Ink Line: Spies, Journalists, Espionage and the Media, David Grant
Through the Eyes of the Enemy: Russia's Highest Ranking Military Defector, Stanislav Lunev
www.cpj.org/attacks96/sreports/cia.html
www.aarclibrary.org/publib/church/reports/contents.htm

EQ: *Should governments use reporters or cameramen as spies? If so, under what circumstances? If not, why not? How could working for an intelligence agency affect how stories are reported? Do you think this puts journalists' lives and integrity at risk? Is intelligence gathering more important than reporting news stories?*

7 PORTFOLIO WRITING

See the Introduction to the Teacher's Guide.

A Sources:
Berlusconi's Shadow: Crime, Justice and the Pursuit of Power, David Lane
Silvio Berlusconi: Television, Power and Patrimony, Paul Ginsborg
www.economist.com/countries/Italy/
http://news.bbc.co.uk/1/hi/world/europe/3034600.stm
www.forza-italia.it/notizie/int_2815.htm

B Sources:
Writing Feature Stories, Matthew Ricketson
Writer's Digest Handbook of Magazine Article Writing,

Michelle Ruberg
www.journalism.org/resources/tools/print.asp
www.cjr.org/tools

8 MEDIA STUDIES *in English* [CLIL]

The idea of a utopian society can be traced back as far as Plato's *The Republic* (360 BC), however, the idea of a dystopian society is much more recent. The first recorded use of the term was by John Stuart Mill in 1868 to the UK Parliament. The idea seems to have gained ground in popular thought and literature, perhaps with the rise in importance of new technologies and the development of the modern state. New technologies were pushing the Industrial Revolution and changing the traditional roles in society. In this new age, Europe experienced a lot of social unrest from the 1840s to 1870s, as the divide between rich and poor began to grow. It is no coincidence that Mills' comments came only a year after the printing of Marx's first volume of *Das Kapital*.

In dystopian visions of the world, several themes emerge that have a direct relationship to this historical period, mostly dealing with control or a lack of it: the influence of machines and technologies as social control; an autocratic, centralised authority that cares little for the individual, but cares a lot for maintaining order; the rise of crime, as social stability and control decreases. Like utopias, dystopias are set in the not so distant future as a warning to change and a general fear of the unknown.

The novels presented in the unit are examples of how controlling the media is part of the formation of a dystopian state and where it could lead.

EQ: *Which do you think is more likely in the future: utopia or dystopia? Why? Do you think these particular dystopias are possible? Is it fair to draw similarities between these novels and today's media and society? Can you see examples today of each of the criticisms mentioned in these novels? What can we do to prevent these dystopias from occurring?*

Sources:
Brave New World, Aldous Huxley
www.huxley.net
Fahrenheit 451, Ray Bradbury
www.raybradbury.com

QSE Advanced See pages 58–61 SB, 106 WB

Unit 13
Teacher's Guide

9 FURTHER DISCUSSION

This section covers the influence of the media, technology and the media, entertainment as news, and the case of *NY Times* journalist Jayeson Blair.

A Try to get students to think about how they form their views on different issues, how the media creates consensus in a society, and how people can affect the media in the age of PR and social activism.

EQ: Which media figures do you respect? Why? How much do they influence your opinions? Is it possible to form opinions independent of or contrary to the media? How important is consensus in your society?

B Try to get students to think about how news travelled before each new technological invention (internet, satellites, TV, telephone, radio, telegraph, ship, printing press).

EQ: How important is speed in receiving news? Give some current news examples. What effect would it have if the story was reported a day, a week, a month or a year later? Do you think technology has given us a better or worse understanding of world events? Why?

C Try to get students to think about how often news covers issues relating to celebrities or the entertainment industry.

EQ: Name five celebrities. What is happening in their lives at the moment? Do you know as much about your neighbours' lives? Does reporting about celebrities trivialise the importance of other stories?

D Try to get students to think about the reality of a high-pressure job like being a journalist, meeting deadlines, and reporting on important people.

EQ: If you might lose your job, would you ever lie to keep it?

10 *Your answer:* DO YOU TRUST THE MEDIA?

This question tries to get students to address the most fundamental question regarding the media in today's society. The media is often seen as an important pillar in democracy. If the media is not providing us with accurate, unbiased information, what does this say about the democracy in our countries? How can we be informed citizens and participate fully in our society without knowing about the reality of the world around us. Does the media actually have much control over individuals?

WORKBOOK

1 WORD POWER

This activity will get students practising the use of colloquialisms and the implying phrases from **Language Bank 13.**

> **1 WORD POWER** Answers
>
> **1** All these documentaries on television are really *daft*. **Based on this, you could get the impression that** people don't want to watch anything more challenging.
> **2** I read in the paper that train fares are going up by 10 per cent. They're going to be really *pricey*. **Some people say that** we are only paying half the real cost.
> **3** I heard there was more hooliganism at the *footie* match last tonight. **I would suggest that** the football league could do more to stop violence.
> **4** Did you see that *telly* programme about that bank manager who *pinched* a million pounds? **I suspect that he knows more** than he is letting on.
> **5** Are you still *keen on* going to see that film tonight? **I would suggest that** the film next week would be better.
> **6** It's such a media stereotype! Not everyone from there is *posh*. **Don't you think it points to** lazy journalism to use stereotypes like that.

2 WRITING

A Sources:
www.thenation.com
www.motherjones.com
www.nationalreview.com
www.conservativenews.org

B Sources:
The Web of Deceit: Britain's Real Role in the World, Mark Curtis
Tell Me Lies: Propaganda and Media Distortion in the Attack on Iraq, David Miller
www.cpj.org
www.freedomhouse.org

Unit 13 — What's in the news? — Teacher's Guide
See pages 58–61 SB, 106 WB

3 SPEAKING STRATEGIES: Use some quotes

This activity is the one of the techniques to help students give better presentations. This provides students with a great way to make their presentations more interesting, more concise and better planned.

3 SPEAKING STRATEGIES				Answers
1 d	2 b	3 a	4 c	5 b

4 IDIOMS

See the Introduction to the Teacher's Guide.

4 IDIOMS				Answers
1 b	2 c	3 d	4 e	5 a

1 to have a thick skin = not be sensitive to criticism **2** to break the story = give the information / tell the story in public **3** to have a sharp tongue = to be very critical, rude **4** on the box = on the television **5** through the rumour mill = from the gossip that goes round

Ask students to use the idioms when answering these questions orally. This can be done as pair work or as a class.

- *Do you think you could handle answering questions at a televised press conference?*
  - I think you would *need a thick skin* to handle some of the questions.
  - I would be nervous. Some news commentators *have very sharp tongues*.
  - I don't see why a press conference *on the box* would be any harder.
- *What would you do if the media printed a false story about you?*
  - I think it happens often when the media is competing to *break a story*.
  - I wouldn't worry. If they printed something from *the rumour mill*, I could just sue for libel.
  - I don't know if my skin is *thick enough* not to be very upset.
- *Can you trust reporters to keep a secret?*
  - I think the papers would print everything. *The rumour mill* is just too powerful.
  - Reporters can't resist *breaking a story*. They just couldn't keep it a secret.

Unit 14 — Heroes and villains — Teacher's Guide

See pages 62–65 SB, 107 WB

WHAT'S NEW?

Communication Objectives:	Students will be able to: – use idiomatic expressions and softening expressions. – use vocabulary, phrases and idioms related to role models.
Educational Objectives:	Students will address the relationship of positive and negative role models to human development.
Connected Topics:	– Teenage role models – Fashion industry and role models – Parents as role models – Literary role models – Eminem and music role models – Male and female role models – Superheroes – Evolving role models
Grammar:	Joining clauses
Key Vocabulary:	advocate, air play, bigot, conglomeration, conjure up, contemporary, deep down, embrace, feat, foul-mouthed, gutter-dwelling, icon, idolise, in your face, invincible, mentor, non-compromising, outrage, paralysis, pressure wound, quick fire, slut, spark, stereotype, surpass, up in arms, vicious

The BIG question: DO WE NEED SOMEONE TO LOOK UP TO?

VIEWPOINT

Fact: The UK teenage girls' magazine, *Sugar*, holds an annual readers' poll of the top 100 inspirational women. The information is in the form of a graphic based on this poll of young women from 13 to 18.

Source: www.sugarmagazine.co.uk

EQ: *Do you think these are positive role models for girls? Why / Why not? What kinds of lessons could these women teach girls? How popular are these women in your country?*

Quote: Albert Einstein (1879–1955) German physicist, who later became a US citizen. Famous for developing his theory of relativity, he won the 1921 Nobel Prize for Physics. Aware of how his theory had laid the groundwork for the later development of the nuclear age and nuclear weapons, he became an advocate of nuclear disarmament after World War II.

Photos: The photos show:
- Kofi Annan (from Ghana), the Secretary-General of the United Nations up to December 2006. He has worked in a number of different areas at the UN, including the United Nations High Commissioner for Refugees (UNHCR).
- Christina Aguilera (from the USA), best-selling pop star who went topless on the cover of one of her albums. She is involved in a YouthAids.org campaign to raise awareness and funds to help protect young people from HIV / Aids.
- Tanni Grey-Thomson, Britain's best-known wheelchair athlete, who has won gold medals at the Paralympics and broken world records at distances ranging from 100 m to the marathon.

EQ: *Do you think Albert Einstein / Kofi Annan / Christina Aguilera / Tanni Grey-Thomson is a good role model? Who would each of them appeal to as a role model?*

Unit 14 Heroes and villains Teacher's Guide   See pages 62–65 SB, 107 WB

1 WORD POWER

A gets students to discuss common adjectives that could be attributed to role models. You can suggest students associate each adjective with a particular person. It is unlikely they will find someone to fit all the adjectives, so there will be room for discussion.

B 1 gets students to practise using the softening expressions from **Language Bank 14**.

---

1 WORD POWER B1   Sample answers

I'm sorry. It's just that I don't see Britney Spears as a good role model. / **It's quite difficult, but** I think Christina Aguilera can be a positive role model. / **If I could just mention one thing,** I think Kofi Annan is a good role model despite the Oil for Food scandal. / **Actually, I had thought that / I often wonder if maybe** Tanni Grey-Thomson wouldn't be a role model if you don't like sport.

ARTICLES

Eminem – Is He A Poet Or Bigot?

This article discusses the influence of Eminem and other popstars on young people. The article was written by a youth organisation, Children's Express, which writes for the *Belfast Telegraph*. Eminem (real name Marshall Bruce Mathers III) is a controversial figure in hip hop and the music industry in general. Beyond the fact that he is one of the few successful white rappers accepted by the black community, his Marshall Mathers LP was attacked for containing misogynistic and homophobic lyrics. To counter these claims, he famously appeared on stage with Elton John at the Grammy Awards to perform *Stan*.

EQ: *What do you think of Eminem? Is his music misogynistic, homophobic or violent? Why is hip hop so popular outside the African-American community where it originated? How popular are rap and hip hop artists in your country?*

Reeve Was Real-Life 'Superman'

This article is a tribute discussing the life and death of Christopher Reeve. After his accident, he did not give up hope for a cure, and became an ardent advocate for people with spinal cord injuries and the possibility that repairing spinal cord injuries would be possible in the future. Reeve was also an outspoken defender of stem cell research and critic of the US government anti-stem cell research position. While he will stay in people's minds as Superman, he will probably be remembered more for his dedicated work after his injury.

EQ: *What made Reeves a role model? Are disabled people generally seen as role models? Why / Why not?*

2 READING

A is a gap completion activity that will help students with Part 2 of the Reading section of the CAE exam.

---

2 READING A   Answers

A 1 D 2 C 3 E 4 B

B 1 requires students to contrast opinions of different people.

---

2 READING B   Answers

1 Drew and Lisa don't think pop stars are not good role models for young people, Mairead thinks Eminem is a good role model because he tells / says it how it is.

2 (Sample answer) The irony is that he played Superman, an invincible superhero, but he was not invincible. In real life, he could be injured like anyone else. / He played a superhuman man of steel but in real life, when he was paralysed in an accident, he showed more courage than an imaginary character.

B 2 The irony is that he played Superman, an invincible superhero, but he was not invincible. In real life, he could be injured like anyone else.

C 1 This question relates to a type of question in the Trinity exam which requires students to speculate and conclude on the unstated feelings of people. You may want to extend the discussion by asking: *If you were a pop star, would you care what others thought of you? Do you think a celebrity's life belongs to them or the media?*

C 2 This question requires students to speculate on the differences between Eminem and Christopher Reeve. Ask students to look at the types of careers both men have had, how their actions are presented in the media and the causes they support.

EQ: *Which person do you think most young people would prefer as a role model?*

3 SPEAK YOUR MIND

This section covers the topics of: personal role models, personal and impersonal role models, messages given by pop stars, popularity of anti-establishment role models, and role models in different groups in society.

A EQ: *How does someone choose a role model? Are role models a question of personal taste, popularity or something else? Can you judge someone without knowing them personally?*

B EQ: *Why are parents and other family members often overlooked as role models? Teenagers often rebel against their parents. Is it possible to idolise and rebel against the same person?*

C EQ: *Who are your favourite music stars? Do you think young people act on the messages sent by pop stars?*

D EQ: *Think about different groups in your country, for example, ethnic groups or people with disabilities. Who are some role models for them? How important is it to have a positive role model in a group?*

4 LISTEN   DVD

While the popularity of comic books has changed over the years, many comic book characters are popular now because of Hollywood films based on comic books. In films, the special abilities of superheroes are brought to life using computer-generated images (CGI). Superheroes in films include: Superman, Batman, the X-Men, the Hulk, Spider-Man, and the Fantastic Four.

A Photos: The pictures are of Batman and Lara Croft, played by Angelina Jolie, from the popular Tomb Raider video games and movies.

B is a CAE-type listening activity.

---

4 LISTEN B, C, D   **Answers**

B Spider-man: complex hero and very human, lots of problems but faces them, an accidental hero; Superman: an early blueprint for superheroes, good guy, helps people; Wonder Woman: independent.

C (Sample answer) Comic book genre dominated by male characters, but some strong female characters such as Wonder Woman.

D 1 1938–1954; **2** His grandfather drew cartoons for comic books / comic book cartoonist; **3** The good guys against the bad guys, fighting crime and helping people. **4** Wonder Woman – independent, Batgirl – helper, extension of a male character like Batman.

5 TEAMWORK

This activity is designed to get students to think how parents concerned about their child's well-being might view teenage role models. There is a deeper meaning to this activity in that many parents' first instinct is often to restrict children's and teenagers' access to negative influences, without consulting the young people themselves. There have been numerous grassroots movements to restrict children and teenagers access to different things. For instance, the Parents Music Research Center in the USA pushed for a film-style rating system on music that led to the 'Parental Advisory: Explicit Content' sticker on many CDs.

Source:
Raising PG kids in an X-Rated Society, Tipper Gore
www.concernedpta.com.gh/index_old.html,
www.ncac.org

EQ: *Should teenagers' access to negative role models be restricted? How do you think your parents would rate your role models?*

6 CONTROVERSY

The fashion industry has been criticised about the kind of body images that they promote, especially for young women. Some people say the fashion industry is simply pandering to the desires of the majority of women when they choose thin models. Thin models reinforce this ideal body image that the majority of women can only hope for. Recently, larger-size models have appeared more in fashion magazines. *Dolly,* an Australian women's fashion magazine, saw a 13 per cent increase in readership after introducing larger models in their fashion

Unit 14 — Heroes and villains — Teacher's Guide

See pages 62–65 SB, 107 WB

spreads. Similarly, a popular TV reality show in the US, *America's Next Top Model 3,* also featured a larger-size model as one of the ten finalists.

Sources:

www.cosmopolitan.com, www.adiosbarbie.com

EQ: *Does the fashion industry affect people's idea of body image? What can be done about this? Do you think men are also affected by men's fashion magazines?*

7 PORTFOLIO WRITING

See the Introduction to the Teacher's Guide.

A Sources:

The Art of Mentoring, Sinclair Goodlad
Students as Tutors and Mentors, Mike Pegg
www.mentoring.org, www.womenswork.org/girls/refs/mentor.html

B requires students to write satirically. It would be worth asking students to review Unit 4's first article *Leave the Poor Psychopath Alone* as an example of writing satire.

8 LITERATURE in English [CLIL]

The two authors represent two of the 20th century's more critically acclaimed American authors. They are generally regarded as 'cool', accessible and appealing to younger readers because they discussed topics that represented a break from the normal narrative in American literature.

Maya Angelou tackled racial issues that were still being worked out in 1970s America, following the rise of the civil rights movement in the 1960s. In addition, she was a woman writing about issues that few women were addressing in contemporary literature: rape, murder and bigotry. Even in the face of these adversities, she maintained an overwhelming sense of hope for the future. And while it was a simple act of autobiographical storytelling, she was clearly breaking new ground.

Jack Kerouac wrote about being young in the 1950s. Trapped by a culture that demanded conformity – a family, a house, a car and a regular job, this younger generation wanted more. In *On the Road* Kerouac discusses travelling the open road, bohemian lifestyles, jazz, race relations, drug use, sexuality and even homosexuality with a compelling, naïve curiosity. Like Angelou, it was a major break from contemporary authors.

Sources:

I Know Why The Caged Bird Sings, Maya Angelou
On The Road, Jack Kerouac
www.mayaangelou.com,
www.jackkerouac.com/index.php

EQ: *What kinds of books do you like to read? Name books and authors who have influenced you? Do you think literature is cool? Do authors make good role models? Why / Why not?*

9 FURTHER DISCUSSION

This section covers the topics of: gender and role models, friends as role models, careers as a basis for being role models, evolving role models, and role models and stereotypes.

A Try to get students to think about role models in terms of gender.

EQ: *Are there role models that are common to both sexes? What is your reaction if a boy has Britney Spears as a role model and a girl has Arnold Schwarzenegger as a role model?*

B Students should think about specific friends and the positive things that they can draw from them.

EQ: *Do your parents see your friends as positive or negative role models? Who has more influence on you: parents or friends?*

C Ask students to list specific careers, for example, lawyers, businesspeople, nurses, firefighters, criminals.

EQ: *Do some careers make for bad role models?*

D Try to get students to think about the role models they had as children. You can brainstorm these as a class.

EQ: *Do you think the role models you had as a child had much influence on you? Do some role models remain the same throughout your life?*

E Ask students about unusual role models to see how these do or do not fit with stereotypes.

EQ: *What is the most unusual role model you have heard of?*

10 Your answer: DO WE NEED SOMEONE TO LOOK UP TO?

There is a phrase often attributed to Isaac Newton often quoted: "If I have seen further it is by standing on the shoulders of giants." It means that he was only able to explore further by having learned from people who came before him. This is true even with the simplest of acts; we are part of those who surround us. The question here tries to get students to consider the basic need for role models. Is it simply an evolving drive in our natural development? Or is it something we could develop without? In the absence of others as possible role models, would we be who we are today?

WORKBOOK

1 WORD POWER

This activity will get students to practise the softening expressions from **Language Bank 14**.

---

1 WORD POWER — Sample answers

1 **I'm sorry. It's just that** I disagree with you about Eminem. – **Well, there's always a first time for everything.** 2 **I often wonder if maybe** parents expect celebrities to be unreasonably responsible. – **You'll have your work cut out for you** if you think you can change their minds. 3 **It's quite difficult to know for certain, but** I think a teenager's friends are their most important role models. – **It stands to reason.** 4 **If I could just mention one thing,** I have always looked up to my father. – **It stands to reason.** 5 **I'm sorry. It's just that** we'll only play if she coaches the team. – **Well, don't hold your breath!** 6 **If I could just mention one thing.** When I was growing up my hero was Spider-man. – **It stands to reason.** He was my hero too. 7 **Actually, I had thought that** most people were shocked with the arrest of the star. – **The bigger they are, the harder they fall.** 8 **I often wonder if maybe** she inspired me to become a doctor. – **There's always a first time for everything.**

---

2 USE OF LANGUAGE: Joining clauses

This activity discusses athletes as role models. The activity is based on an activity type for the CAE and CPE exams.

2 USE OF LANGUAGE — Answers

1 that / which	2 that	3 what
4 who	5 When	6 which / that
7 because / when	8 that	

3 WRITING

A Sources:
Confessions of a Hero-Worshipper, Stephen J. Dubner
www.myhero.com/myhero
www.jerryjazzmusician.com/mainHTML.cfm?page=heroesindex.html

B Sources:
How Not to Write a Screenplay, Denny Martin Flinn
Complete Idiot's Guide to Screenwriting, Skip Press
www.pubinfo.vcu.edu/artweb/playwriting

4 IDIOMS

See the Introduction to the Teacher's Guide.

4 IDIOMS — Answers

1 f 2 e 3 a 4 b 5 d 6 c

1 babes in arms = very young children so not able to do things for themselves 2 to take their cue = to follow the example of 3 to show guts = to show courage, be brave 4 to be in good hands = to be helped by reliable people 5 in someone's good books = in favour with someone 6 to take under someone's wing = to be given someone's protection

- *What would you do if your parents thought your friends were bad role models?*
  – I think my parents would respect my choices. I'm not *a babe in arms* any more.
  – I think it would *take a lot of guts* to follow my parents' wishes.
  – I want to *stay in* my parents' *good books* so I might find some new friends.

Unit 14 — Heroes and villains — Teacher's Guide
See pages 62–65 SB, 107 WB

- *Do you follow everything your role model does?*
  - I *take* some *cues* from her, but I am my own person. I make my own choices.
  - It *takes* more *guts* to follow your own path than to follow a role model.
  - I think it's important for a role model to *take* you *under their wing,* but this doesn't mean you can't be your own person.

- *How are you as a role model?*
  - My younger brother *takes cues* from what I do, so I have to be careful what I do.
  - I've *taken* a younger student *under my wing*. She's doing better at school since I've been helping her.
  - My friends are *in good hands* when they ask me for advice and help. I'm always there for them.

ER 2 — Snowboard nirvana — Teacher's Guide

See pages 66–67 SB

WHAT'S NEW?

Communication Objectives:	Ss will be able to use phrases or grammar from: Units 1–7, Extended Reading 1 Unit 8: Signposting words and phrases: Arguments (1) / Affirming Unit 9: Interrupting / Signposting phrases: Arguments (2) Unit 10: Challenging Arguments and opinions / Intensifiers Unit 11: Evaluating different standpoints / Tentative expressions Unit 12: Deducing / Uncountable nouns (grammar) Unit 13: Colloquialisms / Implying Unit 14: Idiomatic expressions / Softening expressions
Educational Objectives:	Ss will explore how making decisions (career, marriage) lead to different lifestyles.
Connected Topics:	– Snowboarding – Bohemian lifestyle – Cultural differences – Global warming
Grammar / Vocabulary:	Idioms Jargon / slang
Key Vocabulary:	Aussie, awesome, bad conditions, battered, broken English, crack a joke, daze, dodgy, fluorescent, footie, gain a reputation, ingenious, judge a book by its cover, mag, make a mental note, misnomer, park (see Ex. 3) [place for doing snowboard tricks], pipe, plagued by, quick smart, snap out of, spurt out, stock question, stroll v

EXTENDED READING: Background Information

This snowboard blog comes from the website for the *Board the World* magazine. The editors of the magazine travel to different ski or snowboard resorts around the world and give (we)blog editorials on how good or bad a resort was.

It is interesting to note how much the snowboarding has changed within only a few decades. Although it originated in the 1920s, it wasn't until later in the mid-1970s that the sport became popularised. Up until the early 1990s, snowboarding was banned from many ski resorts partly due to its association with teenagers and the skateboarding and surfing culture.

EQ: 1 *What do you think of boarding sports like snowboarding, surfing, skateboarding and windsurfing? Why are they so popular today? Why do you think snowboarding was banned from many ski slopes until the early 1990s?*
2 *Snowboarding was first an official sport at the 1998 Winter Olympics. How are sports chosen for the Olympics? Can you think of any sports that should be added to or left out of the Olympics? Why?*
3 *Some people travel their whole lives for work or by choice. What would it be like to travel round the world all the time? Would it suit you? Why do people need 'roots'?*

1 READING

A is a common skimming activity. It will help students writing the Reading part of the CAE, the Trinity Controlled Writing ISE III section, IELTS Reading Part 2, and IGCSE Reading Parts 1 and 3.

ER 2 — **Snowboard nirvana** — **Teacher's Guide** — See pages 66–67 SB

1 READING A — Answers

1 The snowboarders travel to Laax Crap based on the advice of the snowboard shop guy in Verbier, Switzerland.
2 They are shocked and awed by its size. Later they said, 'Laax rocks!'
3 Swiss Germans were friendlier and drink about ten times as much.

2 IDIOMS

This activity follows the specifications of the Trinity Language Exam Grades 10 and 11 which call for students to have a good understanding of and ability to use various idioms. The correct use of idioms will help students in CAE as well.

2 IDIOMS — Answers

A 1 snap out of something **2** gain a reputation for **3** give something a go **4** pull someone's leg **5** not judge a book by its cover **6** make a mental note of something

B 1 Why don't you *give* surfing *a go*? You'll like it.
2 Ron quickly *gained a reputation* for drinking too much.
3 You're *pulling my leg*. Nobody can hold their breath for six minutes.
4 I *made a mental note of* what she said in case she denied it later.
5 Hey! *Snap out of it!* You almost stepped in front of that bus.
6 You can't *judge a book by its cover*. He's not as mean as he looks.

3 IN THE POWDER

This section follows the specifications of the Trinity Language Exam Grades 10 and 11, which call for students to be able to understand words in context.

EQ: *What do these words mean? In what other areas do people use jargon? How is jargon a positive and negative thing?*

3 IN THE POWDER — Answers

lift station
Mammoth Mountain (major snowboarding resort)
mountain
(rockin') park
rockin' = cool, very good
park = short for snowboard park, an outdoor complex designed for snowboarders with equipment for doing snowboard tricks
peak
(good) pipe
pipe = half-pipe, a semi-circular slope designed for snowboarding aerial tricks
powder
resort
ride
snowboard mag(azine)
snowboard shop
vertical (metres) = height
Whistler Blackcomb (ski resort)

4 PORTFOLIO WRITING

You should remind the students that both activities are from a first-person point of view. Juz might say, 'We went to Verbier. I couldn't board anywhere, though, because of no snow.'

A Sources:
Snowboarding Skills: The Back to Basic Essentials for All Levels, Cindy Kleh
www.snowboarding.com

B Sources:
The Weblog Handbook, Rebecca Blood
www.blogger.com
www.blogwise.com

5 INTERACTIVE TASK

This activity is directly based on the Interactive Task phase of the Trinity Language Spoken Exam Grades 10 and 11. It would also be useful practice for developing stronger communicative skills and confidence for Parts 3 and 4 of the spoken phase of the CAE exam.

This activity requires students to lead the conversation, which can be a challenge for some students. It is important that you go round the room to monitor the students' communicative leadership in this activity. They should be commenting and asking their partner questions. Silence is not an option; it is up to them to keep the dialogue active and flowing if, and when, their partner begins to falter. They should already have experience with leading the dialogue during **Teamwork,** presentation and **Further Discussion** activities in previous units.

To help in general, you can get students to think of the different brainstorming activities they have encountered so far in the Teamwork activities.

Comment 1: If students seem to have trouble beginning, you can help them by suggesting a few cities: London, Paris, Athens, Madrid, Tokyo, Sydney, Rio De Janeiro. You can further suggest a few activities: going to new restaurants, seeing famous places, doing interesting activities (train rides, parasailing).

EQ: *What would you need to know before going on this journey? How much should you know about a culture before you travel to a country?*

Comment 2: If students are having trouble beginning, you can help them by suggesting they brainstorm what they can learn by experiencing other cultures. Some suggestions to help with tourism: income for tourist industry (types of companies depending on tourism), environmental concerns, obnoxious tourists, social problems (illegal immigration, sex tourism, etc.)

EQ: *What would happen if the tourist trade were suddenly stopped (for example, Asian tsunami, border closures, disease epidemic)? What would happen if no one travelled? Can you learn as much about a culture by watching it on TV or reading about it?*

Unit 15 — Family matters — Teacher's Guide
See pages 68–71 SB, 108 WB

WHAT'S NEW?

Communication Objectives:	Ss will be able to: – use expressions for generalising and conditionals. – use vocabulary, phrases and idioms related to roles in the family.
Educational Objectives:	Ss will analyse the cultural meaning and significance of relationships between parent and child, husband and wife and other family members.
Connected Topics:	– Birth rates – Childcare – Household chores – Modern families – Teenage mothers – The extended family – Working mothers – Generation gap – How to be a parent – Fathers' rights in divorce – International adoptions – Arranged marriages – Work-life balance – Large families
Grammar:	Conditionals
Key Vocabulary:	adopted, desert, in-laws, monk, rota, allocate, domestic bliss, job pool, newlyweds, separated, blood ties, droves, juggle, nuclear family, skyrocket, boast, dual, leeway, onslaught, spark, contentious, extended family, liberation, paternity leave, step-children, corporate jungle, frazzled, lobbying, patriarchal, storm, custody battle, frown upon, maternity leave, pelt, tactics, dangle, high-powered, matriarchal, rabid, thwart, descendant, impresario, mirror, recourse, vicar

The BIG question: WHAT'S A NORMAL FAMILY?

Here students should think about the definition of family and family values. Can any family be considered normal when every family situation is unique?

VIEWPOINT

Facts: The significance of these figures lies in the fact that some countries have a low birth rate and that this affects their ability to maintain their population base. Two babies have to be born in every family to maintain population size. It is possible, however, to offset a declining population with more immigration, which is a common solution for many countries.

Source: UN Department of Economic and Social Affairs, Population Division.

EQ: *How does your country compare? Why do some countries have more or less than two children per family? What might these countries' population size look like in fifty years? How might the following affect the estimate: death rates, immigration / emigration rates, poverty and disease rates? What effect would declining / increasing population size have?*

Quote: Delia Ephron is an American author and screenwriter.

EQ: *How accurate do you think this description of an extended family is? Has the concept of family changed much in your lifetime? Is the changing family a good thing?*

1 WORD POWER

A 1 gets students to consider the different relationships within the family construct. Students will need to present an argument for their choices.

A 2 It is important that students should not be pressed to answer this question if they are reluctant to, as discussion about one's family can be difficult for some.

Unit 15 Teacher's Guide

QSE Advanced — See pages 68–71 SB, 108 WB

---

1 WORD POWER A1 — Sample answers

Top picture: whole picture – extended family; back row from left – cousins, nuclear family, newlyweds; middle row from left – divorced / separated, uncle / aunt, adopted child, cousins, in-laws; front row from left – single-parent family, nuclear family, cousins (young children). Lower picture: newlyweds.

B gets students to practise the generalising phrases in **Language Bank 15**.

1 WORD POWER B — Sample answers

It's usually the case that people have extended family. **Most people say that** the nuclear family is not that common, but I think it is. **Everyone seems to think that** adopted children are not common, but I think they are more common than people think. **I don't know anyone who** hasn't got uncles and aunts.

ARTICLES

'New Wives' Opt For Home Life

This article discusses an apparent trend in Australia and other developed countries. Through much of the last half of the 20th century women have worked hard to ensure equality in all areas of society. One of the most contentious was of course equality in the workplace. For most women this meant showing that they were the equals of men in terms of work output and efficiency. Although a great many women managed to create careers for themselves, many men maintained the gender roles of the previous generation. This meant women had to handle both their jobs and the workload at home. Some of today's new mothers have apparently largely decided to abandon this busy lifestyle for a more traditional one, taking advantage of the maternity leave offered. In the UK mothers are entitled to 26 weeks maternity leave. Many other countries offer up to a year.

EQ: How busy do you think your mothers' lives are today? Do you think the trend in the article is widespread? What is more important – having children or having a career? How long should mothers get for maternity leave? How old should children be before they go into childcare?

Fight for Fathers' Rights

This article discusses the issue of fathers' parental rights after a divorce. The divorce rate in many countries has been increasing. In the UK, for example, nearly half of all marriages end in divorce, and the children are caught up in the process. Numerous studies point out some possible effects to these children's emotional, social and mental development. While many countries grant joint custody, UK courts take the view that children should be given solely to one parent, in most cases the mother. As the article states, some mothers can make it near impossible for fathers to have any visiting rights.

EQ: What is the divorce rate in your country? What are some common reasons for divorce? What effect does divorce have on children? In the US, several states have special marriage contracts which make it extremely difficult to get divorced. What do you think of this idea?

2 READING

A 1 is a skimming activity that will help students with the Use of English section of the CAE exam and the Reading section of IGCSE.

2 READING A1, A2 — Answers

1 Many women don't return to paid work until after the children are at school. A small number stay at home and don't go back to work at all.
2 (Sample answers) If I have children, I will put them before career. / If I have children, I will do things differently from my parents. / If they had families and careers, they would be busy but more content. / If I was an older woman, I would point out that women nowadays only had a choice because of what we did before. / If I was an older woman, I would advise my daughter to take it easier.

B reflects on-the-spot discussions that appear in the Trinity Spoken exam. Encourage the students to use vocabulary from the text and try to be concrete in their arguments.

C 1 This question relates to a type of question in the Trinity exam which requires students to speculate on

Unit 15 — Family matters — Teacher's Guide

See pages 68–71 SB, 108 WB

issues that are not explicitly stated. You may want to help the students by suggesting different areas, such as marriage, children, careers, education, fun.

C 2 This question requires students to speculate on the possible benefits of having children with only one parent. You can make this discussion more controversial by asking students to compare how well single mothers would do compared to single fathers.

3 SPEAK YOUR MIND

This section covers the topics of: the meaning of family, work-life balance, childcare, and fathers' versus mothers' rights.

A EQ: *What does family mean to you? Do couples need children to be a family? Are your views on family similar or different to the rest of society?*

B EQ: *Is it possible to have two working parents and a happy family? Can you have it all? Many people are choosing to work fewer hours to balance their lives. What would life be like only working 20–25 hours?*

C EQ: *How expensive are each of these childcare options? Do mothers get maternity leave in your country? If not, why not? If so, how long do / should they get?*

D EQ: *Why are mothers more likely to be given custody of children? Do fathers make good single parents?*

4 LISTEN *DVD*

This audio clip is from a BBC Northern Ireland radio show. The interviewer is from Northern Ireland and Courtney Cassidy, the teenage mother, is from the English Midlands. The issue of single mothers leads to frequent debates in British society. Conservatives often believe that social constraints have become too lax and welfare only perpetuates the problem. More liberal people see the issue as an unfortunate result of poor education and poverty.

4 LISTEN B — Answers
B 1 media 2 three 3 three 4 planned
  5 sister 6 older 7 seventeen 8 career

5 TEAMWORK

This activity is designed to get students to do two things. Firstly, it will allow them to discuss their families, using vocabulary that will be useful in the exam, but they can talk about friends too if this is easier. Secondly, it will give them the opportunity to discuss generational differences. Overall, this activity will prepare the students to discuss their families in a much more concrete way in the exam.

6 CONTROVERSY

In some developed countries the topic of international adoptions is not even discussed, while in others it seems to be an issue that is strongly debated and even resented. It is clear that the people adopting from other countries show their commitment to the child they are adopting by going to great expense to complete often complicated administrative procedures, but it is hard to deny that these adoptions are often made possible only through a large disparity in the standard of living between the developed country and the developing country. Is it in the best interest of the adopted children to remain in their own country with few future prospects or to be adopted by a foreign family with a better standard of living who can offer them more prospects in life?

Sources:
The Complete Guide to Foreign Adoption, Barbara Bascom
From China with Love: A Long Road to Motherhood, Emily Buchanan
http://international.adoption.com
www.dfes.gov.uk/adoption

EQ: *Do you see these international adoptions as baby-buying? How do you think people in the UK or other developed countries would react if individuals from developing nations came to adopt children from their countries?*

7 PORTFOLIO WRITING

See the Introduction to the Teacher's Guide.

A Sources:
From Family History to Community History, W.T.R. Pryce
www.bbc.co.uk/history/familyhistory
www.thefamilyhistoryproject.co.uk

QSE Advanced See pages 68–71 SB, 108 WB

Unit 15
Teacher's Guide

B Sources:
Wedding Invitations, Announcements, Place Cards, and More, Bette Matthews
www.timesonline.co.uk/section/0,,20989,00.html
http://listings.nytimes.com/classifiedsmarketplace/

8 HOME ECONOMICS *in English* [CLIL]

The family was initially a little wary about sharing their particular situation, as they had encountered problems with media interest in the past. Similarly, Catherine has observed that there are often misperceptions about large families. In her family's case, she says on her website that many people assume that she must be religious, not believe in birth control, or be very rich. None of which is true. With a great sense of humour, she states quite simply that she and her husband Reg simply love children.

There are of course some difficulties in managing a large family. They need an extra-large van to take the whole family. Catherine has to do 12 loads of washing, twice a month, but she does get a lot of help from her husband and children. The children have home schooling, mainly because it is too far to go to the nearest English-speaking school every day. The family is English-speaking, but they live in a mostly French-speaking part of rural Quebec.

Source:
www.plomp.com/mabear

EQ: *How common are large families in your country? How are large families viewed in your country? What would it be like to have 10 brothers or sisters? In what other ways would being part of a large family affect your life? Would you want that many children yourself?*

9 FURTHER DISCUSSION

This section covers household chores, members of extended family, parenting skills, and arranged marriages.

A It might be useful to brainstorm vocabulary relating to household chores on the board, for example, washing up, doing laundry / washing, etc.).

EQ: *How do these compare with people your age? Should parents have to pay children a weekly allowance to help with the chores?*

B Try to get students to compare these relationships with other cultures.

EQ: *Do your grandparents or other relatives live with you? What are the advantages and disadvantages of having extended family nearby? Should extended family members have a say in how your family operates?*

C Ask students to think about parenting as another stage in life.

EQ: *If we expect people to behave in a certain way, should we make sure that parenting is standardised? If parenting were regulated, who should decide how it should be done? Is having children a right or a privilege?*

D Try to get students to think about countries that have arranged marriages and what the cultural reasons behind it might be.

EQ: *Why do people marry? Why might people choose not to marry? Do you think parents know better than their children about whom they should marry?*

10 *Your answer:* WHAT'S A NORMAL FAMILY?

This question tries to get students to address a very basic concept of family. Marriage and family are often seen in ideal terms, whereas in many developed countries they have been evolving. Non-standard families from divorce, separation, single-parenting, adoption, step-children, all seem to be in the increase. The question must then be asked: Is it fair to present the nuclear family of father, mother and 2.4 kids as the model for all families to live up to? Or is it simply another variation of family?

WORKBOOK

1 WORD POWER

This activity will get students practising conditionals as shown in **Language Bank 15.**

1 WORD POWER	Sample answers

1 If I need advice, I ask my parents. 2 If I see her, I will tell her. 3 If I won the lottery, my family would be very excited. 4 If it had been me, I would have

Unit 15 — Family matters — Teacher's Guide

See pages 68–71 SB, 108 WB

gone out of the room. **5** If I'm late, my parents get worried. **6** If you love each other, you will have a happy family. **7** If I was / were a divorced father in Britain, I would try to see my children as often as possible / every day / week. **8** If I had known ten years ago what I know now, I would have become a teacher.

2 WRITING

A You can help students by suggesting they start with themselves, then cover each immediate family member's activities over the past five to ten years.

B You can help students by getting them to think about how life might be different. Ask them to think about: technology, politics, world affairs, economy, natural resources and the environment.

3 SPEAKING STRATEGIES: Emphasising a point

This activity is the one of the basic techniques that students should learn to give better presentations. In trying to emphasise modal verbs and negatives, the students will grasp how the rhythms of speech differ when used for emphasising.

3 SPEAKING STRATEGIES		Sample answers
1 do **not**	2 **never** expect	3 **do** place
4 is **not**	5 should **not**	6 **do** function
7 **would** argue	8 **should** matter	

4 IDIOMS

See the Introduction to the Teacher's Guide.

---

4 IDIOMS — Answers

1 e **2** f **3** c **4** a **5** d **6** b

1 a chip off the old block = exactly like your parent **2** Blood is thicker than water = Family is more important than other people **3** a mummy's boy = spoiled, immature man **4** a family man = man who considers his family very important **5** a ready-made family = step-children through marriage, without giving birth to them or adopting them **6** the black sheep of the family = person in family who is not considered respectable or successful

- *Why are some family members more successful than others?*
  - I think it really depends on whether someone is *the black sheep of the family*. Some people just don't seem to do very well.
  - Well, it depends a lot on the success of parents. Children tend to be *chips off the old block* and follow their parents' lead.
  - I suppose it has to do with how much freedom you have as a child. I'm sure that being *a mummy's boy* would stop you from taking risks.
- *Is it easy to be independent from your parents?*
  - I am not *a mummy's boy*, so yes I am very independent.
  - *Blood is thicker than water*. You have to accept that those ties are there forever.
  - I'm *the black sheep of the family*, so I've always been pretty independent.
- *When do you think people are ready to settle down and have a family?*
  - I'm not sure all men are *family men*. Maybe some will never settle down.
  - When I met my husband he already had children, so I had *a ready-made family*.
  - I'm a *chip off the old block* alright, just like my mum, I want kids right away.

Unit 16 — Let's change the subject!
Teacher's Guide
See pages 72–75 SB, 109 WB

WHAT'S NEW?

Communication Objectives: Ss will be able to:
- use expressions for asserting and signposting phrases for sequencing.
- use vocabulary, phrases and idioms related to school curriculum.

Educational Objectives: Ss will address curriculum planning, theory and implementation.

Connected Topics:
- Student needs, parental wishes and the demands of the state
- Favourite subjects
- Academic versus career-oriented education
- Budget constraints
- History: Who tells the story
- State of UK schools
- Evolution versus creationism
- Primary education
- Single-sex schools
- Physical education
- Experiential learning
- Literature
- Well-rounded education
- Testing
- Life-long learning

Grammar: Gerunds and infinitives

Key Vocabulary:

adolescent	echo	literate
allocate	gap	manipulate
apartheid	gender bias	neglect
autonomy	gender-stereotyping	reconciliation
Bantu	hail	reiterate
brains	heritage	scholar
co-educational	hands-on	specialist
condemn	inclusive	standardised testing
creationism	inherit	unmask
diversity	kayak	
dyslexic	literacy	

The BIG question: ARE STUDENTS LEARNING THE RIGHT THINGS?

The idea is to ask the students to think about what they learn / learnt at school.

VIEWPOINT

Facts: This information comes from the same Programme for International Student Assessment (PISA) study produced by the Organisation for Economic Co-operation and Development. The study looked at 41 countries in 2003, testing more than 4,500 15-year-old students in each country.

EQ: *What can this graph tell us and not tell us? Why do you think Italy has three times fewer university graduates than the USA? Does it matter? How common and how important is a university education in your country? Do you think there is a connection between higher education and economic growth?*

Quote: This anonymous quote presents what might seem an odd dichotomy, but what many academics would probably agree with.

EQ: *Is this statement true? Why / Why not? Do you think you know enough? Or will ever know enough? Is it better to be ignorant?*

1 WORD POWER

A gets students to consider some of the key criteria that teachers consider in preparing courses. As this activity is opinion-based, the following are only suggested answers. If time allows, you may ask students to expand on the reason for their choices.

Unit 16 — Let's change the subject! — Teacher's Guide

See pages 72–75 SB, 109 WB

1 WORD POWER A — Sample answers
I'd put student needs first. The next most important is standardised testing. Equally important is the subject matter. And again the curriculum has to follow government policy. Then I'd put the amount of budget available to allocate, and the classroom resources would come next. And finally, the need to understand adolescent psychology.

B This activity gives practice in using vocabulary from A and the phrases from **Language Bank 16**.

1 WORD POWER B — Sample answers
1 **I would put forward the idea that** the teacher would need to give extra lessons for the dyslexic student.
2 **I am confident that** a newly arrived immigrant student would get English / ESL lessons to allow them keep up with regular classes.
3 **We should realise that** a pregnant student is still a student. She should be treated with the same respect and given the same opportunities to learn as others.
4 **It can be argued that** a new teacher might try many new activities until they find a formula that works.
5 **I can confirm that** excessive budget cuts would make it difficult for teachers to include as many activities as they would like.

C More practice in using vocabulary and **Language Bank 16** phrases while discussing what is taught in schools.

ARTICLES

Teary Asmal Hails New History of South Africa

This article discusses South Africa's educational system. From 1948 to 1990, South Africa had a system of racial segregation called apartheid (Afrikaans word meaning 'separateness'). Although the country is today about 60 per cent black, the white minority had established itself through the colonial rule of first the Dutch and later the British. During apartheid, the South African education system spent about ten per cent on each black child compared to each white child. Moreover, it was nearly impossible for blacks to get a university education.

Similarly, textbooks were written to maintain white supremacy. For instance, it was often wrongly suggested that South Africa was largely uninhabited until the Dutch settlers arrived, but the San and Khoekhoe people lived here at the time of the first Dutch arrivals. Some archaeological evidence shows modern human presence there from 100,000 years ago. Another important issue was the language of classroom instruction. Black students had to be taught in Afrikaans, English and Bantu. Later, it was only English and Afrikaans. It should be noted to students that the use of textbooks and the education system to promote political ends is not isolated to South Africa or the past.

EQ: *Do you think your country's textbooks are written well? How can you tell?*
If people are taught incorrect information in school or textbooks, how would people learn about the truth?
Should it be a crime to provide false information in schools or textbooks? Why / Why not?
Can education solve social or racial problems? Has education contributed to these problems?

Call for 'Fairer' Schools System

This article discusses a number of issues in the UK school system. The first point to be addressed was more findings from the OECD's 2003 PISA study (see **Viewpoint**). UK students had a very poor showing compared to other OECD countries. As the article discusses, the British government wants to create more specialist schools, which are often centred around a particular skill. These schools are required to meet certain UK curriculum standards, but are given flexibility in how they achieve these goals and how much each subject is taught. Critics say that these schools force disadvantaged students into vocational areas when they could be better served by attending an ordinary school.

Similarly, many critics are worried by the increasing number of specialist religious schools and the information taught at them. Among these are the schools run by the Emmanuel Schools Foundation sponsored by multimillionaire car dealer and evangelical Christian, Sir Peter Vardy. These schools teach creationism over the dominant UK curriculum which mandates the teaching of evolution. (See **4 Listen**.)

QSE Advanced See pages 72–75 SB, 109 WB

Unit 16 — Teacher's Guide

EQ: *Is it useful or fair to compare different countries' education systems? What might be some reasons for differences in educational levels?*

2 READING

A is a skimming activity that will help students with the Reading section of the CAE exam.

2 READING A		Answers
1 transformation	2 reconciliation	3 inclusive
4 manipulated	5 neglected	

B requires students to identify specific information, but also to provide the supporting arguments to these ideas.

2 READING B   Answers
1 He talks about hunters and lion to describe history, natural history / cultural connection with traditional way of life.
2 Generally negative – gives statistics plus doesn't have what Finland does, but minister is optimistic at end.
3 Up to the students to decide: (Suggested answers) South Africa: government policy, subject matter, student needs. UK: student needs, government policy, adolescent psychology.

C 1 This question relates to a type of question in the Trinity exam which requires students to speculate on issues that are not explicitly stated. You may want to help the students by directing them to think about concrete examples.

EQ: *Who would you not want to write textbooks on ethics, science, religion, or language?*

C 2 This question requires students to speculate on the students' own education system compared to the UK's. This is highly speculative so there is no definite answer. You could of course ask students to research the matter at PISA's website, but the question is more oriented toward looking critically at their own schools.

3 SPEAK YOUR MIND

This section covers the topics of favourite school subjects, practical / vocational versus academic education, budgetary concerns, and re-writing history.

A EQ: *Why are some classes interesting and others boring? Is it the teacher, the subject, the students, personal taste or something else? Can all subjects be interesting or boring? Why are some students better in some subjects than others? How much is determined by their abilities?*

B EQ: *Are vocational or other practical subjects seen positively in your country? Many countries have a shortage of skilled labour. Why do you think this is? Should governments try to meet the needs of industry when they plan a curriculum? Why / Why not?*

C EQ: *Are any subjects expendable? US schools often cut art or music rather than sports. Is this fair? Who should finance schools: the government, parents, industry or someone else?*
Of the different departments in your country's government, how important is education? Should schools be allowed to go bankrupt? Whose fault is underfunding for schools?

D EQ: *Do you believe everything you read? How would your country's history be different if it were written by other countries?*
Some historians argue that history is simply storytelling. The story tends to change with the teller. Do you agree?
Is history about facts or interpretation of facts? How are we able to tell whether something is an historical fact?

4 LISTEN   DVD

This audio clip comes from an Arizona correspondent for the US National Public Radio (NPR). The debate over creationism and evolution has persisted in the United States since Charles Darwin published his 1859 book, *The Origin of Species.* Although widely accepted in much of the Western world and by many different religions, evolution has been passionately resisted especially in the US Bible Belt – the highly religious area in the Southern United States.

Creationism is the belief that humans and the world were created exactly as was written in the Book of Genesis in the Bible. Many southern states had laws which made it illegal to teach evolution. These laws proved unworkable after the 1925 Scopes 'Monkey' Trial overturned an anti-evolution Tennessee law. By 1958, the National Science Foundation created the Biological Sciences Curriculum Study, which stressed the teaching of evolution in biology classes. Since the 1968 'Epperson versus Arkansas' Supreme Court case, the US Federal Government repealed all creationist laws. Today most US proponents of creationism defend their case on grounds of religious freedom.

4 LISTEN B — Answers
B 1 B   2 A   3 A   4 C

5 TEAMWORK

This activity is an attempt to discuss the practicality of basic education. While most people have an understanding about the need for education, the basic knowledge and skills learnt in school are often so fundamental and useful that they are often overlooked as important.

EQ: *Do you think most people are aware of how or how often they use their school education? Do you think people would be able to learn this basic knowledge and these basic skills without a school education? How do you use your school education?*
How has your school education changed you as a person? How important are teachers in society?

6 CONTROVERSY

Although co-educational classes have existed since medieval times due to the practicality of educating in small communities, these examples were often limited to primary education. Single-sex education has been a staple of the primary, secondary and post-secondary education systems in the UK and many other countries.

An important early factor was the Victorian-era assumption that the genders had considerably different educational requirements according to their societal gender roles. Beyond the primary education of reading writing and arithmetic, women's education was largely geared toward domestic tasks such as preparing food, sewing and taking care of babies. Men were accordingly taught much of everything else. However, as the women's rights movement developed through the later 1800s and early 1900s, women showed they had both the interest and talent for the many different fields of study. School systems begrudgingly had to admit women to secondary and post-secondary schools.

Today, however, much debate centres around how the different sexes may or may not benefit from having members of the opposite sex present. Recent studies out of the United States seem to indicate that there is no statistically significant difference in test performance between pupils in co-ed or single-sex schools. That aside, this does little to change the reality that many students and parents simply prefer single-sex schools for their lack of distraction and freedom from gender stereotypes.

Sources:
Beyond the Great Divide: Co-education or Single-sex?, Judith Gill
Going Co-ed: Women's Experiences in Formerly Men's Colleges and Universities, 1950–2000, Leslie Miller-Bernal
Same, Different, Equal: Rethinking Single-Sex Schooling, Rosemary C. Salomone

EQ: *Which kind of school did you attend? What do you think it would have been like to attend the other type? Do you think the opposite sex is a distraction in your studies? Do you think there is gender-stereotyping of certain school subjects?*

7 PORTFOLIO WRITING

See the Introduction to the Teacher's Guide.

A Sources:
Transformative Learning: Educational Vision for the 21st Century, Thomas Berry
The End of Homework, Etta Kralovec
Does Education Matter?: Myths about Education and Economic Growth, Alison Wolf

B Sources:
www.travelcanada.ca
www.australia.com
www.southafrica.net

8 PHYSICAL EDUCATION *in English* [CLIL]

'Tell me, and I will forget. Show me, and I may remember. Involve me, and I will understand.'

QSE Advanced — See pages 72–75 SB, 109 WB — Unit 16 Teacher's Guide

With this advice, Chinese philosopher Confucius illuminates one of the fundamental debates in educational theory and epistemology (philosophy of knowledge).

Some argue that people learn best through abstract conceptualising. Others believe that we need concrete experiences to learn concepts fully. Outward Bound and the Danmark Tall Ship Maritime School follow this idea. By immersing the learners in the experience, the participants are shown how things work and must develop the necessary skills themselves by completing these tasks themselves. Both programmes have a long track record of success and safety.

EQ: *Would you like to take a course like this? Would you learn as much if you read about the experience in ordinary classes? How might these courses benefit you later in life?*

Although both programmes have exceptional safety records, there always remains a small possibility of injury or loss of life. Do you think teenagers are capable of handling the dangers? Should education contain any risk?

Sources:
Principles and Practice of Informal Education: Learning through Life, Linda Deer Richardson
The Outward Bound Earthbook, L. Crenshaw
www.outwardbound-uk.org
http://soefart.inforce.dk/sw232.asp
www.fuldskruefrem.dk/eng.htm

9 FURTHER DISCUSSION

This section covers the influence of literature, balance of subjects at school, value of tests and exams, and life-long learning.

1 Try to get students to discuss concrete examples of books they have read.

EQ: *What can literature tell you about your culture or your country? How does your country's literature differ from other countries? Have you read literature in other languages?*

2 Try to get students to think about how ideas can come from other areas.

EQ: *What ideas could a scientist get from studying English, Anthropology, Music, History or Law? How might studying Astronomy, History, Religion, Psychology or Political Science affect someone studying English at university? Do you agree that people need a well-rounded education? Are there any problems associated with too much specialisation?*

3 Try to get students to think about the types of tests (government or final exams) they have done at school.

EQ: *Is standardised testing fair? Do tests like the IQ test serve any real purpose? IQ tests and other standardised tests are often criticised for having a cultural or racial bias. What do you think? Is it possible to create a standard test for everyone?*

4 Try to get students to think about whether they see finishing school or university as the end of their education.

EQ: *What would people in older age groups (for example, in their thirties or fifties) want to study? Of the older people you know, are they still trying to learn new things?*

10 *Your answer:* ARE STUDENTS LEARNING THE RIGHT THINGS?

This question tries to get students to think about the essential value of their education. While - students are acutely aware that the law requires them to go to school, not all of them appear to appreciate the need for it. Students should be encouraged to critically analyse what they get from their studies. With either positive or negative opinions, students should be asked to justify their opinions with relevant arguments and examples.

WORKBOOK

1 WORD POWER

This activity will get students practising the signposting phrases for sequencing from **Language Bank 16.** These are suggested answers as the list can differ with different opinions.

Unit 16 — Let's change the subject! — Teacher's Guide
See pages 72–75 SB, 109 WB

1 WORD POWER — Sample answers

I'd put 'gather information about different universities' **first.** The next most important would be 'take a tour or look at web pages of prospective universities'. **Then** I would 'send an application to the university'. **Equally important is** to 'apply for a loan and scholarships'. **This would be followed by** 'apply for accommodation if the university is away from where you live'. **Also,** I would 'see an advisor to discuss which classes you should take'. **And finally,** I would 'register for classes'.

2 USE OF LANGUAGE: Gerund and infinitive

This activity introduces the issue of university tuition fees. The activity is based on an authentic test activity used by the University of Cambridge Local Examinations Syndicate in the CAE and CPE.

2 USE OF LANGUAGE — Answers

1 to lead	2 continuing	3 to pay
4 raising	5 being excluded	6 to learn
7 to end up	8 ensuring	9 to decide
10 to live		

3 WRITING

A Sources:
Fair Wind and Plenty of It: A Modern-Day Tall Ship Adventure, Rigel Crockett
Jolie Brise: A Tall Ship's Tale, Robin Bryer
Tall Ship (video), James Lipscomb, director

B Sources:
Lies My Teacher Told Me: Everything Your American History Textbook Got Wrong, James W. Loewen
Archeology of Knowledge, Michel Foucault
www.csulb.edu/~ttl

4 IDIOMS

See the Introduction to the Teacher's Guide.

4 IDIOMS — Answers

1 f   2 a   3 d   4 e   5 b   6 d

1 to speak your mind = to say what you think openly
2 to broaden your mind = to increase your experience through travel, education, contact with other people, etc.
3 to pick up (a language, a skill) = to acquire / learn (a language, etc.)
4 to set the bar high = to have high standards
5 to have a memory like a sieve = to have a very bad memory, forget everything
6 to pass with flying colours = to succeed with very good mark

Ask students to use the idioms when answering these questions orally. This can be done as pair work or as a class.

- *Should students be allowed to voice all opinions in class?*
  – I think it's important for students to *speak their minds.* It motivates them to participate.
  – I think people can help *broaden their minds* by listening to other opinions.
  – You can *pick up* new information if everyone can honestly give their opinions.
- *Should learning be about memorising things?*
  – Some students like me *have a memory like a sieve,* so it's not fair.
  – Say you take a test based on memorising information, what does it prove? If you *pass* it *with flying colours,* you only prove you have a good memory, not that you understand.
  – If you want to *set the bar high,* you should know everything. Memorising helps.
- *If you could do your studies again, what would you do differently?*
  – I would study more to *pass* everything *with flying colours.*
  – I might have taken many different classes, to *broaden my mind* more.
  – I would have *set my bar* a little higher to get better grades.

Unit 17 — **Adventures in science** — Teacher's Guide — See pages 76–79 SB, 110 WB

WHAT'S NEW?

Communication Objectives: Ss will be able to:
- use expressions for developing an argument and expressions used to introduce assertions.
- use vocabulary, phrases and idioms related to scientific developments.

Educational Objectives: Ss will address recent and future concerns in the different fields of science.

Connected Topics:
- History of the Earth compared to the history of humans
- Recent scientific discoveries
- Ethics in science
- Patents and innovation
- Bionics and robotics
- Genetic engineering
- Mission to Mars
- Future devices
- Human cloning
- Use of chemicals in everyday life
- Nanotechnology
- Biometric scanning
- Large engineering projects
- Non-lethal weapons
- Cold fusion

Key Vocabulary:

AI (artificial intelligence)	genetically modified (GM)	non-lethal
alternative energy	greater good	pave the way
amino acid	herd	pouch
applied science / engineering	holy grail	power-assist v
biodegradable	housings	prototype
bioelectric	human genome	purification
bionics	hybrid	purify
body armour	hydrogen fuel cell	retina
building block	ignite	robotics
bulky	integrate	shrunk
cloning	iris	sought-after
compensate	levitation	submerge
cybernics	limb	superconductor
detectable	macro	suture
displace	mass-produce	tendon
embryonic	material science	unclog
exoskeleton	micro	unveil
fibre	mimic	vapour
forensic science	nano	
genetically altered	nurture	

1 *The BIG question:* IS SCIENCE MAKING LIFE BETTER?

VIEWPOINT

Fact: The age of the universe can be measured by measuring the furthest point of the universe and multiplying this by the rate of expansion from the centre. The age of the Earth can be measured several ways. The most common is the measurement of radioactive decay. Uranium (U) is known to decompose into lead (Pb) isotopes at a given rate. By measuring the amount of lead isotopes, we know how much the uranium has decomposed over time and the age of the Earth. *Homo sapiens sapiens* (modern humans) can be dated by carbon dating of the oldest skulls and by studying the rate of mitochondrial DNA mutations.

Unit 17 — Adventures in science
Teacher's Guide
See pages 76–79 SB, 110 WB

Sources:
http://imagine.gsfc.nasa.gov/docs/science/mysteries_l1/age.html
www.nasa.gov/worldbook/earth_worldbook.html
www.mnh.si.edu/anthro/humanorigins

EQ: *What do you think this comparison says about humans? About the Earth? About the universe? How does this compare to the age of human inventions: Gutenberg's printing press (1452), the first telescope (1608), the first telephone (1870), the first computer (1936)?*

Quote: Dr. Magnus Pyke (1881–1958) was a British scientist known for trying to make science understandable to ordinary people.

EQ: *How accurate do you think this description is? How well does the average person understand the different areas of science today? Is it important for average people to understand science? Why / Why not?*

1 WORD POWER

A 1 gets students to consider some scientific developments that have attracted public interest.

---

1 WORD POWER A1, A2 — **Answers**

1 c   2 b   3 e   4 a   5 d

2 (Sample answers) **As you are probably aware,** magnetic levitation trains can greatly improve the flow of traffic in cities. **As a matter of fact,** bionics might lead to technology that would allow paralysed people to walk. **The simple fact is that** hydrogen fuel cells might be the answer to global warming.

B gets students to practise the phrases for developing an argument in **Language Bank 17**.

---

1 WORD POWER B, C — **Sample answers**

B 1 Consequently, this means that we could cure many types of spinal injuries.
2 It follows logically then that we should be careful about how much of it we eat.
3 From here, we can conclude that we should train more people as engineers than scientists.

C 1 The project for mapping the human genome promises many great benefits from genetically customised drugs to identifying the genes responsible for different diseases.
2 This is the classic debate in psychology. What is the greatest influence: our parents and the way they raise us or the genes passed onto us by our parents? The 1990 Minnesota Study on Twins Reared Apart (*Science.* Bouchard et al) found little difference between identical twins brought up together and brought up apart in terms of temperament, career and leisure interests and social attitudes.

ARTICLES

Bionic Suit Offers Wearers Super Strength

This article discusses Yoshiyuki Sankai's invention of the cybernetic exoskeleton. While his design is quite innovative, the premise behind Sankai's invention has a long history in technologies like deep-sea pressure suits as well as in science fiction. Many have also drawn the comparison between Sankai's cybernetic exoskeleton and the one that appears in the 1986 movie *Aliens,* which features an industrial-sized exoskeleton machine for moving cargo. Although the first commercial suits of Sankai's exoskeleton are expected to cost 11,000 to 15,000 euros, they do seem to be out of the price range of many potential users such as the elderly and disabled.

EQ: *How do humans have artificial components already? Do you see the exoskeleton as an extension of artificial limbs (legs, hands)? Do you think using cybernetic parts will be more common in the future?*

'Spider-Goats' Start Work on Wonder Web

This article discusses the issue of transgenics, the movement of genetic sequences from one organism to another, and bioethics. This particular case is interesting in that the new organism's vast potential to benefit humans has made many people overlook transgenic concerns. Firstly, is this manipulation a violation of that organism's rights? Secondly, it raises the issue of transgenic humans. Scientists have already produced transgenic pigs that can be harvested for organ donations. It only seems a matter of time before humans begin to experiment on human DNA to produce more useful models: better immune systems (like rice needing no pesticide), faster development (like salmon which grow six times faster), or increased muscle mass for athletes (like a mouse with double the muscles).

Some scientists believe that we may soon see organisms that may have the ability to talk and reason like humans, which would cause a serious rethink about the rights of animals and humans. In 1998, Jeremy Rifkin and Stuart Newman applied for a patent in the US for a Humanzee (part human, part chimpanzee) to bring attention to this issue. The patent was denied, but the debate was left unresolved.

EQ: *Do you see transgenic animals as monsters, miracles of science or something else? Are we blurring the lines between species?*
The success of the transgenic spider-goats has led to using the milk of different animals to deliver things like drugs and vaccines. Do you think this is a good thing? What might be the effects if transgenic animals escaped into the wild?

2 READING

A is a skimming activity that will help students with the Use of English section of the CAE exam and the reading section in IGCSE.

2 READING A			Answers
1 both	2 spider-goat	3 HAL 3	4 spider-goat

B reflects the on-the-spot discussions that appear in the Trinity Spoken exam. You should encourage the students to use vocabulary from the text and try to be concrete in their visual descriptions.

C 1 This question relates to a type of question in the Trinity exam which requires students to speculate on issues that are not explicitly stated. You may want to help the students by pointing out examples of industry or areas of government which might need this technology: oil, logistics, tourism, agriculture, forestry, aerospace, firefighting, police or military use.

EQ: *Why might business be interested in cybernetic exoskeletons?*

2 This question requires students to speculate on the ethics of transgenic spider-goats. You can give students some help by asking students to give the positive (easy to produce, can be mass produced, can be used to help police, industry) and negative (long-term, unknown health effects to goats and offspring, creating organisms for profit and human benefit) aspects.

EQ: *Do the positive aspects outweigh the negative?*

3 SPEAK YOUR MIND

This section covers the topics of benefits and drawbacks to science, important discoveries (past and future), the ethics of science, and medicine and patenting scientific discoveries.

A EQ: *Give five examples of each. How do you think the public sees scientists (caring / uncaring, analytical / illogical, emotional / unemotional, funny / boring)? Do you think the public generally trusts scientists? Think about the different fields: biologist, nuclear physicist, geneticist or chemist?*

B EQ: *How would your life be different without these inventions? What do you think it takes to make these discoveries? Do you think there are too many technological or scientific discoveries for people to keep up with? Is it possible to learn everything about the world?*

C EQ: *What are the positive and negative aspects of genetic engineering? What are some 'wonders of nature' – unique abilities among plants and animals? Give some examples. How might these special genes help other plants, animals or even humans? Why / Why not?*
Why is it alright to do transgenic work on animals and not on humans? Will we see transgenic humans in our lifetime? Will we need to reconsider what we think of as normal? What would happen if scientists developed animals with human-like intellect, ability to talk or to think?

D EQ: *Some patented medicines (AIDS medicines) could save countless lives in the developing world, but*

are too expensive. Should countries be allowed to override patent law in these cases?
Is it right to patent parts of the human gene? Do patents help or harm innovation? Do you think patent holders (medicine or software) are viewed as innovators who should be rewarded, exploiters of a common good, or something else?

4 WATCH AND LISTEN   DVD

This video clip is from the European Space Agency, which provides public access to media coverage of its space and technology programmes. The video contains an interview with Heiner Klinkrad, an ESA expert on space debris. He explains the problems posed by space debris, which looks set to be an increasing problem for future space exploration. The implications of this problem could be very far-reaching, including an end to all space exploration.

Note: ESA is pronounced [ˈiːsæ].

> **4 WATCH AND LISTEN B, C**   **Answers**
>
> **B** Satellites can run out of energy or fall out of orbit. Fuel tanks are explosive and don't always fall back to Earth. Astronauts could easily be killed in space by this debris, and can create it if they are not careful.
>
> **C 1** 9,500 **2** almost 200 **3** hit by a sphere 1.2 cm in diameter, caused a lot of damage

D You can encourage students to speculate on the impact an end to space exploration would have on a space scientist.

E EQ: *Would you like to travel in space? Why / Why not? Have we really learnt anything valuable from sending people into space?*

5 TEAMWORK

This activity is designed to get students thinking about how scientists, inventors and businesses might approach developing new technology or conducting research. Students should be encouraged to explore any ideas, even wacky ones. Some of the most innovative products were not understood for their potential before they became better known.

To expand the discussion, you can also brainstorm alternative energies before the students address the subject: wind power, tidal power, biomass (agricultural waste, peat), hydroelectric energy, biodiesel. And ask the questions: *Which of these are used to power consumer products today? Which could be used in the future?*

Sources:
Why didn't I think of that?: Bizarre Origins of Ingenious Inventions We Couldn't Live Without, Allyan Freeman
Renewable Energy, Godfrey Boyle
http://inventors.about.com/library/bl/bl12.htm

6 CONTROVERSY

The public have been aware of the prospect of human cloning since scientists announced the birth of Dolly the sheep in 1996. One important downside to cloning is that all cells have telomeres, a sequence of DNA that limits the number of cell divisions. It is widely believed that the length of telomeres indicates the age of a cell, and therefore the organism. Telomeres tend to shrink over time so the number of cell divisions remaining, and therefore the years remaining, continues to grow smaller. Some scientists believe that Dolly's much shorter telomeres indicated that she might have been physically much older than her six-year lifespan. Although it cannot be proved conclusively, her arthritis and early death from a lung infection fit the pattern for much older sheep. Theoretically, a baby born from the DNA of a 70 year-old man may share the life expectancy of a 70-year old.

Sources:
A Clone of Your Own?: The Science and Ethics of Cloning, Arlene Judith Klotzko
Whose View of Life?: Embryos, Cloning and Stem Cells, Jane Maienschein
www.sciencemuseum.org.uk/antenna/dolly/index.asp
www.globalchange.com/sciencestop.html

EQ: *What do you think of human cloning? Would you want to be cloned? Why do you think people are horrified by human cloning, but not animal* cloning? How does religion affect the debate over cloning?

7 PORTFOLIO WRITING

See the Introduction to the Teacher's Guide.

A Sources:
The Elements: A Very Short Introduction, Philip Ball
www.chm.bris.ac.uk/webprojects2002/dean/u.htm
http://c3.org/
http://en.wikipedia.org/wiki/Nitrogen

B Sources:
Some sites have ideas about scientific developments that students can then research further:
www.sciencemap.org
www.newscientist.org
www.seedmagazine.com
http://web.mit.edu/newsoffice/research
http://news-service.stanford.edu
http://news.bbc.co.uk

8 ENGINEERING *in English* [CLIL]

While some fields of engineering, such as software engineering, have existed for relatively short periods, humans have used the principles of nature in practical applications since ancient times. From at least 3000 BC, early humans were already using levers and smelting metals and developing large-scale projects like open-pit mining. The Greeks developed the ratchet and the water wheel. The Romans built roads, aqueducts and sewage systems. They also concentrated a lot of their engineering skills on military uses, such as building fortresses and weapons. These ties between the military and engineering continue to this day.

While this activity includes one example relating to military use, there are thousands of examples of everyday technology that originally had military or aerospace applications. These include GPS, smoke detectors, satellite dishes and zips. The largest advances of engineering, however, came as a result of the scientific revolution and the Industrial Revolution. Many of the engineering work done today follows in this line. Large-scale projects like the Three Gorges Dam are designed to benefit the needs of industry.

In many cases, it does seem that modern engineering attempts to do what people often thought was impossible. Both nanobots and the Three Gorges Dam would have been considered impossible only a few decades ago.

EQ: *Can you see any dangers of using nanobots for medical purposes?*
Do these security measures or any others affect personal freedom?
New evidence suggests that hydroelectric dams are as polluting as coal-burning electricity power stations. Given this and the effect on fish and people along the dam, should we still use hydroelectricity? Why do you think countries are always interested in building the 'biggest __ in the world'?
Should microwave guns be used on people?

Sources:
www.crnano.org
www.biometrics.org
www.wcsscience.com/giant/dam.html
www.au.af.mil/au/awc/awcgate/cst/csat11.pdf

9 FURTHER DISCUSSION

This section covers types of engineering, similarities between animals and humans, forensic science, and how things work.

A Try to get students to think about how different research is from practical applications.

EQ: *What large engineering projects have there been in your country? How important has engineering been to your country's development? Do you have enough engineers in your country?*

B EQ: *Koko the gorilla can use over a thousand signs and understands 2,000 words of spoken English. She has a tested IQ of 75–95 (100 is normal human intelligence). (See: www.koko.org) Does this change your view of animal intelligence? Why do humans place ourselves as superior to animals? Are we? Think about compassion / intolerance, intelligence, ability to create / destroy, or use of resources. If animals are intelligent and can feel emotion and pain, is it right to do experiments on them?*

C Try to get students to think about the popularity of criminal investigations on television and in movies.

Unit 17 — Adventures in science — Teacher's Guide

See pages 76–79 SB, 110 WB

EQ: *Name some high profile crimes or unsolved crimes in your country. What do you think really happened? How would a forensic scientist try to solve the crime? Do you see forensic science as true science?*

D Try to get students to think about the complexities of things we often take for granted.

EQ: *If you had to make these products yourself, could you? Imagine what your life would be like if you had to produce everything: food, shelter, fuel or soap.*

10 Your answer: IS SCIENCE MAKING LIFE BETTER?

This question tries to get students to address the utility of science. The way that science and scientists focus on the rational is often seen by the public as being more focused on the process than on people. It may be worth asking whether this is a fair criticism given the difference between large engineering projects and cures for diseases compared to some genetic engineering and nuclear weapons.

EG: *Do you think scientists are looking at the bigger picture or at the wrong picture? Do the benefits of advances in science outweigh the drawbacks?*

WORKBOOK

1 WORD POWER

This activity will get students practising the phrases for developing an argument from **Language Bank 17**. The phrases are interchangeable, so students could use any of them.

1 WORD POWER	Answers
0 It follows logically then that…	(e)
1 Consequently, this means that…	(c)
2 From here we can conclude that…	(a)
3 Clearly then, this indicates that…	(b)
4 It follows logically then that…	(d)

2 WRITING

A Sources:
A Short History of Nearly Everything, Bill Bryson
www.newscientist.com
www.sciencemuseum.org.uk
www.sciencedaily.com

B Sources:
http://ghr.nlm.nih.gov/ghr/page/Home
www.foodfuture.org.uk
www.who.int/foodsafety/biotech/en
stemcells.nih.gov/index.asp
www.genengnews.com

3 SPEAKING STRATEGIES: Key words

This activity is the one of the basic techniques that students should learn to give better presentations. In trying to summarise arguments in two to three words, they will learn to memorise their presentations and produce better visuals. The following are suggested answers, but other answers may be as acceptable.

3 SPEAKING STRATEGIES	Sample answers

1 The initial experiment. 2 What went wrong.
3 The research continues. 4 300 scientific papers.
5 Evidence of nuclear reactions. 6 Problems remain.

4 IDIOMS

See the Introduction to the Teacher's Guide.

4 IDIOMS				Answers
1 c	2 a	3 d	4 e	5 b

1 to break new ground = to do something other people have not done before **2** to pick your brains = to get information from someone and use it to your own advantage **3** to hit the headlines = to be in the news (literally on the front page of the newspapers) **4** to loom large on the horizon = to appear imminent, likely **5** to be a cornerstone = to be the basis of, be an essential part of

Ask students to use the idioms when answering these questions orally. This can be done as pair work or as a class.

- *Why do you think people know so little about cutting edge research?*
  - I think most research doesn't *hit the headlines* unless it is something that will affect a large number of people.
  - Ordinary, everyday research is *the cornerstone* of science. It just doesn't get reported.
  - I think the mainstream press is not interested in *picking* scientists' *brains* unless it is about genetics or weapons.

- *Should scientific research only be done for profit?*
  - I think you are more likely to *break new ground* when people are motivated by profit.
  - I can't see why we can't *pick* the scientists' *brains* about this.

- *Will humans travel to Mars in your lifetime?*
  - It is definitely *looming on the horizon*.
  - Politicians like to talk about travelling to Mars to *hit the headlines,* but I don't think it will happen.
  - I think Mars Express is intended *to be the cornerstone* of a future European mission to Mars.

Unit 18 — The company we keep — Teacher's Guide
See pages 80–83 SB, 111 WB

WHAT'S NEW?

Communication Objectives:	Ss will be able to: – use expressions used to contradict and summarising information, ideas and arguments. – use vocabulary, phrases and idioms related to social issues.
Educational Objectives:	Ss will address social problems that governments must deal with for the benefit its citizens.
Connected Topics:	– Immigration and refugees – Substance abuse – Crime – Social integration – Healthcare reform – Slums and ghettos – Homelessness – Public transport – Job creation – Affordable housing
Grammar:	Word forms Reported speech Idioms
Key Vocabulary:	assimilate homelessness sciatica audit *n* hostel social integration consultant illegal immigration squat cope imminent statutory crush intolerance stem from digital divide job creation substance abuse drug rehabilitation centre on sufferance utterly era prolapsed disc vandalism *favela* rough sleeper gap scandalous

The BIG question: ARE WE DOING ENOUGH TO HELP?

VIEWPOINT

Facts: These two sets of information are completely unrelated. They were meant to introduce different social issues. It may be worth pointing this out to students in case there may be any possible misunderstanding.

The refugee information comes from the Office of the United Nations High Commissioner for Refugees. Established in 1951 by the Convention relating to the Status of Refugees, the UNHCR has helped over fifty million people.

Source:
www.unhcr.org/cgi-bin/texis/vtx/home

EQ: *Some famous refugees include Albert Einstein, Victor Hugo, Madeleine Albright, Claude Lévi-Strauss, Czeslaw Milosz, Vladimir Nabokov, Haing Ngor, Sitting Bull and Maria von Trapp. Does knowing this change your opinion of refugees? Why do you think negative opinions of refugees persist in developed countries? How does the UN help refugees?*

The crime statistics are from the UK Home Office, which reports that overall crimes have declined from a peak in 1995 of nearly 20 million crimes.

Source:
www.crimestatistics.org.uk/output/Page54.asp

EQ: *Although overall crime appears to have declined since the 1990s, media coverage of crime has increased substantially. Do you think we worry too much about crime? Do people always report crime? If not, why not?*

Quotes: Aristotle (384–322 BC) was an influential Greek philosopher known for his analytical way of studying the natural world.

EQ: *Is this statement true? How are these things connected? Is there much poverty in your country? Do you think most people worry about poverty, or world poverty in general? Is there a gap between poor and rich?*

QSE Advanced

See pages 80–83 SB, 111 WB

Unit 18
Teacher's Guide

John Florence Sullivan – 'Fred Allen' (1894–1956) was an American comedian known for his radio programmes in the 1940s.

EQ: *Why is this funny? Do you think people should feel regret about being human?*

Photos: The photos show a refugee and her child in a refugee camp, and some illegal immigrants who have been stopped by police.

1 WORD POWER

A 1 gets students to consider some of the key social issues facing governments today. It is up to students to decide on the order of importance and whether they are social or individual problems.

---

1 WORD POWER B   **Sample answers**

B Summarising – To sum up, I think the government is doing a great job with job creation. / **For this reason,** I feel social integration is working. / **As I have already pointed out,** we have less homelessness today.
Contradicting – Frankly, I can't see it. Healthcare is worse today than a decade ago. / **Do you honestly think so?** Illegal immigration is continuing to rise. / **In actual fact, it's just the opposite.** Substance abuse is increasing every year.

C 1 This addresses the issue in many Western countries about who should pay for healthcare and how well healthcare is run. The US private healthcare model is often shown as a model of efficiency, but 47 million people do not have health insurance and many more are underinsured.
2 Students should be encouraged to decide whether they see drug addicts as criminals or victims of an illness. Many people continue to blame the individual for their drug addiction and would therefore not like to see their tax money being spent on helping them.
3 This is a touchy issue that should be handled with some discretion. Students should be encouraged to question their own feelings on the matter. However, it may be easier to allow them to explore the issue from the point of view of people around them.

ARTICLES
380,000 Homeless 'Going Unrecorded'

In the UK, especially in the urban areas around London and Manchester there is a chronic shortage of housing. In the London area many people come from other parts of Britain and abroad to look for work. As people have moved into the region, the cost of buying and renting housing has soared, making the London area one of the most expensive places to live in the world. In many cases this has priced many low-paid workers out of the housing market. Add this to the social problems, such as unemployment and family breakdown, as mentioned in the article, and it is not difficult to see why there are so many people living without a fixed address.

EQ: *Why do you think so many people in Britain are homeless? Do you think the situation is the same in your country? What can be done about it?*

Ex-Soldier Told of 70-Week Wait to See Neurologist

This article discusses one of the worst examples of inefficiency in the UK healthcare system. This case was in Scotland, where since devolution the Scottish government has taken control of many aspects of government including healthcare (see Unit 9, Exercise 8). This has meant making a lot of difficult choices to balance the budget, including closing many clinics and hospitals. Some critics believe the Scottish government has in fact made too many cuts, and there have been several cases of pregnant women giving birth on their way to the nearest hospitals over 50 km away. In the rest of Britain, some people also often have to wait a long time for medical treatment.

EQ: *Does your country have public or private healthcare? Which is better? Why? Do you think governments make a good job of running healthcare systems?*

2 READING

A is a skimming activity that will help students with the Use of English section of the CAE exam and the Reading section of the IGCSE.

Unit 18 — The company we keep — Teacher's Guide

See pages 80–83 SB, 111 WB

2 READING A — Answers
1 e 2 c 3 a 4 d 5 b

B requires students to identify specific information, but also to provide the supporting arguments to these ideas.

2 READING B — Answers
B 1 The hidden homeless are hidden because they are not recorded in official statistics as homeless. They are homeless because they do not have a permanent place to live that they can call 'home'.
2 Rough sleepers are people who sleep rough on the street.
3 Here *see* means to have a meeting with; *stem (from)* means to come / originate from; *face* means to confront something or someone, usually a challenge.

C It may be useful to have students work in pairs for question C.
1 This question gives students a chance to practise reported speech. They can make up a story here.
2 Students can role-play this situation, one of them taking the role of Graeme Martin and the other, the role of someone who is one of the hidden homeless.

D 1 This question relates to a type of question in the Trinity exam which requires students to speculate on issues that are not explicitly stated. You may want to help the students by asking them to think about concrete examples.

EQ: *Where would you get food, have a shower or sleep?*

2 This question requires students to make the kind of decisions that people administering a healthcare system must make. Ask students to look at the issue two ways: what if there was no money for expensive treatments, or what if someone close to you was seriously ill?

3 SPEAK YOUR MIND

This section covers the topics of: social responsibility, homelessness, and universal healthcare.

A EQ: *How does your government try to help with social problems? Are they doing a good job? Are they doing enough?*

B EQ: *How big a problem is homelessness in your country? Why? Do you think the hidden homeless are as badly off as rough sleepers? Why / Why not? Should all forms of begging be against the law? Why / Why not?*

C EQ: *How good is your healthcare system? Why? How should the government try to improve healthcare? Do you think doctors, nurses, paramedics and hospital support staff are: not well enough paid, paid enough, paid more than enough? Why?*

4 LISTEN — DVD

This audio clip comes from Interworld Radio, a non-profit organisation that provides free access to radio programmes from around the world. The aim is to give people an international perspective on issues and to stimulate debate on issues relating to different countries. The clip deals with the issue of bridging the digital divide in the *favelas* (slums) of Brazil. There is a significant gap between the rich and poor in Brazil, which means that the poor are often lost or forgotten when it comes to important new advances such as the internet and computers. As a result, a community action group called the Committee to Democratise Information Technology was set up by local *favela* residents to give *favela* dwellers with IT education and access to the internet in the hope of providing employment opportunities. This programme has been so successful that it has spread to many neighbouring countries as well.

4 LISTEN B — Answers
True: They have computer education programmes. They use the internet.

4 LISTEN C — Answers
1 Over one million
2 children's party videos
3 75,000 young people
4 Colombia, Uruguay, Mexico

E You can also encourage students to discuss other issues where people take action themselves rather than wait for the government to do it for them. You can introduce vocabulary such as *grassroots* and *people power*.

5 TEAMWORK

This activity is an attempt to discuss a difficult aspect of globalisation. As companies seek to cut costs and protect their profits, they often have to make difficult decisions such as relocating jobs or production facilities. Relocating to another country can bring advantages from cheaper labour costs to lower business tax rates. For the community losing a large employer, the results can be devastating, especially in small communities with limited employment opportunities. Unemployment rates rise and people move away to look for work. Poverty and crime rates also begin to increase. Like most problems, there are some limited solutions. This activity tries to address some of the more common ones. It may be helpful to get students to discuss any concrete examples they have heard of.

EQ: *How well do small, medium-sized or large communities cope with a loss of a large employer? Do you think globalisation has helped or hurt your country? Why?*
Do you agree that the government should spend money to attract new jobs to an area? Should these be public works projects?

6 CONTROVERSY

Immigration is a major issue for any country. Although it is very complex because each immigrant's case must be looked at individually, it is common for the public, the media and conservative political groups to put all immigrants together as one group. This is often the case where communities have unemployment rates higher than the national average. When people feel their jobs are threatened, they often tend to react negatively towards newcomers, feeling that immigrants are taking away jobs from locals. The reality in many cases is that most immigrants, through necessity, lack of education or not having their qualifications recognised abroad take jobs that many locals would not choose to do. These are often low-paid manual labour jobs. In some countries, entire industries would not be able to operate without immigrant workers, for example, intensive agriculture where fruit or vegetables are picked by hand.

EQ: *Do you see immigration as a positive or negative thing? What do immigrants bring to a country? Many conservative groups like to blame immigrants for many social problems such as crime. What do you think of this?*

7 PORTFOLIO WRITING

See the Introduction to the Teacher's Guide.

A Sources:
Global Report on Crime and Justice, Centre for International Crime Prevention
www.interpol.int, www.uncjin.org/Statistics/statistics.html

B Sources:
Critical Challenges for Healthcare Reform in Europe, Richard Saltman
www.scottish.parliament.uk/home.htm,
www.therightssite.org.uk

8 SOCIAL STUDIES *in English* [CLIL]

Chicago is the third largest city in the United States and the largest city in the state of Illinois. It has had a unique history in US history, serving as the main junction point between the western and eastern US. Most rail lines and truck routes travel through Chicago, making it an important commercial hub.

There has also been a long history of social and political challenges, from racial integration and unrest to organised crime. The city and suburbs of Greater Chicago continue to be divided along racial lines. A case in point is the two areas of Highland Park and Englewood. Highland Park has wealthy celebrity residents like sports star Michael Jordan, while Englewood was the scene of race riots in the 1950s and 1960s.

Sweden generally sees itself to be a model of social integration, priding itself on its social equality and finding consensus among its citizens. The reality is that immigrants have often found themselves socially isolated on the outskirts of larger urban communities. Although, compared to Chicago, the welfare state in Sweden has managed to limit the gap between rich and poor in Stockholm, economic opportunities can still be limited for many immigrants. Many Swedes complain of new Swedish

Unit 18 — The company we keep — Teacher's Guide

See pages 80–83 SB, 111 WB

dialects (such as Rinkeby Swedish) developing, as the socially isolated immigrants begin peppering broken Swedish with words from different languages.

Notes:
- The Fittja statistics include children of non-Swedes born in Sweden. Ethnic Swedes make up only 12 per cent.
- For the state of Illinois there are 722 vehicles per 1,000 people.
- The urban density given is for the city of Chicago.
- Violent crime includes homicide, rape, robbery and assault.

EQ: *How do these cities compare to communities in your country? What solutions to social and racial integration would you suggest? What would life be like in Englewood or Fittja? Highland Park or Ostermalm? How important is it to have parks and lakes or rivers in a city? What effect does population density have on a community?*

9 FURTHER DISCUSSION

This section covers types of social issues in politics, crime, city planning and transport, immigrants, and housing.

A Ask students to discuss concrete examples of issues that are currently in the news.

EQ: *How do social issues benefit and hurt politicians? How much real control do politicians and the government have over social problems?*

B Try to get students to think about crime on a local level.

EQ: *Do you know anyone who has been a victim of crime? How does crime affect people? Do you think the police are doing a good job managing crime in your community?*

C Students should think about different types of transport in their area.

EQ: *How important is public transport in your community or country? How good is it? Who uses it? Is there any way of getting people out of their cars and reducing car use?*

D Try to get students to think about immigration in their community.

EQ: *What effect does immigration to Western countries have on the countries that the immigrants leave? What would it be like to emigrate to another country?*

E You can make this question more concrete by getting students to look at the classified ads of newspapers. Look at house prices or rents and work out how much they would need to pay for mortgage or rent and compare this with the minimum wage in your country.

EQ: *If there is not enough affordable housing available, what options do people have?*

10 *Your answer:* ARE WE DOING ENOUGH TO HELP?

This question tries to get students to think about society and the individual's role in solving society's problems. Students should be encouraged to make a critical assessment of their government's policies for dealing with the social problems mentioned in the unit. With either positive or negative opinions, students should be asked to justify their opinions with relevant arguments and examples.

WORKBOOK

1 WORD POWER

This activity will get students practising new vocabulary in the unit and expressions to contradict from **Language Bank 18.** Sample answers are given, but there may be different opinions.

> **1 WORD POWER** — **Sample answers**
>
> **1** *Intolerance towards foreigners* is the root cause of anti-immigration feelings. – **Do you honestly think so?** I think it is much more complex. **2** *Two-tiered healthcare, for those who can and can't afford to pay* is the way of the future. – **Not if we consider that** this same system has led to big problems in the United States. Many people think the system there is not working there. **3** *Vandalism* only occurs in deprived areas. – **I would argue that it's actually** happening in all areas of the community. **4** *Substance abuse* can lead to involvement with crime. – **In actual fact, it's just the opposite.** It's involvement with criminals selling the drugs that leads to the abuse. **5** Young

QSE Advanced — See pages 80–83 SB, 111 WB — **Teacher's Guide**

people move to large cities to find work but many end up *sleeping rough*. – **Come on, you have to admit** that many of those people don't really want to have a job and responsibilities. **6** The government isn't doing enough to stop *illegal immigration*. – **Frankly, I can't see it.** They spent millions on new border security.

2 USE OF LANGUAGE: Word forms

This activity introduces the issue of anti-immigration policies in different countries. The activity is based on an activity type for the CAE and CPE exams.

2 USE OF LANGUAGE		Answers
1 remains	2 immigration	3 employment
4 falling	5 crashing	6 nationality
7 dangerous	8 shortage	

3 WRITING

A Sources:
Getting By: Begging, Rough Sleeping and the Big Issue in Glasgow and Edinburgh, Suzanne Fitzpatrick
Sleeping Rough Stories of the Night, Christina Dunhill
www.homeless.org.uk

B Sources:
Class and schools: Using Social, Economic and Educational Reform to Close the Black-White Achievement Gap, Richard Rothstein
Effective School Intervention, Enid Lee
Beyond Heroes and Holidays, Natalie Rathvon
http://europa.eu.int/comm/employment_social/soc-prot/index_en.htm

4 IDIOMS

See the Introduction to the Teacher's Guide.

4 IDIOMS					Answers
1 b	2 d	3 e	4 a	5 f	6 c

1 to tighten our belts = to make economies to save money **2** out of the public purse = from public or government funds **3** to throw the book at = to punish severely **4** to fight a losing battle = to try to do / change something but failing **5** to take the drastic step of = to perform a very strong or extreme action **6** to kick the habit = to cure / stop the addiction

Ask students to use the idioms when answering these questions orally. This can be done as pair work or as a class.

- *Should drug users be convicted or treated for their crime?*
  – I think we *are fighting a losing battle against* drugs. It would be better to provide more treatment facilities.
  – I think we need to *take the drastic step of* decriminalising some drugs.
  – It's too hard for some drug users to *kick the habit.* They should go to jail where they can't get drugs.
- *Are immigrants given fair treatment?*
  – Many think we pay too much *out of the public purse* to help them.
  – If you want my opinion, we are *fighting a losing battle against* illegal immigration.
  – If you ask me, they should *throw the book at* illegal immigrants.
- *What would you change about your government's social policies?*
  – I think we should *tighten our belts.* Too much money is spent on frivolous projects.
  – I would take *the drastic step of* making healthcare a legal right.
  – I would make sure that if something is *paid for out of the public purse,* it is something we really need.

Unit 19 — Stressed out! — Teacher's Guide
See pages 84–87 SB, 112 WB

WHAT'S NEW?

Communication Objectives:	Ss will be able to: – use expressions for minimising and the language of empathy and sympathy. – use vocabulary, phrases and idioms related to stress management.
Educational Objectives:	Ss will address sources of stress and assess techniques for coping with stress.
Connected Topics:	– Stressed teenagers – Stress reduction – Post-traumatic stress disorder – Watching fish – Laughing clubs – Phobias – Drugs and alternative treatments – Physical symptoms
Grammar:	Idioms
Key Vocabulary:	at odds with, beneficial, bid, chair(person), contagious, creep back up, criss-cross v, dread, fare better, flutter, frail, giggle v, immune system, impaired, incentive, induce, industrial tribunal, medication, migraine, pebble, pet v, phobia, placebo, post-traumatic stress disorder, pounding the treadmill, red-eye flight, regime, stone (weight 14 pounds), stress-busting, stroke, supraventricular tachycardia, switching off, thyroid, working out

The BIG question: ARE WE SERIOUSLY STRESSED?

VIEWPOINT

Facts: The statistics are from an annual US school survey, *The National Survey of American Attitudes Substance Abuse VIII: Teens and Parents,* conducted by The National Center on Addiction and Substance Abuse (CASA). The three main factors leading to teenage use of drugs and alcohol are high stress, frequent boredom and more than $25 a week spending money.

Source: http://alcoholism.about.com/cs/teens/a/blcasa030819.htm, www.casa.org

EQ: *Why do you think this is the case? Based on your own observations, is this true? Do you know any high stress teens? What causes their stress? How do they cope with this stress?*

There are many factors which can trigger depression: genetic predisposition, environment, medical problems, certain thinking patterns and stressful events in life. About 80 per cent of those who try to get treatment will get better.

EQ: *What kinds of things make you depressed or unhappy? What do you think could cause long-term depression? What do you think life would be like if you were depressed for long periods?*

Quotes: Natalie Goldberg (born 1948) is an American author known for teaching writing through Zen.

EQ: *Why is stress an ignorant state? Do you agree with the quote? Is the stress you feel in proportion to the level of emergency?*

Charles Schulz (1922–2000) was the American cartoonist known for the Peanuts comic strip.

QSE Advanced See pages 84–87 SB, 112 WB Unit 19 Teacher's Guide

EQ: *What is the meaning of this philosophy? Is it meant to be serious or humorous? Why? What do you think of the Peanuts comic strip?*

Cartoons: The pictures are of:
– a patient about to receive some bad news
– a scary plane flight
– giving a speech in public
According to the *Book of Lists,* fear of public speaking ranks number one in fears, even over fear of death or disease.

1 WORD POWER

A 1 is based on a CAE speaking test activity that gets students to comment on pictures.

EQ: *How are these situations the same or different? Have you ever experienced any of these situations? If so, what was your reaction?*

A 2 gives students an opportunity to practise the language of empathy and sympathy in **Language Bank 19.**

1 WORD POWER A2	Sample answers
I know exactly how you feel you feel. I've had my appendix out. It was scary going into the operating theatre. / **I can imagine** what that flight must have been like. I've flown through rough weather too. / **I know exactly how you must feel**. I hate speaking in front of an audience.	

B gets students to analyse the efficacy of some common stress-reducing methods.

1 WORD POWER C	Sample answers
1 Some events which can cause post-traumatic stress disorder: military combat, natural disasters, car accident, near-death experiences or violent personal assaults like rape.
2 When overly stressed, people become burnt out. They can develop depression over feelings of not being able to cope.	

ARTICLES
Blair the Fitness Fan

This article discusses Tony Blair's health and stress-reducing techniques. He was diagnosed with supraventricular tachycardia (SVT). SVT is a heart condition where the upper chambers of the heart (the atria) can be up to 250 times a minute or faster and which can be corrected by surgery or use of a pacemaker. Politics can be one of the most stressful occupations since it involves working long days, always being in the public eye and doing many public speaking engagements.

EQ: *How stressful do you think a politician's life is? What would a day in the life of the British Prime Minister be like? Is bad health linked to stressful occupations?*

Watching Fish Found to Ease Human Stress

This article discusses a recent scientific study that looked at the relationship between stress and watching fish. There is the old saying that a dog is a man's best friend and in terms of stress they are just that. Petting an animal can lower blood pressure and heart rate. A New York City Hospital study found that heart patients were more likely to survive their first year after surgery if they owned a pet. The study of fish and stress-reduction is more recent. Fish have shown to calm children with Attention Deficit Disorder (ADD). Alzheimer patients have also found some benefit. Herbert Benson's Relaxation theory supposes four conditions for relaxation: the presence of an object to focus on, a passive attitude, a quiet environment and a comfortable position, which may be the reasons why watching fish helps reduce stress.

EQ: *Do you have a pet? Do you think pets reduce stress? Do you think some pets reduce stress more than others? Why / Why not?*

2 READING

A is a skimming activity that will help students with the Use of English section of the CAE exam and the Reading section of the IGCSE.

2 READING A				Answers
1 frail	2 procedure	3 random	4 bid	5 proven

B 1 This question relates to a type of question in the Trinity exam which requires students to speculate and

Unit 19 — Stressed out! — Teacher's Guide

See pages 84–87 SB, 112 WB

conclude on the unstated feelings of people. Students should provide some basis for their responses.

> **2 READING B2** — *Sample answers*
>
> People were stressed by reading out loud. Then, blood pressure was measured to see if the presence of fish in an aquarium reduced stress. It did.

C 1 You may want to help the students by pointing out other techniques covered in **Word Power**.

C 2 This question requires students to speculate on the ethics of keeping pets for supposedly selfish reasons. You can give students some help by asking students to look at the interaction between animals and humans, and whether these might change given the circumstances suggested.

3 SPEAK YOUR MIND

This section covers the topics of stress as a natural function of the body, personal stress and stressful occupations, teenage stress, and owning pets.

A EQ: *Why do you think we are equipped to feel stress? Do you think it would be helpful or harmful to have no stress at all in your body?*

B EQ: *If you were overstressed, which treatments for stress would you try? Why do some people find some relaxation techniques helpful, but others do not? What would you consider the ten most stressful jobs? Would you work in these jobs? Would the benefits ever outweigh the stress?*

C EQ: *Is teenage stress 'just a phase' they go through? Does the cause of the stress make the stress more serious; for example, what about exam stress versus divorce?*

D EQ: *If animals communicate through body language, what signs would tell you an animal was stressed? What kinds of stress could animals have?*

4 LISTEN — DVD

This audio clip is from the Australian Broadcasting Corporation (ABC). Laughter Club International was founded by Dr Madan and Madhuri Kataria, with the aim of teaching people 'laughter yoga', a 20-minute session of exercises to make people laugh. As this is done in groups, it is difficult not to laugh when everyone around you is laughing. The health benefits of laughter have been known for some time. Laughter can lower blood pressure, reduce stress hormones, boost the immune system and release endorphins – the body's natural painkillers.

> **4 LISTEN B, C, D** — *Answers*
>
> **B** True: People's health improves; people giggle.
> False: People tell jokes; people talk to each other.
>
> **C** If you see other people laughing, you start laughing yourself / too.
>
> **D 1** 5,000 members. **2** You see other people laughing. **3** On 13 March, 1995, Madan Kataria went to a park and said she wanted to start a laughter club. **4** Laughter yoga.

5 TEAMWORK

This activity is designed to get students thinking about the reality of living with debilitating irrational fears. Each of these phobias are real, although some are much more common and socially acceptable than others. Try to get students to think about all the situations where the illness might have some kind of effect.

Source:
The Anxiety and Phobia Workbook, Reneau Z. Peurifoy
Anxiety, Phobias, and Panic, Edmund J. Bourne

EQ: *Do you know anyone with a phobia? What can be done to help phobia sufferers?*

6 CONTROVERSY

The pharmaceutical industry and medical community is sometimes criticised for seeming to be over dependent on drug treatments when safer alternatives are available. In one US study, 65 per cent of doctors recommended sleeping pills to patients who would have been better off taking exercise or reducing their caffeine intake in the evenings, which the doctors might have found out if they had asked the patients further questions. In several studies published by the Universities of Toronto and Harvard, doctors were found to be treating drug side effects with more drugs.

There have been examples of how over-prescribing antibiotics has led to strains of antibiotic-resistant bacteria. In the US alone, more than 1.5 million people are treated in hospital every year from adverse reactions to drugs; another 100,000 die. Many of these deaths are largely preventable. That is not to say that there is not a place for pharmaceuticals, because many illnesses can only be controlled this way. However, the debate hinges on whether prescribing drugs is the doctor's first or last line of defence.

Sources:
www.abpi.org.uk, www.pharmaceutical-industry.info
Listening to Prozac, Peter Kramer
The Instinct To Heal, David Servan-Schreiber
Dangerous Drug Interactions, Joe Gaedon
www.worstpills.org

EQ: *Do you think we use drugs too often for stress? Do you think alternative treatments might help stress as much?*

7 PORTFOLIO WRITING

See the Introduction to the Teacher's Guide.

A Sources:
Work Stress, Lorne Sulsky
Handbook of Work Stress, Julian Barling
http://stress.about.com/cs/workplacestress/a/jobstress.htm, www.cdc.gov/niosh/stresswk.html

8 BIOLOGY *in English* [CLIL]

Stress has been discussed in this unit as a biological reaction triggered by external, and occasionally internal, stimulae. Our normal state of being is homeostasis, in which our body tries to maintain this balance. It regulates our breathing, our heart rate, our temperature and our stress reactions. The body always tries to be in balance with the environment we are in. When we come under increased stress, our body compensates, and this leads to knock-on effects in other areas. The long-term effects of stress and increased cortisol levels have been linked to physical problems like hypertension, migraines, cancer, arthritis, ulcers and colic. There may also be mental problems, such as anxiety, panic attacks, alcoholism and depression.

Note: In the fight-or-flight response people have feelings of aggression or the need to run away (avoidance).

Sources:
Overcoming Job Burnout, Ellen S. Bernstein
The Physiology Of Stress And Stress Reduction, Beverly A. Potter

EQ: *Are you aware of any health effects when you are very stressed? Have you ever felt the fight-or-flight response? What do you think burnout would feel like?*

9 FURTHER DISCUSSION

This section covers the way stress may change over time, school-related stress, job-related stress and time management.

A Try to get students to think about how stress evolves over time.

EQ: *Is there ever a stress-free period in anyone's life? Why? Why not?*

B Try to get students to consider common school-related stress.

EQ: *How stressful is school and learning for you? How is school fun and stressful?*

C Try to get students to think about reasons for increasing stress – less job security, greater workload.

EQ: *The Japanese have a word –* karoshi *– meaning death from overwork. How would stress be linked to this? What would motivate someone to work that hard? What would you consider the ten most stressful jobs? Would you work in these jobs? Would the benefits ever outweigh the stress?*

D Try getting students to think about how they manage their time.

EQ: *Do you tend to arrive for appointments or class early, on time or late? Is this common in your country? How does your culture view arriving late or on time? Is time management only a business concept? Do you manage your time effectively? If so, how? If not, why not?*

Unit 19 — Stressed out! — Teacher's Guide

See pages 84–87 SB, 112 WB

10 *Your answer:* ARE WE SERIOUSLY STRESSED?

This question tries to get students to address how seriously society takes the effects of stress. In many cultures, it is still not acceptable to talk about being very stressed, especially in countries where men are not allowed to show any signs of weakness.

EQ: *What do the types of programmes for stress reduction say about how seriously your government takes stress? Do you think men and women react to stress differently?*

WORKBOOK

1 WORD POWER

This activity will get students practising vocabulary from the unit and the phrases from **Language Bank 19**.

> **1 WORD POWER** — **Sample answers**
>
> **1** I injured my back while I was *working out* at the gym. – **You must be feeling absolutely terrible.** Have you seen the doctor? / **There's nothing to worry about.** Take some painkillers. **2** I took the *red-eye* flight to Lisbon and feel really tired and stressed today. – **I can see how difficult it must be** for you to stay awake. You look really tired. / **It's not such a big thing.** Have some coffee. **3** My doctor said I need to *watch my diet* if I want to improve my health. – **I know exactly how you must be feeling.** My doctor said I needed more exercise. / **Let's try to keep things in perspective.** Just eat smaller portions. **4** I felt better after taking those *anti-depressants*, but I didn't like the side-effects. – **That must have been very hard for you.** Is there anything I can do? / **Everything's going to be fine.** You'll soon get used to them. **5** I'm worried about my husband – he finds it difficult to switch off and gets stressed. – **I feel so sorry for** both of you. It can be hard to leave work behind. / **Try to calm down; worrying won't help.** He just needs a hobby. **6** After serving in the army, my father developed *post-traumatic stress disorder*. – **I can imagine how painful it must have been** for him. Can he get any help for that? / **There's nothing to worry about.** It's a common reaction.

2 WRITING

A Sources:
The Complete Idiot's Guide to Dealing with Stress for Teens, Sara Jane Sluke
Pressure? No Problem, Michelle Steele
www.stress.org.uk

B Sources:
http://health.msn.com
http://news.bbc.co.uk/1/hi/health/default.stm
www.cnn.com/HEALTH
www.menshealth.com

3 SPEAKING STRATEGIES: Anticipating questions

This activity is one of the basic techniques that students should learn to give better presentations. In trying to anticipate questions, students will be better prepared for the presentation in the Trinity or CAE exams.

> **3 SPEAKING STRATEGIES** — **Answers**
>
> **1** f **2** c **3** d **4** b **5** a **6** e

4 IDIOMS

See the Introduction to the Teacher's Guide.

> **4 IDIOMS** — **Answers**
>
> **1** b **2** d **3** c **4** a **5** f **6** e
>
> **1** to lose the plot = to feel stressed or out of control **2** to pay the price = to suffer the consequences **3** to compare notes = to check each other's information about something **4** just what the doctor ordered = exactly the right thing **5** to let off steam = to express strong feeling, release pent-up emotion **6** an emotional rollercoaster = lead to very strong swings / variations in feelings / emotions

Ask students to use the idioms when answering these questions orally. This can be done as pair work or as a class.

- *What would you do if you felt your life was out of control?*
  – If I was beginning *to lose the plot,* I would seek professional help.

- I think I would need to do something *to let off steam*, like sports.
- I would say a few days off would be *just what the doctor ordered*.

• What happens if you work too hard?
- You will *pay the price* with poor health and high stress.
- I think overwork can take you on *an emotional rollercoaster*.

- I haven't *compared notes* with others, but I tend to get sick and need time off.

• What is your number one stress-reducer?
- I like to go for walks *to let off steam*.
- I begin *to lose the plot* if I can't spend a few hours by myself from time to time.
- A weekend away from the kids is always *what the doctor ordered*.

Unit 20 **Shock tactics** **Teacher's Guide** See pages 88–91 SB, 113 WB

WHAT'S NEW?

Communication Objectives:	Ss will be able to: – use expressions for language of caution and eliciting feedback. – use vocabulary, phrases and idioms related to youth behaviour.
Educational Objectives:	Ss will critically assess common examples of positive and negative youth behaviour.
Connected Topics:	– Straight Edge – Tattoos and piercings – Young people and drugs – Poetry and music – Young people and crime – Behaviour relativism – Typical male and female young people – Age of consent – Reputations – Experimenting – Group mentality – Life lessons – Binge drinking – Youth rebellion – Youth programmes
Grammar:	Word choice Collocations Idioms
Key Vocabulary:	abstain holiday rep promiscuous sex adhere hostile recruit all-terrain vehicle illicit rep / reputation attire intimidating seizure close-minded Latino skip school consume lure thrashing cult mosh pit vegan do-gooder off the mark vice drive-by shooting patch vigilante free-for-all picker hardcore music politically correct

The BIG question: ARE ALL TEENAGERS REBELS?

VIEWPOINT

Facts: The statistics on teenage drinking are from the Waltham Forest Crime and Disorder and Drug Audit 2004. UK schoolchildren are the heaviest teenage drinkers in Europe.

Source: www.lbwf.gov.uk/8.5.6-alcohol.pdf

EQ: *Why do you think this is the case? How does this compare to teenagers in your country? What effect can drinking at this age have?*

The statistics on cannabis are from the British Crime Survey 2001.

Source: www.drugscope.org.uk/druginfo/drugsearch/ds_report_results.asp?file=%5Cwip%5C11%5C3%5C008chapter6.html

EQ: *What is the attitude to cannabis use in your country? Has anyone you know every tried it? Do you think there is a difference between soft drugs (like marijuana) and hard drugs (like cocaine)?*

Quotes: Robert MacKenzie (1928–) is a retired politician from the Ontario, Canada, provincial legislature.

EQ: *How do you think adults see teenagers? Is this a fair stereotype?*

George Bernard Shaw (1856–1950) was an Irish playwright and winner of the 1925 Nobel Prize for Literature.

EQ: *Do you think this is true? How do the youth of today shock the old?*

1 WORD POWER

A 1 gives students an introduction to some new vocabulary.

> **1 WORD POWER B**   Sample answers
>
> **1** Straight-A students have problems too. **If I were to hazard a guess, I might say that** we all need help sometimes. **2** There is a generation gap between parents and young people today. **It could be the case that** there is one, but every generation thinks the same thing. **3** Something needs to be done about these yobs. **I would be a little concerned that** people will overreact about this. **4** Peer pressure pushes young people into risky behaviour. **It seems as if** peer pressure is very strong, but parents can play their part.

ARTICLES

Walking the Straight Edge

This article discusses the US teenage movement called Straight Edge. The movement originated in the mid to late 1980s out of the hardcore punk rock movement. It is widely believed that the movement takes its origins from the lyrics of Ian MacKaye of Minor Threat, and later of Fugazi, fame. His song *Straight Edge* was written about a friend who had overdosed on heroin and is a warning to young people about avoiding dangerous activities.

Much of the movement's image is related to the larger hardcore punk rock movement: tattoos, black clothing, piercings and loud aggressive music. What makes the movement different is the abstinence from sex, drugs and alcohol. Many of its followers are also vegans. The movement is largely non-violent, but there have been incidents specifically among male members, who tend to travel in groups. Several police organisations including the Salt Lake City Sheriff's office identify Straight-Edgers as being involved in gang activity (in relationship with the Animal Liberation Front, an extremist animal rights group).

EQ: *Is there a relationship between people who believe very strongly in an idea, religion or philosophy and violence? Do the positive aspects of Straight Edge outweigh its negative aspects?*

Marijuana Growers Hire Rural Quebec Students

This article discusses marijuana growing in the Canadian province of Quebec. Canada is developing a reputation as a major producer and exporter of marijuana, especially to the United States. The marijuana industry is estimated to be worth $7 billion, second only to oil and gas extraction ($15.3 billion). The largest producing provinces are British Columbia, Ontario and Quebec with much of the production now being done in 'grow-ops' (small-scale indoor cultivation inside houses). This is the reason why organised crime has such a big stake in Quebec and is willing to pay so much to helpers. Canada is considering de-criminalising marijuana possession with the hopes of moving production out into the open where it could be taxed. The United States Department of Justice is not happy with this development.

EQ: *Should cannabis use or production be illegal? What is the best way to combat drug taking? If you were approached to do illegal work for very large wages or work at a boring job for low wages, which would you do? How important is it to have money as a teenager? Is it important enough to risk going to jail?*

2 READING

A is a skimming activity that will help students with the Reading section of the CAE and IGCSE exams.

> **2 READING A**   Answers
>
> **A 1** no   **2** yes   **3** yes   **4** no

B This question relates to the type of question in the Trinity Exam where students must determine feelings or thoughts that are not explicitly stated.

C 1 You can give students some help by getting them to look at the different aspects of the Straight Edge image and philosophy.

EQ: *What can you do in a group that you couldn't do alone?*

C 2 You can give students some help by looking at the values of people at this age and the prospect of a large income to people with limited opportunities.

3 SPEAK YOUR MIND

This section covers the topics of typical teenagers, reputations, group membership, and youth crime.

Unit 20 — Shock tactics
Teacher's Guide
See pages 88–91 SB, 113 WB

A EQ: *How are / were you similar to other teenagers? Would you describe yourself as typical? Is there anything positive or negative about being typical?*

B EQ: *Do you care what others think of you? Can someone ever change their reputation? How important is personal / family honour in your country? Is a reputation or honour worth dying for?*

C EQ: *Why do you think police might consider Straight-Edgers to be gangs? Are there any groups in your country which might get labelled as gangs? What would be the appeal of joining a gang?*
Do you consider yourself an extrovert or introvert? Which do you prefer: more spending time with people or by yourself?

D EQ: *What attracts people to crime? Are youth criminals treated differently from adult criminals? What are the purposes of prison: keeping criminals away from the public or rehabilitating criminals? Which does your country favour? Can criminals go straight?*

4 LISTEN — DVD

This audio clip features a meeting among holiday reps for a travel company that organises package holidays for young people. Many of these package holidays have a focus on partying and drinking. The issue of binge drinking is an important issue in the UK, where many young people go out to drink large quantities of alcohol on Friday or Saturday nights. Holiday trips to other countries where alcohol is much cheaper than in the UK often leads to bouts of drunkenness and violent behaviour.

4 LISTEN B — Answers
Swimming: not mentioned. **Responsible drinking:** Not mentioned, they want to bring enough alchohol so they don't run out. They provide only nachos and light snacks. And they are only concerned about the drinking in terms of the impact on locals. **Fun party games:** Yes, Mexican theme. **Sightseeing:** Yes, they visit a nearby island.

4 LISTEN C — Answers
1 Mexican (Getaway). **2** Mexican music, trance and deep house. **3** A lot to drink, but only a little food (including nachos with salsa and guacamole). **4** People getting into trouble with the police for carrying open bottles of alcohol through the town and being fined (50 euros), or making too much noise. **5** They don't really seem to be.

D In the event that students cannot think of anything, you can get them to discuss: *What kinds of evening activities do they have in Ibiza or other resorts? What sort of activities would appeal to you?*

5 TEAMWORK

This activity is designed to get students to think about the very real situation that can affect any community with large-scale economic or social problems. It may be wise to avoid discussing rates of youth crime, suicide and unemployment directly in this context.

Sources:
Handbook on Counseling Youth, John McDowell
Community Youth Development, Francisco A. Villarruel

EQ: *Do you have youth programmes or youth centres in your community? Do these programmes work? Are programmes designed by adults for young people always appropriate? What kinds of programmes would young people want to create?*

6 CONTROVERSY

Tattooing originated in Asia and is still a much admired cultural practice among the island states of the Pacific. It spread to the West with sailors who travelled to these ports of call. From a Western perspective, tattoos were historically worn only by prisoners and sailors, however, this has begun to change as tattoos have become a much more common way of expressing individuality. Many cultural anthropologists point to the role that music videos and MTV have had in making tattoos popular as so many rock and pop stars and other celebrities now have them.

© Brookemead Associates Ltd 2009 — BROOKEMEAD ENGLISH LANGUAGE TEACHING

QSE Advanced   See pages 88–91 SB, 113 WB   Unit 20
Teacher's Guide

Sources:
Bad Boys and Tough Tattoos: A Social History of the Tattoo with Gangs, Sailors and Street-Corner Punks 1950–1965 Samuel, M. Steward
The Tattoo Encyclopedia, Terisa Green
Modern Primitives, V. Vale
Return of the Tribal, Rufus C. Camphausen

EQ: *Is tattooing and piercing just a trend? Why do some people find tattooing and piercings intimidating?*

7 PORTFOLIO WRITING

See the Introduction to the Teacher's Guide.

A Sources:
See your country's government website for examples of information pamphlets.

B Sources:
The Girl's Book of Love: Cool Quotes, Super Stories, Awesome Advice and More, Catherine Dee
52 Lessons on Communicating Love, Dr. Ruth Westheimer
www.loveadvice.com/LIBRARY.HTM

8 POETRY AND MUSIC *in English* [CLIL]

This activity could be made more personal for the students by asking them to bring examples of music they like. The lyrics can be analysed in the same way as the song in the activity. The example can be considered more as a back-up in case students do not have time to research and bring in examples. There are many places online which offer lyrics to songs for free.

Sources:
www.azlyrics.com
www.lyrics.com
www.sing365.com

EQ: *Why does music evoke and appeal to our emotions? Why is music such an important part of youth culture? What would youth culture be without music, music stars or MTV?*

9 FURTHER DISCUSSION

This section covers relative behaviour, youth experimentation, life lessons, and youth rebellion.

A Try to get students to think in concrete terms about their own behaviour. If you are daring enough, you can discuss the use of swearwords in different circumstances.

EQ: *Would you use swearwords in each situation (school, work)? Why / Why not? What motivates you to do good? Do you think your parents, friend or, co-workers know how you act when you're with other people? Why / Why not?*

B Try to get students to discuss the reasons behind experimenting.

EQ: *Why do young people experiment? Is it a natural process?*

C Try to get students to think about the lessons they have learnt.

EQ: *Do you think you could learn these all on your own? Do you think we rely on TV too much for educating young people? What would someone who learnt about life only from television be like?*

D EQ: *Who do you find more interesting: rebels or conformists? What does this tell us about ourselves? Is youth rebellion healthy?*

10 *Your answer:* ARE ALL TEENAGERS REBELS?

This question tries to get students to address how young people behave. While there are many different viewpoints among young people, society often works from the Hollywood stereotypes of the 'rebel without a cause'. What are young people rebelling against? Should young people rebel? Will teenagers always rebel? How does youth rebellion become adult conformity?

WORKBOOK

1 WORD POWER

This activity will get students practising the language of caution from **Language Bank 20.**

Unit 20 — Shock tactics — Teacher's Guide
See pages 88–91 SB, 113 WB

1 WORD POWER — Answers

1 Young people say they want to be individuals, but they just copy each other. **I'm not sure I would** say that, they are just doing their best.
2 Young people should be allowed room to make mistakes. **It seems as if** that is the case.
3 Young women are never as bad as young men. **I'm not sure I would** agree with your statement. What about girl gangs?
4 Television is responsible for making young people behave badly. **I would be a little concerned that** we blame television for everything. Parents have a role to play as well.
5 Teenagers can always get drugs or alcohol if they want. I don't think anything can stop that. **I would be a little concerned that** that if you give up hope, it won't help.
6 We can only hope a good education will keep young people safe. **If I were to hazard a guess, I might say** education is the most important thing in helping young people find the right path in life.

2 USE OF LANGUAGE: Word Forms

This activity introduces the brief history of skateboarding and it being banned on the streets of many US cities. The activity is based on an authentic test activity used by the University of Cambridge Local Examinations Syndicate in the CAE and CPE. It will also help in the Reading section of the IELTS.

2 USE OF LANGUAGE — Answers
1 sharpen   2 revolutionised   3 increase
4 banned   5 fear   6 remains
7 organised 8 requesting

3 WRITING

A Sources:
www.vanishingtattoo.com
http://tattoo.about.com

B Sources:
www.drugscope.org.uk
www.drugs.gov.uk/Home
www.nida.nih.gov

4 IDIOMS

See the Introduction to the Teacher's Guide.

4 IDIOMS — Answers
1 were   2 saw / sees   3 open
4 nip   5 kept   6 scratching

1 to be on the same wavelength = to understand each other and think alike **2** to see everything in black and white = to see things in very clear terms, not in nuances **3** to open the floodgates = to allow something to get out of control **4** to nip something in the bud = to stop something before it really starts **5** to keep his nose clean = to behave well **6** to scratch their heads over = to worry about what to do, to be confused about what to do

Ask students to use the idioms when answering these questions orally. This can be done as pair work or as a class.

- *What do you think of very conformist young people?*
  – I think there's nothing wrong with *keeping your nose clean*.
  – I guess if they've been raised a certain way they just *see everything in black and white*.
- *Why are some young people into binge drinking?*
  – When some young people are suddenly given too much freedom, it just *opens the floodgates*.
  – I'm just left *scratching my head*.
  – I think some parents don't *nip it in the bud* early enough with proper discipline.
- *If you could give parents advice on rowdy teenagers, what would it be?*
  – I would tell them to try and *be on the same wavelength*. They need a lot of empathy for teens.
  – I think you should *nip problems in the bud* by openly discussing things.
  – They should not *open the floodgates* on their teenager's freedom too early.

ER 3 | **Not all Natives are created equal** | **Teacher's Guide** | See pages 92–93 SB

WHAT'S NEW?

Communication Objectives:	Ss will be able to use phrases or grammar from: Units 1-7, Extended Reading 1 Units 8-14, Extended Reading 2 Unit 15: Generalising / Conditionals Unit 16: Signposting words: Sequencing / Asserting Unit 17: Developing an argument / Expressions used to introduce assertions Unit 18: Summarising information, ideas and arguments / Expressions used to contradict Unit 19: Calming expressions / Language of empathy and sympathy Unit 20: Eliciting feedback / Expressing caution
Educational Objectives:	Ss will explore how stereotypes shape our views and understanding of the world.
Connected Topics:	– Native American stereotypes – Interacting with strangers – African-American stereotypes – Hollywood stereotypes
Grammar / Vocabulary:	Idioms Non-standard English grammar and vocabulary
Key Vocabulary:	a cold chill, ain't, big deal, bigotry, blurt out, booming, chatter, comfort zone, contemplate, crack a smile, crack (voice), curl one's lip, dead silent, dimly, dimple *v*, drop dead, engulf, frown *n*, glow, harsh, 'hood, ignorant, Injun, jerk, jut out, loathing, malcontent, melt away, naive, not going to bite you, prejudice, profiling, real world, reservation, scowl, sincerity, smart ass, stink *v*, stroll, stutter, tip back, unclinch, unwittingly, warm and fuzzies, will, worrisome

EXTENDED READING: Background Information

This text is part of an editorial column called 'Bee in the Bonnet,' which appears in Canada's *First Nations Drum* magazine. It highlights the take that the Native American humourist, B.H. Bates, has on many different issues from the perspective of First Nation people. (Note: In Canada, Native Americans are called First Nation people.) Other topics in the series have included Canadian politics, life on the reservation, poverty among First Nations, residential schools, Aboriginal achievement and so on.

The title is a play on words that echoes 'All men are created equal' from the United States Declaration of Independence (1776).

Note: Paragraph 1, line 7 should read 'dimly lit'.

Sources:
www.firstnationsdrum.com

EQ: 1 *What is a stereotype? Why do we create stereotypes?*
2 *What stereotypes exist about your country? Are stereotypes harmful, helpful or something else? When do stereotypes become racism?*
3 *Imagine you meet a foreigner in your city. They know little about your country. How would you*

ER 3 Not all Natives are created equal — Teacher's Guide

See pages 92–93 SB

explain what your country is like? What is it like to come from your country? What customs, habits or traditions are unique in your country?

1 READING

A is a common scanning activity. It will help students writing the Reading part of the CAE, the Trinity Controlled Writing ISE III section, IELTS Reading Part 2, and IGCSE Reading Parts 1 and 3.

---

1 READING A — Answers

1 He has preconceptions of African-Americans as dangerous. Without realising it, he walks into a bar where there are only African-Americans.
2 He speaks to Big Glenn, who makes him feel at ease and changes his perception of blacks.
3 If he could feel like he did about blacks even after meeting Glenn, he wonders how whites would see him.

---

2 IDIOMS

This activity follows the specifications of the Trinity Language Exam Grades 10 and 11 which call for students to have a good understanding of and ability to use various idioms. The correct use of idioms will help students in CAE as well.

---

2 IDIOMS — Answers

A 1 big deal 2 comfort zone 3 the real world
4 blurt out 5 smart ass 6 to put *someone* at ease

B 1 put everyone / at ease 2 the real world
3 smart ass 4 comfort zone 5 blurted out
6 big deal

---

3 WHAZZUP?

This section follows the specifications of the Trinity Language Exam Grades 10 and 11 which call for students to be able to understand words in context.

EQ: *Some linguists have begun to speculate that non-standard English may become the norm in the future, as the number of speakers of English as a second language increases. What do you think of this? If English is used as the global language, can anyone claim ownership of the language?*

3 WHAZZUP? — Answers

Grammar
Where you from, boy? – Where (are) you from, boy?
Hi, where ya from? – Hello, where (are) you from?
I ain'a goin'a bite you – I('m not) going (to) bite you
Yo, cool! – Oh, cool!
Where you from, boy? – Where are you from, sir / mister?
You'z sure in'a hell ain't from round here. – You are sure in the hell not from around here.
Ya'll take care now! – You take care now.
What the __ you lookin' at? – What the __ (are) you looking at?

Words
hood – neighbourhood
Injun – Indian
ain't – is / are not
yo – you / you're
ya – you
you'z – you are
y'all – you (all)
hi – hello

4 PORTFOLIO WRITING

You should remind the students that activity **A** is in the third person 'He went into a bar.' and activity B is in the first-person point of view. 'I saw B.H. outside talking to some boys.'

A Sources:
A Native American Encyclopedia: History, Culture and Peoples, Barry Pritzker
Stereotypes and Prejudice: Essential Readings, Charles Stangor
www.firstnationsdrum.com
www.afn.ca
www.si.edu/resource/faq/nmai/naster.htm

B Sources:
Countering the Conspiracy to Destroy Black Boys, Jawanza Kunjufu
Black Youth, Racism and the State, John Solomos
Black like Me, Robert Bonazzi
African-American Lives, Henry Louis Gates

5 INTERACTIVE TASK

This activity is directly based on the Interactive Task phase of the Trinity Language Spoken Exam Grades 10 and 11. It would also be useful practice for developing stronger communicative skills and confidence for Parts 3 and 4 of the spoken phase of the CAE exam.

This activity requires students to lead the conversation, which can be a challenge for some students. It is important that you go round the room to monitor the students' communicative leadership in this activity. They should be commenting and asking their partner questions. Silence is not an option; it is up to them to keep the dialogue active and flowing if, and when, their partner begins to falter. They should already have experience with leading the dialogue during **Teamwork,** presentation and **Further Discussion** activities in previous units.

To help in general, you can get students to think of the different brainstorming activities they have encountered so far in the **Teamwork** activities.

Comment 1: If students are not sure where to start, ask them to say what they expect a working environment to be like and what they expect from relationships with other co-workers.

Comment 2: If students seem to have trouble beginning, you can help them by suggesting: people from different countries – Japanese, Spaniards / Spanish, Swedes, Indians; people in different occupations – doctors, teachers, janitors, models.

EQ: *Why do filmmakers use stereotypes in film? Who are more often stereotypes – main or supporting actors? Why? Imagine what movies would be like today if all the white characters in films were played by actors of different ethnic groups.*

QSE — Using the Student's DVD-ROM — Teacher's Guide

QSE Advanced Student's DVD-ROM

The *QSE Advanced* Student's DVD-ROM contains all 20 audio and video clips to go with Exercise 4 (**Watch and Listen,** or **Listen**) for each Unit of the Student's Book. There are also PDF files of the transcripts of the audio and video clips that can be printed out.

The DVD-ROM can be played on a DVD player or a personal computer with a DVD player. From the main menu students can access all the different parts of the DVD-ROM. To return to the main menu at any time, students click on the BACK button in the bottom right-hand corner of the screen.

Units 1-20 Audio and Video Clips

The audio and video clips are each approximately three to four minutes long. There are six video clips and 14 audio clips. Units 2, 6, 12 and 19 have a pause in the clip linked to an activity in which the student is asked to speculate on what will come next or what people may be thinking about a situation. Just before the pause, the words *PAUSE coming up* appear on the screen. After the pause, the clip continues. To hold the pause for longer, press the pause button on the DVD. To continue, press the play button on the DVD.

Online Material for Teachers

Downloadable material for teachers is available online as **PDF** files (printable) or as **MP3** files (audio) at http://www.brookemead-elt.co.uk/downloads/ The PDF files contain the complete Teacher's Guide, exam materials (CAE, IELTS, IGCSE), audio and video transcripts, and answer keys. The MP3 files contain the audio for the Exam Practice Audio (Tests 1–7).

Student's DVD-ROM contents

Units 1-20 Audio/Video Clips

(*American*=type of English)
Unit 1 Using photo health warning labels on cigarette packets (Interviews with **British** people).
Unit 2 Interview with Gunther von Hagens, creator of the *Body Worlds* exhibition (**British English** commentary and voiceover of interview with **German** person).
Unit 3 Interviews with various **American** people about the American Dream.
Unit 4 Bullying in the workplace (Interviews with **British** people).
Unit 5 PETA's *I'd rather go naked* campaign against wearing fur (**American** commentary).
Unit 6 Talking about beauty contests (Interviews with **British** and **American** people).
Unit 7 Is war good for the economy? **British** teenagers talking.
Unit 8 Bjorn Lomborg, author of *The Skeptical Environmentalist* (**American** interviewer talking to **Danish** scientist).
Unit 9 Behaviour-modification camps for teenagers (**British** teenagers talking).
Unit 10 Hanni, the seeing-eye dog (Interview with an **American**).
Unit 11 Tropical storm causes flooding in Haiti and the Dominican Republic (**British** newsreader).
Unit 12 Click kanji: Is English the only language for the internet? (**British** commentary, interviews with people from **Australia** and **SE Asia**).
Unit 13 Extract from the film *Outfoxed* containing interviews with **Americans** (*The O'Reilly Factor* interview with Jeremy Glick).
Unit 14 Radio programme about comic book superheroes (Interviews with **British** people).
Unit 15 A teenage single mother talks about her life (**Northern Irish** interviewer talking to a girl from the **British Midlands**).
Unit 16 The science curriculum in Arizona (Interviews with **Americans**).
Unit 17 Space debris – European Space Agency (**British** commentary, interviews with **Germans** speaking English).
Unit 18 Brazil: Bringing computers to the children of the *favelas*. **Brazilian** interviewer talking to **Brazilians** in American English and translation – voiceover in **British English**.
Unit 19 A laughter therapist talks about Laughter Clubs (**Australian** interviewing English-speaking people in **India**).
Unit 20 Holiday company representatives meet in a Spanish seaside resort (People from **Britain, Australia** and **New Zealand** talking).

PDF files (printable text computer files)

- About QSE
- Using the DVD
- Audio and video transcripts for the text of each audio and video clip.

Unit 1 Using photo warning labels on cigarette packets

Interviewer: Around four million people worldwide die every year from smoking-related illnesses according to the World Health Organisation. It is estimated that some 360,000 people are admitted to hospitals in the UK every year because of smoking-related illnesses. Cancer groups from Britain and the EU have begun demanding the introduction of warning labels similar to those introduced in Canada in 2001. So we went out on the streets of London to find out what Londoners feel about this.

Interviewer: Excuse me, could I ask you what do you think about smoking?
Woman 1: Well, I don't smoke, but my boyfriend smokes and, to be honest, I'd like to see him stop. Like a lot of people, I think he smokes 'cause it's cool.
Man 1: What? I thought that was part of my appeal. No, but seriously, I don't see anything wrong with smoking. It's a question of personal freedom.
Interviewer: British anti-smoking groups are pressuring the government to introduce photographic warning labels like these ones used in Canada on cigarette packets. What do you think of them?
Man 1: *(coughing)* Oh, this is too much.
Woman 1: Wow, I think these are brilliant, a really good idea. I think it would be pretty hard to look cool with a photo of mouth cancer sitting on the table in front of you.
Man 1: I'm not so sure. I don't spend much time thinking about whether to give up smoking or not. She does most of that for me. *(laughs)*
Interviewer: Hello...what are your views on smoking?
Woman 2: Well, I'd like to quit...sure, but it's not easy when so many of my friends smoke.
Man 2: I hate it. Every time you go out with people who smoke, you come out reeking of smoke. It's really a nasty habit.
Interviewer: Here are some anti-smoking warning labels from Canada. Would you like to see them on cigarette packets here?
Man 2: Um, well, I think we should have them here, but the problem is that the Government makes about £8 billion a year from cigarettes. I think it's a question of whether the UK government can give up its addiction to taxes on cigarettes.
Woman 2: Mmm... These are certainly very graphic. Are they for real?
Interviewer: Yes, they are. Do you think these might convince you to give up smoking?
Woman 2: Well, I think they might. I'd hate to have to look at one of those labels every time I reach for a cigarette.
Interviewer: To date, the Canadian government has had considerable success with its anti-smoking programme. Smoking rates among young people dropped from 28 per cent to 18 per cent between 1999 and 2003. The question remains, do the EU and the British government have the courage to follow Canada's lead? It may just come down to a question of image. Reporting from London, this is Patricia Connelly for Channel Six news.

Unit 2 Interview with Gunther von Hagens, creator of the Body Worlds exhibition

Von Hagens: Remember that you are mortal. That is what is suggested to everyone who attends the exhibition, especially by the gestalt plastinates themselves. I was what you are. You can become what I am. And that brings us to body donors. The people who are exhibited here made a very conscious decision during their lifetimes to be available to the next generation for the sake of anatomical instruction.

First, people attending the exhibition should get a clearer idea of their own bodies. We live in an artificial world. Normal persons are no longer conscious that they themselves are nature. Secondly, the intention was to present anatomy in a very concrete way.

This exhibition is not about art or science, it's about instruction. Instruction in the fullest sense of the word in that people attending the exhibition can realise their own vulnerability. In a prophylactic sense, since if people see how unhealthy habits or lifestyles concretely affect their own bodies, for example smokers' lungs, heart attacks, or meniscus damage, it will help them to gain a greater appreciation and perhaps a renewed sensitivity toward their bodies.

My models are the Renaissance anatomists who pioneered the initial enlightenment in this field: Leonardo da Vinci and Andreas Vesalius. For the first time, they discovered the beauty of bodily interiors at

a time when the beauty of bodily exteriors was the focus of an entire artistic epoch.
[PAUSE]
In the late Middle Ages, Andreas Vesalius was the first to assemble a skeleton. He literally took it from the grave and returned it to society.

I see myself in this tradition and I am continuing it with the possibilities of plastination. By making it possible to solidify soft tissue, plastination permits bodies to be exhibited not only as skeletons, but also as skeletons with muscles and organs at the same time. And I do not display people as incomplete specimens. I do not use dissection to remove organs. Instead, I provide insights into bodily interiors. People can look inside.

Unit 3 The American Dream

Interviewer: What is the American Dream?
Girl (15 years): My American Dream is to be a famous musician.
Man 1: I perceive it as the opportunity or equal opportunity to set goals and to be able to achieve them and have an education and an environment that's equal for everyone so everyone can work and set their goals and live the lifestyle in the environment they wish to live in.
Man 2: The American Dream means different things to different people depending on their background, their experiences they've had in life so far and their heritage. For me the American Dream is to preserve the freedoms that our ancestors have worked so hard to acquire for us and to leave a situation that continues to better for the generations that follow.
Interviewer: Do you think you are living the American Dream?
Woman 1: I have no complaints. I have a family, a home, an education, privilege of going to church when I want to.
Man 3: Well, I don't know if I'm living the American Dream, but I'm certainly striving to get there. Right now, I'm in college to obtain my degree so that I can get a better job and provide a better life for my family.
Interviewer: According to a recent study, 79 per cent of African Americans will only experience poverty in their lifetime. For white Americans, the percentage is only 24. Why do you think this is?
Woman 3: The number of individuals who have broken families within the African-American community is much greater than within the white community. Education is another big part of it. Having a good education will allow someone to go further within this country. And unfortunately, African Americans...the number of individuals in that group having higher education is much lower.
Man 3: There are a lot of African Americans that are born into poverty. And a lot of them don't get out of the environment. They succumb to the environment and become a part of the environment rather than trying to seek a life outside of it. I think also, too, the system in some ways there are some advantages that are handed down to folks that the African-American community doesn't get to experience.
Interviewer: How would you describe a successful person?
Girl: Having a job, having a family, making money, not exactly being rich but at least having some food and shelter.
Woman 2: Someone who's happy and productive in whatever capacity they choose, law-abiding. I think someone who has chosen an outlet, creative or otherwise, and is working towards fulfilling it.
Woman 1: Living the good life of friends, security, that sort of thing, but it's not how many playthings you have.
Interviewer: How important is success to you?
Woman 3: Very important. For me, there are a lot of different areas of success. And for me, it's more building a stable community, family and being able to contribute something back.
Man 1: I think success is the American Dream. So I would rank it number one for me to be successful and (that) raising my family and providing for my family.

Unit 4 Bullying in the workplace

Cynthia Banks: Welcome to *Straight Talk*. I'm Cynthia Banks. When someone brings up the subject of bullying, people often think of school playgrounds and badly behaved children. But there is another type of bullying that is nearly as widespread — bullying in the workplace. To talk about it, we are joined today by management consultant Martin Halverson.
Martin Halverson: Hello, Cynthia.

C. Banks: Hello, Martin. First, let's hear from Gemma, an executive assistant whose boss bullied the whole office.
Gemma: As far as I'm concerned, this guy was really over the top. Some of us were actually wondering whether he had some kind of mental problem. Take meetings, for example. If someone started to make a comment or a suggestion, he'd just shout, 'Shut up! Who's talking to you?' And worse, you know, swearing at people. Personally, I felt traumatised. Even when he wasn't in the office there was no let-up, he was calling every two minutes to scream at people about something or other.
C. Banks: So Martin, what do you make of this?
M. Halverson: Well, this behaviour certainly seems to be extreme, although incidents can take many forms, not just the more obvious ones like shouting, making someone look small, or humiliating them in front of others.
C. Banks: Such as?
M. Halverson: There's also a lot of passive-aggressive behaviour, for example, spreading negative rumours about somebody, or simply not talking to them, not returning phone calls, or delaying action on something a co-worker needs to do a job.
C. Banks: How widespread would you say this problem is?
M. Halverson: A number of studies have looked at this in depth. In a recent University of North Carolina study, researchers followed 1,600 workers over four years. The results were fascinating. There is a definite lack of social stability in the US workplace; rudeness, disrespect and bullying – all of these are becoming more and more common. Lots of swearing, even fighting. We even heard of scientists throwing equipment at colleagues.
C. Banks: Where does this problem originate?
M. Halverson: Researchers say that intense competition and rapid change are often to blame. And we have to remember that the bullies often have a special status in the company, perhaps they are higher up the corporate ladder, or they have some special talent or skill. Most companies usually have a well-defined policy about bullying in the workplace. The problem tends to be a lack of will to enforce these anti-bullying rules, especially against people in positions of authority.

C. Banks: Are you saying management sometimes makes exceptions for these people? What effect does this have?
M. Halverson: Yes, there can be serious side-effects if the policy is not enforced. It causes a lot of mental and emotional stress. In the North Carolina study, 22 per cent of people said they actually worked less hard when they were bullied. About half said they lost work time worrying about an incident or whether the bully would target them again. And most dramatically, 12 per cent of the people who responded actually changed their jobs to get away.
C. Banks: That's a big loss to the company. What can be done about it?
M. Halverson: Basically it's best to adopt a zero-tolerance policy. No exceptions, no matter how small the offence is, no matter who the person is. Companies really should become aware of how much this kind of behaviour costs them – just how much it reduces efficiency.
C. Banks: Well, now let's hear from Roger, a former computer technician for a software company, who has experienced…

Unit 5 PETA's I'd rather go naked campaign against wearing fur

Narrator: The 'I'd rather go naked than wear fur' campaign began in 1990. *The Wonder Years* were on TV. Nelson Mandela was out of jail. And the Go-Gos were planning a reunion.
Go-Gos: We're the Go-Gos and we'd rather go naked than wear fur.
Dan Mathews: And when the Go-Gos announced that they were having a reunion tour and they're all PETA supporters. We asked them if they would pose for a poster.
Narrator: The poster 'I'd rather Go-Go naked than wear fur' was inspired by an activist in Florida.
D. Mathews: There was an activist down there named Holly Jensen who had a fur protest. And she outfitted herself in a flesh-coloured leotard and made a sign with a magic marker that just said I'd rather go naked than wear fur. And she sent us photos of this protest, as a lot of activists do. And when I was going through the photos, I saw that one and I thought, you know, there's something there.

Narrator: There was definitely something there. The poster was used by newspapers nationwide. And soon the whole country was talking about the fur issue. A 'Go' was dropped and the campaign spread with protests in Italy, Germany and Japan. Celebrities were enlisted. Singers, supermodels, actors all bravely disrobed. PETA staffers volunteered by the dozens: interns, campaigners, founders.

And a funny thing happened, fur sales slipped. From *Fur Industry Magazine*, *the Trapper* and *Predator Caller*, Sept. 2001, fur industry directories reveal that in 1972, there were 779 established fur garment makers in the United States. Twenty years later, in 1992, that number had dwindled to only 211.

But what is this craft that sparked a decade of naked activism? Simply put, it's a billion-dollar-a-year industry that has taken fur-bearing animals out of the forests of fairytales and the Discovery Channel and dropped them straight into the middle of a horror novel.

On a fur farm, what you first notice is the pacing, round and round in psychotic circles. Animals crazed with boredom and stress. Next, you see the filth. Urine and faeces encrust the cages of fastidious animals, who, in the wild, would spend hours cleaning themselves. Finally, the mutilations sink in. Legs gnawed to the bone. Eyes and ears lost to infection. Cage mates cannibalised. The cage doors do eventually open. But the world outside is brief and horrible.

The animals whose lives have been lost to the fur industry can't be brought back. But over ten thousand fur coats have been donated to PETA from people sickened by animal cruelty. Over the years these furs have been distributed to homeless people who can't afford to buy their own coats, have been used to make bedding for orphaned wildlife, have been distributed to refugees in frozen, war-torn Afghanistan.

Woman: Don't go out in the woods. Them animal activists will get you.

Unit 6 Talking about beauty contests

Commentator 1: ...yeah, yeah, beauty pageants, or contests as you call them in the UK, have been around for over eighty years.

Radio presenter: Yes, they still seem to be going strong, although we don't see the Miss World contest on TV in the UK anymore, because a lot of people here see it as old-fashioned and out of date. Even adding intelligence and personality tests to the Miss World contest didn't keep the UK TV audiences interested, although the show is still broadcast around the world. But how did beauty contests start?

Commentator 1: The first beauty pageant took place in Atlantic City in 1921. Called the National Beauty Tournament, it was basically to get tourists to stay in Atlantic City after the end of the summer season – after the Labor Day holiday in early September.

Radio presenter: So how exactly have the beauty contests changed since those days?

Commentator 1: Well, it took several decades for many of the basic rules to become established, such as only being able to win a competition once, not being married and having no children, well, with the exception of the Mrs America beauty pageants...

Radio presenter: Why exactly is it that contestants need to be unmarried and have no kids?

Commentator 2: Well, that's a good question... I mean, as the beauty contest has developed these early rules have stayed the same.

Commentator 1: There were a number of highly publicised scandals over the years involving Miss America contestants. Several early winners ran off with their male chaperones. One Miss USA winner in 1957 actually turned out to be married with two children.

Commentator 2: There were problems with some Miss World contestants too. The 1974 winner turned out to be a single mother, and in 1980 Miss World resigned after posing naked for a magazine!

Radio presenter: I find it quite interesting that the contest doesn't have a rule against plastic surgery, given the other strict rules.
[PAUSE]
Commentator 1: Yes, it does seem a little hypocritical, but how are you supposed to prove someone has breast implants or other cosmetic surgery? It would be quite difficult to do.

Commentator 2: Well, I tend to think that the beauty contest is more about some kind of 'ideal' world, and not the real world. And I think a lot of the newer beauty contests you see today are a reflection of that.

Radio presenter: Such as?
Commentator 1: Well, to go back to the question of plastic surgery. China has recently had its first Miss Artificial Beauty contest for plastic surgery patients, one of whom used to be a man. But she didn't win though.
Commentator 2: True, it seems to me that that's a good example of how the beauty pageant is being used today to promote acceptance of different people...the idea that 'everyone is beautiful'. In Botswana, they hold the Miss HIV Stigma Free, which I think is a brilliant way to promote the issue of AIDS and acceptance. The contest shows just how far beauty contests have come today...

Unit 7   Is war good for the economy?

Teacher: Hello, everyone.
Class: Hi.
Teacher: OK, in this session we're going to look at another aspect of economics – how war can affect the economy of a country. Carla and Steve are doing a presentation on this for us today. Carla, Steve...
Carla: The question is: Is war good for the economy? Well, it's an interesting question, but like most economic issues, it's difficult to answer it with a simple 'yes' or 'no'. The truth of the matter is that although wars can be both a positive and negative economic stimulus, economies are often driven forward by wars.
Class: That's true.
Steve: If you look back to the 19th century and World War 1, you will find that governments paid for war by printing more money. And, of course, printing money tends to increase inflation. People need more and more cash just to pay for basic necessities, like food. In Germany after World War I, in the 1920s, there was such hyperinflation that prices went up every day.
Carla: While the US economy survived World War I intact, it faced its own crisis with the stock market crash of 1929. This led to huge unemployment when many companies went bankrupt, and later non-stop deflation as the price of goods began dropping, but no one was buying because they had no jobs or money. To counter this, President Franklin D. Roosevelt's government adopted a key idea of economist John Maynard Keynes...increasing government spending.
Steve: It's a bit like jumpstarting a car, when the battery's dead. You need a huge jolt to get the engine roaring again. US government money was the huge jolt of cash needed to get the economy going again, and large-scale New Deal projects, such as the Tennessee Valley Authority, gave work to thousands of people. When World War II came, many more jobs were created in arms manufacturing and related industries like steel and coal.
Carla: While the number of manufacturing jobs does go up during a war, war often still leads to heavy damage to industry and infrastructure in war-torn regions. Also, there is the high cost in human life. Many European countries lost nearly a whole generation of men in the two World Wars. More women entered the workforce, but there were still significant labour shortages as a result.
Steve: And we come back to the issue of inflation. Since 1945, you can see a pattern of increased inflation with each war. The Korean War began in 1950. In that year wholesale prices increased by 12 per cent in the US and 21 per cent in Britain. Vietnam was arguably even worse. The US government spent about 15 per cent of its GDP on the war, and this led to a deep recession in the 1970s.
Carla: If we take the example of more recent wars, like the one in Iraq, war has certainly been bad for the Iraqi economy, but for America the biggest impact has been on oil prices, which were pushed up to record levels. There may have also been some effect on consumer and business confidence, which is much harder to calculate.
Teacher: Thank you, Steve and Carla. Does anyone have any questions...

Unit 8   Bjorn Lomborg: The Skeptical Environmentalist

Peter Heinlein: The Earth's environment is steadily improving. Global warming is nothing much to worry about. The real danger is the Kyoto Treaty, which will cost too much and do almost no good. Those are the ideas of a Danish professor and former Greenpeace activist who has written a book titled, *The Skeptical Environmentalist*. The book, which has recently been published in English, is causing outrage in the environmental community.

His fans call Bjorn Lomborg an outstanding representative of a 'new breed of scientists – mathematically-skilled and computer-adept'. One favourable review predicts his new book will overturn our most basic assumptions about the world's environment. But to his detractors he is not a scientist at all, but a fraud: a statistics professor who they claim makes selective use of statistics to support a right-wing, anti-environment agenda.

He explains that he started out as an environmental activist.

B. Lomborg: I'm an old Greenpeace, left-wing kind of guy and thought basically, yes, things were getting worse and worse. When I read an interview with Julian Simon, an American economist, that tells us things were actually getting better and better, contrary to common knowledge. I thought, No, it can't be true. But then he said, 'Go check it yourself,' ... so I'll have to get his book, to see that it was probably wrong. And it was sufficiently good, and it looked sufficiently substantiated that it would actually be fun to debunk. So I got some of my best students together and we did a study course in the fall of '97.... We wanted to show, you know, this is entirely wrong, this is just right-wing American propaganda. As it turned out over the next couple of months, as we did this, we were getting debunked for the most part.

P. Heinlein: Professor Lomborg says the project convinced him that environmental groups, the so-called Greens, are exaggerating their claims of global environmental gloom and doom.

But he says those exaggerations and sometimes, he adds, even outright falsehoods, often become part of conventional wisdom, often accepted by a majority of people because he says green groups seem to enjoy more credibility than government or business lobbies.

B. Lomborg: Now everybody knows that businesses, you know, when they come and say 'don't worry about the environment,' that may be true, but they might also have a good reason for saying this, profit reasons, ulterior motives. So we're sceptical about them. But we're not in the same way sceptical about green groups, but they also have an agenda. They are also lobby groups.

P. Heinlein: One of Professor Lomborg's favorite targets is the Kyoto Treaty on global warming. A host of recent studies predict catastrophic consequences for the environment from a rise in global temperatures. The United Nations Panel on Climate Change, backed by 3,000 scientists, has thrown its full weight behind the argument that global warming is happening faster than expected, and that ratification of the Kyoto Protocol is urgent.

Professor Lomborg concedes that global warming is real, but calls the Kyoto Treaty a monumental waste of money.

B. Lomborg: Basically, Kyoto will do very little to change global warming. On the other hand, Kyoto will be incredibly expensive. It will cost anywhere from $150–350 billion a year, now that's a lot of money that should be compared to the total global aid of about $50 billion a year. And so basically the idea is to say just for the cost of one year of Kyoto we could give clean drinking water and sanitation to every single human being on Earth. This would avoid two million deaths a year, and would help half a billion people from not getting seriously ill.

P. Heinlein: That argument has sparked a furious outcry from environmentalists. Klaus Heinberg, a professor of environmental sciences at Denmark's Roskilde University, accuses Professor Lomborg of twisting facts and manipulating statistics.

Klaus Heinberg: His main argument is that we can use the money we have earned through industrialism to repair all the bad things going on, and that kind of argument is dangerous. And he made these weird comparisons which normal people make to make fun, I mean, like 'if all children in Europe would stop eating ice cream, then we could have enough money for eliminating some diseases in Africa.' He uses that kind of argument seriously, and he does that in the climate and Kyoto connection.

P. Heinlein: Peter Heinlein for *VOA News*...

Unit 9 Hanni, the seeing-eye dog

Presenter: Traversing the busy streets of Chicago isn't always easy, especially in the winter. On any given day, a pedestrian has to deal with unpredictable traffic, sidewalk holes, snow, ice and city buses. Now, imagine that you're blind. Writer Beth Finke navigates Chicago's many obstacles with the help of her seeing-eye dog Hanni. Hanni is a tail-wagging mix of yellow Lab and Golden Retriever. She was schooled at the Seeing Eye in Morristown, New Jersey.

It's the oldest school of its kind in North America and tomorrow it celebrates 75 years of training dogs as companions to the blind. Hanni's eyes and Beth's patience have formed an effective bond that make an ordinary walk home from the gym an example of true collaboration. We accompanied Beth and Hanni recently as they walked home from Michigan and Balbow in Chicago's South Loop.

Beth: I think most people think you're standing at an intersection; you're with a dog; the dog looks up, sees the green light and then pulls you ahead. What really happens is you're at an intersection; you listen to your parallel traffic so that is the traffic that's going with you, the same direction you want to cross. When you hear the parallel traffic going forward and you sense that the traffic in front of you has stopped, then you tell the dog. In Hanni's case, I would say: 'Hanni, forward.' And then she'll look right and left to make sure it's safe and then she'll go.

Okay, here, I can hear parallel traffic, but I don't know how long they've been going so I'm going to wait and let the whole cycle begin, because I can hear the car idling in front of me. And when he goes, then I'll know...I'll know to listen until we go parallel again. There are some intersections where I actually count...one, one thousand, two, one thousand, but I haven't done it at this one. At Clark and Pope, I count sometimes to get a general idea about when it's going to cycle again. This one's a fairly easy one to cross because it's...there's a steady flow of traffic in both directions. And it's generally pretty predictable except for when the L (train) comes by. *[To Hanni]* Leave it! Thatta girl.

There are certain times when the dogs will stop. And you'll feel in front of you with your foot and there's not a kerb there. And you feel in front with your hand and there's not an obstruction there and you don't know why they're stopping.

It must be a car pulling out of a garage, I guess? Or a parking lot? It's never happened before. I usually...actually, it's not exactly rush hour, but I do try not to walk at this time of day, because there's more traffic. If I can avoid it... *[To Hanni]* Hanni, can you go forward? No? Good girl. There you go. Good girl, Hanni! That was perfect. What a good girl you are. You pretty proud of yourself? You should be. You should be. That was very good. Because I didn't know what was going on.

I feel kind of bad for Hanni. Sometimes we're at a corner and she...it's green and she's not going. And I think the people around me are thinking: 'What a loser seeing-eye dog!' But really, she's waiting for me. I'm waiting to hear the people going.

Unit 10 Behaviour-modification camps for teenagers

Peter: I don't believe it! Have you read this article?
Mary: No, why?
David: What article are you talking about?
Peter: Well, it's about this school in Jamaica called Tranquillity Bay. If you want to call it a school, it sounds more like a maximum security prison to me. It's a 'behaviour-modification programme for troubled teenagers'.
Mary / David: Oh!
Mary: Oh, wait a second, I think I've heard about that. Isn't that the one where really strict American parents send their kids?
Peter: Yeah, most of the kids are American, but a few come from Canada and the UK. Let's see, it's part of some larger group called the 'Worldwide Association of Specialty Programs and Schools', or 'WWASP' for short.
David: Never heard of it.
Peter: It's just so harsh. Listen to this 'the children are often taken from their beds in the middle of the night by private guards, handcuffed, and flown off to Jamaica.' Oh, and then, get this, when they get there 'they are put in isolation for up to a week until the staff think the child is under control. Then, they're given a uniform, a haircut and join a 'family' of 20 students. Boys and girls are kept separate. And an older student, a 'buddy', is given complete control over the new student.
Mary: Family? Sounds a bit like a cult.
David: Well, I think brainwashing is par for the course. This got me thinking...my sister wrote me about this guy she met on an exchange visit in Massachusetts who'd been to a behaviour modification camp in the US. It really messed him up. He said staff members beat him and used pepper spray on him.

When his parents came six months later, they didn't believe anything he told them. Anyway, he was 18 the next year and the school couldn't hold

him anymore, so he left. He's in university now, but he still gets nightmares about the place. And he doesn't speak to his parents any more.
Mary: How can they get away with this kind of stuff?
Peter: Well, the article said that most parents gave their permission, not knowing or maybe not even caring what the staff did so long as they got results. And I guess it does work for some 'troubled teens'. Well, I guess it'd better, since it costs $40,000 a year.
David: Uh, I suppose if you have a choice between getting nightmare treatment or conforming to their rules, most people eventually give in… But I mean what does that do to someone's mental state to be treated that way.
Mary: So are these like the worst teenagers in the world or what? Tell me they're murderers or heroin dealers or something really bad.
Peter: That's actually the worst part. Many children were sent there for doing things like playing truant, not working at school… oh, and trying cigarettes or even cannabis. Oooooh. And sometimes, if they're girls, they might have become 'sexually active' or had a boyfriend the parents didn't approve of.
David: Really?
Mary: That makes me really angry. How could parents do that to their children?
David: Yeah.

Unit 11 Tropical storm causes flooding in Haiti and the Dominican Republic

Reporter: On May 24th, excessive tropical rain showers drenched the Caribbean island shared by the Dominican Republic and Haiti. NASA's weather satellites reported that within 24 hours, over 60 centimetres of rain had fallen on the central mountain regions dividing the countries. By early morning on the 25th, several rivers had burst their banks sending walls of mud, water and debris down into the low-lying areas. This was the worst disaster to hit Haiti in over a decade.

In the two countries more than three thousand people have died in the floods. In Haiti, there were 1,191 dead and 1,484 have 'disappeared'. In the Dominican Republic, 691 are reported dead or missing. And more than 50,000 people have been left homeless in both countries.

The situation in Haiti was made much worse for a number of reasons. As the poorest country in the Americas, the majority of Haiti's 8 million people have been cutting down the island's limited forest resources for fuel and shelter. It is estimated by officials that over 90 per cent of the forests in the country are gone. The United States Agency for International Development reports that it has planted some 60 million trees in the region, but it estimates that 10 to 20 million trees are being cut down every year. Without the trees and their root systems to hold back the deluge of water, small streams quickly became torrents, carrying with them gravel, silt and mud.

US forces had been sent to Haiti to provide security after the fall of Haiti's President Jean-Bertrand Aristide, and US Marine helicopters airlifted 100,000 tonnes of food and water in the first few days of the disaster. However, some international aid agencies have complained that the US helicopters stopped their relief efforts too soon. A Marine spokesman said it was due to pilot fatigue. As a result, the rest of the aid supplies had to be carried by foot into the areas affected. United Nations forces which have just arrived are expected to aid in this effort.

In a cruel irony, the floods came on the tail end of one of the country's worst droughts. A large number of crops had already failed and many Haitians were by now in dire need of food aid. Officials are also concerned about the possible outbreak of disease with the large number of bodies unaccounted for.

Haitian officials and international governments are now looking at solutions to the problem of Haiti's deforestation in an effort to alleviate future floods in the region. Some solutions proposed have included importing wood from Canada, the United States and Guyana, and possibly propane from Venezuela or Trinidad. This is Jenny…

Unit 12 Click kanji: Is English the only language for the internet?

Jonathan
Kent: Kuala Lumpur, in many ways, it's rather like the internet. In the early days, it was English-speaking people, in this case, it was the British who built much of its infrastructure, like the railway station and the

courthouses. But as it's grown, people of many races have left their mark, and its future is without doubt multicultural. And like the internet, communication in Kuala Lumpur takes place in many different languages. But when you want to find your way around, the street signs in Kuala Lumpur all use Western letters. It's the same on the net. It makes things simple for those familiar with the 26 letters of the English alphabet, but more difficult for everyone else. People from countries that use their own scripts are demanding equal treatment. The biggest group are Chinese speakers. They want email and web addresses including top level domain names like '.cn' for China in Chinese characters – characters, which are very close to Chinese people's hearts.

Tso Yu Ling: It's a part of our life, our culture and everything that we do every day. And take for example, the name in Chinese cannot be translated into other languages, you know, the same as it is. So why couldn't it be allowed on the internet? We want our name. That's our identity.

J. Kent: But that's a task in itself. These characters may have originated in China but variations are used right across East Asia – 150,000 in all – and the number keeps growing. The internet's old 16-bit coding wasn't up to the task, so programmers have had to upgrade to cope with the thousands of symbols. To make matters worse, there are often clashes between one country's set of characters and another's.

James Seng: Because the Chinese characters are used in different languages from Chinese, Japanese, Korean and Vietnamese, some characters that look the same mean different things in different languages. Some characters that look different actually mean the same thing in some languages.

J. Kent: In Japan, these characters mean 'male' – in China, 'napkin'. These ones mean 'modern'. In China, they say 'zian dai'; in Japan 'gendai'; in Korea 'hyundai' – each the name of a major corporation, but the characters are the same. So who will get to use them on the internet? These are major headaches for the people who make the net work smoothly. So the Internet Corporation for Assigned Names and Numbers, or ICANN, has been meeting in Kuala Lumpur to try to find a solution. It's partly a technical problem. Some languages, for instance, are written right-left, not left-right. But mainly, it's a people problem.

Paul Twomey: How do we get communities to come together and agree that you express certain characters in similar ways across countries or even across languages? *[PAUSE]*

J. Kent: That means getting agreement on a standard way of writing things in Chinese, Arabic, Thai, Tamil and other scripts, perhaps 300 languages in all. And that's the hard part, not least because some people think the internet's framework should stay in English. They say that by allowing internet addresses in different scripts, you'll destroy the web's ability to connect. Others disagree, saying that if you don't, countries like China will simply set up their own internet, inaccessible to the rest of the world. However, most believe that common sense will win out.

P. Twomey: I got a business card today in Japanese, but in this part of the world they also give it in English. Because the person who's giving it to me knows that they are interacting with people in Japanese and people in English. We'll probably have people having email addresses potentially in both, but the key question is: 'Does the mail system still work in either case?'

J. Kent: And that's going to matter to a lot of people. There are now more than 100 million broadband users worldwide and almost half of them are here in Asia. In a few years' time, most internet users will live here. And experts say it's set to transform the economy of the region. Like it or not, the internet is fast outgrowing its Western roots.

Unit 13   Extract from: *Outfoxed: Rupert Murdoch's War on Journalism* with The O'Reilly Factor interview with Jeremy M. Glick

B. O'Reilly: In the Personal Story segment tonight we were surprised to find out that an American who lost his father in the World Trade Centre attack had signed an anti-war advertisement that accused the USA itself of terrorism.

Al Franken: Jeremy Glick is the son of a Port Authority worker who died in 9/11. He had signed an anti-war petition and O'Reilly had to have him on.

Jeremy Glick: And they were so persistent about getting me on the O'Reilly show 'cause they found out that I was on the advisory board and signed a statement that was against the war and that I was

directly impacted by 9/11. The success that I had on the O'Reilly show had to do with just practice and preparation. I taped the shows and what I did was I took a stop watch that I used to use for running sprints in high school and I would see when he has a hostile guest and I would time how long it takes for him to cut them off.
B. O'Reilly: I was surprised and the reason I was surprised is that this ad equates the United States with the terrorists.
J. Glick: I said I'm shocked that you're surprised, and basically just made the only point I wanted to make.

Our current president now inherited a legacy from his father and inherited a political legacy that's responsible for training militarily, economically and situating geopolitically the parties involved in the alleged assassination and murder of my father and countless of thousands of others, so I don't see why...
B. O'Reilly: Let me stop you here. Alright...
J. Glick: ...it is surprising that I would want to come back and want to support escalating Bush's aggression to that area...
B. O'Reilly: It is surprising and I'll tell you why. You are (espousing) a far-left position...
J. Glick: It was extremely intimidating sitting down the studio, 'cause he's really tall, and like dude, he lords over you.
B. O'Reilly: You see, I'm sure your beliefs are sincere, but what upsets me is I don't think your father would be approving of this.
J. Glick: Well, actually my father thought that Bush's presidency was illegimate.
B. O'Reilly: Maybe he did, but I don't think he'd be equating this country as a terrorist nation as you are.
J. Glick: Well, I wasn't saying that it was necessarily like that.
B. O'Reilly: Yes, you were. You signed this and it absolutely said that.
A. Franken: Jeremy was pretty cool during it and he was giving his political views, which were very to the left of O'Reilly's.
J. Glick: And he said I don't really care what you think politically. And I said obviously you do care because: a) you brought me on the show, and b) I told him that he uses 9/11 and sympathy with the 9/11 families and the lives lost to rationalise his narrow right-wing agenda.

J. Glick: You evoke sympathy with the 9/11 families.
B. O'Reilly: That's a bunch of crap.
J. Glick: ...so that means...I'm a 9/11 family...
B. O'Reilly: I've done more for the 9/11 families..., by their own admission, I've done more for them than you will ever hope to do.
J. Glick: OK.
B. O'Reilly: So you keep your mouth shut.
J. Glick: Well, you're not representing me...
B. O'Reilly: You shouldn't be exploiting those people.
J. Glick: You're not representing me.
B. O'Reilly: And I'd never represent you. You know why?
J. Glick: Why?
B. O'Reilly: Because you have a warped view of this world and a warped view of this country.
J. Glick: Well, explain that. Let me give you an example of a parallel experience...
B. O'Reilly: No, I'm not going to debate this with you.
J. Glick: ...let me give you an example of parallel experiences...
B. O'Reilly: No...
J. Glick: ...on September 14th, on September 14th.
B. O'Reilly: Here's the record, here's the record. Alright. You didn't support the action against Afghanistan to remove the Taliban. You were against it.
J. Glick: Why would I want to brutalise and further punish the people in Afghanistan?
B. O'Reilly: Who killed your father!
J. Glick: The people in Afghanistan...
B. O'Reilly: Who killed your father!
J. Glick: The people in Afghanistan didn't kill my father.
B. O'Reilly: Sure, they did! The Al Quaeda people were trained there.
J. Glick: The Al Quaeda people, well what about the Afghan...
B. O'Reilly: See, I'm more angry about it that you are!
J. Glick: So what about George Bush?
B. O'Reilly: What about George Bush? He had nothing do with it.
J. Glick: The director, senior, as director of the CIA.
B. O'Reilly: He had nothing to do with it!
J. Glick: So the people that trained a hundred thousand mujahadeen, who were...

B. O'Reilly: I hope your mom is not watching this.
J. Glick: Ah...
B. O'Reilly: I hope your mother is not watching this.
J. Glick: It was unfair for O'Reilly to evoke both my mom and my father in the interview, especially when I wasn't.

Unit 14 Talking about comic book superheroes

Presenter: We're coming to you live today from the Comic Book Expo. In this part of the show, we'll be looking at comic book superheroes. Are they good role models for children? Joining us today, we have comic book cartoonist Jim Bailey.
Jim Bailey: Hello.
Presenter: ...and comic book historian Dr. Joanne Sykes.
Joanne Sykes: Hi.
Presenter: I'd like to start with you, Joanne. Maybe you can give us some background on comic book superheroes.
J. Sykes: Probably we should start with the golden age of comics...that's from 1938, when Superman first appeared, to 1954. We find the basic blueprint for this group of heroes was along the same lines as Superman. Mostly, they were superior beings...invincible. In fact, it's not until about ten years later that Superman's only weakness, green kryptonite, was introduced.
Presenter: Jim, your grandfather was a comic book cartoonist at this time. What did he tell you about this period?
J. Bailey: Well, a lot of these characters were created during World War II. The types of characters and plots often reflected the uncertainty of this time. I mean, you could argue they were really propaganda pieces, you know, invincible heroes versus evil-doers... and the heroes always win. A good example is the cover of the first Captain America comic in 1941 showing him punching Hitler.
Presenter: What about these early superheroes as role models for young readers?
J. Sykes: To put it simply, these early superheroes would have helped children to learn about society's values early on. I mean it's quite straightforward – good guys against bad guys. It's good to fight crime and help people. Vulnerability aside, they're not very different from the heroes in Ancient Greek mythology.

Presenter: How does this change as comics develop?
J. Sykes: By the 1960s, we have characters like Spider-man... He's a teenager...
J. Bailey: Yeah, with a lot of problems in his life.
J. Sykes: That's right. He lives with his Aunt May because his parents are dead, and he worries about everything...about the women in his life, his career as a photographer and paying the bills. He even becomes a hero by accident, after getting bitten by a radioactive spider.
Presenter: You're a big Spider-man fan, Jim. What do think about him as a role model?
J. Bailey: Spider-man is a very complex character. He's the super teen, facing all the same problems teenagers face, but even more so. And in terms of what kind of role model he represents, I think it's a very positive one. He's human, just a kid really.
Presenter: Joanne, are comic book superheroes just for boys?
[PAUSE]
J. Sykes: Do comic book superheroes appeal to everyone? Well, yes and no. Obviously, as a genre comic books are dominated by male figures. In terms of the female characters you find two basic types. There's the Wonder Woman type, an independent character like the men. Then, there's the Batgirl type, which tends to be just a helper, an extension of a male character like Batman.

Generally, in terms of the empowerment of girls, many critics point out that these women all have a Barbie-doll look – an ideal that can't be met. Well, I wonder... how many men could have or would want to have a body like the Incredible Hulk?
J. Bailey: If I could just mention one thing...

Unit 15 A teenage single mother talks about her life

Stephen Nolan: Now, Courtney Cassidy has been creating quite a stir recently. The young blonde lady has had the press queuing up for interviews in the past. She does not have an agent. She does not have a public relations company. She doesn't have a record deal. She doesn't have a film deal. She doesn't have a television deal. She has no rich, famous or well-connected parent, or friend or lover. She's simply had three lovers who've produced children with her. And, well, she's very young. Courtney had her first kid aged fourteen years. Good morning, Courtney.

Courtney
Cassidy: Hello. Good morning.
S. Nolan: Courtney, nice to talk to you today. Obviously, I've been reading about you in the papers. You first became pregnant at fourteen.
C. Cassidy: Yeah, that's right. I was in a relationship for four and a half years. It took me two and a half years before I actually fell pregnant or had intercourse.
S. Nolan: And how was that for you?
C. Cassidy: Um, I planned the pregnancy myself so it wasn't so shocking because I wanted a baby.
S. Nolan: And did you not think at fourteen years of age you were too young?
C. Cassidy: No, my sister is...become pregnant at the same age as well. So I thought if she could do it, I could.
S. Nolan: Now, obviously, some people will be feeling very, very sorry for you. They will be giving you a lot of sympathy. Do you think it's sympathy that you need, Courtney?
C. Cassidy: I don't want people to feel sorry for me or give me sympathy. I can do it on my own. I don't need people to feel sorry for me.
S. Nolan: Do you think you can be a good mother at fourteen years of age?
C. Cassidy: I can give my babies as much loving as a 34, 38-year-old woman could.
S. Nolan: You might be able to give them as much love but you can't really give them experience. You're still developing yourself at the age of fourteen, aren't you?
C. Cassidy: Yes, but...I don't know, I bring my children up...I've brought all my children up as good as any other woman could, if not better.
S. Nolan: What makes you think that?
C. Cassidy: 'Cos...I don't know, I gave them stability. I've gave them love. I've gave them caring. I've gave them what they wanted basically in life.
S. Nolan: Now of course, what you haven't given the first child is a father because you've fallen out with him, haven't you?
C. Cassidy: Yeah, I fell out with him. That was no fault of my own though. He had another girlfriend whilst I was pregnant and me not knowing. Two weeks after my little girl was born, he finished with me to go out with this girl.
S. Nolan: Did you not feel like getting married to him?
C. Cassidy: I wanted to get married, yeah. But obviously he'd got another girl...sorry, a girlfriend with him by that time.
S. Nolan: So that was your first child, age fourteen. Then, you had your second child, what age were you then?
C. Cassidy: I was fifteen or sixteen. Sixteen, I was.
S. Nolan: Two children by sixteen. And you didn't know the father's last name?
C. Cassidy: No.
S. Nolan: Why not?
C. Cassidy: 'Cos it was one night out after having my first daughter, I was going out with all my friends. I got too drunk, gone home, had intercourse with someone I don't know. Woke up the next morning and he wasn't there.
S. Nolan: Do you regret doing it now?
C. Cassidy: Yes.
S. Nolan: So that was the second child. Have you tried to seek out the father? Have you tried to find him?
C. Cassidy: No, 'cos my partner I'm now with brings up all my three children the same.
S. Nolan: And you had the third child, aged?
C. Cassidy: My third child, how old was I when I had it?
S. Nolan: Yes.
C. Cassidy: I was seventeen.
S. Nolan: Now obviously Courtney, when you get to seventeen years of age and you've three kids, you're surely saying to yourself the majority of my friends are not like this. I am doing something that is rather extraordinary here. Should I be doing this?
C. Cassidy: Well, I don't care what people think of me. At the end of the day, this is the life that I wanted. I can live my career when I'm older and my children are older. I'll still be young at the end of the day. So that's what I think...
S. Nolan: What kind of sex education were you given in school?
C. Cassidy: By the time, I had sex education, I was already pregnant with Laina, my first daughter. So...

Unit 16 The science curriculum in Arizona

Anne Minard: Late last month, the Arizona department of education visited Flagstaff as part of a quick series of public meetings around the state to get input for classroom standards for science. They got an earful from people you might expect to care, like science teachers. Julie Bias, a teacher at Granite Mountain Middle school in Prescott, showed up to tell the department she worries about the proposed buffet-style plan for middle schools which would touch on a variety of science topics each year, rather than going in depth into one area per grade level like the schools do now.

Julie Bias: We're teaching an incomplete unit in cells, where genetics is not covered and then, moving on to a weather unit, doesn't make much sense. On number three, this seems to be surface sampling of the science areas instead of learning an area in depth.

A. Minard: Some local teachers worry about the effects of the new standards on existing in-depth programmes like the third-grade focus on astronomy at Flagstaff's DeMiguel School. Another teacher complained that the fourth grade is too soon for students to get a lesson on the parts of an atom like the new standards suggest. But not everyone was there to criticise the nuances of the standards. Just like it has in every other state that's grappled with new science standards, the process in Arizona has brought out the age-old debate between creation and evolution. Al Scott is a Flagstaff resident who says evolution has no place at all in the science curriculum.

Al Scott: The theory of evolution is not science. And I submit to the board that it ought to be removed from the scientific curriculum and placed in philosophy or some other curriculum, not in science. Because it's not science, it is in fact a religion. It believes that the origin of life started with a rock. Now, I don't know whether any of you here evolved from a rock, but I didn't. And my ancestors aren't monkeys.

A. Minard: Others took a gentler approach and simply asked the committee to present the theory of evolution in such a way that students are invited to critique it and not just accept it as fact. Tom Horne, Arizona's superintendent of education, seems to agree. He says he thinks his department has found a pretty good solution that will work for people on both sides of the debate. It has to do with changing a couple of key words in the teaching standards themselves, like in this example.

Tom Horne: Reforms Objective 9, the original one was: 'Use patterns in the fossil records to support the theory of organic evolution.' The proposed revision is: 'Evaluate patterns in the fossil records that support the theory of organic evolution.' I think the use of the word 'evaluate' helps convey the idea that you can both support and criticise different forms of evidence.

A. Minard: Horne says supporters of evolution need not worry about the future of science education in Arizona as long as he's in charge.

T. Horne: Well, as long as I'm state superintendent of schools, we are going to have generally accepted scientific knowledge in our science classrooms. And evolution is part of that.

A. Minard: But Skip Evans, network project director with the National Center for Science Education, is wary. His group's main focus is keeping an eye on the nation's science classrooms to make sure creationism doesn't get any more time at the chalkboard. But he says the proponents of creationism and its sister theory called 'intelligent design' are sneaky.

Skip Evans: Creationists have switched their tactics over the last couple of years. In the past, they've wanted to bring in some kind of alternate theories, you know, even traditional biblical creationism or maybe now it's sort of the next evolutionary step in creationism – intelligent design creationism. But that's largely failed so what they've done is resorted to this sort of fall-back procedure and say, you know: 'We want to teach both the evidence for evolution and the evidence against evolution.' Now to the average person that sounds very reasonable. However, what they'll bring in to the curriculum as evidence against evolution is bad science. It used to be a lot easier just to knock down, you know, creation science. But like any organism that's going to survive it's going to have to adapt. And anti-evolutionism has adapted very well to its current environment.

A. Minard: Evans worries that changes like some of those proposed for Arizona's curriculum are a foot in the door for sacrificing good science in favour of religion.

The three-week public comment period on the new science teaching standards has come and gone with hardly any public notice and no press coverage. And that alarms Skip Evans. The revised standards are expected to go to the state board for final approval as early as next month. And they could be phased into classrooms over the next several years. For Arizona Public Radio, I'm Anne Minard in Flagstaff.

Unit 17 Space Debris – European Space Agency

Narrator: Space. This is the year 2005 when satellites have been launched into space for nearly fifty years. Thousands of these manmade objects are orbiting the Earth. And most will remain there for decades. Only a few are still in use. The rest are space debris.
Heiner Klinkrad: What one can say is the number of space objects that we know of is in the order of 9,500. And these objects are typically larger than 10 centimetres in the low Earth orbit, up to 2,000 km. And they are typically larger than about one metre in the geostationary orbit. Now if you go to smaller sizes, the number of objects increases dramatically. And if you go to one-centimetre objects, then probably we have half a million objects up there.
Narrator: The dramatic increase of space debris – the result of a lack of awareness during the early phases of space exploration. Back in the 1980s, several hundred satellites per year were put in orbit around the Earth, mostly as spy satellites. With them came the upper stages of rockets that lifted them in space. Today, even fuel tanks and old astronaut gloves are migrating in space around the Earth.
H. Klinkrad: Space debris is a big problem because there are many objects, sometimes very small objects which have a very high velocity and a high kinetic energy, which can cause lots of damage.
Narrator: Space debris or micrometeorites sometimes crash into abandoned rocket fuel tanks or batteries orbiting Earth. This causes explosions, creating clouds of new space debris with innumerable tiny bits and pieces. Since the beginning of the space age, there have been almost 200 explosions in orbit, under half of which involve old rocket bodies. Because space debris is travelling so fast, even pieces of one centimetre or less in size can cause big damage.

H. Klinkrad: The object that we see here is an aluminium block, a solid aluminium block which was hit by a tiny sphere which is 1.2 centimetres in diameter. And you see that this caused quite a bit of damage. This bullet, if you like, was fired at this block at a velocity of 6.8 km a second, which is less than the orbital speed. You don't just have this crater morphology, but you can also have detachments like this. So in a worse case, this could have separated. And with high velocity, this detachment could have moved through a cabin of a space station and might have caused lots of damage.
Narrator: So space debris is not only an aesthetical or an environmental problem, if the debris increases further, there is danger that even space exploration could suffer dramatically, says Heiner Klinkrad.
H. Klinkrad: If you do not enforce space debris mitigation measures in very near future, it may happen that collision events become prevailing in the long term. And then you may reach a situation where collisions totally dominate and whatever you do, you cannot get control of the situation anymore. Ultimately, this may lead to a situation where in certain altitude regions you cannot conduct any safe space missions anymore.

Unit 18 Brazil: Computers in the *favelas*

Paula Gobbi: This small courtyard in front of the church is the only recreation area in the San Carlos *favela* – a slum of forty thousand people. This hillside shanty town is one of the 630 *favelas* in Rio De Janeiro, where poverty, unemployment and drug dealers reign. Over a million people live in Rio's infamous *favelas* surviving on little more than the minimum wage of 80 dollars a month. Yet this information technology school set up in a small room of the church is helping the poor strive for a better future.

A simple clicking on the keyboard, two dollars inscription tuition and five dollars monthly fee has transformed life for 21-year-old Eloisa Fajeira. Eloisa makes a living filming children's party videos. And with the newly acquired computer skills, her business is growing.
Eloisa Fajeira: I work with my brother filming parties. We have a video and a karaoke. And the

computer has helped us because we can now make brochures and attractive covers for the videos. We can now put the child's photo on the front of the video along with our name and address to get more business. We can also add graphic designs to make it look better. Before we only had local clients here in the poor areas. Now we get work from other neighbourhoods, even from rich people.

P. Gobbi: Eloisa says it's hard for her and her brother to find traditional jobs because nobody wants to employ people from the *favelas*. And it's also hard to get qualifications if you live in the slums. Former computer analyst Rodrigo Baggio set out to close that gap six years ago when he founded the Committee to Democratise Information Technology. He started out with just five PCs donated by a big international company. Today, nearly 75,000 young people have been trained in basic computer skills. Some have gone on to higher training programmes in one of over 240 schools in the slums where the scheme operates.

Rodrigo Baggio: In our project, we have a very concrete product, the information technology citizenship school. Each school needs to be a self-sustainable and self-management school. With the technology, we talk about citizenship, human rights, ecology, sexuality, non-violence. The idea is to use information technology like a citizenship tool to change lives and to change poor communities.

P. Gobbi: Rodrigo Baggio confirms that change is possible.

R. Baggio: About eighty-six per cent of our students said they changed their lives after our class. This means things like they come back to the public school. They change their behaviour inside the public school. They change their behaviour inside their families. They didn't work more in drug dealers. They have a productive way to spend their time.

P. Gobbi: Rodrigo Baggio's next goal is to provide internet access for all the schools participating in this scheme – creating an online exchange for the poor communities to discuss their problems, and providing more opportunities for people to better themselves and their communities through better employment prospects. And following on from the success of this project in his homeland, Baggio's ambition has gone global with similar schemes in Colombia, Uruguay, Mexico and Chile.

Unit 19 A laughter therapist talks about Laughter Clubs

Mark Colvin: India's giggling guru, Doctor Madan Kataria, is no stranger to ABC audiences, our Delhi Bureau discovered him more than a decade ago, and he's appeared on ABC Radio, TV News, and the Foreign Correspondent programme. But he's never brought his laughing gear to our shores till now.

This weekend, Doctor Kataria will touch down in Melbourne to kick-off a belly-laughing tour, which will also take in Sydney and Brisbane. South Asia Correspondent Geoff Thompson spoke to Doctor Kataria today, after visiting a laughter club in New Delhi this morning.

Geoff Thompson: Laughter Club starts with a warm-up, as about 15 people standing in a New Delhi public park begin their day with a giggle about... well, anything really. Leading this group is local giggling guru, Doctor Umesh Sahgal, who balances his stressful daily life as a dentist with morning of cackling and silly movements – a bit like an exercise group in which everyone's as a high as a kite.

Umesh Sahgal: But we do it in a different way. We do all by laughing, we don't do it seriously, we keep on laughing through all the exercises for 20 minutes, and after that we just laugh for no reason. So that everyone is happy, you know, when they leave this place. They are just fresh for the whole day. They can go and fight their own stress and tension in a good, better way.

G. Thompson: Is it difficult to laugh on cue early in the morning?

[PAUSE]

U. Sahgal: Well, on your own you can't laugh, but when you see others laughing you start laughing yourself.

G. Thompson: And laugh you do. It's hard not to when surrounded by complete strangers all giggling themselves stupid, jumping on one leg or pretending to make milkshakes or even flapping and squawking like birds.

Mumbai-based Doctor Madan Kataria is the founder of Laughing Clubs and has spread his guffawing enthusiasm for laughter's health benefits all over the world. This weekend, Doctor Kataria kicks off a new tour of Australia in Melbourne. But the laughter bug is already booming in Australia, with 30

clubs and about five thousand members. And it all started with Doctor Kataria's idea nine years ago.
Madan Kataria: The idea of Laughter Club came to my mind on 13th March 1995, and I went to a public park and told people, 'I want to start a Laughter Club', and they started laughing at me, they said, 'Doc, are you all right?' I said, 'No, I'm serious about it. Let's start a Laughter Club.' And they ridiculed, they said, 'This is not a good idea', and then I could find four people who were ready to laugh at me. That was the beginning of the Laughter Club.
G. Thompson: Laughter Clubs are sometimes called Laughter Yoga, and do involve breathing exercises. But for the most part you just stand around and laugh, something which even cynical journalists can't help finding contagious. You got anything that can make Australian people laugh?
U. Sahgal: Yes, I think we can. We can. We can make everyone laugh. See we made you laugh also...weren't you laughing...?
G. Thompson: Yes, you did.
U. Sahgal: That's what I told you. This is a contagious disease, you know. Even if you are not laughing, when you see others laughing you start laughing yourself. So at least you have a smile on your face when you see others laughing, and when you join the stream, you start laughing yourself.
Club member 1: But start laughing with me. And now you laugh more. You see, this way the laugh is spread all over world, not only in India, all over the world, this is pretty.
Club member 2: Now you have to laugh and record your voice.

Unit 20   Holiday reps meet in a Spanish seaside resort

Andrew (Manager): Well, we can't wait any longer. Let's get started.
Justin: Sorry, sorry. I overslept, must have forgotten to set the alarm.
Andrew: Alright, you're here now. Look can everyone try to be here on time tomorrow? I mean, how hard is it to get up in time for a meeting at 11? Now, let's talk about today. Lindsay, what's on for today?
Lindsay: OK. Today things begin at one o'clock. I've organised a boat trip over to Las Salinas. The theme is Mexican Getaway. To get them in the mood everyone gets a cheap Mexican sombrero as they go on the boat. Nicole is handling the activities on board.
Andrew: Nicole, what have you got?
Nicole: Well, I hired a local DJ...Tom 'Mega' Watts...he plays mostly trance and deep house. Those girls from Bristol were wanting more deep house, so I think he fits the bill. We've found some CDs of Mexican music, so we can have some of that on the way back. And we've got Mexican costumes for all of the reps.
All: Oh, right.
Andrew: Okay, that sounds about right. What are they going to do besides dance and drink?
Nicole: Well, Lindsay and I've got a few party games lined up too, with shots of tequila for the winners.
Andrew: Yeah, well, that'll liven things up. Which reminds me Justin, what else will they be drinking?
Justin: Well, it goes with the Mexican theme...margaritas, two kinds of light Mexican lager, and the tequila too, of course.
Andrew: Anything to eat?
Justin: Oh...yeah,...some nachos with salsa and guacamole and a few other things.
Andrew: OK...Just remember when we get back that the local cops don't want anyone carrying open bottles of alcohol through the town. It's a 50-euro fine on the spot. We want people to have a good time but we need to try and keep the noise down too. We don't want them coming off the boat shouting and yelling and throwing up all over the police like last time...and we definitely don't want anyone to get arrested.

Oh...and I had an email from Head Office, saying there's been a lot of bad publicity at home about Brits binge drinking in Spanish holiday resorts, so I have to remind all you reps that we have to keep on good terms with the people who live here, and the police too.
Justin: No worries. I'll be sticking with those Scottish lads to keep 'em in check. Remember those two guys who passed out after a drinking bout in the main street in June. Someone took all their clothes and they got their pictures all over the papers. Mind you, the police were pretty restrained about that one.
All: That's true.
Andrew: That's what I like to hear. Oh, I need to say something about the rep show...

Test 1   Exam Practice Listening Scripts   Teacher's Guide

Test 1   IELTS only: IELTS Listening Section 1

Narrator: You will hear a woman named Jane talking to a colleague at work about a concert she saw the previous evening. Look at the map. The boxes with the letters A-H indicate the location of Jane and her friends. You have some time to read Questions 1 to 5. *[PAUSE: 30 seconds]*

Narrator: For Questions 1 and 2, write the correct letter A-H next to the questions. You will see that an example has been done for you. Jane was standing in front of the stage, so C is her location and has been written in the space. Now we shall begin. You should answer the questions as you listen because you will not hear the recording a second time. Listen carefully and answer Questions 1 to 5.

Mike: Hi, Jane...Jane...I said, 'Hi'.

Jane: Oh, hi, Mike. Sorry, my ears are still buzzing from last night's concert.

Mike: So how was it?

Jane: It was fantastic. I went with some flatmates. You remember meeting Katie and Rebecca, right?

Mike: Sure. Was it at the Centre Space?

Jane: Yes, I love that place.

Mike: So where did you watch it, inside?

Jane: Well, it was really crowded. We all ended up in different places while the concert was on. I think I had the best place though. I followed this guy and ended up only a few feet from the lead singer.

Mike: So where were Katie and Rebecca?

Jane: Well, Katie still hasn't managed to give up smoking, so I think she went out for a cigarette. She said she met a friend there. When the concert started though, they made their way to the corner bar to the left of the dance floor. She has a crush on the bartender so she stayed there the whole time flirting with him.

  I guess Rebecca met some friends and sat with them in the booth nearest the entrance. That was until her new boyfriend showed up. By the time the band started, she had wandered over to the main bar with him. I guess they were just off the dance floor so they had a really good view.

Mike: So what happened after the concert?

Jane: Well, I went looking for them for about half an hour. But I gave up because it was so crowded and decided to have a drink and sit with Rebecca's friends. Ten minutes later, Katie and Rebecca arrived. Katie was very upset.

Mike: Oh, why?

Jane: Katie said she must have left her pink designer handbag on a table on the patio. Katie went to look for it, but it wasn't there. She was so upset. She had found Rebecca and they went to the bar to ask if someone had handed in a handbag, but nothing. Katie looked like she was going to cry.

Narrator: Before you hear the rest of the conversation, you have some time to look at Questions 6 to 10. *[PAUSE: 30 seconds]*

Narrator: Now listen and answer Questions 6 to 10.

Mike: Did she have much in it?

Jane: Luckily, she said that she had left her wallet at home, so she didn't lose her credit cards or her bank card. Unfortunately, she had about £40 in it for her taxi fare home. She thought she had lost her mobile phone too, but it was in her back pocket. She did have her keys in the bag, but that was okay because we all had keys to the flat. I guess it was mostly that the handbag itself was really expensive.

Mike: Well, did she ever find it?

Jane: Well, that was the funny part. She'd completely given up and said she wanted to go home. When we went to get our coats, she gave the coat check person her number. When the man came back he had her coat in one hand and her bag in the other. She had completely forgotten she'd left it there.

Mike: That's pretty funny.

Jane: I know. Katie's always doing stuff like that.

Mike: But tell me, what was the band like?

Jane: They were great live, maybe better than their album. And they looked really wild.

Mike: What do you mean?

Jane: Well, the lead singer had his trademark long brown hair under a cowboy hat. He was wearing just black leather pants so you could see he had a big Japanese samurai tattoo on his chest. The lead guitarist was another story. He had a red Mohawk. And he was wearing these crazy pants made of cuddly animals. When he turned around you could see he had tattoos on his back that looked like two angel wings. It's funny, we each had our favourite band members. Rebecca liked the drummer, Katie thought the lead singer was really good-looking and I liked the guitarist best.

Mike: Sounds like you had a good time.

Narrator: That is the end of Section 1.

Test 2 IGCSE only: IGCSE Listening Part 1

For Questions 1–6 you will hear a series of short sentences. Answer each question on the line provided. Your answer should be as brief as possible. You will hear each item twice.

1 Benny is travelling to Paris next week. According to the weather forecast, on which weekday morning would it be best for him to sit outside at a café?
Weather presenter: And now the weather for our holiday travellers. Berlin should be hot and sunny all week with a high of 25 degrees. Amsterdam might experience some thunderstorms, as a cold front moves in from the west. And Paris will continue to see rain until mid-week, but this should clear up by Thursday afternoon.

2 Your English class is planning a trip to London this Friday. Where must you meet your class and when?
Alex: Sorry Peter, I came late to class today. What's the plan for the London trip on Friday?
Peter: Oh, well, Mr. Ferguson suggested we meet in Terminal 1 by the information desk. He said you need to be there two hours before we take off at 4 pm.

3 Pamela is going to the cinema. When will her film start?
Cinema: Good afternoon. This is the New Haven cinema hotline. How may I help you?
Pamela: Oh hello, I was wondering if you still have any tickets available for the late show.
Cinema: Let me see, was that for the film in Studio One or Two?
Pamela: Studio Two.
Cinema: OK, that would be the 9.25 show. Just let me check. Yes, we still have a few tickets available.

4 Richard needs a map of the Underground. How much does he pay for it?
Richard: Hello, I'd like a packet of crisps and I'd like to buy a London Underground map please.
Kiosk assistant: Well, that will be one pound for the crisps. The maps are free to the public.

5 Scott is going to play a game of football with his friends. What three things does he need to bring with him?
Dharmash: Oh, hi, mate. Are you still coming to the pitch tomorrow?
Scott: Hi, Dharmash! Yeah, definitely. I was just going to call you to ask whether I should bring anything with me.
Dharmash: Well, it'll be pretty hot out, so you better bring a bottle of water. Other than that, just make sure you've got a good pair of football boots. The grass is slippery. Also, we usually go for some chips after so remember to bring some money with you.

6 Sharon and her friend are out shopping. Why does her friend suggest she buy some shoes?
Sharon: Beth, what do you think of these?
Beth: Mmmn, those are okay. Do they come in blue?
Sharon: I don't know. I could ask.
Beth: Hey Sharon, what do you think of those pumps? They're red, so they'd go with your favourite top.
Sharon: Yes, but...they're a bit pricey.
Beth: You'll get a lot of use out of them though, trust me.
Sharon: Well, alright, I'll try them on.

Test 3 IGCSE / IELTS

Nina: Hello, and welcome to London Heathrow Airport. My name is Nina and I'm here to give you a tour of our facilities. Now if you'll just follow me, we will start off in Terminal 2.

Heathrow is the busiest airport in Europe and the third busiest in the world just behind Atlanta and Chicago. To accommodate the flow of more than 67 million passengers who pass through the airport every year, we stay open 24 hours a day, 365 days a year. We have four terminals right now, with our big new fifth terminal scheduled to open in 2008.

In case this is your first time here, I'd like to give you a few statistics to show just how vast this place is. We have a total retail space of 48,000 square metres, that is, about six and a half times bigger than the football pitch at Manchester United.

Every year nearly half a million planes land here. To make sure passengers reach their planes on time, we have over 500 check-in desks. And Heathrow employs the equivalent of a small city, around 68,000 people. There are also over 34,000 car parking spaces, with about half reserved for staff. Speaking of staff, how many of you have seen the BBC TV documentary *Airport*?

Okay, that's quite a few of you. Well, as many of you are probably aware, that programme was filmed here on location at Heathrow, using some of our very own staff. Although some of the staff have moved on, many of the people who appeared in it still work here. And before you ask, Jeremy Spake wasn't a professional actor when he was on the programme. But I must say, he has managed a fairly successful career as a presenter since then.

At any rate, I saw at least two people you might recognise from the show earlier today. If you're lucky, you might get a chance to say hello to one of them later in this tour.

Now, I'll tell you a little bit about the history of London Heathrow. The land that was used to create the first airstrip in this area was originally owned by the Vicar of Harmondsworth. He sold the land to Fairey Aviation, an early British aeroplane manufacturer, who used the airstrip to test their aircraft. In 1944, the Ministry of Air took control of the site for use in World War Two, although it never in fact saw any military use.

The airport itself gets its name after the small village of Heath Row, which was where Terminal 3 stands now. The village was demolished in 1945 when the airport site was developed.

On 1 January, 1946, the Royal Air Force gave control of the airport to the Ministry of Civil Aviation, and the airport officially opened. The first plane to leave that day was a flight headed for Buenos Aires.

The terminal that we are in now, Terminal 2, is in fact the very first terminal building. It was originally called Europa Building and was opened by the Queen in 1955.

If you'll look over here, you can see...

Test 4   IGCSE / CAE / IELTS

Presenter: Welcome to *Science Today*, your weekly science news and interviews show. I'm your host Jonathan Peel. On our show today, we are going to look at a subject that everyone seems to be talking about – stem cells. To help us understand this a bit better, I've asked cellular biologist Dr Veronica Randall to join us. Welcome Dr Randall.
V. Randall: Please just call me Veronica.
J. Peel: OK. Well, Veronica. Let's begin with the basics. What are stem cells?
V. Randall: Well, stem cells are basically unspecialised cells. They have not yet 'quote-unquote' been told what to become. They are also remarkable in that they will continually renew themselves through cell division for long periods.
J. Peel: So why are these cells so special?
V. Randall: The best way to think about these cells is that they are literally blank slates. Under certain physiological or experimental conditions, these cells can become any kind of specialised cells you want. You just need to tell them what they are going to be and they become it. Now some of your listeners might already be thinking what the potential of this discovery might be. Well, to tell you the truth, the potential does seem limitless.
J. Peel: Well, could you give us some examples?
V. Randall: Sure. Take for example the case of Parkinson's disease. It affects about 2 per cent of the population over 65 years.
J. Peel: Yes, and some people much younger than that. The actor Michael J. Fox developed Parkinson's, if I'm not mistaken?
V. Randall: Yes, that's true. Along with the boxer Muhammad Ali. With Parkinson's disease, in the brain there is progressive degeneration and loss of neurons which produce the hormone dopamine. Eventually, the decreasing levels of dopamine cause a whole host of problems from tremors and rigidity to less mobility. It can start with the hands shaking, then later the head and legs.

However, Parkinson's has also been shown to be one of the first diseases to benefit from stem cell therapy. In a recent study on mice, embryonic stem cells were made to become specialised dopamine neurons. When these were introduced into mice with Parkinson's-like neurological problems, the cells began working, producing dopamine and improving the motor function of the mice. Scientists are currently working on a way to do the same in humans.
J. Peel: That's fantastic.
V. Randall: And the same possibilities exist for

everything from creating insulin-producing cells for diabetes sufferers to regenerating nerve-cells for spinal cord injuries. Before he passed away, the actor Christopher Reeve had become a major proponent of stem cell research for finding a cure for spinal cord injuries.

J. Peel: I understand there is still a lot of opposition to this research. Why is that?

V. Randall: Well, it comes from the fact that there are two types of stem cells – embryonic stem cells and adult stem cells. The embryonic stem cells are cells formed in the earliest stage of life and they are capable of developing into any cell in the body. It should be noted that these cells come from embryos which have been created in the lab, mostly by *in vitro* fertilisation clinics, and have been donated for research purposes. Many religious groups oppose the use of embryonic stem cells because the cells come from embryos.

J. Peel: Does it make a difference if we use embryonic or adult stem cells?

V. Randall: Actually, it does. Embryonic stem cells are widely available and can become any cell in the body. Adult stem cells are very rare in mature tissue and seem to only be able to become specific types of tissue. As far as we know, bone marrow cannot produce heart tissue, for example. As well, the embryonic stem cells can be grown easily in the lab, but a way to do this for adult stem cells has yet to be discovered.

On the other hand, adult stem cells from a transplant patient would not carry the risk of transplant rejection. However, it has not been determined whether embryonic stem cells would in fact cause tissue rejection.

Presenter: So what does the future hold for stem cells?

Test 5   IGCSE / CAE / IELTS

S. Law: Welcome to this week's *London Business Review podcast*. I'm your host Steve Law. This week, we'll be discussing the life and work of someone who had a huge impact on the advertising world – David Ogilvy. To discuss his extraordinary influence, we have brought in two advertising executives, Stanley Montgomery and Lauren Mackenzie. I'd like to thank you both for coming.

Let me start this discussion with you, Lauren. How would you describe Ogilvy's impact on advertising?

L. Mackenzie: Well, I think you could call him the 'father of advertising'. Besides creating some of the most innovative advertising campaigns of the 20th century, Ogilvy also helped develop many techniques in print and television advertising that are today considered standards in the business.

S. Montgomery: I'd certainly agree with Lauren on that. He was one of the first to apply a more scientific approach to advertising.

S. Law: Why was that so important?

S. Montgomery: Well, one of the biggest challenges with any advertising campaign is to find out whether or not your work is actually having an effect on sales. Are people buying more because of it? If so, why? If not, why not? I think the famous department store owner, John Wanamaker, put it best when he said: 'Half the money I spend on advertising is wasted; the trouble is I don't know which half.' And Ogilvy made it one of his key aims to find this out.

L. Mackenzie: Yes, I think a lot of this goes back to when he worked for George Gallup's Audience Research Institute. As you probably know, Gallup was the statistician responsible for modern polling for market research surveys. And it was through Gallup that Ogilvy became very aware of just how useful doing meticulous research could be.

S. Law: What kind of research do you mean?

S. Montgomery: Well, he would get all kinds of research on simple, yet important things. Take print ads for newspapers. For example, when you put a headline in quote marks, readers will be able to remember your headline 28 per cent better. Or if you don't hit the readers with what a product is or what it can do for you immediately, they will remember it 20 per cent less than with normal adverts.

L. Mackenzie: Yes, the same goes with the USPs, or unique selling points. We all know how important this can be. If you wait to explain a product's USP until the main text of an advert, you should remember that only 5 per cent of people bother to read this far. This means you are losing 95 per cent of your readers, who won't read about the USP at all. Mind you, nowadays most print ads tend to be just headlines anyway.

S. Law: But have all of Ogilvy's ideas about advertising been correct?

L. Mackenzie: That's a good question. Some have dated, others have taken time to become fashionable. Take, for example, using celebrities for endorsing products. Now, there have been some brilliant examples of matching the product to the celebrity. I mean, look at Nike and Michael Jordan. However, there has been a recent development that Ogilvy was aware of. Pepsi is a good example of this. A few years back, they decided to drop Britney Spears and Beyoncé Knowles from Pepsi ads on the grounds that these commercials tended to promote these stars' own brand identity and did little to help Pepsi.

S. Montgomery: I agree. While many companies continue to use celebrity endorsements like David Beckham and Gillette or Bill Cosby and Jell-O, there has been a steady shift away from them.

S. Law: So you're saying the stars are getting paid to promote their own brand?

S. Montgomery: Well, yes,...

TEST 6   CAE only: CAE Listening Part 4

Narrator: You will hear five short extracts in which different people are talking about science. Look at Task One. For questions 21-25, choose from the list A-H each speaker's occupation. Now look at Task Two. For questions 26-30, choose from the list A-H each speaker's aim for the future.

You will hear the recording twice and while you listen you must complete both tasks. You now have 40 seconds to look at Part 4. [PAUSE: 40 seconds]

Narrator: Speaker 1

Speaker 1: Well, I've been working on this issue for the company for the last twelve years. We have developed several concept models in recent years and are pleased to see a growing interest in the media. As the public becomes more aware of the possibilities, I think we will see an increased demand among consumers for a cleaner alternative. By making a shift away from fossil fuels to a fuel based on water, we will ensure that we can cut carbon dioxide emissions. And I am very pleased to know that I will be making a contribution to helping make the Earth a better place.

Speaker 2: Actually, I'm very concerned about traffic in my city. My son has asthma so I know first hand the effect too much air pollution can have. I'm glad that in my work, I can make a positive difference. Our department is in charge of many things such as building new roads. Many people would say that creating more roads leads to more cars on the road. But I would counter that cars left idling in slow traffic lead to much greater fuel consumption and air pollution. Cars aren't going away any time soon. The better you can manage traffic in a city, the better the air quality and way of life.

Speaker 3: Honestly, I don't give global warming much thought. My entire livelihood depends on moving goods from one city to the next. Diesel fuel powers my truck and my truck pays my bills so I've got no problem using oil. What I am concerned about though is the rising price of fuel. Just a few years ago, it seemed the price of oil was about half what it is today and every week the cost of litre of diesel goes up. If these prices keep rising, I might need to consider some other line of business.

Speaker 4: I lead a team of experts who have been investigating this issue for the government since the mid-1970s. In the past two decades, technology such as infrared satellite imaging has provided us with fairly conclusive evidence that, indeed, temperatures on Earth are warming. And it is becoming clearer that human activity in the form of transport and energy production is a significant driving factor behind this. I would have to assume at some point we will be forced out of necessity to switch to some other fuel than oil. Unfortunately, by then, it may be too late to stop the changes in the climate.

Speaker 5: Think about it for a minute. Carbon dioxide is a part of the cycle of life. We breathe it out and plants take it in. It's ridiculous to label carbon dioxide a pollutant. If it was, everyone including environmentalists would be polluters. Don't get me wrong, I'm worried about the environment as much as you are. Our industry is looking at the possibility of developing new modern fuels like hydrogen and sugar ethanol. But let's be realistic. Until these fuels can be supplied at a reasonable price, society will need to continue using oil. And we will continue to provide this valuable commodity.

(See page 256 for **TEST 7 CAE Listening Part 1**.)

QSE Introduction to Exam Practice — Teacher's Guide

Using the Photocopiable Resources

The **Photocopiable Resources** section includes exam practice material pages in the style of the IGCSE, Cambridge Advanced English (CAE) and IELTS exams. There is also a **Placement Test** for assessing students' levels. These pages are also downloadable as PDF files from: http://www.brookemead-elt.co.uk/downloads/

You can use these pages at the same time as the main units, or separately for homework. In the materials map at the beginning of this Teacher's Guide, each of the units is cross-referenced to exam practice materials, so you can choose exam practice material according to the topic area.

Each set of materials can be marked by the teacher, using the **Exam Answer Key** on page 253.

The **Exam Practice** pages, **Placement Test** and **Answers** are available online as PDF files that can be printed, as well as the **Exam Listening Practice** audio clips as MP3 files.

IGCSE Exam Practice (pages 176-203)

These 28 pages are in the format of the IGCSE, covering reading and writing, listening and speaking.

IELTS Exam Practice (pages 204-223)

These 20 pages are in the format of the IELTS, covering reading, writing, listening and speaking.

CAE Exam Practice (pages 224-250)

These 27 pages are in the format of the CAE, covering reading, writing, listening and speaking.

Placement Test (pages 251-252)

This test can be used to give an approximate assessment of the students before you use **QSE Advanced**.

Exam Practice Photocopiable Resources

A full list of the **Exam Practice Photocopiable Resources** is given on page 175. Note that many of the exams are more than one page and some may have up to four pages depending on the exam format.

Exam Listening Practice

There are seven listening practice recordings, which are available as MP3 files online at http://www.brookemead-elt.co.uk/downloads/ with written scripts on pages 169-173 (Tests 1-6) and 256 (Test 7) in this Teacher's Guide. Two of the recordings are used for IGCSE, CAE and IELTS exam practice. One of the recordings is used for IGCSE and IELTS but not CAE. And the other four recordings are dedicated to a single exam style, either IGCSE, CAE or IELTS. This allows practice of the different requirements for each of the exams. The table below shows which test is used for each exam. (See also the contents list for **Photocopiable Resources**.)

Audio	IGCSE	CAE	IELTS
Test 1	–	–	Section 1
Test 2	Part 1	–	–
Test 3	Part 2	–	Section 2
Test 4	Part 3	Part 2	Section 3
Test 5	Part 3	Part 3	Section 4
Test 6	–	Part 4	–
Test 7	–	Part 1	–

Placement Test

The **Placement Test** can be used to establish an approximate assessment of the students' levels before starting **QSE Advanced**.

Part 1A is based on the Cambridge Advanced English (CAE) exam Part 3, Use of English. Part 1B is a general reading comprehension test similar to aspects in different exams which requires students to give brief responses (1-2 sentences) to open questions. Part 2 is an open writing activity based on the CAE and Trinity Integrated Skills in English III exam. Part 3 is a speaking test which should be conducted individually with each student. You may start with simple opinions, but you should try to elicit longer and more detailed responses.

For all parts, you can refer to the Council of Europe's Common European Framework for a list of acceptable skills. The pass mark is 60%.

http://www.coe.int/t/dg4/linguistic/CADRE_EN.asp

Exam Practice Photocopiable Resources – Contents

IGCSE Exam Practice

	Page
IGCSE Reading and Writing 1: Exercise 1	176
IGCSE Reading and Writing 2: Exercise 2	177
IGCSE Reading and Writing 3: Exercise 2	179
IGCSE Reading and Writing 4: Exercise 3	181
IGCSE Reading and Writing 5: Exercise 3	183
IGCSE Reading and Writing 6: Exercise 4	185
IGCSE Reading and Writing 7: Exercise 4	187
IGCSE Reading and Writing 8: Exercise 4	188
IGCSE Reading and Writing 9: Exercise 5	190
IGCSE Reading and Writing 10: Exercise 5	191
IGCSE Reading and Writing 11: Exercise 6	192
IGCSE Reading and Writing 12: Exercise 6	193
IGCSE Reading and Writing 13: Exercise 7	194
IGCSE Reading and Writing 14: Exercise 7	195
IGCSE Speaking 1: A, B, C, D, E, F, G, H	196
IGCSE Speaking 2: A, B, C, D, E, F, G, H	198
IGCSE Listening 1: Part 1 (use Test 2 audio script on page 170)	200
IGCSE Listening 2: Part 2 (use Test 3 audio script on pages 170-171)	201
IGCSE Listening 3: Part 3, Exercise 1 (use Test 4 audio script on pages 171-172)	202
IGCSE Listening 4: Part 3, Exercise 2 (use Test 5 audio script on pages 172-173)	203

IELTS Exam Practice

	Page
IELTS Listening 1: Section 1 (use Test 1 audio script on page 169)	204
IELTS Listening 2: Section 2 (use Test 3 audio script on pages 170-171)	206
IELTS Listening 3: Section 3 (use Test 4 audio script on pages 171-172)	207
IELTS Listening 4: Section 4 (use Test 5 audio script on pages 172-173)	208
IELTS Reading 1: Part 1, Passage 1	209
IELTS Reading 2: Part 2, Passage 2	213
IELTS Reading 3: Part 3, Passage 3	217
IELTS Writing 1: Task 1	221
IELTS Writing 2: Task 2	222
IELTS Speaking: Tasks A and B	223

CAE Exam Practice

	Page
CAE Reading 1: Paper 1, Part 1	224
CAE Reading 2: Paper 1, Part 2	227
CAE Reading 3: Paper 1, Part 3	229
CAE Reading 4: Paper 1, Part 4	231
CAE Writing 1: Paper 2, Part 1	234
CAE Writing 2: Paper 2, Part 2	235
CAE Use of English 1: Paper 3, Part 1	237
CAE Use of English 2: Paper 3, Part 2	239
CAE Use of English 3: Paper 3, Part 3	240
CAE Use of English 4: Paper 3, Part 4	241
CAE Use of English 5: Paper 3, Part 5	242
CAE Listening 1: Paper 4, Part 1 (use Test 7 audio script on page 256)	244
CAE Listening 2: Paper 4, Part 2 (use Test 4 audio script on pages 171-172)	245
CAE Listening 3: Paper 4, Part 3 (use Test 5 audio script on pages 172-173)	246
CAE Listening 4: Paper 4, Part 4 (use Test 6 audio script on page 173)	247
CAE Speaking 1: Paper 5, Part 1	248
CAE Speaking 2: Paper 5, Part 2	249
CAE Speaking 3 and 4: Paper 5, Part 3 and 4	250
Exam answer key	253

Placement Test

	Page
Placement Test	251

Exam Listening Practice

	Audio	Page
IGCSE Listening 1: Part 1	Test 2	200
IGCSE Listening 2: Part 2	Test 3	201
IGCSE Listening 3: Part 3, Exercise 1	Test 4	202
IGCSE Listening 4: Part 3, Exercise 2	Test 5	203
IELTS Listening 1: Section 1	Test 1	204
IELTS Listening 2: Section 2	Test 3	206
IELTS Listening 3: Section 3	Test 4	207
IELTS Listening 4: Section 4	Test 5	208
CAE Listening 1: Paper 4, Part 1	Test 7	244
CAE Listening 2: Paper 4, Part 2	Test 4	245
CAE Listening 3: Paper 4, Part 3	Test 5	246
CAE Listening 4: Paper 4, Part 4	Test 6	247

QSE Advanced — **IGCSE Exam Practice Reading & Writing 1**

Name:
Class:

IGCSE Reading and Writing 1: Exercise 1

Read the advert about travel packages to Finland and answer the questions that follow.

Go Wild! Travel Tours
The best travel packages from the UK!
Summer Package Tours in Finland

Early bird special: Book before 1 March and get a 10% discount.
All inclusive* package (Air fare, accommodation, event tickets, meals)
Depart London Heathrow June 21st – Return Helsinki-Vantaa Airport 28 June
*Travel insurance extra.

Adrenaline Package
€2199
Ages 18-30, suitable for individuals/groups
Max: 60 people

Clubbing, Sea-kayaking, Provinssirock Rock Festival, Rally School, Scuba diving, Beach party

Day 1: Arrive in Helsinki, city sightseeing tour, nightclubbing.
Day 2: Learn to kayak. Sea-kayak with guides around Helsinki Archipelago. Evening train to Seinäjoki.
Day 3: Provinssirock: the largest rock festival in Finland.
Day 4: Second day of Provinssirock. Evening coach to Savonlinna.
Day 5: Scuba diving in Lake Saimaa with wild seals. Evening train to Mustola.
Day 6: Car rally school in Mustola. Evening train to Helsinki.
Day 7: Private beach party. Party under the Midnight Sun.
Leave on the morning of Day 8.

In Style Package
€2899
All ages, suitable for couples
Max: 40 people

Golfing, Cruise, Savonlinna Opera Festival, Hot Air Ballooning, Hiking, Tango dancing, Spa & Sauna

Day 1: Arrive in Helsinki. Deluxe sightseeing tour.
Day 2: 18 holes at Finland's best golf course. Dinner at clubhouse.
Day 3: Champagne cruise from Helsinki to Turku. Sightseeing. Evening train to Savonlinna.
Day 4: Savonlinna Opera Festival performance at the beautiful Olavinlinna Castle. Evening train to Tampere.
Day 5: Hot air balloon ride. Sightseeing. Overnight train to Rovaniemi.
Day 6: Hiking in the Lappland Fells. Romantic tango dancing under the Midnight Sun.
Day 7: Flight to Helsinki. Day spa and sauna. Leave on the morning of Day 8.

---

a List **four** water-related activities. _____
b What is not included in price of the package tours? _____
c How can you save €219.90? _____
d Which package takes you to a medieval fortress? _____
e Which package has you behind the wheel? _____
f Which Finnish cities are visited in both packages? _____

IGCSE Reading and Writing 2: Exercise 2

Read the article below and answer the questions that follow.

Art versus Sport

Across the United States local school boards are having to weigh up the comparative merits of the arts versus sports. And sports are winning out.

Local school boards have seen cuts in both state and federal funding for education. One underlying reason has been the 'No Child Left Behind' programme signed into law in 2002.

The NCLB was meant to give more money to schools that perform well in national standardised testing, but the NCLB does not cover the cost of buying new sophisticated data management systems, employing highly qualified personnel to manage these computers and software, or even paying for the intensive efforts needed to improve the schools. This has put many school boards in the difficult position of having to make large cuts to their education budgets.

Streamlined through the 1990s by earlier cuts, the schools are now making some tough decisions about cutting programmes considered as not essential for the curriculum. This has inevitably led to a choice between funding physical education programmes, such as the quintessential high school football teams, and fine arts programmes, such as art, music and drama.

Given the popularity of professional sports in American culture, few elected politicians have chosen to axe sports programmes. In New Mexico, the Education Secretary Veronica Garcia sought out $4 million in the state budget for new physical education spending, while freezing arts programmes. (The state's governor, Bill Richardson, had initially wanted to cut money from the arts programme, but faced serious protests from arts groups.) Ms Garcia cited high rates of obesity as a driving factor for her decision.

A similar result was seen in Florida's local school boards as they tried to meet the criteria set by the state's Florida Comprehensive Assessment Test (FCAT), based on the NCLB testing criteria. One interesting difference with the NCLB is that the FCAT leaves out arts as one of its main testing subjects. Many critics believe that rigidly adhering to passing the NCLB tests has led to curriculums across the US to become more focused on testing than on 'real' learning.

Perhaps fuelled by the stereotype of the starving artist, there appears to be many misconceptions about how useful funding the arts is from an economic perspective. A study by Kennesaw State University compared the economic impact in Atlanta, Georgia, of the arts community versus Atlanta's three professional sports teams, the Braves, the Falcons and the Hawks. Based on numbers of attendees, some 36 million people attended arts events across metro Atlanta in 1995 compared to 2,561,831 for the Braves, 496,679 for the Hawks and 456,640 for the Falcons. In economic terms, the arts bring $624 million per year to the city's economy compared to only $300 million for all three professional sports teams. However, until local voters are willing to see their taxes increased to pay for a wider-ranging education, students wanting to study art, music and drama are going to be left behind.

IGCSE Reading and Writing 2: Exercise 2 (continued)

a What **three** things does the 'No Child Left Behind' programme **not** cover?
   _____
   _____

b What must many local school boards choose between?
   _____

c What reason does New Mexico's Education Secretary give for supporting physical education?
   _____

d What is the difference between the FCAT and NCLB testing?
   _____

e How much more money do the arts bring in to Atlanta compared to professional sports?
   _____

IGCSE Reading and Writing 3: Exercise 2

Read the article below and answer the questions that follow.

The Science of Love

Do you like what you see in the mirror? According to the current science of human attraction, the answer is probably 'yes' if we are speaking of the mirror figuratively. Researchers have found that 'mirroring' or synchronising your movements with those of your object of desire, such as tilting your head at the same time, is one of those subtle cues that tells the other person you like them.

It should be no surprise, though. Researchers have known for quite some time that a larger portion of our communication is transmitted by body language. When we meet someone for the first time, 55 per cent of the message that person gets from us is transmitted by our appearance and body language. In fact, only 7 per cent of what you actually say ever counts. The remaining 38 per cent is taken up by your way of speaking.

Hair-Raising Attractions

It appears that one of the best aphrodisiacs is adrenaline. In a study led by psychologists Arthur Aron and Don Dutton, they placed an attractive 'female' researcher on two bridges. The first bridge was the well-built Capilano Suspension Bridge in Vancouver, Canada. Looking something straight out of an Indiana Jones adventure, the cable bridge sways in the wind about 70 metres above a rocky riverbed. The second was a very sturdy design just a few metres above sea level. Whenever a single man walked across the bridges, he was approached by the woman halfway for a brief survey. Afterwards, she gave her phone number. The men on the scary bridge were more likely to call her and more likely to ask her out on a date. So, if you want to create sparks on a date, you should skip the chat over coffee and go straight for a scary movie or a rollercoaster ride.

The Sweetest Smell

It is often joked that women want to meet someone like their father. Oddly enough, this may in fact be more correct than most women would like to admit. In a study by the geneticist Carole Ober, women were asked to smell t-shirts of various scents choosing the shirt they liked the smell of best. What was surprising was that in case after case, the women tended to choose a smell that was closest to their own father.

While this information might make a few men ponder whether or not to buy the cologne worn by their new love's father, other chemicals have shown to have even more dramatic effects. A study on prairie voles has shown that injecting the males with the hormone vasopressin can cause them to become strongly bonded to females. Similar research has not been done on humans (yet). Some illegal drugs have also been found to increase the supplies of neurotransmitter dopamine in the brain believed to trigger the euphoria felt when falling in love. But a person doesn't need to take cocaine or amphetamine when they could get the same level of dopamine quite legally from taking exercise. Another neurotransmitter in the body, phenylethylamine (PEA), has been dubbed the 'love molecule' as it causes strong feelings of excitement. Chocolate has been shown to be a good source of PEA. So after a good workout and a bar of chocolate, you would be more than ready for anyone Cupid might want to send your way.

IGCSE Reading and Writing 3: Exercise 2 (continued)

a What amount does spoken language account for in communication?

b What is the connection between romance and horror movies?

c Who was not as likely to ask the research woman on a date?

d Name **two** things that can create dopamine.

e How is chocolate a good way to create romance?

IGCSE Reading and Writing 4: Exercise 3

Read the information about what to do in the event of a hurricane and complete the notes that follow.

Hurricane Survival Guide

You should only plan to stay if you…
- do not live in a mobile home.
- do not live in an area vulnerable to storm surges and flooding.
- have trimmed or removed dead or diseased trees near your home.
- have hurricane shutters on your home.
- have prepared a disaster survival kit that includes two weeks of food, water and one month's supply of prescription medication.
- have a disaster plan for your family and pets.
- have a battery-powered TV or radio and extra batteries.

You should go if you…
- receive an evacuation order.
- live in a mobile home.
- live in an area vulnerable to storm surges and flooding.
- can leave early enough for regional evacuation times. It is hazardous to travel on highways in a storm.

In both cases, you should…
- review your home owner insurance for adequate coverage.
- notify a friend, relative or emergency management agency of your whereabouts.
- keep important documents near you (driver's licence, medical information, insurance documents, etc.).

When the storm approaches…
- turn off electricity, if rising water levels threaten your home.
- turn off major appliances if you lose power.
- check for weather updates on the TV or radio.
- avoid rooms with windows or glass doors.
- get cash. Banks or cash machines may not operate without electricity.

After the storm…
- check for weather updates on the TV or radio.
- use a generator or barbecue grill outdoors.
- don't touch fallen power lines.
- avoid driving. Roads are often littered with dangerous debris.
- use telephones for emergencies only.
- assess and photograph any damage to your home.
- contact your insurance company if repairs are needed.
- if flooding is widespread, boil tap water or add 2 drops chlorine per litre.

During clean-up, you should…
- get professionals to get rid of fallen trees.
- use proper safety equipment such as goggles, heavy boots and gloves.
- tie back long hair when working outside.
- drink lots of fluids and rest when needed.
- lift with your legs, not your back.
- avoid fallen power lines.

IGCSE Reading and Writing 4: Exercise 3 (continued)

Survival Kit

Groceries
- Tinned goods (meat, fruit, vegetables and drinks)
- Drinking water (6 litres per person per day for two weeks)
- Ice

Other
- Gas-powered generator
- Battery-powered TV or radio with extra batteries
- Medication (one month's supply)
- Cash (Cash machines and credit card terminals won't work without electricity.)
- Non-electric can opener
- Flashlights and batteries
- Cell phone, charger and 2 charged batteries
- First aid kit
- Charcoal or gas for outdoor barbecue grills
- Plastic tarpaulin for holes in roof or windows
- Tools (hammer, nails, etc.)
- Paper supplies (toilet paper, moistened towelettes)
- Mosquito repellent
- Water purification kit
- Camera, film and batteries

Pets
- Proper ID collar and rabies tag or license
- Pet carrier
- Leash
- Food supply (at least 2 weeks)
- Water / Food bowls
- Veterinary medications
- Cat litter, newspaper and plastic bags for waste
- Proper vaccination within the past 12 months

a What place should you **not** live in if you want to be safe in a hurricane?

b What item should you have more than a two weeks' supply of in your survival kit?

c How should you treat polluted tap water?

d Name **three** survival kit items that would require batteries.

e How do you prevent pets from becoming ill after a hurricane?

IGCSE Reading and Writing 5: Exercise 3

Read the article about Justin's lifestyle and complete the information sheet to show what Justin is doing now and what changes he could make for a healthier lifestyle.

Getting Fit with Britain's Kids

Meet Jimmy. He's your average British 15-year-old. Like a lot of teens, he loves watching the telly, playing video games, hanging out with his mates and eating fast food. He plays the occasional game of football with his friends, but he doesn't participate in any amateur sports. According to the National Diet and Nutrition Survey (2000), he's among the 40-69% of children over six years old who spend less than the recommended minimum hour of moderate physical activity.

Today at lunchtime, Jimmy is eating with his friends at McDonald's. He's having a burger, large fries, a large Coca-Cola, and cookies for dessert. These have 530, 570, 320 and 270 calories respectively, making a grand total of 1,690 calories. For his height (170 cm), weight (70 kg), age and sedentary lifestyle, Jimmy should get a total of about 2,300 calories every day. So in one meal, he's consumed almost three-quarters of his entire daily intake. Combined with his breakfast of breakfast cereal with whole milk and two slices of toast (670 calories) and the dinner that his mother will make him tonight, roast beef and roast potatoes (870 calories), he's taken in about 930 more calories than he needs.

While this shouldn't matter if this was an occasional thing, it isn't. Jimmy averages between 200 and 400 calories more than he needs every day. This means that he is on target to become overweight by the time he becomes an adult. He would have a higher risk of heart attack and stroke, Type 2 diabetes, bowel cancer and high blood pressure.

What can be done about this? The good thing is that Jimmy need not have to worry about a shorter lifespan if his parents make some fairly simple changes to his diet, eating habits, and physical activity.

In terms of diet, he should get about half his calories from complex carbohydrates such as potatoes, bread, and pasta. They have a high weight-to-energy ratio. He should avoid high-fat foods like burgers, fish fingers, deep-fried French fries, crisps, chocolate and biscuits and sugary foods and fizzy drinks, many children's breakfast cereals, sweets and doughnuts. At the same time, Jimmy's parents can make some changes to their eating habits. Mealtimes should be family events with set meal and snack times to avoid snacking throughout the whole day. Even though Jimmy likes watching TV, he shouldn't be allowed to eat in front of it. Jimmy should also not associate food with comfort. This means that he shouldn't be rewarded for good behaviour or good marks in school by going out for fast food or sweets.

At the same time, a key change is needed in Jimmy's level of physical activity. His parents should suggest kicking a football around or walking to and from school. Jimmy would see exercise as a fun treat if his parents reward him with special trips to an ice skating rink, adventure play or swimming pool. His family should try to make physical activity a family affair with group bike rides or in-line skating together.

IGCSE Reading and Writing 5: Exercise 3 (continued)

LIFESTYLE PROFILE: Jimmy

Breakfast

Calorie intake:

Lunch

Calorie intake:

Dinner

Calorie intake:

Average excess calorie intake per day:

Vegetables/Fruit consumed:

Physical activity
Present activity:

Should aim for:

How can Justin's parents help him? (Three ways)

IGCSE Reading and Writing 6: Exercise 4

Read the information about celebrity chef Jamie Oliver and complete the task.

CELEBRITY CHEF

James Trevor Oliver, MBE (born May 27, 1975), better known as Jamie Oliver and The Naked Chef, is a British celebrity chef.

Biography

Jamie grew up in a small Essex village called Clavering where his parents own a pub called The Cricketers. He had some difficulties in school due to dyslexia, and left school with no qualifications. When he was 16, he attended Westminster Catering College. Later, he spent several years working alongside the London chef, Gennaro Contaldo, whom he regards as one of his culinary 'mentors'. His first TV break came in 1996 when he was 'discovered' by television producer Patricia Llewellyn while working at the River Café in London. She saw him on a documentary called *Christmas at the River Café* and recognised his star potential immediately.

Two highly successful series of *The Naked Chef* were filmed in 1998 and 1999. On June 24, 2000 he married Juliette Norton, also known as Jools. The couple met in 1993, and currently have two daughters. The daughters are named Poppy Honey (born in March 2002) and Daisy Boo (born in April 2003).

In June 2003 he was appointed an MBE in the Queen's Birthday Honours List. He set up Fifteen, a charity restaurant where he trains 15 disadvantaged young people to work in the hospitality industry.

Television shows

The first series that featured Jamie Oliver was *The Naked Chef* on BBC Television. The title was a reference to the simplicity of Oliver's recipes, and has nothing to do with nudity. Oliver has frequently admitted that he wasn't entirely happy with the title, which was devised by producer Patricia Llewellyn. The success of the programme led to the books *Return of the Naked Chef* and *Happy Days with the Naked Chef*. His work on the Fifteen restaurant was shown as *Jamie's Kitchen* and *Return to Jamie's Kitchen* on Channel Four. His programmes are shown in over forty countries, including the USA's Food Network, where he is the second most popular presenter. His latest show in the United States is *Oliver's Twist*.

In 2005 Channel 4 screened *Jamie's School Dinners*, in which Oliver took over responsibility for running the kitchen meals in Kidbrooke School, Greenwich (the UK's first comprehensive school), for a year. Disgusted by the unhealthy food being served up to schoolchildren and the lack of healthy alternatives on offer, Oliver began a campaign to improve the standard of Britain's school meals. Public awareness was raised, and following on from the campaign, the UK Government pledged to spend more on school dinners (spread over three years). Tony Blair himself accepted that this was a result of Jamie's campaign. Following the success of the campaign, Oliver was named 'Most Inspiring Political Figure of 2005' in the Channel 4 Political Awards 2006.

Advertising deals

Since 2000, Jamie Oliver has been the public face of the Sainsbury's supermarket chain in the UK, appearing on television and radio advertisements and in-store promotional material. The deal earns him an estimated £1.2 million every year. In the first two years, these

IGCSE Reading and Writing 6: Exercise 4 (continued)

advertisements are estimated to have given Sainsbury's an extra £1 billion of sales, or £200 million gross profit.

In 2003, fellow chef Clarissa Dickson-Wright criticised Oliver for endorsing Sainsbury's Scottish farmed salmon and accused him of 'selling his soul' to the supermarket chain. In 2005, Oliver fronted Sainsbury's new advertising slogan urging customers to try something different by suggesting recipe ideas. In October, the company claimed sales of some featured products had more than doubled.

In North America and the UK, Oliver markets his own line of cookware as well as a line of upmarket cutlery.

You are planning to give a short presentation about Jamie Oliver to your class at school. Make two brief notes under each heading as the basis of your talk.

JAMIE OLIVER

a Origins
b TV stardom
c Popularity
d Commercialism

IGCSE Reading and Writing 7: Exercise 4

Read the following article about an incident of workplace bullying, and then complete the notes.

£800,000 for Six Years of Harassment

In a decision that is likely to send shockwaves through London's financial district, a City worker from Deutsche Bank Group Services (UK) Ltd. was awarded over £800,000 for enduring what she described as 'a department from hell'.

Helen Green, 36, began her job as a secretary at Deutsche Bank in 1997. She said that almost immediately she became a target of harassment at the hands of four of her colleagues, Valerie Alexander, manager of the insurance division, and her PA, Fiona Gregg, telephone directory administrator Daniella Dolbear, and Jenny Dixon, PA to Ms Green's department head Richard Elliston.

According to Mr Justice Owen, at London's High Court, the attacks were 'a relentless campaign of mean and spiteful behaviour designed to cause her distress'. As such, he awarded Ms Green £640,000 for future loss of earnings including pension, £128,000 for lost income, £25,000 for her disadvantage in the labour market, and £35,000 for pain and suffering, totalling £817,000. The bank must also pay Ms Green's legal expenses.

The campaign by the four women according to Ms Green was 'so vindictive and so deliberate. They were discussing how to make me cry'.

In one telling incident, the four women arrived at the office and Ms Dolbear said in a very loud voice to the others: 'What's that stink? It's coming from over there,' while she pointed at Ms Green. The others laughed.

They would make sure to exclude Ms Green from group activities such as restaurant lunches. And they would often stare silently at her, with their arms crossed or wait until she was walking past them and begin laughing loudly. On other occasions, Ms Dolbear would hover near Ms Green's desk and speak very loudly making it impossible for her to answer the phone.

As a result, Ms Green began to develop a major depressive disorder. By November 2000, she had a nervous breakdown and had to be hospitalised on suicide watch. In April 2001, she returned to work, but her condition worsened again in October. Deutsche Bank kept her job open until September 2003 when her employment was terminated.

Ms Green was not alone in this matter. There were five other victims in the department. Several of whom had complained to management over the behaviour. 'Deutsche Bank knew what was happening at the time but they are continuing even today to diminish and deny it,' says Ms Green. 'Bullying is a big problem for the City and now all City businesses will have to pay more than lip-service to this hidden menace.'

Elaine Bartleet, a spokesperson for Deutsche Bank, stated after the verdict that no internal action was taken over the bullying, but Valerie Alexander was the only one of the four women still working there. She also said that Deutsche Bank has not decided whether to appeal or not.

You are going to give a short talk to your class at school about an incident where bullying has taken place in the workplace. You have decided to base your talk on this article. Make **two** short notes under each heading.

WORKPLACE BULLYING

a The behaviour of Ms Green's colleagues

b The effects on Ms Green

c The bank's response to the bullying

d The Court's decision

IGCSE Reading and Writing 8: Exercise 4

Read the information about Jammu and Kashmir and complete the notes below.

JAMMU AND KASHMIR

The land dispute over Jammu and Kashmir is the oldest unresolved land dispute in the world. It has lead to three separate wars between Pakistan and India in 1947–48, 1965 and 1971.

JAMMU AND KASHMIR
Population: about 8 million (1981 census) **Size:** 84,471 square miles
Indian-administered Kashmir
The Kashmir Valley: 3 million (95% Muslim, 4% Hindu) **Jammu:** 2.7 million (66% Hindu, over 30% Muslim) **Ladakh:** 134,000 (over 50% Buddhist, 46% Shia Muslim, over 3% Hindu)
Pakistan-administered Kashmir
Northern Areas: 500,000 (mostly Shia Muslim) **Azad Kashmir:** 2 million (mostly Sunni Muslim)

History of the Region	
653–1346	Hindu Rulers
1346–1586	Muslim Rulers
1586–1757	Moghul Rulers
1757–1819	Afghan Rulers
1819–1846	Sikh Rulers
1846	British defeated the Sikhs. The British sold Kashmir to Ghulab Singh of Jammu for 7.5 million Rupees
1846–1947	Jammu and Kashmir ruled by Hindu Maharajahs (independent of British India)

IGCSE Reading and Writing 8: Exercise 4 (continued)

Source of Conflict

The plan for the British Partition of India (1947) that divided up the Indian subcontinent into Pakistan and India at independence had a special provision for princely states like Jammu and Kashmir. These states had three choices: join India, join Pakistan, or remain independent. Pressured by both India and Pakistan, the Maharajah decided to sign the 'Instrument of Succession' to make Kashmir a part of India. The British Governor General of India, Lord Mountbatten, stressed that this decision would only become final once the people of Jammu and Kashmir voted on it. A UN Security Council resolution (1948) following the first war reconfirmed the need for a vote by the people of the region.

Economy

The Kashmiri region's main source of revenue comes from agricultural exports. It first became recognised in the early 1800s for its ultra-soft cashmere wool, which was exported around the world. The Cashmere goat has since become largely extinct in the region.

The Kashmir people are also well known for their highly-skilled weaving ranging from woven rugs to shawls. The region is also home to the most sought-after saffron in the world. Saffron is a very flavourful, aromatic spice derived from the saffron crocus flower, and is easily more valuable than gold with retail prices ranging from €1,000 to €10,000 per kilo.

Tourism has also been a major part of the economy for centuries. The mountainous scenery is often described as 'Heaven on Earth'. However, the region has suffered from increasing political instability since the 1990s. The region's economy was also greatly affected by the strong earthquake that hit in October 2005, with an estimated 70,000 dead in the Pakistani-controlled area and 1,500 dead in the Indian-controlled area.

You are planning to give a short presentation about Jammu and Kashmir to your class at school. Make two brief notes under each heading as the basis of your talk.

JAMMU AND KASHMIR

a History of the region
b Demographics of the region
c Main sources of income
d Problems for the economy

IGCSE Reading and Writing 9: Exercise 5

Read the following article about internet blogging. Then, **write a summary** explaining what a blog is. **Your summary should be about 100 words.** Try to use your own words as much as possible.

Blogging

Web logging, or blogging as it is more commonly known, is a way of keeping a diary online. One unique feature is that it is in a reverse chronological order, meaning that the newest entry always appears first. Although blogs are sometimes described as diaries, they can be so much more than just an online version of what was traditionally a hand-written record of personal thoughts and ideas. Blogs do present an individual's thoughts, but blogs can also contain video clips, photos, MP3 sound clips, links to news articles, and much more.

One way of understanding the difference between a blog and a diary could be in looking at the difference between newspapers and television. While you can get a mental picture about the force of a hurricane from a written description in a newspaper, this does not compare to the vivid realism that you get from a television clip showing the hurricane in action. A blogger can simply present so much more information in a very concise way.

Like many technological innovations, blogging can trace its origins back to earlier innovations. Its development came after the development of new types of software and ways of communicating online in the early 1990s. Email lists and bulletin board systems (BBS) allowed people to post messages that a large group of people could read and respond to with their own messages. In short, the new media allowed users to carry on conversations over time and distance. When early bloggers, such as Justin Hall and James 'Kibo' Parry, began posting, the 'blogosphere' was a fairly limited space. Many early bloggers created journals by updating their webpages. It was not until 1997 when developments in blogging software appeared that made blogging more accessible to the general public. Today, blogs are everywhere. In 2005, the Blog Herald estimated the number of blogs to exceed 100 million worldwide.

So what are all these blogs about? Blogs are about as varied as the number of people writing them. Blogs can be about anything and, in some cases, nothing at all. Besides the countless individuals digitally detailing their daily existence, many in the media spotlight have turned to this medium to help get their own message out. From celebrities like Madonna to companies like Microsoft, brands are now using them to help communicate with their audience. It has proven a relatively cheap way to handle PR and marketing.

A significantly large number of blogs also deal with news and political issues. These tend to represent one side of an issue or another. These sites become beacons for people who hold similar beliefs and are in some cases viewed regularly by millions. Yahoo, the internet search engine, has included blogs amongst its news searches. This is a double-edged sword, though. In many cases, blogs can distribute news more widely than traditional news agencies. But blogs may not adhere to the traditional strict ethical standards that most Western news agencies do. This means information can sometimes be inaccurate, false or misleading.

IGCSE Reading and Writing 10: Exercise 5

Read the information about becoming an astronaut, then write a summary explaining the job of a pilot astronaut and what training is involved. **Your summary should be about 100 words.** Try to use your own words as much as possible.

BECOMING AN ASTRONAUT

Astronauts are divided into three main groups: pilot/commander astronauts, mission specialists and payload specialists.

Commanders oversee the success of the mission, as well as the safety of the crew and the vehicle. The pilots are second-in-command and responsible for manoeuvring the vehicle. For both roles, there are several prerequisites before applicants can even be considered. To begin with, a successful applicant needs to have a first degree in engineering, biological science, physical science or mathematics. A further degree is desired, but not essential.

The second major prerequisite is flying time in a jet aircraft. Pilot or commander astronaut hopefuls must have at least a thousand hours in the air. Test-pilot experience is also desired, but not essential.

Applicants must then pass a strict physical examination with eyesight no greater than 20/50, correctable to 20/20. The applicants must also be 162 to 193 cm in height. Then, they need to pass strict psychological examinations, as the living conditions in space can be very stressful, including small enclosed spaces, being far from family and lack of privacy.

Mission specialists are responsible for operations on board, including crew management, use of food/water, conducting experiments and carrying out payload activities. The requirements are somewhat similar to pilots except for the flying time, eyesight of 20/100, correctable to 20/20, and a minimum height of over 152 cm.

Payload specialists are usually chosen to conduct specific experiments or operate some specialised equipment. They need not be US citizens, but must go through the same strict physical examination. Payload specialists are often sponsored by the organisation that is having a payload carried into space, but they must still be approved by NASA.

Astronaut Training

The training process is very intensive and complex, requiring hundreds of personnel to conduct it. The training is in two parts: basic and advanced training. In basic training, new astronauts must follow advanced academic education, covering mathematics, Earth resources, meteorology, guidance and navigation, astronomy, physics and computer science. Pilots and mission specialists receive training in T-38 high-performance jets. From here, these astronauts are given hands-on simulation training in the single systems trainers (SST), which lets them develop work procedures and learn how to deal with malfunctions.

All groups will spend many hours in a neutral buoyancy tank called the Weightless Environment Training Facility (WETF). Here they will experience similar weightless conditions to space.

The advanced training programme follows the one-year basic training. The astronauts will take courses ranging from guidance, navigation and control systems to payload deployment and retrieval systems. The programme can take anywhere from seven months to a year, depending on the flight mission. Ten weeks before the scheduled launch, the crew will begin working in the Shuttle Mission Simulator (SMS). Completed in 1977 at a cost of $100 million, the simulator can recreate all phases of a mission from launch to landing starting at T-minus 30 minutes.

IGCSE Reading and Writing 11: Exercise 6

World Television Productions
www.wtp.com

Become a Television Star and a Millionaire!

We are looking for 20 people from around the world to join a new Reality Television show. These 20 contestants will be locked into a BIOSPHERE for 20 weeks. Each week a contestant will be eliminated from the competition based on a challenging task relating to global issues. The winner will receive 1 million euros.

If you are interested, send us an email for more information.

You've seen this leaflet all over the city.
Write an email (100–150 words Core tier / 150–200 words Extended tier) to the company.

- Describe yourself.
- Explain why you would be interested in joining the TV show.
- Ask for more information.

To:	
From:	
Subject:	Become a Television Star and a Millionaire

IGCSE Reading and Writing 12: Exercise 6

> ## Want to hang out with celebrities? Interested in seeing the world?
> ## Want free tickets to the best music concerts anywhere?
>
> *Rage* is the new online music magazine for today's global music scene. And we are looking for a few good writers to report on the world of music from hip hop to pop to metal. We cover it all and so will you. You will travel the world interviewing musicians, critiquing new albums and attending music concerts. You'll get to live the rock and roll lifestyle.
>
> If you think you've got what it takes, send us an email telling us about yourself. Be sure to include a 50-word review of your favourite album.

You've seen this advertisement on TV, posters and the internet for weeks now.
Write an email (100–150 words Core tier / 150–200 words Extended tier) to the company.

- Describe yourself.
- Explain why you would be a great music journalist.
- Ask for more information.
- Include a 50-word review of your favourite album in the email.

To:	writers@rage.co.uk
From:	
Subject:	I'd make a great music journalist

Review:

IGCSE Reading and Writing 13: Exercise 7

Money can't buy you happiness

Write an article for your school or college magazine giving your views on whether money can bring you happiness or not. The comments below may give you some ideas, but you are free to use your own ideas. Your article should be about 150 words (Core tier) / 200 words (Extended tier) long.

- Money does pay for things we like, such as trips to foreign countries.

- People who like you for your money are not true friends.

- Money isn't bad in itself. It's how you use it that counts.

- People can become selfish if they have lots of money.

IGCSE Reading and Writing 14: Exercise 7

> 'Actions speak louder than words'
> when it comes to role models.

Write an article for your school or college magazine giving your views on what makes a good role model. The comments below may give you some ideas, but you are free to use your own ideas. Your article should be about 150 words (Core tier) / 200 words (Extended tier) long.

- Many people in power don't practise what they preach.

- You can only judge a person by what they do.

- People are human and make mistakes.

- Setting examples of good behaviour is the most important thing.

QSE Advanced — IGCSE Exam Practice Speaking 1

Name:
Class:

IGCSE Speaking 1: A, B, C, D

A ADVERTISING

Discuss with the examiner the impact that advertising has on people today.

You may wish to consider the following:
- Style of adverts – funny, persuading, flashy
- Some examples of the best adverts you have seen
- Some things you want to buy and the reasons why
- Types of advertising - TV, radio, internet, newspaper
- Whether there is too much advertising
- Whether advertisers should advertise to children

You are free to consider any other ideas of your own.

You are not allowed to make any written notes.

B THE ARTS

Discuss with the examiner the role of creativity in our society.

You may wish to consider the following:
- People who are thought to be very creative
- The most creative ideas you have seen, read, or heard about
- Whether we value creative as much as earlier generations
- Whether creativity is a sign of intelligence
- Where you find creativity in your own life
- Should ideas always be about making money?

You are free to consider any other ideas of your own.

You are not allowed to make any written notes.

C AMBITIONS

Discuss with the examiner what sort of career you would like to have.

You may wish to consider the following:
- The types of jobs have you had in the past
- The kind of education would you like or need to take in the future
- How money influences our career choices
- Which jobs would you never consider and why
- How your friends and family can influence your career choices
- Whether everyone has a dream job

You are free to consider any ideas of your own.

You are not allowed to make any written notes.

D BULLYING

Discuss with the examiner how someone should defend themselves against an aggressive person, whether verbal or physical.

You may wish to discuss:
- Whether humour is an effective defence
- The disadvantages of using violence to solve problems
- Situations people your age could find themselves in
- How safe you feel where you live
- Whether parents, teachers or society can help
- Whether pacifism is always the best solution

You are free to consider any other ideas of your own.

You are not allowed to make any written notes.

IGCSE Speaking 1 (continued): E, F, G, H

E DESIGNER GOODS

Discuss with the examiner the influence that fashion designers have on teenagers.

You may wish to consider the following:

- Whether you can be an individual if you buy mass market goods
- Whether seeing thin fashion models leads to anorexia in young people
- The influence of celebrity fashion on your choices
- Whether clothes say something about a person
- Some fashions that you find interesting or funny
- Whether creating fashion is just about making money

You are free to consider any ideas of your own.

You are not allowed to make any written notes.

F COMPETITIVENESS

Discuss with the examiner the advantages and possible disadvantages of competing in sports.

You may wish to consider the following:

- The health benefits of regular exercise
- Your own experience in playing sports
- How you felt having won or lost competitions
- Any risks involved in different sports
- Whether sports are only for young people
- Whether sportsmanship is dying in sports today

You are free to consider any ideas of your own.

You are not allowed to make any written notes.

G ECONOMIC ISSUES

Discuss with the examiner the influence oil has today on everyday life and what the world would be like without it.

You may wish to consider such things as:

- Who controls the world's oil today
- Who uses the most oil today
- How would we power cars, lorries, airplanes, boats without oil
- How are world politics affected by oil today
- Whether the world economy would stop without oil supplies and how this would affect the environment

You are free to consider any ideas of your own.

You are not allowed to make any written notes.

H EQUAL OPPORTUNITIES

Discuss with the examiner some of the causes of inequality between men and women.

You may wish to consider the following:

- The roles of men and women in your society
- The physical differences between men and women – for example, strength, size
- Whether you have experienced inequality
- Whether your country promotes equality or inequality
- Whether religion helps or hinders equality
- The effect of having children

You are free to consider any ideas of your own.

You are not allowed to make any written notes.

IGCSE Speaking 2: A, B, C, D

A FREEDOM

Discuss with the examiner the reasons why children want to move away from their parent's home.

You may wish to consider the following:
- Whether your society has certain rules about this
- How parents can help or hinder this change
- How personal finances affect this move
- Places that someone would move to
- The effect of independence on relationships
- The types of changes that happen to someone aged 18 to 25

You are free to consider any other ideas of your own.

You are not allowed to make any written notes.

B INDIVIDUAL RIGHTS

Discuss with the examiner what you would like to do or change if you were elected to government.

You may wish to consider the following:
- What effects government policy has had on you and your community
- How the economy has been helped or hurt by different government decisions
- Whether you agree or disagree with current foreign policy
- The effects of corruption or mismanagement
- How you envision a perfectly run government

You are free to consider any other ideas of your own.

You are not allowed to make any written notes.

C INTERNATIONAL EVENTS

Discuss with the examiner what international events in the past decade have had the most impact on you and your country.

You may wish to consider the following:
- What changes have happened in your life
- The effect of less activity in the economy or prices changes
- The effect of different wars around the world
- How politics has changed internationally/domestically
- Which people have been in the headlines
- Whether terrorism has had an impact

You are free to consider any ideas of your own.

You are not allowed to make any written notes.

D USING THE INTERNET

Discuss with the examiner how the internet has changed and is changing the world.

You may wish to discuss:
- How you use the internet
- Who uses and doesn't use the internet and why
- The advantages and disadvantages of so much information
- Whether it develops understanding between nations
- How it affects different businesses
- The effect of viruses and hackers

You are free to consider any other ideas of your own.

You are not allowed to make any written notes.

IGCSE Speaking 2 (continued): E, F, G, H

E THE MEDIA

Discuss with the examiner the role that violence in the media (movies, TV, video games) has on young people.

You may wish to consider the following:
- The types of media available to young people
- Why violence in media is attractive to some people
- Whether children / young people understand the reality of violence
- Whether media in the violence is more for boys or girls
- Who commits youth violence
- Whether there should be restrictions on the media

You are free to consider any ideas of your own.

You are not allowed to make any written notes.

F ROLE MODELS

Discuss with the examiner the importance of role models in creating well-adjusted citizens.

You may wish to consider the following:
- Who the role models in your life are
- The values your parents have taught you
- How different teachers have affected you
- How celebrity role models affect young people
- Whether we need role models to be ordinary people
- What a bad role model might be like

You are free to consider any ideas of your own.

You are not allowed to make any written notes.

G ROLES IN THE FAMILY

Discuss with the examiner the advantages and disadvantages of close ties between family generations.

You may wish to consider such things as:
- Your family and how close you are to older relatives
- Whether there is a generation gap in your society
- The value of older people in your society
- Whether there are conflicts between generations
- How older people are cared for in your society
- How different generations see the world differently

You are free to consider any ideas of your own.

You are not allowed to make any written notes.

H SCHOOL CURRICULUM

Discuss with the examiner the importance of learning about technology at school.

You may wish to consider the following:
- Types of new everyday technology
- Whether technology is a subject or a tool for learning
- Whether technical knowledge can be learned outside school
- The types of occupations that require computer knowledge
- How soon today's technology will be out of date
- Whether technology will replace other subjects in school

You are free to consider any ideas of your own.

You are not allowed to make any written notes.

IGCSE Listening: Part 1

(Use *QSE Advanced* Exam Practice Audio, **Test 2**)

Questions 1–6

For Questions 1–6 you will hear a series of short sentences. Answer each question on the line provided. Your answer should be as brief as possible.

You will hear each item twice.

1   Benny is travelling to Paris next week. According to the weather forecast, on which weekday morning would be best for him to sit outside at a café?
    _____

2   Your English class is planning a trip to London this Friday. Where must you meet your class and when?
    _____
    _____

3   Pamela is going to the cinema. When will her film start?
    _____

4   Richard needs a map of the Underground. How much does he pay for it?
    _____

5   Scott is going to play a game of football with his friends. What **three** things does he need to bring with him?
    _____

6   Sharon and her friend are out shopping. Why does her friend suggest she buy some shoes?
    _____

IGCSE Listening: Part 2

(Use *QSE Advanced* Exam Practice Audio, **Test 3**)

Listen to the following tour of London Heathrow Airport, and then fill in the details below.

You will hear the interview twice.

HEATHROW INTERNATIONAL AIRPORT

GENERAL INFORMATION

- Busiest in Europe
- Busiest airports in the world: Atlanta, Chicago, London Heathrow
- Number of passengers: _____
- Open: 24 hours a day, _____ a year

Size

- Total retail space:
- 48,000 sq. m, or _____ bigger than Manchester United's football pitch
- Total staff: _____
- Total parking space: 34,000

Airport documentary

- Filmed at Heathrow
- Jeremy Spake, now a television presenter

History

- Originally owned by the Vicar of Harmondsworth
- Fairey Aviation built the first airstrip to _____
- The airport officially opened _____
- Terminal 2 originally called _____

IGCSE Listening: Part 3, Exercise 1

(Use *QSE Advanced* Exam Practice Audio, **Test 4**)

Listen to the following interview with a cellular biologist about stem cells, and then answer the questions below.

You will hear the interview twice.

a What are stem cells?

_____
_____

b What kind of cells do they become?

_____
_____

c What is lost in Parkinson's disease?

_____
_____

d What positive development was shown with the mice?

_____
_____

e Name **two** other medical conditions that may be helped by stem cell research.

_____
_____

f Give **two** ways in which embryonic and adult stem cells differ.

_____
_____

IGCSE Listening: Part 3, Exercise 2

(Use *QSE Advanced* Exam Practice Audio, **Test 5**)

Listen to the following interview with two advertising executives about the noted advertiser David Ogilvy, and then answer the questions below.

You will hear the interview twice.

a Give **two** reasons why David Ogilvy is considered the father of advertising.
　_____
　_____

b What did John Wanamaker think about his spending on advertising?
　_____
　_____

c What was George Gallup's occupation?
　_____
　_____

d Why should an advertising headline include quote marks?
　_____
　_____

e How are print ads different today?
　_____
　_____

f Why did Pepsi drop Britney Spears?
　_____
　_____

IELTS Listening: Section 1 Questions 1–10

(Use *QSE Advanced* Exam Practice Audio, **Test 1**)

Questions 1–2

You will hear a woman named Jane talking to a colleague at work about a concert she saw the previous evening. Look at the map. The boxes with the letters A-H indicate the location of Jane and her friends. You have some time to read Questions 1 to 5.

For Questions 1 and 2, write the correct letter A-H next to the questions. You will see that an example has been done for you. Jane was standing in front of the stage, so C is her location and has been written in the space. Now we shall begin. You should answer the questions as you listen because you will not hear the recording a second time. Listen carefully and answer Questions 1 to 5.

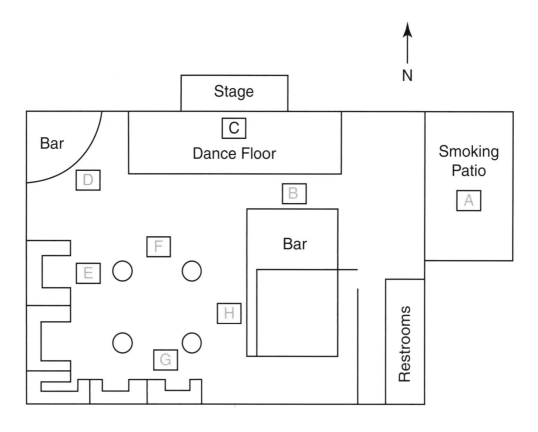

Example: **Jane**   __C__

1   **Katie**   _____

2   **Rebecca's boyfriend**   _____

IELTS Listening: Section 1 (continued)

Questions 3–5

3 When the concert was finished, Jane immediately

- **A** hung out with Rebecca's friends. ☐
- **B** looked for her flatmates. ☐
- **C** had a drink. ☐

4 When Jane saw Katie again, she was

- **A** crying. ☐
- **B** angry. ☐
- **C** very upset. ☐

5 Katie found her handbag when she

- **A** wanted to go home. ☐
- **B** got her jacket. ☐
- **C** was ready to leave. ☐

Question 6

Choose **TWO** letters, **A-F**.

6 The bag contained

- **A** a wallet ☐
- **B** a credit card ☐
- **C** a house key ☐
- **D** a mobile phone ☐
- **E** a bank card ☐
- **F** £40 ☐

Questions 7–10

Complete the table below.

Write **NO MORE THAN TWO WORDS AND/OR A NUMBER** for each answer.

	Hair	Pants	Tattoo	Their biggest fan
Lead singer	(7) _____	black leather	Japanese samurai	(10) _____
Lead guitarist	red Mohawk	made of (8) _____	two (9) _____	Jane

IELTS Listening: Section 2 Questions 11–20

(Use *QSE Advanced* Exam Practice Audio, **Test 3**)

Questions 11–13

Choose the correct letter: **A**, **B** or **C**

11 Heathrow is the busiest airport

    A in the world ☐
    B in international flights ☐
    C in Europe ☐

12 Heathrow will have

    A 4 terminals in 2007 ☐
    B 5 terminals in 2007 ☐
    C 4 terminals in 2008 ☐

13 Total retail space is

    A 48,000 m² ☐
    B 6 times larger than a professional football pitch ☐
    C 60,000 m² ☐

Questions 14–15

Choose **TWO** letters, **A-E**.

Which **TWO** airport facilities are mentioned?

    A information desks ☐
    B car hire agencies ☐
    C check-in desks ☐
    D waiting lounges ☐
    E car parking spaces ☐

Questions 16–20

Complete the table below.

Write **NO MORE THAN THREE WORDS AND/OR A NUMBER** for each answer.

Owner	Use
(16) _____ of Harmondsworth	– never mentioned
Fairey Aviation	– to (17) _____
Ministry of (18) _____	– took control for (19) _____ – never used it for military purposes
Ministry of (20) _____	– commercial flights

QSE Advanced — IELTS Exam Practice Listening 3

Name:
Class:

IELTS Listening: Section 3 Questions 21–30

(Use *QSE Advanced* Exam Practice Audio, **Test 4**)

Questions 21–22

Complete the sentences below.

Write **NO MORE THAN TWO WORDS AND/OR A NUMBER** for each answer.

21   Stem cells are simply _____ cells.

22   They constantly renew themselves using _____ over long periods of time.

Question 23

Choose **ONE** letter, **A-E**.

Which celebrity might benefit from stem cell research?

   A   Magic Johnson   ☐
   B   Michael Jackson   ☐
   C   Muhammad Ali   ☐
   D   Michael Jordan   ☐
   E   Mahmoud Abbas   ☐

Questions 24–30

Complete the notes below.

Write **NO MORE THAN TWO WORDS AND/OR A NUMBER** for each answer.

How stem cells might help

- Transplanted stem cells helped produce dopamine in (24) _____
- People with (25) _____ could receive specialised stem cells that produce insulin.
- Christopher Reeve supported stem cell research for (26) _____ injuries.

Differences between embryonic and adult stem cells

- Two kinds of stem cells: embryonic and adult
- Embryonic stem cells are created in the (27) _____
- Many (28) _____ are against the use of embryos for research.
- Embryonic stem cells can become any cell in the body.
- On the other hand, adult stem cells in bone marrow can not produce (29)_____
- Adult stem cells from the same patient would not have the risk of transplant (30)_____

QSE Advanced — IELTS Exam Practice Listening 4

IELTS Listening: Section 4 Questions 31–40

(Use *QSE Advanced* Exam Practice Audio, **Test 5**)

Questions 31–33

Complete the sentences below.

Write **NO MORE THAN THREE WORDS** for each answer.

DAVID OGILVY

31 The discussion is taking place in _____.

32 Ogilvy is responsible for some of the most _____ through the last century.

33 Ogilvy took a more _____ approach to advertising.

Questions 34–37

Complete the table below.

Write **NO MORE THAN THREE WORDS AND/OR A NUMBER** for each answer.

Headlines in Print Advertising	The Facts
Use of quote marks there	People remember the headline (34) _____ better.
Describing a product's use there	People will remember the product (35) _____ more.
Placing the unique selling point there	Only 5% of people will actually read (36) _____ of the advert.
Today	(37) _____ today are just headlines.

Questions 38–40

Complete the notes below.

Write **NO MORE THAN THREE WORDS** for each answer.

Celebrities in Advertising

1900–1950	David Ogilvy believed that celebrities should not be used in advertising. His idea was not (38) _____ at the time.
1950–2000	Celebrities are used extensively to (39) _____ products. Many examples show that the advertising can benefit both product and celebrity.
2000–	Ogilvy's ideas about celebrity (40) _____ are taken on board by many companies.

IELTS Reading Part 1: Reading Passage 1

Not-So Secret Messages

A

Subtlety is the new codeword in advertising since the industry has found that younger generations are no longer responsive to the stream of commercial images they are exposed to on a daily basis. Having grown up on a steady diet of MTV, glossy magazines and the web, they have essentially become immune to 'in-your-face' adverts of yesterday. As a result, many advertisers are turning to more subtle forms of advertising, such as product placements.

B

A product placement could be a company logo or product. The most common places for product placements are in television and films, but lately there have also been some inroads to video games. At times, these placements are intentional, and the company will often pay a hefty sum to producers for their inclusion. For example, near the judges on *American Idol* Coca-Cola cups surreptitiously appeared. At other times, the product placement is much less deliberate and there is simply a mention, but always with the desired outcome of viewer consciousness of the product.

C

In both cases, the advertisers hope that whether the viewers see the product in the background or hear it mentioned in the context of the programme, the placement will leave a positive impact on them. The goal is not so much to push people to run out and buy the product straight away, but to instill that positive feeling that will eventually translate into a purchase of their product. Some companies have had such success with product placement that they have started to 'cross-pollinate' their business areas. For example, a conglomerate company like Sony has taken advantage of its varied media empire and has been using one of its products, the Sony Playstation, to help promote other Sony products like music or films.

D

In the past, television and film producers were reluctant to have products marketed through them unless the product was a corporate sponsor. As such, most products were often 'greeked', which meant that their names or logos were changed to avoid trademark infringements. For example, a Nokia phone might be labelled Nokio. Today, 'greeking' goes even further since products can be digitally blurred or removed. This manipulation has led to some unusual court cases such as the lawsuit between the Times Square billboards' owners and the *Spider-Man* film producers who digitally replaced adverts filmed in Times Square to include the name of one of the film's sponsors.

E

Although product placements have been around for decades, the recent surge of them in TV programmes seems to be invariably linked to the ascendance of reality television and the threat of new recording technologies like TiVo. TiVo allows viewers to record TV programmes without TV commercials. Consequently, many networks are seeing a decline in advertising revenues and are turning to TV scriptwriters to write in segments about a company or product. What this translates to is either the direct use of a product or reference to a specific company by the characters in a programme, such as in the NBC series, *Friends*, where one of the main characters, Rachel, works for the company, Calvin Klein.

IELTS Reading Part 1: Reading Passage 1 (continued)

F

In the case of reality TV shows, producers have found it much easier to use product placements effectively. The competitive nature of reality shows like *Survivor* provides ample opportunity for direct product placement since contestants actually win gifts from various companies. Meanwhile, other reality shows function more as glorified infomercials. For example, *The Cut* gave audiences 13 weeks of Tommy Hilfiger's fashion and brand. These more documentary-style reality TV shows offer viewers some emotional attachment to the brand, but the underlying message is still to buy the products.

G

With the successful rise and solid presence of product placement in television and films, it was simply a question of time before marketers would reach the literary world. Literary critics have resoundingly voiced their dismay at not just the mere appearance but the blatant focus on brand names like Bulgari in what has become the product placement novel. The Italian luxury jewellery maker reportedly commissioned UK author Fay Weldon to write a promotional novel called *The Bulgari Connection*, which was to include 12 mentions of the company. While the book was only supposed to be for just 750 of the company's most important customers, it wasn't long before it was snapped up by publisher HarperCollins for general distribution.

H

It should come as no surprise that there has been some growing opposition to product placements, principally because the industry is currently not regulated by the government. Hollywood's Writers Guild and Screen Actors Guild have been especially outspoken on this point. Both groups claim that the government has an obligation to establish standards for this $1 billion industry or certain ethics will be compromised with blatant advertising. Furthermore, they are not being paid to sell these products. For example, in an episode of *Desperate Housewives*, the writers of the show had a character take a job as spokesperson for Buick's LaCrosse sports car, and she devoted a significant part of her on-screen time to discussing the merits of the car.

I

Many parent groups are equally outspoken about the subtle and not-so-subtle attempts to sell to their children via product placements. One recent piece of legislation sponsored by Commercial Alert was presented to the Federal Trade Commission in which they called for a Parents' Bill of Rights. The bill, if it had become law, would have required media outlets to fully disclose any and all product placement agreements made for a TV show, film or video game. But it was voted down on the grounds that only claims about a product, not the images of a product, could be deceptive. Commercial Alert responded on their website with a study showing that teenagers are indeed negatively affected by product placement; an example was teenagers who had viewed lots of smoking in films being three times more likely to start smoking themselves.

IELTS Reading Part 1: Reading Passage 1 (continued)

Questions 1–5

The passage has nine paragraphs labelled **A-I**.

Which paragraph contains the following information?

Write the correct letter **A-I** for numbers 1-5.

1. the spread of product placements into new media areas
2. television programmes that are based entirely on promoting a product
3. the development of cross-promotions between media groups
4. the disagreement between writers and producers of films
5. the changes made in a TV programme to hide the product of a non-sponsor

Questions 6–11

Complete the sentences below with words taken from the passage.

Choose **NO MORE THAN THREE WORDS** from the passage for each answer.

6. Teenagers can react negatively to _____ adverts.
7. Sony's large media empire allows it to _____ between its business areas.
8. Digital images were the cause of a lawsuit brought by owners of the _____.
9. Critics argue that Hilfiger's reality TV programme was nothing more than _____.
10. Bulgari's product placement was originally intended only for _____.
11. Hollywood's actors and writers complain that they are not paid for helping _____.

IELTS Reading Part 1: Reading Passage 1 (continued)

Questions 12 – 14

Do the following statements agree with the information given in Reading Passage 1?

TRUE   *if the statement agrees with the information*
FALSE   *if the statement contradicts the information*
NOT GIVEN   *if there is no information on this*

12 Public TV stations in the US have banned the use of product placements. _____

13 New technology and TV programmes have increased product placements. _____

14 The product placement industry is heavily regulated by government. _____

IELTS Reading Part 2: Reading Passage 2

You should spend about 20 minutes on **Questions 15-27,** which are based on Reading Passage 2.

PHILANTHROPY

Unless you are an avid reader of the financial or business news, you were probably unaware of the name of Warren Edward Buffett. That was until 2006. That was when the world's second richest man made the announcement that he was planning to donate 85 per cent of his current $44-billion fortune to the $30-billion charity run by the world's richest man, Bill Gates. Besides the fact that this was the largest single act of charitable giving in all of history, Buffett's donation represents a significant sea change in attitude to philanthropic deeds. In the past, it was much more common for men of substantial means to leave a portion of their estate to a charitable foundation upon their death. The late 1800s and early 1900s saw the birth of numerous new foundations dedicated to various causes: the Ford Foundation, the Lilly Endowment Corporation, J. Paul Getty Trust, the Wellcome Trust and others.

However, the super-wealthy's relationship with money has changed significantly since Henry T. Ford ran his company. Many have come to embrace two core values within American culture: success based on hard work and giving to the betterment of humanity.

Regarding the former, the nouveau riche are making a definite break with the past. It's more than likely that they are aware of the notorious tales of ugly infighting that have erupted in families when an extremely wealthy patriarch dies. Bill Gates has made it clear that his children will only inherit $10 million each out of his vast billion dollar fortune. Buffett shares his sentiments. While his children will not inherit much of his money, they will be comfortably looked after and will continue to oversee charities in their names.

The second major difference is the personal attention that many of the current philanthropic giants take in the actual targeting of the funds. Rather than use their money to build new art galleries or opera houses, many of the famous US philanthropists have a deep belief that their wealth needs to be used to help shape society for the better.

IELTS Reading Part 2: Reading Passage 2 (continued)

A Even with the loss of $7 billion in the ill-fated AOL takeover of TimeWarner, billionaire Ted Turner continued his pledge of $1 billion to support United Nations causes.

B Hungarian-born money speculator George Soros created the Open Society Institute, which the PBS network suggests has given over $4 billion. The OSI supported many dissident movements during the Cold War in different Eastern Bloc countries.

C Bill Gates made the announcement in 2005 that he would be stepping aside from his role in Microsoft to dedicate his time to the Gates Foundation. This foundation donates money to a variety of causes, including medical research into diseases that ravage the developing world — from malaria to tuberculosis. It also supports organisations that are trying to alleviate international poverty and promote childhood education, both internationally and within the United States.

D Gordon and Betty Moore are committed to giving over $7 billion to the Gordon and Betty Moore Foundation, which is dedicated to international biodiversity conservation. They have been involved in causes that range from preserving the North Pacific wild salmon ecosystems to protecting the rainforests of the Andes and Amazon.

E Another foundation created by a married couple is the Michael and Susan Dell Foundation, which has given $1.2 billion to helping children who are suffering in urban poverty.

F James and Virginia Stowers created the $1.5-billion Stowers Institute for Medical Research. The institute focuses all of its energies into researching DNA. Their hope is to find cures for many genetic and microbial afflictions.

The self-reflective attitude of these philanthropists has also sparked a debate in the general public. The baby-boomer generation (those born after World War Two) is one of the wealthiest on record. And it is estimated by Paul G. Schervish of Boston College that anywhere from $41 to $136 trillion will be transferred between parents and their offspring in the next fifty years. A growing portion of them believe that a significant part of this amount should be given to charity. Schervish believes that about $6 trillion may eventually reach the outstretched hands of charities.

But while Gates and Buffett make headlines for the size of their contributions, even their contributions pale in comparison to the giving by a less obvious group. Who might this be? It is, in fact, lower and middle income families. According to Indiana University's Center on Philanthropy, people who earn less than $100,000 gave 59 per cent of all donations. It seems that while we can look to the wealthy for inspiration, the true giving begins surprisingly with those who have less to spare.

IELTS Reading Part 2: Reading Passage 2 (continued)

Questions 15–18

Do the following statements agree with the information given in Reading Passage 2?

TRUE   *if the statement agrees with the information*
FALSE   *if the statement contradicts the information*
NOT GIVEN   *if there is no information on this*

15   Bill Gates convinced Warren Buffett to donate to his charity. _____

16   Philanthropists used to give all their money to charity trusts on their death. _____

17   Bill Gates believes too much money would hurt his children. _____

18   Warren Buffett plans to give more money to his children than Gates. _____

Questions 19–23

Look at the six famous US philanthropists **A-F** in Reading Passage 2 and the statements below (Questions 19-23).

Match each philanthropist with the statement that has a shared meaning.

This philanthropist

19   is helping find possible cures for diseases in Africa.

20   maintained his philanthropic commitment despite personal loss.

21   has helped research into human health with a strong focus on genetics.

22   has strong political beliefs that have led him to support democratic movements.

23   is committed to developing opportunities for underprivileged city children.

IELTS Reading Part 2: Reading Passage 2 (continued)

Questions 24–27

Choose the correct letter **A, B, C** or **D**.

24 Warren Buffett has

   A given his money to more than one charity.
   B not given his children any money.
   C tripled the capital value of the Gates Foundation.
   D been a widely recognised figure in the US.

25 Bill Gates believes strongly that his wealth should be

   A used to create more wealth.
   B spent more on other people's children.
   C given away entirely.
   D spent on his own children.

26 Baby boomers might

   A be the largest group of philanthropists.
   B give less to charity than the Gates Foundation.
   C be against the idea of family proposed by Gates.
   D give over $35 trillion to their families.

27 The author suggests that Bill Gates and Warren Buffett

   A have not made enough of an effort.
   B have given only a small part of all donations.
   C should support more philanthropy among billionaires.
   D should give more money in the US.

IELTS Reading Part 3: Reading Passage 3

You should spend about 20 minutes on **Questions 28-40**, which are based on Reading Passage 3.

Questions 28–32

Reading Passage 3 has six sections, **A-F.**

Choose the correct heading **i-x** for sections **A-E** from the list of headings below.

List of Headings

i	Violent groups in vogue
ii	Breaking through the mainstream
iii	The 70's fashion revival
iv	Bling-bling backlash
v	B-boys and flygirls
vi	Uncertain origins
vii	Cropped, braided or undercover
viii	Designer labels all the rage
ix	The four cornerstones of the culture
x	The hip hop market opens up

28 Section **A** ☐
29 Section **B** ☐
30 Section **C** ☐
31 Section **D** ☐
32 Section **E** ☐

IELTS Reading Part 3: Reading Passage 3

HIP HOP FASHION

Section A

Hip hop culture can trace its origins back to street parties in New York City in the 1970s. While DJs were changing the soul, funk or R&B records, MCs started to fill in the pauses to keep the crowds excited. Eventually, the talk became more stylised with MCs speaking over the music and rap music was born. The birth of rap music happened to coincide with the popularity of break-dancing, a stylised gymnastic dance form, and the development of graffiti into a street art form. Together, all four became the core elements of hip hop culture. As hip hop evolved and spread across the US and the rest of the world, the different genres within the culture prompted many different periods of fashion.

Section B

As rap music moved into the 1980s, there was one group who established the dominant hip hop fashion. Run DMC created the classic rap look. The group's most notable fashion contribution was their Adidas sportswear. Wearing sportswear as regular clothing became a trend and brought into the hip hop fashion scene many more manufacturers from Russell Athletic to Nike. Run DMC were often seen wearing Adidas tracksuits and sneakers (without laces). The group even wrote a song entitled 'My Adidas' in 1986, leading the company to create a pair of shoes in their honour. This was the first time fashion was connected commercially to hip hop. Soon after, the brother of Run DMC's Joseph 'Run' Simmons and co-founder of Def Jam records, Russell Simmons, created the first commercial hip hop clothing line – Phat Farm. Another major hip hop label, FUBU, appeared the same year. Its name is an acronym of 'for us, by us' which suggested its political stance of employing mostly African-Americans. Both labels continue to have tremendous success to this day.

Section C

Jewellery also became an important component in the image of these early rappers and those of later years. There are several theories to its origins. In ghetto culture, which rap music is closely tied to, wearing expensive jewellery is a way of showing your status. Rather than invest their money in banks or real estate, drug dealers and criminals often wear their wealth to avoid tax and other legal issues. Others suggest that the wearing of gold has a cultural connection to the African continent where gold is both widely extracted and used in many traditional art forms. Furthermore, many artists of 1980s, such as Queen Latifah, Boogie Down Productions and Public Enemy, promoted other traditional African ties by wearing red, green and black clothing.

Section D

Many rappers through the 1980s made other jewellery popular, including necklaces and multi-finger rings, as worn by LL Cool J, who had a gold and diamond-encrusted 'Cool J' across his knuckles. This is part of the wider trend of bling-bling, or showing off wealth with diamond or platinum jewellery, expensive champagne (Krystal), designer fur coats and even customised vehicles. This lavish behaviour has been widely criticised by the mainstream media for promoting the wrong values. It is also being criticised within the industry by several prominent artists. Chuck D of Public Enemy narrated a recent documentary about the diamonds coming from war-torn regions in Africa, and Missy Elliot publicly expressed her concern about young black men feeling the pressure to spend irresponsibly.

IELTS Reading Part 3: Reading Passage 3 (continued)

Section E

By the late 1980s and through the early 1990s, gangsta rap began to develop bringing very distinctive styles that originated from street gangs. The Chicano gangsters (of Mexican descent) in Los Angeles contributed loose trousers that are thought to come from Latin dance fashion. These oversized trousers are often worn without a belt, which tends to show the wearer's underwear – a prison reference since inmates have their belts taken away when they go in.

Colour is also important in gangster clothing. In Los Angeles and elsewhere, colours signified connections to particular gangs: red was associated with the Bloods and blue with the Crips. These connections were sometimes obvious in rap groups, such as the prominent NWA who tended to wear all black despite criticism that the group was associated with the Compton Crips. NWA often wore the paraphernalia of the Los Angeles Raiders football team. Today, most rappers are seen wearing the jerseys of different professional basketball, baseball or football teams.

Gangsta rap is often criticised for, among other things, being responsible for the negative image of women in hip hop culture. Women are often envisaged as another possession to own in the bling-bling lifestyle. Women in hip hop videos and even some female rap artists are often seen wearing very revealing clothing. However, this is not always the case. Many women from Lauryn Hill to Missy Elliot have chosen more conservative clothing.

Section F

Hairstyles and hats are a notable component of hip hop fashion as well. Early on, many artists chose to wear hats, such as the soft Kangol bucket hats worn by LL Cool J and the black fedora hats worn by Run DMC. Gangsta rappers often wore black knit ski caps (a possible reference to the balaclavas worn in robberies) like Eazy-E or bandanas (a common item among street gangs) like Tupac Shakur. Today, the flat-rimmed trucker's cap (a mesh-back baseball cap) as worn by 50 Cent and Pharrel Williams tend to predominate. The other popular hip hop headwear is the doorag. Similar to the bandana, the polyester doorag was an early method of keeping moisture in the hair.

Hairstyles too could identify a rapper with a particular genre. The popular 'high top fade', a hairstyle that was high and flat on top, was worn by pop rappers the Fresh Prince and Kid of Kid N Play. Several gangsta rappers like Ice Cube and Eazy-E chose the jheri curl, which left their hair in long, hanging curls. Today, there are several popular hairstyles. Most commonly seen are cornrows, a type of braiding that runs close to the head from front to back. They have been worn by many diverse rappers from Snoop Dogg to Andre 3000. These two rappers have also worn their hair in afros, a style from the 1970s.

IELTS Reading Part 3: Reading Passage 3 (continued)

Questions 33 – 40

Complete each sentence with correct ending **A-L** from the box below.

33 MCs began rapping because
34 The first commercial hip hop relationship developed
35 FUBU was so named
36 Gold necklaces became popular
37 Bling-bling has been criticised
38 Many youth avoid wearing certain colours
39 The media have criticised gangsta rap
40 Eazy-E was recognisable as a gangsta rapper

A	because they wanted the attention of the audience.
B	because hip hop has long had an association with street culture.
C	because it can be made from products that involve human suffering.
D	because they needed to fill the time between records.
E	because he was often seen wearing a black ski hat.
F	because Run DMC created a song praising their favourite brand.
G	because they portray the opposite sex in a negative light.
H	because rap artists wore them.
I	because Run's brother started his own clothing company.
J	because they are symbols of violent gangs.
K	because he wore his hair in cornrows.
L	because it reflected their desire to support African-Americans.

IELTS Writing: Task 1

You should spend about 20 minutes on this task.

This graph shows the gap in earnings for full-time United States workers 25 years and older with a high school diploma, bachelor's and master's degrees.

Write a report for a university lecturer describing the information below.

Write at least 150 words.

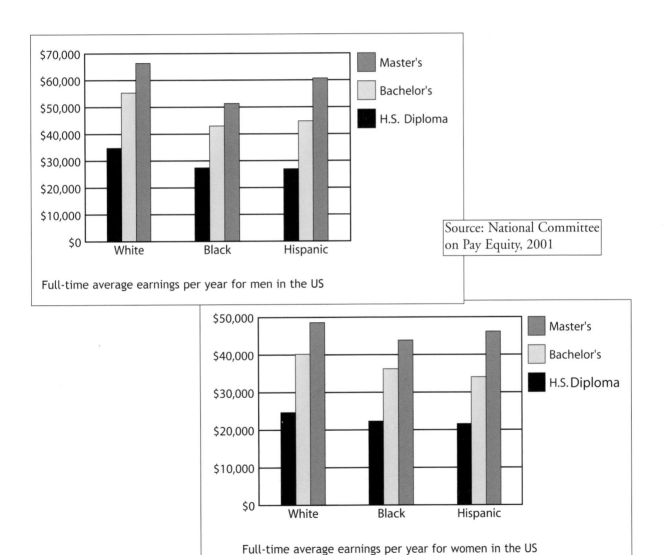

IELTS Writing: Task 2

You should spend about 40 minutes on this task.

Present a written argument or case to an educated reader with no specialist knowledge of the following topic.

> *The internal combustion engine has allowed for the rapid transport of people and goods across far distances. The entire global economy is based on this. At the same time, these engines produce CO and CO_2 gases, which have been identified as a significant factor in the growing global warming problem.*
>
> *What are your opinions on this?*

You should use your own ideas, knowledge and experience and support your arguments with examples and relevant evidence.

Write at least 250 words.

IELTS Speaking: Parts 1-3

PART 1 (4-5 minutes) ***For examiner use only***

Ask the student the following: 1) Give a brief introduction about yourself. 2) Ask about these familiar topics. (Example questions) **Homes / Families** • Tell me about your family. • Tell me about the accommodation you live in. • What's your favourite place in your community? • Is it a good place to live? Why / Why not?	**Jobs / Studies** • What do you do in your job? • What are you studying? Why? • What are your future career goals? **Interests** • What do you do in the evenings / at weekends? • What books have you read lately? • What is your favourite kind of music? Why?

PART 2 (3-4 minutes)

Photocopy the following Task Cards. Give only one to each student.

Task Card A	Task Card B
Describe a sport you like to watch or play. You should say: – why you started playing it – how long you have played it – how popular the sport is and why and explain why it is important to you. • You will have to talk about the topic for 1-2 minutes. • You will have 1 minute to think about what you're going to say. • You can take notes to help you if you want.	Describe a job you would like in the future. You should say: – what the job is all about – what qualifications you need for it – how important the job is and explain why you would enjoy it. • You will have to talk about the topic for 1-2 minutes. • You will have 1 minute to think about what you're going to say. • You can take notes to help you if you want.

PART 3 (4-5 minutes) ***For examiner use only***

1) Ask the student 1-2 round-off questions for either Tasks A or B.	2) Discuss the following points with the student for either Task A or B.
Task Card A • Is it easier / harder than other sports to play? • Who / What is your favourite player / team? **Task Card B** • What company would you like to work for? • Does the job pay well?	**Task Card A In-depth discussion** • What do you think about drugs in sports? • How has the sport changed over the years? • Are professional athletes paid too much? **Task Card B In-depth discussion** • How important is income / job / status in your society? • How well is the economy doing in your area? Compare jobs today with your parents' or grandparents' generations.

CAE Reading: Paper 1, Part 1

You are going to read three extracts which are all concerned in some way with architecture. For questions **1–6**, choose the answer (**A**, **B**, **C** or **D**) which you think fits best according to the text.

CIVIL ENGINEER ASSOCIATION PRESENTS
THE ANNUAL POPSICLE STICK BRIDGE COMPETITION

HOW TO ENTER: If you are under the age of 30 and are enrolled in, or planning to enrol in, a university-level civil engineering program, you have a great opportunity to show off your engineering skills and win €5000 towards your education.

General Rules:

- You must build a bridge that can span a gap of one metre. The bridge must be designed to carry as much weight as possible. You are allowed to use any number of unmodified popsicle sticks and standard wood glue. However, the winning bridge will have the best bridge weight to load-bearing ratio.
- The competition will take place from 10am to 2pm on 2 June in the University Auditorium (98 University Boulevard). Entrants must be present with their bridge by 9:30am at the latest. The winner will be chosen and announced at 2:30pm.
- The decision of the judges is final. This year's panel of judges are comprised of: Dr Jonathon Banks, Chairman of the Civil Engineering Association; Professor Nick Stevens of the Civil Engineering Dept.; and Samantha Ward, a local radio personality from WKRP.
- Last year's winning design by Sandeep Singh, a local Civil Engineering student, weighed just 1.348 kilograms and held a weight of 276.662 kilograms before reaching breaking point.
- The Grand Prize winning design this year will receive a €5000 bursary and a new laptop computer (Value: €500). The second place entrant will receive a €1000 bursary. The third place entrant will receive a €500 scholarship.
- The winning entrant will also be featured in an article for the Civil Engineering Association's monthly magazine.

---

1 The winning entry

    A must carry twenty times its weight before breaking.

    B can be comprised of any combination of popsicle sticks and glue.

    C will carry the most weight.

    D could have fewer popsicle sticks than its competitors.

2 The competition rules state that

    A a controversial judges' decision cannot be appealed.

    B the second place award is worth one-fifth that of the first place prize.

    C the winner must write an article for the Association's magazine.

    D the entrants must be present at nine in the morning.

'BURJARIFIC'

With some estimates of over one million words, English has the largest vocabulary among the world's 2700 tongues. And yet even this linguistic behemoth at times fails to measure up to the task. Namely, what word could truly describe the amazing engineering marvel that is the Burj Dubai? I'm of the mind that this building is in such a class by itself that it deserves a word of an equally unique purpose. I propose 'Burjarific'.

Standing at 818 metres, the 160-floor Burj Dubai dwarfs its nearest competitor by nearly 200 metres. The coveted tallest title had long been divided between the tallest freestanding structure, Toronto's CN Tower (553.3 m); the building with the most floors, Chicago's Sears Tower (110 floors); and the tallest structure, North Dakota's KVLY-TV Mast (629 m). In one knockout blow akin to Iron Mike unifying the WBA, WBO and IBF titles in 1987, the Burj Dubai can now lay claim to all three tallest titles.

Since the construction of New York's Empire State Building in 1932, building tall has been a point of national pride and international swagger. In lockstep with their rising financial fortunes, countries across Asia have been in a race to the ostentatious top of the national ego heap. Taiwan had briefly asserted its own tallest with the Taipei 101 located in Xinyi financial district. Malaysia had a likewise brief stint in the front runner position with the Petronas Towers from 1998 to 2004. Now, Dubai has pushed its way into the record books.

---

3 The writer makes a connection between boxing and tall buildings because
   A the writer believes the race to be the tallest building is violent.
   B there had previously been different contenders for the title.
   C Mike Tyson owns part of the Burj Dubai.
   D the tallest building title is as important as undisputed heavyweight boxing champion.

4 In the third paragraph the writer suggests that Asian countries are
   A showing that they have financial resources on par with their western counterparts.
   B demonstrating their appreciation of American architecture.
   C investing heavily in basic infrastructure projects.
   D building these towers to satisfy the demand for more office space.

CAE Reading: Paper 1, Part 1 (continued)

> *(Extract from a novel)*
>
> As two local constables cordoned off the stone steps of the medieval cathedral with yellow police tape, Inspector Marsh knelt down beside the mayor's crumpled body. Click, whirr, click, whirr. To his left, the forensics inspector was slowly circling the body, taking photos at different angles. The intermittent flashes cut through the twilight dim, leaving a macabre silhouette.
>
> Inspector Marsh looked towards the spire of the church. It had recently been renovated in preparation for the city's 800-year anniversary. 'Bad luck that,' interjected the forensics man. Marsh followed the man's gaze toward the heavy marble cornice that lay next to the body. It was blood-splattered, but still intact. The body had absorbed the impact. Flash.
>
> 'Oi, what do we have here?' Marsh muttered to himself.
>
> Marsh drew his torch from the inside pocket of his mac and shone it on the bottom of the marble block. There were clear scratch marks and chips around the cement. He looked up toward the entablature depicting the Last Supper. The missing block formed part of the parapet of the observation deck. Clenching his jaw, he thought the worst, 'Could this have been deliberate?'

5   The forensic inspector and the police inspector

   A   shared the same view as to the cause of death.

   B   were called there to investigate the mayor's murder.

   C   both felt sorry for the mayor.

   D   were used to the sight of a dead body.

6   Inspector Marsh suspects foul play because

   A   the block showed indications it may have been chiselled.

   B   the church was recently renovated with poor craftsmanship.

   C   the missing block fell on the mayor from the parapet.

   D   the mayor had many political enemies.

CAE Reading: Paper 1, Part 2

You are going to read an extract from a biography. Six paragraphs have been removed from the extract. Choose from the paragraphs A-G the one which fits each gap (**7–12**). There is one extra paragraph which you do not need to use.

Henri Dunant

It was to be the defining moment in his life and career. Jean-Henri Dunant arrived in the small town of Solferino, in Italy, on the evening of June 24, 1859. He had come to the town on business; what he witnessed was to change not only his life, but the lives of countless others. On that day 118,000 French and Sardinian troops had waged a victorious battle against the 100,000-strong Austrian forces. Some 30,000 men from both sides were left wounded or dying on the battlefield.

| 7 |

When he returned to his home in Geneva, he wrote a personal account of the event titled 'A Memory of Solferino' and published 1,600 copies at his own expense. In the book, Dunant described the inhumanity of the conflict and outlined a remedy to the situation.

| 8 |

Among those to receive a copy was the President of the Geneva Society for Public Welfare, Gustave Moynier, who was impressed by the book's ideas. His organisation agreed to create the neutral organisation that Dunant had been petitioning for. On February 17, 1863, the five-person committee consisting of Dunant, Moynier, Swiss general Henri Dufour, Dr Louis Appia and Dr Théodore Maunoir met to consider how best to put Dunant's ideas into practice. This was considered the first meeting of the International Committee of the Red Cross (ICRC).

| 9 |

In the years following the start of the ICRC, it was Dunant's commitment to this charity work that finally led to the failure of his businesses in Algeria. His bankruptcy created a scandal in Switzerland, leading to him being ousted from both the ICRC and the YMCA.

| 10 |

Although ostracised by the parent organisation, Dunant continued to promote the efforts of the Red Cross in the different countries he visited.
   However, things were to take a turn for the better. In 1895, the editor of *Die Ostschweiz* published an article about Dunant. The article entitled 'Henri Dunant, the founder of the Red Cross' was eventually reprinted in many newspapers across Europe.

| 11 |

As the culmination of his career in charitable work and his endless support for humanitarian relief, Dunant was awarded the first ever Nobel Peace Prize in 1901. It was given jointly to Dunant and the French pacifist Frederic Passy, who had founded the Peace League. The International Committee sent their congratulations:

| 12 |

Dunant spent the remaining years of his life in a nursing home in Heiden, Switzerland. He died on October 30, 1910 and was buried in Zurich. In his will, he donated part of the 104,000 Swiss francs he received with the Peace Prize to ensure that a free bed was available in the nursing home for any poor citizen in the region.

CAE Reading: Paper 1, Part 2 (continued)

A
Much has been written of the resulting tumultuous early years of the organisation and Dunant's subsequent removal from the organisation. The best way to assess how this happened is to first look at Dunant's upbringing. From a very early age, he had two competing influences on his life: Calvinism, which led him to join the Geneva Society for Alms and to found the Geneva YMCA, and his interest in business which he developed from his father, a businessman.

B
The Czechoslovakian Red Cross had originally called for a three-day truce to fighting at Easter. While many in the ICRC supported the move, it would take another 26 years for the idea to take hold. The ICRC eventually set the date of the World Red Cross and Red Crescent Day on May 8th, Dunant's birthday.

C
This led to a revival of interest in his work. In the years that followed, he received the Swiss Binet-Fendt Prize and financial support from many notable European aristocrats including the widow of the Russian Tsar.

D
On seeing this horror, Dunant took it on himself to rally the town's citizens, especially the women, to help the victims on both sides. Under a rallying cry of *Tutti fratelli* ('All are brothers'), he personally arranged to buy sufficient medical supplies and even negotiated the release of captured Austrian doctors from the French.

E
There is no man who more deserves this honour, for it was you, forty years ago, who set up the international organisation for the relief of the wounded on the battlefield. Without you, the Red Cross, the supreme humanitarian achievement of the 19th century would probably have never been undertaken.

F
His idea was to establish a charitable organisation that would care for wounded soldiers regardless of which side they were on. Dunant went on a tour of Europe presenting copies of his book to many leading political and military leaders across Europe.

G
With his reputation and financial affairs in tatters, Dunant moved to Paris and a life of poverty, but it was not to be a quiet life as he continued his charitable work. Between 1874 and 1886, he moved to many different cities in Europe including Stuttgart, Rome and Corfu.

CAE Reading: Paper 1, Part 3

You are going to read a magazine article. For questions **13–19**, choose the answer (**A**, **B**, **C** or **D**) which you think fits best according to the text.

Brother, Can you PayPal me a Dime?

When you think of someone asking for a handout, what comes to mind? The lady on the corner waving a used coffee cup under your nose or the squeegee guy assaulting your car at the stoplights? Well, times have changed and so has the approach. If you want to be a successful beggar today, you need to have media savvy and of course a website.

Like most things today, it was only a question of time before begging began infiltrating cyber-space. Cyber-begging, or e-panhandling as it also known, made itself visible with a bang in 2002. That year, Karyn Bosnak was facing dire financial prospects having run up her credit cards on designer goods to the tune of $20,000. It was a bit hard to understand. The high-living, former Manhattanite made nearly $4000 a month in her job as a television producer, but paying the credit cards had drained her savings account. The final blow came when she bounced a cheque on groceries. Rather than declare bankruptcy like many would have in a similar situation, she set up a website, explaining her situation and asking for people to help her out. Karyn figured that if 20,000 people each gave $1 each she'd have enough to pay off her debts. While she confesses to receiving many negative emails about her motives, the philanthropists came in droves. In 20 weeks, she had made enough money and had become a bit of US national celebrity with over 2 million visitors to her website and coverage by a US national morning TV show and a national magazine. She has since written a best-selling book about her begging adventure with a Hollywood movie deal in the works.

The success of her story has spawned dozens of other hard luck cases from the comedic to the strange to the truly heart-wrenching. A quick search of Yahoo's e-panhandling directory will give you at least three women asking for money for breast enhancement surgery with one happy individual claiming to have received enough to have gone ahead with the operation. Numerous university students have posted pleas to help offset the cost of their tuition or at least make a little beer money. And a few desperate entrepreneurs are seeking start-up capital. As in real-life, it is somewhat difficult to distinguish the freeloaders from the forlorn.

One case that falls into the latter category is that of Jacqui Saburido. Born in Caracas, Venezuela, the beautiful college student decided to study English in Texas in 1999. One night, driving home from a party her vehicle was struck by a drunk driver killing the two female passengers with her. Unable to escape the burning car, she sustained horrific third-degree burns over sixty percent of her body. While Saburido continues her recovery, her family has posted an information website that lets people donate money for her numerous costly surgeries.

But not every person looking for generosity online is necessarily seeking financial help. A case in point is that of Canadian Kyle MacDonald who sought out generosity purely for the adventure. Kyle set himself the task of trying to 'get a house...or an island...or a house on an island' by trading up. He started with a red paperclip. After a year and more than a dozen trades, he reached his goal with a two-storey house in Kipling, Saskatchewan. His travelled to many places across North America meeting the people he traded with along the way. Some of the items included a snowmobile, a role in a Corbin Bernsen Hollywood movie and an afternoon with Alice Cooper.

CAE Reading: Paper 1, Part 3 (continued)

13 The writer assumes that the readers are
    A scared of people begging on the streets.
    B angered by the constant pleas from beggars.
    C very generous with people who ask for money.
    D aware of people begging in the streets.

14 Karyn Bosnak got into financial trouble
    A when she became a television producer.
    B after spending excessively on clothes.
    C when she went to buy some groceries.
    D after she decided to become bankrupt.

15 What led to Bosnak's success online?
    A She wrote a book about her story.
    B She found many very generous people.
    C She would not give up after negative emails.
    D She was interviewed by the national media.

16 Since Bosnak became a celebrity,
    A dozens of people have asked her for financial help.
    B there have been others who have found similar success.
    C several companies have been started to help people online.
    D she began trying to help others in need.

17 Jacqui Saburido's family set up a website because
    A they wanted to bring attention to Jacqui's situation.
    B they are seeking justice against the person responsible.
    C they are trying to inform people about the dangers of drunk driving.
    D they want to help Jacqui return to Caracas.

18 Kyle MacDonald started trading items online in the hopes that
    A he could meet a lot of famous people.
    B he'd have an adventure meeting different people.
    C he could finally have his dream house in Saskatchewan.
    D he could finally get rid of his red paperclip.

19 Corbin Bernsen offered MacDonald
    A some Hollywood memorabilia.
    B a chance to spend the afternoon with Alice Cooper.
    C a roundtrip plane journey to Hollywood.
    D an opportunity to act in a feature film.

CAE Reading: Paper 1, Part 4

You are going to read a newspaper article about the media. For questions **20–34**, choose from the sections (**A-D**). The sections may be chosen more than once.

Which section mentions the following?

the largest constant source of funds for the fledgling TV station	20 ___
the effect that satellite technology has had on governments	21 ___
the management has been changed to update the network's focus	22 ___
the size of the TV network's audience compared to others in the market	23 ___
the belief that the network might be controlled by agents from other countries	24 ___
the issue of information control in the Middle East	25 ___
the station likes to present view of the ordinary Arab people	26 ___
the accusations of anti-Semitism levelled against the TV station	27 ___
the audience grew with its coverage of two big events related to the United States	28 ___
the fact that one of their offices was forcibly closed	29 ___
the televising of the person responsible for atrocities in the United States	30 ___
the fact that TV stations with specialised content were doing so well	31 ___
the TV station maintains its right to show graphic images of victims of war	32 ___
the confidential report that disclosed a possible reason for the bombing of Al Jazeera	33 ___
the staff had some experience in a rival news agency	34 ___

Al Jazeera: Television News on the Edge

A

Al Jazeera first launched its television broadcasting in November 1996 with a $150 million grant from the emir of Qatar, Sheikh Hamad bin Khalifa Al Thani. The concept of the station was to emulate the success that Western media groups have had with specialised content stations such as all-news networks like CNN or BBC World. At the time, there had been no such specialised TV content on most TV networks across the Arab World. Most Arabic TV stations in the region were operated by the different government Information Ministries. With their traditional autocratic style, these Information Ministries sought to control all content shown in the country through strict regulation and censorship. However, by the mid-1990s, the wide-spread ownership of satellite dishes was making this nearly impossible. The emir in consultation with the Qatari Ministry of Information chose a fairly progressive route and decided to end the Ministry in favour of a politically independent channel. The start of broadcasting coincided rather fortuitously with events at the ill-fated BBC World Service's Arabic TV Station. That channel was a joint venture between the BBC and the Saudi government-controlled Orbit Communications Corporation. There were constant clashes between BBC and Orbit notably over the strict censorship imposed by the Saudi Arabian government. It eventually closed on April 1996. The majority of the former BBC staff joined Al Jazeera.

B

Al Jazeera's business plan had proposed financial self-sufficiency by 2001 through its advertising revenue, but it continues to receive roughly 60% of its estimated $85 million annual revenue from the emir according to *Time* magazine. The largest barrier to Al Jazeera reaching its goal of profitability has been the unspoken economic embargo imposed by different countries in the region. Since Al Jazeera is independent and does report stories that are at times highly critical of different countries, these countries are rather reluctant to see their state-owned businesses advertise with Al Jazeera. Despite this, Al Jazeera is now one of the largest TV networks in the Middle East and a medium-size player in the world with an estimated 40 million regular viewers. There have been several reasons for the relative success of the channel. Early on, it took a fairly adversarial position against many of the countries in the region. They asked a lot of difficult questions from government officials not used to this journalistic style. Then, there was their coverage of the World Trade Center attacks in 2001 and the War in Iraq in 2003. Both events led to an explosive upsurge in its popularity.

CAE Reading: Paper 1, Part 4 (continued)

C

While the station continues to enjoy a high level of popularity, Al Jazeera does have its detractors from many sides. In the Middle East, it has been criticised by both Israel and Arab countries alike. Many in Israel were incensed over the TV station's coverage of the second Palestinian Intifada beginning in September 2000. Al Jazeera has developed a unique reporting style that tries to show everything under the premise of free speech. This means that it has at times shown extremely gruesome images of people killed in the Palestinian territories, Iraq, Afghanistan and elsewhere. On the other hand, many in the Arab world have accused Al Jazeera of being an agent of the Mossad, the Israeli Secret Service, or the US Central Intelligence Agency citing the fact that the network regularly interviews US and Israeli politicians. Al Jazeera has also had a difficult relationship with Iraq since the Iraq War began in 2003. Al Jazeera's coverage of the war and its aftermath painted a poor picture of Iraq and was seen by the new Iraqi government as supporting the insurgency. In August 2004, the Iraqi government closed the Iraq offices of the TV network, but Al Jazeera promised to continue covering the story from outside the country.

D

Given its insistence on presenting international news from the view 'on the Arab street', Al Jazeera has drawn much ire from the United States. The US grievances relate in large part to Al Jazeera's broadcasting of full footage communiqués by 'terrorists' like Al Qaeda leader, Osama bin Laden, broadcasting images of US hostages during the Iraq War and graphic reporting of civilian war casualties. Al Jazeera, on the other hand, is quite angered over a memorandum from April 2004 which cited a conversation between then US President George W. Bush and UK Prime Minister Tony Blair. The London tabloid *The Daily Mirror* reported that in the memo Bush had said that the US should bomb Al Jazeera's Doha headquarters and other locations. Although the White House denied this by suggesting it was likely just a joke taken out of context, the memo implies that there may have been some nefarious intent in the previous US bombings of Al Jazeera's headquarters in Kabul, Afghanistan in 2001 and in Baghdad, Iraq in April 2003. However, Qatar's emir, a staunch US ally, has tried to soft any anti-American rhetoric from the station by replacing the managing director Mohammed Jassim Ali. Likewise this softening of their image coincides with Al Jazeera's overall business plans. These include Al Jazeera International, a 24-hour English language news network to rival CNN and BBC World.

CAE Writing, Paper 2, Part 1

You **must** answer this question. Write your answer in **180–220** words in an appropriate style.

1 For the past year, you have been working as a personal assistant to a famous movie star. Your friend Chris has written to you asking about it. Read the extract from you friend's letter and from your diary below, and write a letter to your friend saying whether or not you would recommend the job to your friend and giving your reasons.

> Do you think I'd like the job? I especially want to make lots of good film industry connections. I'd like to eventually become a film director. If I could use my knowledge of film and get some work experience at the same time, that would be fantastic!
>
> Cheers,
> Chris

> **Feb 2**
> Picked up drycleaning. Arranged a limo. At least 100 phone calls today – typical.
>
> **Feb 4**
> Pay day! At least the pay's great. Five minutes small talk with Mr. Scorcese today—real gentleman.
>
> **Feb 10**
> Got yelled at by the boss. She's stressed about the Academy Awards and her designer gown.
>
> **Feb 15**
> Only a few more days until the Awards. Can't wait to meet more stars!

Write your **letter**. You do not need to include postal addresses.

CAE Writing, Paper 2, Part 2

Write an answer to **one** of the questions **2–5** in this part. Write your answers in **220–260** words in an appropriate style. Put the question number in the box at the top of the page.

2 You see this announcement on a community bulletin board.

> ### BEST CITIZEN AWARD
>
> We want you to nominate someone in your community who you think deserves the title best citizen. Your entry should mention:
>
> - what this person has done for the community
> - why this person is different from other good citizens
> - what we can learn from this person

Write your **competition entry**.

3 A new student magazine is looking for a new music reviewer. You need to submit a review of a music group you are familiar with. You should describe the band and its music; what makes the group different, interesting or exciting; the impact you think they have made on music and popular culture.

Write your **review**.

4 You have been picked to become a salesperson in your company. Your first task will be to write a letter to a possible new customer. You should introduce yourself, explain what your company does and how they do it and how this customer would benefit from using your company's products or services.

Write your **letter**.

CAE Writing, Paper 2, Part 2 (continued)

5 Answer **one** of the following two questions based on **one** of the titles below. Write the letter **(a)** or **(b)** as well as the number 5 in the question box.

(a) *Lucky Jim* by Kingsley Amis
A famous film director is thinking of making a film of *Lucky Jim*, but he hasn't read it. Write a report for him about the main characters in the book and explain why certain actors (either imaginary or famous such as Brad Pitt and Angelina Jolie) would or would not be suitable as members of the cast.

Write your **report**.

(b) *The Pelican Brief* by John Grisham
A friend of yours is teaching English in a remote town with no bookshop or library. He needs some ideas for books he can order over the internet. Write him a letter explaining why he would (or would not enjoy) *The Pelican Brief*.

Write your **letter**.

The above set texts are valid for 2008–09, 2009–10.
The set texts for 2010–2011 are *Of Mice and Men* by John Steinbeck and *Through a Glass, Darkly* by Donna Leon.
Set texts change every two years. Future titles are available online.

Other appropriate level books could include the following:

The Firm by John Grisham
Ripley's Game by Patricia Highsmith
On the Road by Jack Kerouac

CAE Use of English: Paper 3, Part 1

For questions **1–12**, read the text below and decide which answer (**A, B, C** or **D**) best fits each gap. There is an example at the beginning **(0)**.

Example:

0 **A** celebrate   **B** share   **C** encourage   **D** perpetuate

Example: | 0 | <u>A</u> | <u>B</u> | <u>C</u> | <u>D</u> |

Religious Holidays in Schools

While 1950s British parents would have thought discussing whether or not to **(0)**___ Christmas in schools a rather absurd **(1)**___ , it is **(2)**___ a question which gives great pause to many today. Post-WWII Britain has **(3)**___ several waves of immigration from the 1950s Caribbean, India and Pakistan immigrants under the British Nationality Act of 1948 to Irish immigrants throughout the century looking for employment to Eastern European refugees **(4)**___ Communist regimes to even some German prisoners of war. This has given rise to the increasing amount of ethnic **(5)**___ in most metropolitan areas and even in many rural districts. While Protestant Britain remains the **(6)**___, the UK Ministry of Education has set up guidelines to encourage greater **(7)**___ of different religions. The goal **(8)**___ to teach students about the world's religions and religious festivities in the hopes that this will **(9)**___ understanding in today's mixed communities. So today, December and January become a **(10)**___ point for classroom discussion about the world's many religions. The Christian holiday of Christmas can be **(11)**___ alongside the Jewish holiday of Hanukkah, the Hindu holiday of Makar Sankrant, the Sikh celebration of the birthday of Guru Gobind Singh, the Muslim celebration of Eid-Ul-Adha and many others. So rather than just celebrating one point of view to the exclusion of some students, everyone gets **(12)**___ a potluck of different world views.

CAE Use of English: Paper 3, Part 1 (continued)

1	A	belief	B	notion	C	assumption	D	expression
2	A	unwillingly	B	legally	C	not actually	D	in fact
3	A	shown	B	dealt	C	experienced	D	included
4	A	escaping	B	running	C	evading	D	confronting
5	A	divergence	B	diversity	C	dissimilarity	D	distinction
6	A	most	B	majority	C	opposition	D	superiority
7	A	hope	B	tolerance	C	equality	D	cooperation
8	A	has	B	is	C	should be	D	was
9	A	foster	B	make	C	pacify	D	educate
10	A	focus	B	focal	C	pin	D	setting
11	A	discussed	B	conversed	C	talked	D	spoken
12	A	to enjoy	B	enjoying	C	join	D	to join

CAE Use of English: Paper 3, Part 2

For questions **13–27**, read the text below and think of the word which best fits each gap. Use only **one** word in each gap. There is an example at the beginning **(0)**.

Write your answers **IN CAPITAL LETTERS**.

Example: **0** B O R N

Charles Darwin

Charles Robert Darwin was **(0)** _____ in Shrewsbury, England on 12 February 1809. In 1825, he began **(13)**_____ medicine under his father's guidance. However, the horror of 19th century surgery led him into other pursuits. He eventually developed an **(14)**_____ in taxidermy, collecting beetles and learning **(15)**_____ natural history. His father enrolled Charles in theological studies at Christ's College, University of Cambridge. **(16)**_____ was thought that attaining this degree **(17)**_____ allow Charles to become a clergyman, a career which would **(18)**_____ him a reasonable income and allow him to pursue his interest in natural history. Most clergymen at the **(19)**_____ thought the study of nature was part of their duty to understand the miracle of **(20)**_____ creation. Under the advice of Cambridge professor Reverend John Henslow, Charles delayed taking his holy orders. **(21)**_____, he joined an expedition to map the coastline of South America on the HMS Beagle. This five-year **(22)**_____ undertaken in two parts was to be a watershed in the field of biology. During the trip, Charles was **(23)**_____ catalogue hundreds of species of animal, plants and fossils. Among the many places he visited from South America through to Australia **(24)**_____ the Galapagos Islands off the **(25)**_____ of Ecuador. It was here that he identified slight variations in what appeared to be the same species from one **(26)**_____ to the next in the Galapagos Islands. It was these observations which led **(27)**_____ to formulate his ground-breaking 1859 thesis *On the Origins of Species by the Means of Natural Selection, or The Preservation of Favoured Races in the Struggle for Life*.

CAE Use of English: Paper 3, Part 3

For questions **28–37**, read the text below. Use the word given in capitals at the end of some of the lines to form a word that fits in the gap **in the same line**. There is an example at the beginning **(0)**. Write your answers **IN CAPITAL LETTERS**.

Example: | 0 | C | O | M | M | O | N | L | Y |

The Largest Predator

Thanks in no small part to movies like Jurassic Park, it is a **(0)** _____ **COMMON**
held **(28)** _____ that the Tyrannosaurus Rex was the largest of all the **ASSUME**
(29) _____ dinosaurs. However, even the largest known specimen of **PREDATOR**
this thunder lizard, a 6.4 tonne, 12.8 metre long fossil held by the Field
Museum in Chicago pales in **(30)** _____ with others of the **COMPARE**
period. In 1995, one such dinosaur, the Giganotosaurus **(31)** _____ **LITERAL**
'Giant Southern Lizard') was **(32)** _____ by palaeontologist Rodolfo **EARTH**
Coria in Argentina. The 13.7 metre specimen lived about 100 million years
ago. It is believed to have hunted the 40 metre long herbivore
Argentinosaurus in packs. However, even this dinosaur **(33)** _____ to be **BE**
relegated to a second place finish with the reassessment study conducted by
Cristiano Dal Sasso of the Civic **(34)** _____ History Museum in Milan, **NATURE**
Italy. Sasso based his new **(35)** _____ on the work of German **FIND**
palaeontologist Ernst Stromer. In 1912, Stromer discovered an exceptional
example of the Spinosaurus which he estimated to be much larger
than T. Rex. **(36)** _____ this skeleton was destroyed **FORTUNATE**
when the allies bombed the Munich museum in WWII. Sasso took
(37) _____ of two partial Spinosaurus skull fragments and compared **MEASURE**
it to the skulls of other similarly-shaped spinosaurs. The new spinosaurus
were 17 metres long and weighed as much as 9 tonnes.

CAE Use of English: Paper 3, Part 4

For questions **38–42**, think of **one** word only which can be used appropriately in all three sentences. Here is an example **(0)**.

Example:

0 I've tried several times, but I can't seem to get this software to _____.

You're a futurist? Wow, what kind of _____ does that entail?

If you want to lose weight, you'll have to _____ harder.

Example: **0 | W | O | R | K |**

---

38 The club holds an annual _____ to raise money for charity.

Pass me the instruction manual. I can't figure out the _____ of this button.

I think national defence is the most important _____ of government.

39 Who was the first man into _____?

It's still cold in here. Should we buy a _____ heater?

We have a lot more _____ since we moved house.

40 The hubcap came off when they hit a _____ in the road.

He got a painful _____ on the head when he was struck by a cricket ball.

We saw a _____ in our share price after launching the new software.

41 The _____ of the alleged gang leader took more than a year.

Early _____ research suggests the new formula of the medicine is more effective.

They found a solution through _____ and error.

42 The school board was worried about teen pregnancy. It decided to begin _____ education a year earlier.

They just had a baby, but I forgot to ask about the baby's _____.

Many parents worry that there is too much _____ and violence on television.

CAE Use of English: Paper 3, Part 5

For questions **43–50**, complete the second sentence so that it has a similar meaning to the first sentence, using the word given. **Do not change the word given**. You must use between **three** and **six** words, including the word given. Here is an example **(0)**.

Example:

0 I can't understand why you would ask her to come on holiday. She hates the beach.

POINT

I don't _____ trying to convince her to come on holiday. She hates the beach.

The gap can be filled with the words 'see the point in', so you write:

Example: | 0 | S | E | E | T | H | E | P | O | I | N | T | I | N | | |

Write your answers **IN CAPITAL LETTERS**.

---

43 We've had our share of good and bad times like most married couples.

DOWNS

Like most married couples, we've had _____.

44 The wind howled outside as the tornado approached.

ONLY

As the tornado approached, _____ heard outside.

45 Do you think you could help me move on Saturday?

WONDERING

I _____ me a hand moving on Saturday?

46 Help yourself to coffee and biscuits.

FREE

_____ to take some coffee and biscuits.

CAE Use of English: Paper 3, Part 5 (continued)

47 The protestors demanded the minister's resignation in the wake of the scandal.

FOR

The protesters _____ the minister in the wake of the scandal.

48 The plane failed to depart on schedule due to an engine malfunction.

OFF

The plane _____ as planned due to an engine malfunction.

49 There were not as many tourists this year due to the economic downturn.

SIGNIFICANTLY

Compared to previous years, we had _____ due to the economic downturn.

50 I really don't know what to say about that news.

WORDS

I am at _____ about the news.

QSE Advanced — CAE Exam Practice Listening 1

Name:
Class:

CAE Listening, Paper 4, Part 1

(Use *QSE Advanced* Exam Practice Audio, **Test 7**)

You will hear three different extracts. For questions **1–6,** choose the answer (**A, B** or **C**) which fits best according to what you hear. There are two questions for each extract.

Extract One

You hear two people on a current affairs programme discussing a controversial television advertisement.

1   What do the two speakers agree about?
     A   The ad is targeted at men.
     B   The Super Bowl ads are getting worse.
     C   The ad failed to win new customers.

2   What did the advertisement feature according to the speaker?
     A   a man presenting a box of flowers to a woman
     B   a gift that turned out to be rather rude
     C   talking flowers in a decorative glass vase

Extract Two

You hear an interview of a woman discussing New York designer Zac Posen at New York's Fashion Week.

3   How does the interviewer describe the temperature at Fashion Week?
     A   It's cold.
     B   It's exciting.
     C   It's getting warmer.

4   How does Posen differ from his peers?
     A   He is more creative than them.
     B   He started his own business early.
     C   He draws his inspiration from nature.

Extract Three

You hear an interview of the painter Paul Rimmington who lives in Helsinki, Finland.

5   How does the host expect listeners to examine Rimmington's work?
     A   by visiting his website
     B   by coming to Helsinki
     C   through in-depth interviewing

6   How does Rimmington still feel connected to Britain?
     A   His painting commissions mostly come from the UK.
     B   Finns treat him more as a Brit than as a Finn.
     C   His painting technique is influenced by working in Sheffield.

CAE Listening, Paper 4, Part 2

(Use *QSE Advanced* Exam Practice Audio, **Test 4**)

You will hear a conversation on the radio about stem cell research. For questions **7–14,** complete the sentences.

STEM CELLS

As opposed to regular cells, stem cells are [___7___]

They can become any kind of cell under specific physiological or [___8___] conditions.

Roughly 2 per cent of people [___9___] are affected by Parkinson's disease.

Parkinson's disease attacks the part of the [___10___] that produces dopamine.

Scientists discovered that transplanted stem cells will produce dopamine in [___11___]

Christopher Reeve wanted to use stem cells to help [___12___] injuries.

Many [___13___] are against using embryonic stem cells.

[___14___] stem cells cannot be easily grown in the lab.

CAE Listening, Paper 4, Part 3

(Use *QSE Advanced* Exam Practice Audio, **Test 5**)

You will hear a radio interview with two advertising executives about David Ogilvy, known for his work in advertising. For questions **15–20**, choose the answer (**A, B, C** or **D**) which fits best according to what you hear.

15 Ogilvy is known as the father of advertising because he

    A started the first advertising company of the 20th century.
    B developed important new methods for advertising.
    C created the advertising industry standards.
    D made the best adverts in the business.

16 According to John Wanamaker, advertising has a major flaw in that

    A it only attracts half as many people as it should.
    B it is difficult to judge how effective it really is.
    C it is half as effective on people as it was earlier.
    D it costs a lot of money.

17 What did Ogilvy learn from George Gallup?

    A He learned to do statistical mathematics.
    B He learned about how advertising affects people.
    C He learned to find the cause behind the statistics.
    D He learned to interview people for useful information.

18 Ogilvy noticed that people can remember more of an advert

    A if its headline contains a quote from a famous person.
    B if it has 20 per cent larger type.
    C if its headline explains what the product is.
    D if it has a headline like in a newspaper.

19 Ogilvy believed that a product's unique selling point should

    A be included as soon as possible.
    B be shown at the beginning of a newspaper.
    C make up 95 per cent of an advert.
    D be the main part of the advert.

20 Ogilvy had thought that celebrities

    A were fashionable ways of advertising products.
    B endorsing a product helped that product's brand identity.
    C were one of the weaker ways to advertise products.
    D should continue to be used for adverts.

CAE Listening, Paper 4, Part 4

(Use *QSE Advanced* Exam Practice Audio, **Test 6**)

You will hear five short extracts in which different people are talking about science.

TASK ONE

For questions **21–25**, choose from the list **A–H** each speaker's occupation.

TASK TWO

For questions **26–30**, choose from the list **A–H** each speaker's opinions on transportation and the environment.

You will hear the recording twice. While you listen you must complete both tasks.

A a science teacher

B a car designer

C a climatologist

D a local government official

E an environmentalist

F an oil industry spokesperson

G an urban planner

H a lorry driver

Speaker 1 [ ] 21
Speaker 2 [ ] 22
Speaker 3 [ ] 23
Speaker 4 [ ] 24
Speaker 5 [ ] 25

A Carbon dioxide is a part of the cycle of life.

B Traffic congestion is a pressing problem.

C Limiting traffic in cities would be unpopular.

D People should walk, bicycle or use car pools more.

E The price of fuel might affect jobs.

F Hydrogen is going to replace petrol as a major fuel.

G Global warming is real and humans are partly responsible.

H Using public transport is better than private cars.

Speaker 1 [ ] 26
Speaker 2 [ ] 27
Speaker 3 [ ] 28
Speaker 4 [ ] 29
Speaker 5 [ ] 30

QSE Advanced — CAE Exam Practice Speaking 1

Name:
Class:

CAE Speaking: Paper 5 **Part 1 (3 minutes)**

> Good morning/afternoon/evening. My name is...(and this is my colleague...).
> And your names are?
> Can I have your mark sheets, please?
> Thank you.
> First of all, we'd like to know something about you.

Select one or two questions and ask candidates in turn, as appropriate.

- Where are you from?
- What do you do?
- How long have you been studying English?
- What do you enjoy most about learning English?

Select one or more questions from any of the following categories, as appropriate.

Work and study

- What would be your ideal job? ...(Why?)
- Which jobs are popular in your country at the moment? ...(Why?)
- How important is to continue studying throughout your lifetime? ...(Why?)

People

- Tell us about a good friend ...(Why are they a good friend?)
- Who has been the most important influence on your life so far? ...(Why?)
- Which teacher have you liked the most? ...(Why?)

QSE Advanced — CAE Exam Practice Speaking 2

Name:
Class:

CAE Speaking: Paper 5   Part 2 (4 minutes)

Stress (Describe, speculate and hypothesize)

Interlocutor: In this part of the test, I'm going to give you each three pictures. I'd like you to talk about them on your own for about a minute.

Which picture would be the most stressful? Why?

How do you think the people are feeling in the picture?

Interlocutor: I'd like you to compare two of the pictures, and decide which would be the most stressful and why, and how do you think each person is feeling in each picture.

QSE Advanced — CAE Exam Practice Speaking 3 & 4

Name:
Class:

CAE Speaking: Paper 5 **Part 3 (4 minutes)**

Interlocutor: Now I'd like you to talk about something together for about three minutes. (*5 minutes for groups of three.*)
Here are some pictures showing different ways in which young people get around. First, talk about **how each of these pictures show the behaviour of young people today.**

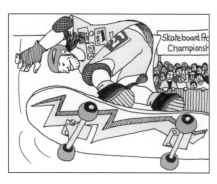

How do these pictures show social mobility through hard work?

Which picture represents the best possibility for a successful future?

Now talk to each other about **how these pictures describe the concept of social mobility through hard work.** Then decide **which picture represents the best possibility for a successful future.**

CAE Speaking: Paper 5 **Part 4 (4 minutes)**

Interlocutor *Select any of the following questions as appropriate.*
- Some people say young people are more concerned with having fun than having a job. What's your opinion?
- What are the advantages and disadvantages of companies hiring young people?
- In what ways could the government help young people find work?
- What problems are associated with youth unemployment?
- Should young people have to travel inside or outside your country to find work?....(Why? / Why not?)

Thank you. That is the end of the test.

Part 1A Grammar

Read the text below and then decide which word best fits each space. See example (0).

Forced Marriage

Every year, the UK Foreign and Commonwealth Office (FCO) **(0)**_____ about 250 cases of forced marriage of UK nationals. A forced marriage is any marriage where one or both **(1)**_____ are forced to marry against their will usually under emotional or physical **(2)**_____ from family members. This is different **(3)**_____ arranged marriage which happens between two consenting parties. The FCO has established a Forced Marriage Unit (FMU) in an attempt **(4)**_____ with this problem. While **(5)**_____ cases have arisen among African, East Asian, European, Middle Eastern communities, forced marriage is most prevalent among South Asian communities (for example, India, Bangladesh, Pakistan). Here, the custom of arranged marriage sometimes leads a few families to believe **(6)**_____ they have the right to forcefully impose their choice in marriage on their children. These children, some **(7)**_____ 13, are often sent overseas for marriage. Some **(8)**_____ or held against their will. Others experience sexual abuse and forced pregnancy or abortion. In some cases, a refusal of marriage has even resulted in the death of the individual. **(9)**_____ so-called 'honour killings' are most often carried out by close male family members such as the father, brother, uncle or cousin. The FMU works vigorously with local authorities in other countries to ensure the safe return of UK nationals who have been abducted **(10)**_____.

0	**A** studies	**B** *investigates*	**C** hinders	**D** searches
1	**A** partners	**B** participants	**C** plaintiffs	**D** humans
2	**A** pressing	**B** impulsiveness	**C** encouragement	**D** pressure
3	**A** to	**B** from	**C** on	**D** for
4	**A** in dealing	**B** which deals	**C** for dealing	**D** to deal
5	**A** a few	**B** most	**C** some	**D** three
6	**A** that	**B** which	**C** since	**D** though
7	**A** as young as	**B** as old as	**C** as young like	**D** as old like
8	**A** abducted	**B** are abducted	**C** will be abducted	**D** will have been abducted
9	**A** Those	**B** Every	**C** These	**D** Some
10	**A** in the way	**B** on the way	**C** in this way	**D** on this way

Part 1B Reading

Answer these questions based on the text above.

1 How does the UK government deal with forced marriage?

2 How are arranged marriages and forced marriages different?

3 What is meant by honour in 'honour killings'?

Part 2 Writing

Choose one of the following. Write approximately 250 words.

1 Imagine a teenage friend of yours has flown abroad with her parents. Before she left, she told you she was worried that she was going to be forced to marry someone. Write a letter to the Forced Marriage Unit about your friend.

2 Write an article about marriage in your country. You can compare it to the situation in the article.

Part 3 Speaking

How do you think marriage has changed over the years? Why do people get married in your country? How common is divorce in your country? Why?

QSE Advanced — Teacher's Guide

Exam Practice Answers

IGCSE answer key

Reading and Writing 1: Exercise 1

a Sea-kayaking, scuba diving, beach party, champagne cruise, sauna. **b** Travel insurance. **c** Order Adrenaline before 1 March. **d** In Style. **e** Adrenaline. **f** Helsinki, Savonlinna. (1 mark for each correct answer. Total: 5 marks.)

Reading and Writing 2: Exercise 2

a New data management systems, highly qualified personnel, or school improvements. **b** Physical education or fine arts programmes. **c** Obesity levels in the state. **d** FCAT does not include arts in its testing. **e** $324 million. (1 mark for each correct answer. Total: 5 marks.)

Reading and Writing 3: Exercise 2

a Spoken - 45%. **b** Fear causes adrenaline which makes a man more aware of a woman sexually. **c** The man on the safer bridge. **d** Illegal drugs (cocaine, amphetamines) and exercise. **e** It contains phenylethylamine (PEA) which gives feelings of excitement. (1 mark for each correct answer. Total: 5 marks.)

Reading and Writing 4: Exercise 3

a One that is vulnerable to storm surges or flooding. **b** Medication. **c** Boil it or add 2 drops chlorine per litre. **d** Battery-powered TV or radio, flashlights, cell phone. **e** Food supply (at least two weeks), veterinary medications and proper vaccination within the past 12 months. (1 mark for each correct answer. Total: 5 marks.)

Reading and Writing 5: Exercise 3

Breakfast: Cereal and whole milk, two slices of toast. Calories: 670. **Lunch:** Burger (530 calories), large fries (570), large Coca-Cola (320), cookies / biscuits (270). Calories: 1,690. **Dinner:** Roast beef and roast potatoes. Calories: 870. Excess calories: 930. **Average excess calorie intake per day:** 200 to 400 calories. **Vegetables/Fruit consumed:** None. **Physical activity: Present physical activity:** Watching television, playing video games, sometimes playing football. **Should aim for:** minimum of one hour of moderate physical activity a day. **How Jimmy's parents can help him?** Not serve high-fat foods and sugary foods and drinks. Have family mealtimes, so Jimmy doesn't snack between meals. Not reward Jimmy for good behaviour or good marks in school with fast food or sweets. Play football with Jimmy or take him ice/in-line skating, swimming, bike riding, or to an adventure play park. (Total: 8 marks.)

Reading and Writing 6: Exercise 4

(Sample answers) **a Origins:** grew up in Essex village; parents owned pub; dyslexic, went to catering college at 16. **b TV stardom:** First break in 1996, was in Christmas documentary about restaurant where he worked; Two series: *Naked Chef*, 1998 and 1999 on BBC Television; programmes shown in over 40 countries, including USA. **c Popularity:** Voted 'Most Inspiring Political Figure of 2005' after campaign to improve standards of school meals in UK schools. Did TV programme *Jamie's School Dinners* to make people aware of the problem. **d Commercialism:** Appears in TV and radio adverts for supermarket chain, earning over a million pounds a year. (Total: 5 marks.)

Reading and Writing 7: Exercise 4

(Sample answers) **a The behaviour of Ms Green's colleagues:** Caused her distress by saying she smelled, excluded her from group lunches, stared at her silently, spoke loudly so she couldn't make phone calls. **b The effects on Ms Green:** Became very distressed, had a nervous breakdown in 2002 and was on suicide watch in hospital. Went back to work, but got worse again. Bank sacked her in 2003. **c The bank's response to the bullying:** No action taken over the bullying, but only one of four women still works in bank. **d The Court's decision:** Awarded Ms Green £800,000 in compensation. (Total: 5 marks.)

Reading and Writing 8: Exercise 4

(Sample answers) **a History of the region:** Oldest unresolved land dispute in the world; was

QSE Exam Practice Answers — Teacher's Guide

independent of British rule from 1846–1947. **b Demographics of the region:** 8 million people – over 6 million Muslim. **c Main sources of income:** Agricultural exports (saffron); woven goods; tourism – major money earner. **d Problems for the economy:** Political instability; earthquake in October 2005 (estimated 70,000 dead). (Total: 5 marks.)

Reading and Writing 9: Exercise 5

(Sample answers) Could mention:
– what blog includes (text, video clips, photos, MP3 sound clips, links) / what's in a blog (subject matter)
– difference between blog and diary
– how blogs developed
– uses for blogs
(Total: 8 marks.)

Reading and Writing 10: Exercise 5

(Sample answers) Could mention:
– three kinds of astronaut
– what need to apply
– training (how long, what includes)
– weightlessness training
(Total: 8 marks.)

Listening 1: Part 1

1 Friday morning. **2** In Terminal 1 by the information desk at 2 pm. **3** At 9.25. **4** He doesn't pay anything. **5** Bottle of water, football boots, money. **6** The red pumps will go with her favourite top. (1 mark for each correct answer, except 2 and 5, which are 2 marks each. Total: 8 marks.)

Listening 2: Part 2

67 million; 365; six and half times; 68,000; test aircraft; 1 January 1946; Europa Building. (1 mark for each correct answer. Total: 7 marks.)

Listening 3: Part 3, Exercise 1

a Unspecialised cells. **b** Any kind of specialised cells you want them to be. **c** Neurons, leading to lower dopamine level and mobility. **d** Dopamine was produced and motor function of mice improved (they could move better). **e** Diabetes and spinal cord injuries. **f** Embryonic stem cells can become any cell in the body while adult stem cells can only be specific types of tissue / embryonic stem cells can be grown easily in the lab; this is not true with adult stem cells yet / with adult stem cells there is no risk of rejection for transplants but it is not yet known if embryonic stems cells could cause rejection. (1 mark for each correct answer. Total: 6 marks.)

Listening 3: Part 3, Exercise 2

a He made many innovative ad campaigns and developed many techniques that are standards. **b** He wasted half his money in advertising. **c** He was a statistician. **d** Because readers remember the headline 28% more. **e** Print ads tend to be just headlines today. **f** The star's brand identity was being promoted more than the product. (1 mark for each correct answer. Total: 6 marks.)

IELTS Answer key

Listening 1 (Section 1)

1 Katie (D) **2** Rebecca's boyfriend (B) **3** B **4** C **5** B **6** C / F **7** long brown **8** cuddly animals **9** angel wings **10** Katie (1 mark for each correct answer. Total: 10 marks.)

Listening 2 (Section 2)

11 C **12** A **13** A **14** C **15** E **16** Vicar **17** test aircraft **18** Air **19** World War II / World War Two / WWII **20** Civil Aviation (1 mark for each correct answer. Total: 10 marks.)

Listening 3 (Section 3)

21 unspecialised **22** cell division **23** C **24** mice **25** diabetes **26** spinal cord **27** lab **28** religious groups **29** heart tissue **30** rejection (1 mark for each correct answer. Total: 10 marks.)

Listening 4 (Section 4)

31 London **32** innovative advertising campaigns **33** scientific **34** 28% **35** 20% **36** the main text **37** Most print adverts **38** fashionable **39** endorse/promote **40** endorsements (1 mark for each correct answer. Total: 10 marks.)

Reading 1 (Part 1)

1 G **2** F **3** C **4** H **5** D **6** in-your-face **7** cross-pollinate **8** Times Square billboards **9** an infomercial **10** 750 customers / its

important customers / 750 important customers
11 sell the / these product (s) **12** *NOT GIVEN*
13 *TRUE* **14** *FALSE* (1 mark for each correct answer. Total: 14 marks.)

Reading 2 (Part 2)

15 *NOT GIVEN* **16** *FALSE* **17** *TRUE* **18** *NOT GIVEN* **19** C **20** A **21** F **22** B **23** E **24** A **25** B **26** D **27** B (1 mark for each correct answer. Total: 13 marks.)

Reading 3 (Part 3)

28 ix **29** x **30** vi **31** iv **32** I **33** A **34** F **35** L **36** H **37** C **38** J **39** G **40** E (1 mark for each correct answer. Total: 13 marks.)

CAE Answer key

Reading 1: Paper 1, Part 1

1 D **2** A **3** B **4** A **5** D **6** A
(1 mark for each correct answer. Total: 6 marks.)

Reading 2: Paper 1, Part 2

7 D **8** F **9** A **10** G **11** C **12** E (B was not part of the text.) (1 mark for each correct answer. Total: 6 marks.)

Reading 3: Paper 1, Part 3

13 D **14** B **15** B **16** B **17** A **18** B **19** D (1 mark for each correct answer. Total: 7 marks.)

Reading 4: Paper 1, Part 4

20 B **21** A **22** D **23** B **24** C **25** A **26** D **27** C **28** B **29** C **30** D **31** A **32** C **33** D **34** A
(1 mark for each correct answer. Total: 15 marks.)

Use of English 1: Paper 3, Part 1

1 B **2** D **3** C **4** A **5** B **6** B **7** B **8** B **9** A **10** B **11** A **12** A (1 mark for each correct answer. Total: 12 marks.)

Use of English 2: Paper 3, Part 2

13 studying **14** interest **15** about **16** It **17** would **18** earn / give **19** time **20** God's **21** Instead **22** voyage / journey **23** to **24** many **25** coast **26** island **27** him (1 mark for each correct answer. Total: 15 marks.)

Use of English 3: Paper 3, Part 3

28 assumption **29** predatory **30** comparison **31** literally **32** unearthed **33** was **34** Natural **35** findings **36** Unfortunately **37** measurements (1 mark for each correct answer. Total: 10 marks.)

Use of English 4: Paper 3, Part 4

38 function **39** space **40** bump **41** trial **42** sex (1 mark for each correct answer. Total: 5 marks.)

Use of English 5: Paper 3, Part 5

43 our ups and downs **44** only the wind could be **45** was wondering if you could give **46** Please feel free **47** called for the resignation of **48** did not take off **49** significantly fewer tourists **50** a loss for words (1 mark for each correct answer. Total: 8 marks.)

Listening 1: Paper 4, Part 1

1 C **2** B **3** A **4** B **5** A **6** C (1 mark for each correct answer. Total: 6 marks.)

Listening 2: Paper 4, Part 2

7 unspecialised / unspecialised cells **8** experimental **9** over 65 **10** brain **11** mice **12** spinal cord **13** religious groups **14** Adult (1 mark for each correct answer. Total: 8 marks.)

Listening 3: Paper 4, Part 3

15 B **16** B **17** D **18** C **19** A **20** C (1 mark for each correct answer. Total: 6 marks.)

Listening 4: Paper 4, Part 4

21 B **22** G **23** H **24** C **25** F **26** F **27** B **28** E **29** G **30** A (1 mark for each correct answer. Total: 10 marks.)

Placement Test

Part 1: 1 A partners **2** D pressure **3** B from **4** D to deal **5** C some **6** A that **7** A as young as **8** B are abducted **9** C These **10** C in this way (1 mark for each correct answer. Total: 10 marks.)

Test 7 — Exam Practice Listening Scripts — Teacher's Guide

(continued from page 173)
TEST 7   CAE only: CAE Listening Part 1

You will hear three different extracts. For questions 1–6, choose the answer (**A, B** or **C**) which fits best according to what you hear. There are two questions for each extract.

(*Extract One*)
You hear two people on a current affairs programme discussing a Super Bowl advertisement.
Andrea: I'm not sure if any of you watched the Super Bowl ads this year. As always, there was a mix of some exceptional ads, some mediocre ones and some downright terrible ones!
Patsy: Yes, I saw quite a few of them later on YouTube. I must say, there was at least one ad that I really hated.
Andrea: Let me guess, Teleflora?
Patsy: Exactly. What were they thinking?
Andrea: For the sake of those who haven't seen Teleflora's ad, it featured a woman in an office who receives a box of flowers in front of her colleagues. When she opens the box, the flowers begin insulting her. Something like 'Look at the mug on her. You're a train wreck. Go home to your fat stinking cat.' The ad then finishes off by suggesting that you should buy Teleflora's flowers in a glass vase to prevent insulting the person.
Patsy: Personally I'll never use Teleflora after seeing this horrible ad. I realise that the Super Bowl's target audience is, for the most part, men, but I have to believe that modern men would also find this in bad taste.
Andrea: To think they paid 3 million dollars in order to lose customers!

(*Extract Two*)
You hear an interview of a woman discussing New York designer Zac Posen at New York's Fashion Week.
Interviewer: We're here in Bryant Park in the heart of Manhattan for the opening salvos in the Mercedes-Benz Fashion Week. It's a chilly four degrees this February afternoon, but inside the tent behind me, it is definitely hotting up. The precocious young designer Zac Posen has just finished showcasing his Fall collection. To discuss it, I'm joined by famed London fashionista, Beverly Saint Germaine. So Bev, was it a hit or a flop?
Bev: Oh, it was a tremendous hit. I loved it. His designs are so romantic, so old-Hollywood glamour and chic. Silk and chiffon dresses drawing inspiration from nature like seashells and raffia palms. It's the kind of work you expect from an alumnus of Saint Martins College of Art and Design which has produced so many creative talents over the years like John Galliano, Stella McCartney and Alexander McQueen. However, unlike his peers, he never went to work for one of the leading fashion houses. With backing from rap mogul, Sean 'P. Diddy' Combs, Posen started marketing his own line of jeans and hosiery right out of college. Maybe it's a sign of the times; the fashion industry is entering the new marketing era.

(*Extract Three*)
You hear an interview with the painter Paul Rimmington who lives in Helsinki, Finland.
Interviewer: On today's Art World, we're in Helsinki, Finland – joined by artist extraordinaire, Paul Rimmington. Paul originally hails from Sheffield, England, but has lived in Helsinki for over a decade. For our listeners, we've set up a link to Paul's website, paulislost.com, so you can see his artwork. (*pause*)
So, Paul, you've developed a reputation in Finland for your wild and imaginative abstract paintings. Is painting your favorite medium?
Paul: Yes, I love liquid colour and what it can do for me. I began painting about 18 years ago when I first attended Sheffield College. In the last few years, I've been taking painting into other areas of contemporary art. For example, I've been making sculptures from paint using found objects, recycled paint objects and repetitive applications of paint. At the moment, I'm working on a commissioned sculpture for a private collector.
Interviewer: Do you still see yourself as a British artist?
Paul: Sheffield is a working class city, very industrial. You can say there was a direct influence from my working on a production line as a young man to the mechanical and repetitive way I apply paint. I wouldn't say that I'm a British artist anymore. But I'm not Finnish either. I don't think it's easy to be a foreign anything in Finland, but as an artist, being foreign has its advantages. My work seems foreign to Finns, so it stands out from the crowd.